# Additional Praise for
## *BRINGING BEN HOME*

"As a member of the San Antonio Four who served thirteen years in a Texas prison for a crime that never occurred, this book dredged up a lot of feelings and memories—frustration, helplessness, and finally hope when someone on the outside believes you."

—ANNA VASQUEZ, director of outreach
and education, Innocence Project of Texas

"A spellbinding story of resilience and faith. It's a fascinating account of a broken justice system and what people are doing to help mend it."

—JAMES MARTIN, SJ, author of *Jesus: A Pilgrimage*

"*Bringing Ben Home* achieves a rare feat: it is simultaneously infuriating, fascinating, and inspiring. The author's personal commitment to her subject and his family filled me with awe. This is a luminous book."

—ALLISON LEOTTA, author of *The Last Good Girl*

"Barbara Bradley Hagerty brings her keen eye to the phenomenon of wrongful convictions in this beautifully written and accessible exploration of an injustice in Texas. As she makes clear, when an innocent person is convicted, the harm transcends that individual's suffering and affects all of us."

—DANIEL S. MEDWED, author of *Barred:
Why the Innocent Can't Get Out of Prison*

"There are valuable lessons here about the reasons for wrongful convictions and the immense difficulty of obtaining justice. With drama, insight, and conviction, Barbara Bradley Hagerty describes how a remarkable team proved Ben Spencer's innocence and won his freedom."

—STEPHEN BRIGHT, Yale Law School,
veteran death penalty attorney

# BRINGING BEN HOME

# Bringing Ben Home

*A Murder, a Conviction, and the Fight
to Redeem American Justice*

+———+

**BARBARA BRADLEY HAGERTY**

RIVERHEAD BOOKS
NEW YORK
2024

RIVERHEAD BOOKS
An imprint of Penguin Random House LLC
penguinrandomhouse.com

Library of Congress Cataloging-in-Publication Data

Names: Bradley Hagerty, Barbara, author.
Title: Bringing Ben home : a murder, a conviction, and the fight to redeem
American justice / Barbara Bradley Hagerty.
Description: First edition. | New York : Riverhead Books, 2024. |
Includes bibliographical references and index.
Identifiers: LCCN 2023056643 (print) | LCCN 2023056644 (ebook) |
ISBN 9780593420089 (hardcover) | ISBN 9780593420102 (ebook)
Subjects: LCSH: Judicial error—United States. | Compensation for judicial
error—United States. | False imprisonment—Law and legislation—United
States. | Prosecutorial misconduct—United States. | African
Americans—Legal status, laws, etc. | Discrimination in criminal justice
administration—United States. | Spencer, Ben (Benjamine),
1965– —Trials, litigation, etc. | Trials (Murder)—Texas—Dallas.
Classification: LCC KF9756 .B73 2024 (print) |
LCC KF9756 (ebook) | DDC 345.764/077—dc23/eng/20231214
LC record available at https://lccn.loc.gov/2023056643
LC ebook record available at https://lccn.loc.gov/2023056644

Printed in the United States of America
1st Printing

Book design by Amanda Dewey

*For Jim McCloskey, who changed the world*
*And for Wade Goodwyn (1960–2023),*
*who graced our lives with his stories and friendship*

# CONTENTS

+——+

## PART 2. APPEAL

## PART 3. DARKNESS AND LIGHT

I am not quite sure where to begin with the details of this case, but I can assure you that wherever I start, that it will be the truth. The proverbial problem for me has been trying to figure out, what's significant and what's insignificant? My fervent prayer is that I will not fail in my objective in pointing out the serious wrong that has been imposed upon me, my family and the family of the victim, Jeffrey Young. My prayer is that after reading about the details in this particular case, that you can find it in your heart to help come up with a solution to this problem of injustice. May God bless you richly and grant us favor in this request.

+——+

BENJAMINE SPENCER
Inmate #483713
*Coffield Unit, Tennessee Colony, Texas*
*September 5, 2016*

# INTRODUCTION

## *A Specimen in Amber*

+————+

On July 13, 2016, at ten thirty in the morning, I called Jim McCloskey and asked a simple question.

"Jim, what's the case that haunts you?"

"Oh, that's easy," he replied. "Ben Spencer's case. There's not a day that goes by that I don't think about Ben."

At the time, I did not foresee the catalyzing effect his answer would have—for me, for people I did not yet know, for a long-settled murder conviction. Why would I? I was just chatting with a source, an exercise I had conducted thousands of times in my thirty-five years as a journalist. But I should have anticipated this, for McCloskey specialized in necessary upheavals. He had been haunted by stories like Spencer's since the early 1980s, when he left his studies at Princeton Theological Seminary to re-investigate the case of a prisoner he believed was wrongly convicted, and persuaded a judge that the man was innocent. A decade before the Innocence Project was founded, McCloskey was already freeing innocent prisoners and launching a revolution in criminal law from his rented bedroom in Princeton.

By the time we spoke on this July day in 2016, McCloskey had won the freedom of fifty-four men and women, some within days of execution.

Benjamine Spencer, who had been in prison in Texas for twenty-nine years, was McCloskey's unfinished business, his heartbreak.

The story of Benjamine Spencer, a Black man convicted of robbing and killing a white man in Dallas in 1987, unfolds on two levels: the procedural and the personal. Procedurally, his experience mirrors that of thousands of innocent men and women in prison. It boils down to this settled fact: Convicting an innocent person is easy; undoing the mistake is almost impossible.

His journey also spans the modern innocence movement that began with Jim McCloskey. One year after Spencer was sentenced to life in prison, DNA exonerated a prisoner convicted of rape—the first time the technology was employed to free an innocent person in the United States. Suddenly, the judicial system, the media, and the public at large saw that the foundation on which prosecutors had always built their cases was rickety at best. DNA could offer irrefutable evidence that someone else, almost certainly not the suspect in custody, had raped or killed the victim. DNA proved that evidence such as eyewitness testimony, ballistics, hair comparisons, fingerprinting—even confessions from the suspect—could be flat-out wrong. But if DNA is the deus ex machina for innocent prisoners, it is a selective god, visiting only 10 to 20 percent of crime scenes. Like the vast majority of prisoners who claim to be innocent, DNA could not help Ben Spencer. Without unassailable forensic evidence, Spencer's several appeals failed.

Even as some states have tried to avoid mistakes with new procedures and better science, they cannot fix two problems at the root of the US criminal justice system: the human mind and the human body. Can a witness accurately record and replay a crime that takes place in a split second on a dark, moonless night? What if the witness is poor or has an axe to grind; can science erase the motive to lie? Jailhouse informants play a leading role in murder convictions, an astonishing fact unique to the United States: What is to stop these criminals from trading bogus "confessions" from the suspect for a shorter sentence for themselves? Police, rushing to find the culprit while the trail still has scent, have been known to discard or ignore evidence that points away from their suspect. Prosecutors have rationalized burying a piece of evidence because it muddies the clear story they are trying to tell in the interest of serving justice.

If convicting the innocent is the natural result of human error, undoing the mistake is thwarted by the legal system—specifically, by the concept of "finality." Appellate judges rarely overturn jury verdicts; after all, they did not sit in court listening to evidence and assessing witnesses, so who are they to second-guess the jury? And while Americans now recognize that the government routinely convicts innocent people, Congress and the US Supreme Court have narrowed the path to freedom for the wrongly convicted by systematically blocking the federal courts' ability to review a jury verdict, even in the face of obvious innocence.

On a personal level, Ben Spencer was twenty-two years old when he was arrested, newly married to Debra, and expecting a child. At first confident that the police would sort things out, he watched in disbelief as he was indicted, convicted, sentenced to life in prison, and denied parole year after year. The toll on Spencer, on his wife and son, on his family and friends, on their faith in God and in the law can never be calculated. These private narratives are almost always hidden. But Ben and Debra Spencer have allowed us the rare privilege of surveying the wreckage the system has wrought.

For several months during 2020 and 2021, I lived in Dallas, trying to uncover new evidence and solve the murder of Jeffrey Young. My efforts felt futile at times. Once the Texas legal system found Ben Spencer guilty, it was as if that judgment sealed him in amber, and he needed an extraordinary instrument, such as DNA, to free him. Without this scientific cudgel, Spencer's lawyers and investigators had to make do with something akin to an ice pick, trying to chip away at his conviction, filing writs and parole applications, petitioning one district attorney after another, hoping that these efforts would eventually crack apart his case and release him as an innocent man.

The thirty-seven years since Spencer was incarcerated have seen a reckoning. Defense attorneys across the country began publicizing wrongful convictions. The public noticed, as did judges, legislators, and a new breed of prosecutor. Rather than simply denying the mistakes, most states began to recognize that prosecutions can go off the rails, and some have tried to eliminate the most egregious flaws. In a happy surprise, on this issue the most progressive state in the country is Texas. In part because the cost of error is so high—the state executes more people than any other—Texas has set up a number of guardrails and is by far the state that most generously recompenses its exonerees.

Thus Texas is the perfect starting point to begin and end the story of Ben Spencer, the logical place to examine the failure of American justice and the incipient attempts to redeem it. For this journey, Ben Spencer is a consummate guide.

# BRINGING BEN HOME

*Part 1*

# Conviction

+———+

# Chapter 1

# A MURDER IN DALLAS

+———+

**You let the man lay there, like a dog in the street?**

—GLORIA FAYE CHILDS, *West Dallas witness*

What were those last minutes like for the man locked in the trunk of his car? Was he awake, aware, terrified? Did he open his eyes, blind in the cramped space, and grope for a lever, a tool, anything that might release the lid to his escape? Or had the savage blows to his head hurtled him into unconsciousness?

As the stolen BMW turned right onto Inwood Road and crossed over the Hampton Road Bridge spanning Dallas's Trinity River, did he recognize that he was crossing a boundary, from affluence to poverty, from safety to peril? As the car carried him into West Dallas—a poor neighborhood reeling from the relentless violence unleashed by crack cocaine—did he know that his brain was swelling and slowly shutting down, his fragile life caught in a riptide inexorably sucking him down and out to sea? Maybe he was tempted to surrender—maybe, that is, until he imagined his wife, whom he had loved since high school; his daughter, only eight years old; his middle child, a ten-year-old son; his oldest, a boisterous, twelve-year-old boy.

Whatever he was thinking, the man managed to find the lever that opened the trunk and, in a burst of strength, hoisted himself out, falling headfirst onto the unforgiving pavement of Puget Street. There he lay, in this neighborhood riven by gangs, where a young man risked his life by walking down the wrong street. A small crowd gathered around the man, who was wheezing and struggling to sit up. In that moment, Puget Street became a demilitarized zone, any urge toward violence stilled by the sight of a man whose life was ebbing away.

W hen Jeffrey Young unlocked the door to 1127 Conveyor Lane at 8:21 p.m. on Sunday, March 22, 1987, he had no reason to think this would be his last trip to the office.[1] The warehouse for FWI, a clothing importer, was Young's domain. At thirty-three, he would soon run the company as its new president. It was his habit to spend Sunday evenings preparing for the week and sending faxes to his suppliers in Asia, where the Monday workday had begun. Often, his sons would accompany him, but this was spring break, and his wife and three children had left for vacation.

Young lit an Antonio y Cleopatra cigar, and at 8:45 p.m., he called Troy Johnson, a friend whose company managed FWI's computer software. He said he needed access to the computer, but Johnson told him he would have to wait an hour until the weekly system maintenance was finished. They chatted for five or six minutes. At 9:45 p.m., the maintenance complete, Johnson called his friend to say he could now access the computer. Johnson let the phone ring twenty times before hanging up. He tried again, five times in all, before deciding that Young had left the office for the night.

No one witnessed the sequence of events leading to that final unanswered call. Dallas police and prosecutors believe that two men either crouched behind Jeffrey Young's BMW in the empty parking lot or flattened themselves against the far side of the stairwell, waiting for Young to come out. When he did, the thieves forced him back inside. They hit him on the head with a blunt instrument, grabbed his wallet and extracted his cash, slid the watch off his wrist, yanked the wedding ring off his finger, and snatched a portable TV-radio from the back room before dragging him down the concrete stairs and toward his car.

If this was supposed to be a robbery, it was going badly. According to his wife, Young had less than a hundred dollars in his wallet.[2] The assailants decided not to leave him in the parking lot, where he could call police, but placed him in the trunk of his car. The men had to subdue him, for Young was strong, five foot eleven and 170 pounds, fit and in the prime of life. They slammed him on the forehead with a blunt object, hit him on both temples, smashed the base and the back of his skull—the latter which is, the medical examiner later testified, "the thickest part of the bone and would require an extraordinary amount of force to cause it to shatter the way it has."[3] It was a frenzy of blows, and when the assailants were done, they had cracked his skull in five places.

During the struggle, it is possible that Young scratched one of the thieves and snagged a tiny bit of skin. This would not matter in 1987, before DNA technology began solving crimes, but would matter two years hence. Once he was subdued, they closed the BMW's trunk and drove to West Dallas.

O nly the killers know precisely what happened that night in March 1987. No security cameras recorded the assault. No neighbors pulled out cell phones to capture who was riding through West Dallas in a late-model, two-door BMW, as the technology had not yet been invented. There isn't even agreement on whether there was one culprit or two, much less their identities. For some time, at least, there was no conclusive evidence to indicate how Jeffrey Young exited the car: Was he dumped from the passenger's door, as one witness told police? Or did he manage to escape from the trunk?[4]

Details begin to fill in the picture around ten thirty that night. Seventeen-year-old Donald Merritt, who lived in West Dallas, was walking his girlfriend home when a neighbor ran toward them—and away from something on Puget Street. *Don't go down there*, he warned them, and hurried away. Curiosity piqued, they continued down Puget and soon came upon a white man lying in the middle of the empty street, struggling to breathe. They were terrified.

Donald Merritt's cousin, Charles Stewart, was not. He was walking home from Warner's Pool Hall. The twenty-year-old noticed a light gray BMW driving slowly, perhaps fifteen miles an hour. When the car turned onto Puget Street, he saw "a man get pushed out of the car," he testified a year later in court. Stewart kept walking: "I had tickets at the time and I didn't want to stop."[5] Residents began to gather around the injured man, among them Gloria Faye Childs, then thirty-two years old, who was riding in the bed of a truck with her coworkers from Church's Chicken. "He was already dying when we got to him," she recalled thirty-five years later. "I've never seen a person die. I'll never forget it. I looked over and I say, 'You all right?' He was trying to say something to us." She paused, reliving the moment. "'*Help me*,'" she croaked. "All these goddamn people looking, ain't nobody saying shit. I say, 'Y'all ain't call no goddamn police or nothing?! You let the man lay there, like a dog in the street?!'"

Finally, at 10:46 p.m., someone—officials don't know who—called 911. By the time paramedics arrived on the scene and examined the man, Jeffrey Young's eyes were not reacting to light—a sign of a head injury or oxygen deprivation for an extended period of time.

"This individual had massive head and possibly internal injuries," a paramedic testified later. "I checked his chest, his ribs. His ribs were pretty well bashed in. No external trauma per se, where there was a loss of blood, but you could tell from the injuries as they existed that he—he had been beat up pretty bad."[6]

While Jeffrey Young was loaded into an ambulance, two young Dallas patrol officers arrived. Nancy Felix, the more seasoned officer with two and a half years' experience, began canvassing the dozen or so witnesses gathered near the body. She got nothing from the crowd. "People saw it, they ain't gonna talk," Gloria Childs noted. Finally, one witness told the police he saw a white man being thrown out of a small sports car. He couldn't tell the color of the car or how many people were inside. The officer elicited no other information.

At twenty-three minutes past midnight, Robert Mitchell called police and reported a BMW abandoned in an alley about two blocks from where the white man lay. By then, the victim had been rushed to Parkland Memorial Hospital, the same hospital that had received the city's most famous murder victim, President John F. Kennedy, in 1963. When the two officers arrived in West Dallas, Jeffrey Hutchinson called in the BMW's information and learned the car belonged to Jeffrey Young. Hutchinson's partner, Aaron Perkins, began interviewing witnesses and found these spectators chattier than the ones who had surrounded the victim on Puget Street.

Witnesses in the area state that complainant Young had been thrown out of the vehicle," Perkins wrote in his report, "and suspect, a black male, parked the vehicle in the alley and got in a small sports car and fled in an unknown direction."[7] One person thought the driver might be a thirty-nine-year-old man named Van Mitchell Spencer, who had served time for robbery and had just been released on parole. Unfortunately, Officer Perkins failed to ask witnesses for their names.[8]

The BMW was towed to a police lot sometime between 1:00 a.m. and 1:15 a.m. By this point the police knew that the victim was close to death. Jeffrey Young died at 3:05 a.m., and at that moment a robbery became a homicide.

The investigation into Jeffrey Young's death could hardly have been more highly charged: the murder of a white man dumped in a poor Black neighborhood at the height of Dallas's drug wars. It was off to an inauspicious start. Police investigators could not persuade witnesses to talk. When they did elicit some details, they failed to gather names and could never find the witnesses again. They neglected to take pictures of where the BMW was parked in the alley or even draw a crude map. They did not protect the crime scene: Forensic experts never secured the alley; rather, they allowed the BMW, itself a crime scene, to be towed to an impound lot where it was left outside in the rain before they dusted for fingerprints.[9]

Three decades later, private investigator Daryl Parker asked Jesus Briseno, the lead detective on the case, why no one took pictures or drew a map of the alley before they towed away Young's car. For violent crimes, experts from the Physical Evidence Section (PES) are supposed to secure and memorialize the crime scene, taking fingerprints, photographs, and gathering any other evidence that may be important in the case.

"Because he wasn't dead," Briseno said. "He was still alive."

"But he had still been assaulted," Daryl observed.

"Well, yeah. But most of the time they don't call the PES out there because they figure: Well, he's going to be okay," Briseno explained.

What's surprising is not that the police botched the crime scene; what's surprising is that they were *discovered* to have done so. Early mistakes in an investigation create blisters, like a pebble in one's shoe, which can become infected. Within hours of Young's death, the investigation was infected. Just how catastrophically was not yet clear.

Still, investigators had collected two critical pieces of information: The killer was determined to be a lone Black man who fled in a sports car. And the prime suspect was Van Mitchell Spencer.

*Chapter 2*

# THE DAY AFTER

+———+

**At the age of twelve, I became an adult overnight.**

—JAY YOUNG, *son of victim Jeffrey Young*

W hen he was twelve years old, Jay Young often accompanied his father to the office on Sunday nights. Jeffrey Young would prepare for the week ahead as his son entertained himself, content to be in his dad's presence. But in March 1987, his parents decided Jay would spend his spring break in Arkansas with family friends. Which is why, on the evening of March 22, Jeffrey Young was alone when he entered his office, sent a fax, made a phone call, and completed some paperwork before he was accosted, robbed, beaten, and killed.

"I was supposed to be there," Jay recalled. "That's the thing that I've dealt with for a while."

His younger brother, Jimmy, nodded and sipped his coffee. It was a steamy Dallas evening in June 2017, but blessedly cool and still inside Jimmy's town house, elegant with its muted gray walls, a two-story ceiling with skylights, sleek wood furniture, and glistening chrome kitchen appliances. At forty, Jimmy was lean, with an easy, earnest smile and thick brown hair combed straight back. Forty-two-year-old Jay Young was conventionally handsome with a wide face, stocky but fit, recently divorced and pining for his children.

They began the story that has haunted them for three decades. By

7:45 on the morning of March 23, 1987, James Coyle had identified his son-in-law in the morgue. He and his wife drove to Galveston, Texas, where their daughter Jamee, Jeffrey Young's wife, had brought her two younger children for spring break. Jimmy, then ten years old, recalls seeing his grandparents slowly getting out of their car and thinking, Oh, cool, what are they doing here? As they approached their daughter and hugged her, Jimmy noticed fear flicker across his mother's face. "They grabbed my mom and they were like, 'Something's happened,'" Jimmy recalled. She began to weep, and the adults explained to Jimmy and Jordan, his eight-year-old sister, that their dad was gone. The family caught the first flight back to Dallas.

Jay Young was permitted a few more hours of untroubled childhood. He was lounging around at his friend's house in Arkansas, the two boys contemplating a day at the lake, when the phone rang. "And all of a sudden, [his friend's parents] started rushing around saying, 'Hey, we got to go,'" Jay remembered. He picked up the phone to let his dad know he was coming home. His friend's father rushed into the room. "Who are you calling?" he asked. "I'm calling my dad," the boy replied. The man grabbed the phone and replaced it in the cradle. "Your dad knows you're coming home," he said. They piled into the car and headed toward Dallas, the parents sitting silently in the front, Jay and his friend in the back, laughing, a five-hour drive home toward unimaginable grief.

Jay's two grandfathers intercepted him at the front door and sat him down on the outside step of their home. An accident had happened to his father, they said. Jay waited, lying down on the stoop, allowing the silence to stretch. Finally he asked, "What hospital is he in? Is he okay?" "He didn't make it," one answered quietly. In a daze, Jay walked inside to a living room crowded with family and friends crying softly and speaking in hushed voices. It was the raw, unbridled grief, not the grandfathers' words, that broke his confusion.

That night, after everyone had slipped away and they were left alone, Jamee and the three children slept in the same bed. "I remember waking up the next day and thinking, Did that really happen? Was this a night-

mare?" Jay remembered. He could hear his mom, brother, and sister snif-
fle and begin to cry. "At the age of twelve, I became an adult overnight,"
he said. "I just remember going, I'm at a fork in the road. I can either let
this define me or I can go down the right path. And I didn't want that to
define me."

The two men had never spoken to a journalist about their father's
murder, the trial, or the emotional aftermath. They distrusted reporters,
with their boom microphones and promises to tell their side of the
story—a story that has been hijacked with accusations of racism, ineptitude, and corruption, leaving the victim and his family on the side of the
road. They insisted all reporters have an agenda, and as the conversation
unfolded, the air in the room vibrated with tension. Finally, I asked: Why
did you agree to talk with me?

Jay sighed, a little impatiently. "I want to make him more human," he
explained. "I want someone from his family to say what type of person
he was, and what was lost. Father, husband, friend, brother, cousin, all the
titles that go with all that. I want to make him not . . . *invisible.*"

This is my goal as well. I have written and called his family and friends,
knocked on their doors, slipped letters through their mailboxes. All these
attempts have met with silence, or anger. I am confined to the memories
of a twelve- and a ten-year-old, which can hardly paint a rich portrait of a
vibrant adult. It's not how this story should be told. It is inevitable, and it
is unfair.

A more fundamental question has dogged me from the start: Who
should tell the story of a young Black man accused of murder and fed into
the criminal justice system? Do I, a privileged white woman, have any
such right? Because, I *am* white and I *am* privileged, raised in a middle-
class family that prized education (and faith) above all else. I received a
superb education at Williams College and enjoyed a meaningful career
as a journalist. Indeed, several people who spent years trying to free the
accused man were white, and virtually everyone involved enjoyed some
measure of privilege, possessing advanced degrees in law or theology.
Perhaps this is understandable. When you are rowing against a strong

current, when you are working to overturn a criminal conviction, you are struggling against superhuman forces. Perhaps you need every hand on the oars, no matter what color, to challenge a rival as storied, powerful, and streamlined as the American justice system.

Who should tell this man's story? One day, I hope he will. But in the interim, he has entrusted that remarkable task to me. And of all the many privileges I have enjoyed in my life, this is the finest of all.

B efore Jeffrey Young's sons learned of his death, even before their father had been identified at the morgue, Dallas Police Detective Jesus Briseno was assigned to find the killers. Arriving for his shift at downtown headquarters at 7:00 a.m., he learned that he would lead the investigation. It would require finesse and quick resolution to identify a suspect and arrest him: Not every day is an affluent white man beaten and dumped on the streets of one of Dallas's poorest Black neighborhoods. Although he was in his thirties, Briseno had worked homicides for only a little more than a year. This would be the first high-profile case he would lead.

To begin their investigation, Briseno and his colleague drove to the victim's office and met with an investigator from the Physical Evidence Section. The crime-scene investigator snapped photographs, which captured an office that was messy but not obviously ransacked, except for a cigar on the floor and the victim's scattered credit cards. He dusted for latent fingerprints and lifted what were known as "prints of value" from a chrome rail near the victim's desk. He collected several items for processing at the Dallas police lab: the victim's credit cards, driver's license, petty cash receipts—objects that might determine the killer's identity.

From there, they drove to the Dallas Police Department Auto Pound, where they found the 1982 BMW, still wet from rain, in row 14. The forensic investigator photographed the inside and outside of the car and lifted prints of value inside the driver's-side window, the passenger's side, the back windows. He gathered a few items—a checkbook, a tube of lipstick—to test at the laboratory.[1]

When he finally arrived in West Dallas, Briseno found the residents afflicted with what he says are common maladies in this part of town: blindness, deafness, and amnesia. He knocked on door after door, paying special attention to the houses around the alley where the assailants had parked the BMW and fled. Just the night before, a dozen people had gathered around the body on the street, and later, near the car in the alley. Someone must have seen something. When Briseno quizzed the residents the next day, they shook their heads, claiming they saw nothing, or refused to answer the door. This was the standard reception in West Dallas. "The only thing we could do was pass out our business cards, and hopefully they would call you sometime later on," Briseno remarked years later. They rarely did. Most murders went unsolved.

As a kid, Briseno wanted to be an FBI agent, and later, a Dallas cop, but he was too short for the five-foot-eight-inch height requirement until the police department rescinded it. He grew up in West Texas, in a tiny town called Marathon. "No crime there whatsoever," he said. He was shocked at the rampant violence of Dallas as a tsunami of slayings washed over the city in the late 1980s and early 1990s, triggered by the crack epidemic. One year, he recalled, the city's twelve homicide detectives handled nearly five hundred murders. "It was very difficult," he observed dryly.

In 1987, the term "superpredator" had not yet been coined, but the fear underlying it was fermenting, with its connotation of remorseless young Black men hopped up on cocaine, mowing down competing gangs and killing women and children as collateral damage. The superpredator theory was later debunked when crime rates fell, but back then, violence soaked poor neighborhoods in blood.

West Dallas was at war not only with itself but with police as well.[2] Officers tried to eradicate the drug-related violence with an approach more hatchet than scalpel, conducting random raids—ten a day in parts of Dallas—and routinely detaining "suspicious" people. Nor were the police reluctant to use their guns, particularly when aiming at Blacks. From 1980 to 1986, Dallas police killed sixty people, thirty-six of whom were Black, twelve white, and twelve Hispanic.[3] In 1987 alone, at the time Briseno and his colleagues were seeking information from the Black residents of West Dallas about Jeffrey Young's murder, Dallas police killed twenty-nine people, more then half of whom were Black.[4]

"They see a Black person and they shoot," says Michael Phillips, author of *White Metropolis: Race, Ethnicity, and Religion in Dallas, 1841–2001.* "No one trusts them." Black residents dared not call 911 when a crime took place. "They actually are more in danger at the hands of police than at the hands of un-uniformed criminals."[5]

"The whole idea was to try to make arrests quickly," says Bob Ray Sanders, who covered the Dallas area as a newspaper reporter and television host for fifty years. "Often making arrests quickly means you made mistakes, but it didn't matter. Not if the defendant was Black."

Jesus Briseno's notes detailed a frenetic, frustrating investigation. One man swore that Young was thrown out of the car, which then backed up and ran over him. Evidence contradicted that. Several others claimed that a neighborhood woman lured the victim with the promise of drugs and sex; this too was debunked. But other leads appeared more promising. Fourteen-year-old Sandra Brackens had been sitting on her porch when a fire engine and ambulance screamed through the neighborhood on their way to Puget Street, where Jeffrey Young lay. A few minutes later, Briseno wrote in his notes, Brackens noticed the BMW and an unknown Black man rummaging through the car. According to the teenager, "that same person came running around the front of the house carrying a silver jambox and some other box-looking item," Briseno reported. (A jambox is a portable TV-radio.) "She gave the following description: 5'8"–6', slender build, dark complexion, wearing a black baseball cap, black leather jacket, dark color pants, and possibly wore dress shoes. She claims she did not see his face good enough to make an identification."[6]

According to Briseno's notes, "several people" stated that the description given by Sandra Brackens matched the physical description of Van Mitchell Spencer—his height, his build, and the clothing he was wearing the previous night. This accorded with statements from witnesses at the crime scene on the night of the murder, whose names the police did not bother to get, and who identified Van Mitchell Spencer as the driver of the BMW.

Van Mitchell Spencer liked to steal things. His known burglary career began in 1969. On the weekend in question, according to Briseno's notes, he had been released on parole after being sent to prison on a "high bitch for burglary"—that is, his multiple arrests should have sent him away for years. But he was out now, and was their prime suspect. On Monday, Briseno interviewed him and searched the houses of his mother and his girlfriend. Police found no incriminating items—no jambox, wedding ring, or watch. He denied he was involved with Jeffrey Young's homicide. That was good enough for Briseno. "I don't think that Van Spencer was involved," Briseno concluded in his notes.[7]

As for Sandra Brackens, the notes are silent as to why the detective believed a convicted criminal over a fourteen-year-old girl who offered a detailed description of the man fleeing the scene. Years later, he explained his reasoning to private investigator Daryl Parker. "She was one of those crack whores," he said.

When I spoke with him, Briseno retreated from that assessment, saying he didn't remember every detail three decades after he closed the case. What he remembered well, and what galled him still, was the way the crime scene was handled. Actually, there were three crime scenes. There was the office. There was the alley where the car had been parked, then towed, before any official photographed the exact position of the car. The resulting imprecision allowed the state to claim facts—namely, that witnesses could see the car—that the defense was unable to decisively rebut. The third crime scene was the vehicle itself, which was towed and left in the rain at the Dallas Police Department Auto Pound.

The patrol officers arrived late Sunday night, Briseno recalled. "They transport the body to the hospital because [the victim] was apparently still alive. And they tow the car off to the auto pound and they don't put no hold on it or nothing." Under normal procedure, police put vehicles involved in a criminal investigation in a protected area of the pound. That didn't happen with the BMW. Worse, Briseno said, the day after Jeffrey Young was killed, the Dallas Police Department opened the pound to the public for an auction of abandoned vehicles. There's no telling how many prospective buyers touched the car and left their fingerprints, nor how badly this crime scene was contaminated, if at all. But one fact is clear: The investigation was off to a sloppy start, and that pattern would continue.

# Chapter 3

# DEFYING GRAVITY

+———+

**He was just that gentlemen that your dad
wants you to meet and marry.**

—Debra Spencer

B en Spencer threaded his way through the Dallas Police Department
Auto Pound, searching for a car for his mother. On the morning of
March 23, 1987, Spencer was twenty-two, newly married, and he and Debra
were expecting a baby in two months' time. Spencer doesn't recall seeing the
1982 BMW sports car that had been towed from his neighborhood to the
pound early that morning. Valued at twenty-five thousand dollars, it was
too rich for his wallet. Among the many strokes of bad luck Spencer would
encounter over the next three decades, this was an aberration, a lucky break.
Had he touched that BMW, had he opened its door and slid inside to get a
feel for it, had he checked out the trunk—in short, had he left his fingerprints anywhere on Jeffrey Young's BMW—his fate would have been sealed.

But Spencer did not touch the car that day. He left the auction empty-
handed around 10:00 a.m. On the way home, Charles Stewart flagged
him down. His neighbor owned an Alpine amplifier that Spencer wanted
to buy for his 1976 Ford Gran Torino. They drove to the pawnshop with
$128 in Spencer's wallet, flush with cash from Friday's paycheck and a tax
refund. The amp cost $30 to redeem. Spencer broke a $100 bill to buy it.
Stewart took notice of the large bill.

In the early evening, Spencer drove to his job at Mistletoe Express, where he worked the night shift loading and unloading trucks. On his way he saw Robert Mitchell playing dominoes on the front step of his grandmother's house. Mitchell waved him over.

"You hear what happened last night?" Mitchell asked. "Man, they found a white guy up on Puget and they found a stolen car in the alley behind the Brackens' house. The police was everywhere."

"I didn't see anything," Spencer said. "That's the first I've heard of it."

Later, it struck Spencer as peculiar that Charles Stewart had failed to mention the incident when they drove to the pawnshop. The crime was roiling the neighborhood, and Stewart had seen the body of the dying man and the BMW. Unaware of this, Spencer drove to work, finished his shift, returned home after midnight, and went straight to bed.

It's remarkable how facts gain or lose importance when viewed through the lens of a capital murder charge. The events you thought were significant—the day you fell in love, the day you got married, the day you learned you were having a baby—recede into the background. The most mundane details—breaking a hundred-dollar bill, having a pointless spat with your spouse, giving a neighbor a ride to church—suddenly loom improbably large.

But on that cool March morning, Ben Spencer envisioned only good things. He had a decent job loading trucks at night. His wife earned a good salary. He could hardly believe he had persuaded this whip-smart, beautiful, if strong-willed woman to marry him. He was thrilled about becoming a dad. He was looking for a second job to plump up their savings, and they were setting aside money for a deposit to buy their own home. "Little did I know," he wrote later to a friend, "that evil was lurking about and that I was about to become the victim of vicious lies, that would completely disrupt my life and plans for my future."[1]

There is a famous story within the Spencer family. When Benjamine Spencer was eleven or twelve years old, he gathered his brothers and sisters and all the kids in the neighborhood up and down the street to the

Spencer home for a performance. His family had recently seen *Mary Poppins* at the movie theater, and he had marveled at the iconic flight of a woman in a long, black coat and skirt, clutching an open black umbrella. She floated gracefully through the air above London, propelled toward the house as her future charges, a young brother and sister, watched in wonder, until she alit ever so gently in her black-laced boots on their front step and rang the bell. The grace, the weightlessness, the magic—it was his, the boy thought, if he only believed.

"He went to the backyard, and he got on the roof with an umbrella," his younger sister, Juanita, recalled. He opened the umbrella and jumped off the roof. "And the umbrella flipped up, and he came crashing down!" she hooted, dabbing her eyes. All those people, waiting to see him fly. Dazed, his glasses crooked on his face, his skinny legs akimbo, nothing was hurt except his ego. The audience howled.

Ben Spencer thought he could defy gravity. He didn't know then, not yet, that poor Black boys in Dallas could not escape their geography or their skin color, that only white children could thwart the downward forces, that the world was ordered such that sniffing cocaine earned white teens a stern lecture while smoking cocaine sent Black teens to prison for years. At eleven or twelve, he did not yet realize that Black boys fall like a stone. He still nurtured ambitions to preach, to drive long-haul trucks, to marry and raise a family. Prison had no part in his plan. And for twenty-two years, Ben Spencer defied the fate of his peers, until the death of Jeffrey Young.


B enjamine John Spencer III was born five days before Christmas in 1964, the third of five children, raised in the modest Black neighborhood of Oak Cliff, a suburb of Dallas. His father worked at General Motors for twenty-one years, and on the weekends preached occasionally at Sunnyvale Church of Christ. "We were never in need of anything while my father and mother were together," Spencer recalled. His mother, Lucille, cleaned houses and offices, and ran the youth group at church. "An idle man is the devil's workshop," she used to say. Keep the kids busy and you keep them out of trouble. When she worked, they did. "Ben can clean a house or an office as good as I can, or maybe even better," she noted.

Their lives revolved around church, Juanita Spencer recalled. "We went to church every day, it seems like," she said. "Ben knows his Bible. All of us know it, but he *knows* it." Everyone thought he'd become a preacher. As a boy, Spencer assumed pastoral duties whenever the need arose. "Like if the dog died, we'd have a ceremony," Juanita recalled. "We'd have crackers and juice. He was always the preacher. He always presided over the funerals of the pets."

His parents' divorce when Spencer was thirteen unwound the family's settled life; he was cut loose suddenly, unwillingly. They stopped attending church and his mother moved the children from Oak Cliff to West Dallas, where drugs, gangs, and violence marred the landscape of their lives. Yet Ben Spencer seemed oblivious to the pressures to join a gang. Fights broke out every day at Pinkston High School, but Spencer paid no notice. "If somebody was fighting, Ben went on about his business, he didn't even stop to watch the fight," his friend Jerry Fuller recalled. "It wasn't like he was afraid. He just wasn't that type of person."

On a summer evening in 1983, Spencer, recently graduated from Pinkston, stopped by the Pizza Inn on his way home from work. Stylish and handsome, his high cheekbones sloped down to a narrow chin and a wide, open smile. With his lanky six-foot-four frame, clothes seemed designed with Spencer in mind. He favored Ralph Lauren, Perry Ellis, and ostrich boots. Every Friday, he went to the barber for a fresh "Clark" cut—named after Clark Kent, Superman's alter ego. He was, in truth, a little vain: On those rare occasions that Spencer went clubbing, he would take extra shirts. If someone was wearing a similar shirt, he'd change outfits.

"He didn't want nobody in there with the same shirt he had on," Juanita Spencer observed. Soft-spoken and polite, Spencer attracted young women like a magnet, but he wouldn't date. His mother laid down the law: If you got a girl pregnant, you married her. "He said my mama had just put the fear of God in him," Juanita said. "She gave the same story to all of us, but for some reason he took it a little more seriously than we did."

No surprise, then, that when Spencer settled into a booth at the Pizza Inn by himself, he drew the gazes of Debra Childs and her three friends. "I was like, 'Aw, he's kind of cute,'" Debra remembered. "One of my friends said, 'Well, I'm going to go over there and tell him to talk to you.'" A minute later, he was sitting awkwardly in the booth with the four young women. Self-conscious, he lingered only a couple of minutes, long enough to take in the tall, slim, arresting girl with straight black hair who seemed stricken with reticence. "I can almost remember that night as if it was last night," he wrote Debra some twenty years later. "You were acting all shy, and wouldn't say one thing."

As it happened, they lived around the corner from each other. He visited her house, and Debra was hopeful; but a few weeks later, he disappeared. He had moved to his father's home in Karnack, three hours east of Dallas, putting distance between him and his best friend, Ray Lee.

Ray Lee lived in Oak Cliff and was not an obvious choice for Spencer. Spencer steered away from trouble; Ray Lee embraced it. He had been running with all the thugs in the neighborhood, breaking into houses, and Spencer's father, ever the pastor, encouraged his son to befriend the troubled teenager and influence him for the better. The two became inseparable. Ray Lee ceased breaking into houses, until Spencer moved to Karnack. When Spencer returned, they resumed their friendship, but now they were older, nineteen, and his friend had acquired some bad habits.

On February 13, 1985, Ray Lee stole a Chevrolet Camaro Z28. Stealing cars and joyriding was Ray Lee's favorite pastime—one that Ben disapproved of but deemed better than burglarizing homes. The next morning, the two young men were joyriding when Ray Lee decided to stop by his house to pick up a bottle of Crown Royal whiskey. He asked Spencer to drive around the block. "As I was making a block, this police [car] fell in behind me," he recalled in a letter. Spencer had no intention of being caught in this stolen car. "So I led the police on a chase," he wrote. "I was terrified."[2] He managed to bail out of the car and hide at another friend's house. The next day he moved back to Karnack.

After a few months, Debra Childs drove to Karnack and brought him back. "I wanted to date that guy," she explained. "Ben was quiet, sweet." He was *tall*—a bonus, since Debra topped six feet—handsome, a beautiful dresser, and respectful. "When he came to my parents' house, he was just that gentlemen that your dad wants you to meet and marry."

"Against my better judgment," Spencer said, on his return, he picked up his friendship with Ray Lee where it left off. "One day while I was hanging out with him, I realized something," Spencer reflected. "I was still possibly a wanted man. And I'm like, If I keep running with this guy here, I'm either going to wind up dead, or in prison. So, I made a decision that I was going to stop hanging out with my best friend and get my life together." Spencer's good intentions did not satisfy the law, of course. In May 1986, Dallas police arrested him for a UUMV—unauthorized use of a motor vehicle. He pleaded guilty and was sentenced to six years' probation.

An equally pressing motive beyond the prospect of prison ended the friendship. Spencer left Ray Lee's orbit to join Debra's. "You had stolen my heart," he wrote her years later, "I just had to have you in my life."[3] He wasn't ready for marriage. But she was unlike the other girls he knew. Smart, confident, and reserved, she wanted her own career and gravitated toward the sciences and computers. And unlike Spencer, she came from a stable, happy family. Her parents cared deeply for each other. "They never fought, they never raised their voices," she recalled. The family ate every meal together. "I mean, it was just what you wanted in a family. We had two cars, a nice house, and Christmas was always good. Birthdays were good. Almost perfect."

Debra expected her life with Spencer to include all this and more.

While her father never attended church, Spencer never missed it. "I had actually found a guy that goes to church. He would make sure our kids went to church. I felt really lucky." Spencer had developed a separate relationship with her father, who after retirement indulged his passion and worked as a car mechanic. Spencer often spent afternoons with Mr. Childs at the garage helping him with repairs. Her dad called him Brother Ben, introduced him as his son-in-law, and shared his tools.

In late 1986, the couple moved into a house in West Dallas that Lucille Spencer owned. One memory remains among his favorites. A few days before Christmas, they shopped for gifts for all their family and friends, even though they had little money to spare. When they returned home, they realized that they had forgotten to buy gifts for each other. "We had each other, which to me was a perfect gift," Spencer wrote in a letter to Debra years later. "I had what I wanted for Christmas: You were with me. That was the best Christmas ever for me."[4]

A few days later, the couple learned that Debra was four months pregnant. "I was like, 'What are we going to do?'" Debra recalled asking. "And he said, 'Well, I'm going to take care of the baby.'" Spencer asked her father for permission to marry her. "Will you take care of my girl?" Mr. Childs asked. "Yes, sir, I will," Spencer replied. "Then you can marry her," he said, and shook his hand. They married at the Childs home a week later. Spencer wore a borrowed suit and his ostrich boots.

In Debra's telling, their days glided by on a quiet sea of expectation and hope. Every evening after Debra returned from work and before Spencer left for the night shift, "he would get right next to my belly and talk to the baby," Debra said. "That baby would just be kicking all over the place. Ben just loved that." He would run her bathwater, make sure she had something to eat, and settle her into bed before he left. "We just had each other. And family. We had a real quiet life."

But in Spencer's telling, theirs was a bumpy transition. He recalls downpours of arguing followed by droughts of silence. "My relationship with Debra was constantly off and on," he wrote in one letter.[5] He was persuaded she was torn between him and another man. Years later, he wrote Debra: "I would go from Mountain highs to Valley lows with you constantly. I was miserably in love."[6] At the same time, other women began approaching Spencer, sometimes offering to pay his bills if he would spend time with them. Spencer was perplexed that his wife seemed unhappy with him while other women found him so attractive. His insecurity would be his undoing.

# Chapter 4

# A BREAK IN THE CASE

**Benjamine was acting nervous, rubbing his chin.**

—GLADYS OLIVER, *the state's star witness*

Aa was their routine, Ben Spencer drove his wife to work on Tuesday, March 24, at 7:40 a.m., and returned home. His dominant memory involved a migraine that worsened throughout the day until it was almost unbearable as he began his shift at Mistletoe Express. After about an hour of "pain that intensified every time that I would bend over to pick up something," Spencer asked his supervisors' permission to leave work. They agreed, after he finished helping with that truck, and the next, and just one more. He finally left after 2:00 a.m.

Detective Jesus Briseno, too, was faring poorly in his investigation into Jeffrey Young's homicide. His notes record that a crime-scene investigator lifted fingerprints from the interior of the BMW—all four windows, front and back—as well as on the roof of the car above the driver's side. He also found a palm print on the trunk, where someone had closed the lid—possibly the assailant when he secured Jeffrey Young inside for the ride across the Trinity River. But Briseno doubted the forensics would crack the case.

"We really didn't have that much luck with fingerprints for some reason," Briseno later admitted. "Maybe the guys weren't doing a good job, I don't know, but we really very seldom got hits on fingerprints from the crime scene back then."

Briseno's break would come from an entirely different source. Early Tuesday morning, flyers appeared stapled to telephone poles across West Dallas and on a bulletin board at a nearby grocery store. They offered up to one thousand dollars from Crime Stoppers for information leading to the arrest of Jeffrey Young's assailants. Word of an even larger reward— ten thousand dollars from Jeffrey Young's company for information that led to an indictment—quickly spread throughout the neighborhood. At nine fifteen Tuesday morning, a West Dallas resident placed a call to Crime Stoppers, reporting that she had seen two men exiting the victim's BMW and running away. Better, she could identify them.

Crime Stoppers relayed the information to the Dallas Police Department, and Briseno made arrangements for an unmarked police car to pick up the woman and bring her to police headquarters. Gladys Oliver was about to become the star witness for the prosecution.

At forty-two, Oliver struggled to walk into police headquarters. Her asthma was bothering her and polio had ravaged her left leg, making it nearly impossible to climb stairs. Before the polio, Oliver had worked as a private nurse; now she depended on welfare, earning a little side money selling barbecue sandwiches on the weekend.

But Oliver could tell a story. She told Detective Briseno she knew exactly who killed Jeffrey Young. Her house overlooked the alley where the BMW had been parked, and she identified Ben Spencer and Robert Mitchell as the two men she saw running from the car. Given her strategic vantage point, police had asked her at least twice before if she had seen anything that night. She had seen nothing, she said. Then she heard around the neighborhood that police suspected her friend Van Mitchell Spencer, and that there was a sizable monetary reward. She reconsidered her silence and called Crime Stoppers.

Briseno listened calmly as Oliver laid out the very best kind of eyewitness evidence. She was not trying to identify a stranger—or worse, someone of another race, which goes wrong so very often. The accuser and the accused were neighbors. Spencer lived across the street from her, and Mitchell lived down the block.

According to her signed affidavit, Oliver said that "around 10:00 or 11:30 p.m.," while she was in bed trying to sleep, she heard noises in her backyard. "So I peeped out of my bedroom window and saw Robert Mitchell get out of the driver's side and go around toward the back of the car," her affidavit stated.[1] "I also saw Benjamin Spencer get out of the passenger side and start running toward the Brackens house," past fourteen-year-old Sandra Brackens, who was sitting on her porch. (Spencer spells his first name Benjamine, but in official documents, such as affidavits, legal filings, or trial transcripts, the state used the traditional spelling of Benjamin.) Oliver recalled that Spencer was wearing a black jacket, black cap, and dark pants—the same clothes that Brackens had recalled. But Spencer had a light complexion, stood six feet four inches tall, and weighed 180 pounds—nothing like the dark-skinned, slender man between five foot eight and six feet tall whom Brackens had described to Briseno earlier in the week.[2] Oliver stated that Mitchell was wearing a dark, V-neck shirt and dark pants. But at five foot nine and 255 pounds, Mitchell could not be described as slender.

Even with these discrepancies, Briseno was impressed by Oliver's command of detail, particularly for someone peering out her window more than a hundred feet away from the car on a moonless night. Quizzed about this, she explained that the streetlight stood at the foot of the alley, and her neighbor's back light was on.

Oliver continued her story. She closed the curtains, slipped on a dress, and looked out the front door. She saw Spencer walking from behind her house through the driveway. "Benjamin was acting nervous, rubbing his chin," she stated in her affidavit. He entered the house next door, and when Oliver checked again, Debra Spencer's red Thunderbird, which had been parked in front of her house, was gone. She suggested the detective talk with two teenage boys to corroborate her story. She hadn't talked to them, she said. It was just a hunch.

Gladys Oliver was no drug-addled teenager with a fuzzy memory who could be attacked at trial, Briseno later explained. "She was an older person, not a young kid. I figured that she was trustworthy. I didn't think that she had anything to lie or get out of it."

T hursday morning, Briseno and a fellow homicide detective spoke with three more witnesses. At the recommendation of Gladys Oliver, they pulled eighteen-year-old Jimmie Cotton out of class at Pinkston High School, where he was a junior. Cotton told them he remembered the evening well. After playing basketball in the park, he was cooking a late dinner for himself, moving from the stove to the sink and back, when he looked out the window and spotted an expensive sports car turning slowly into the alley across the street. He watched—cars like this did not frequent his neighborhood—and after one second, two, three, the passenger's door opened and Ben Spencer climbed out. He ran toward the Brackens house, and a second later, Robert Mitchell clambered out from the driver's side.

Although Gladys Oliver and Jimmie Cotton viewed the event from opposite angles, the details dovetailed seamlessly. Cotton signed an affidavit, which has since been lost.

In addition to Cotton, Gladys Oliver had steered the detectives to Donald Merritt. They were settling in to question the seventeen-year-old at his home when Merritt's cousin, who was living in the house as well, spoke up. It turned out that twenty-year-old Charles Stewart had seen *everything*. The detectives split up and interviewed the young men in separate rooms. Briseno talked with Merritt, who said he had spotted Jeffrey Young lying on the street, and a few minutes later, had walked by Robert Mitchell standing next to the BMW in the alley. But he had not seen anyone driving the car or running from it. Merritt signed an affidavit. It, too, has disappeared.

In his affidavit, Charles Stewart allegedly stated that he had seen Robert Mitchell driving the BMW with Ben Spencer riding as passenger. He had seen them push the victim out of the car. Later, he swore, he watched as they maneuvered the BMW into the alley, and recognized Spencer and Mitchell leaving the car. This affidavit is gone as well.[3] In July 1990, prosecutors petitioned the court to dispose of the document, along with nonessential items such as newspaper clippings and photographs.

This might not matter, except that Charles Stewart would later testify at trial to something very different. Under oath, he denied several damaging statements in the lost affidavit. He denied that he saw Spencer and Mitchell riding in the BMW. Without placing the two men in the car—without Stewart's testimony that he later recanted—the police had little to tie the suspects to the assault, and nothing to say they murdered Jeffrey Young and dumped his body in the street. Spencer and Mitchell could argue they were merely examining the car, as others in the neighborhood had done.

Stewart provided police with another damning detail. According to the detective's notes, which do still exist, Stewart claimed that while he was driving with Spencer on Monday to redeem his amplifier from the pawnshop, "Benjamin also said something about picking up a white dude off of Inwood." Inwood is the street closest to Jeffrey Young's office. The notes continue, quoting Stewart: "Benjamin was wearing a nugget ring on his little finger that he didn't have before."[4]

Later that day, Briseno secured arrest warrants for Ben Spencer and Robert Mitchell. The warrants rested entirely on Charles Stewart's affidavit—not on Gladys Oliver's, Jimmie Cotton's, or Donald Merritt's. Only Stewart had claimed to see Spencer and Mitchell riding inside the BMW, pushing the body from the car, and parking the car in the alley. Briseno's warrant also contained a statement that was not in his notes: that Spencer told Stewart that he had "beat the white dude."[5] In three days, Briseno had solved the case.

The US justice system is fairer than most, particularly if you are white and relatively affluent. But for others—people of color, people with low incomes—it is deeply flawed from top to bottom. Spencer, like most citizens in the 1980s, trusted the system to vindicate the innocent and convict the guilty. Not until 2012, when a group of law professors formed the National Registry of Exonerations and began tallying the number of wrongful convictions, did the scope of the problem emerge, as well as the personal cost. More than thirty-four hundred innocent people have been convicted and exonerated in the past thirty-five years. Each man or woman wasted on average nearly a decade of their lives incarcerated, years that would never be recovered. The Registry has identified the reasons for the wrongful conviction in each of those cases, and this allows a glimpse into the psychological and structural reasons the system punishes the innocent.

Far and away the largest cause of wrongful convictions is faulty eyewitness testimony. People fail *miserably* at recalling events or faces—particularly when watching a crime take place, a fact that psychologists chronicled starting in the 1970s. Even before that, in 1967, US Supreme Court Justice William Brennan Jr. famously observed in *United States v. Wade*: "The vagaries of eyewitness identification are well-known; the annals of criminal law are rife with instances of mistaken identification."[6] DNA grounded Brennan's observation in scientific fact. Beginning with the first DNA exoneration in 1989, the science showed dispositively that eyewitnesses often identify the wrong person. Since then, of the first 375 cases in which an innocent person was convicted but later absolved of guilt through DNA testing, seven out of ten erroneous convictions involved mistaken eyewitness identification.[7] Yet eyewitness identifications—even those believed to be unreliable—are rarely excluded in court.[8]

In general, an eyewitness may present flawed testimony for one of two reasons: she honestly made a mistake, or she intentionally lied.

Consider the honest mistake. Although it is benign in motivation, it is pernicious in result. A victim may point at the suspect and swear, *"I'll never forget that face,"* but this certainty often dissolves under scientific scrutiny. We've known this for more than a century, thanks to the work of a Harvard psychologist named Hugo Münsterberg. His 1908 book, *On the Witness Stand*, chipped away at the foundational assumptions of the trial system.

In his most famous essay, "The Memory of the Witness,"[9] Münsterberg begins his demolition of eyewitness testimony with a disarming anecdote at his own expense. One summer, he and his family were vacationing when he received word that his home had been burgled. He rushed back and, blessed with an exceptional memory—he had delivered three thousand lectures without a single note[10]—he confidently stated his keen observations before a jury: where the burglars entered the house, what rooms they investigated, what items they took, and what items they didn't. A few days later, police caught the perpetrator. "Every one of these statements was wrong,"[11] he confessed—including the number of burglars (one, not two).[12]

"How did all those mistakes occur?" he asks. He concludes that even under the best circumstances, our recollections are fragile, fragmented, malleable. "Justice would less often miscarry if all who are to weigh evidence were more conscious of the treachery of human memory."

To prove his point, he cited an experiment at the University of Berlin in 1902.[13] A famous criminologist was lecturing when suddenly a fight broke out between two students, becoming more and more heated until one took out a revolver and pulled the trigger. The professor ordered the rest of the students to write down an exact account of what happened: the sequence of events, who said what, what each was wearing, and other details. The entire scene had been rehearsed by actors as a test of the students' powers of observation and recollection. When all the accounts were examined, the most accurate student was wrong in 26 percent of his statements; the worst was 80 percent wrong. In other experiments, trained observers, such as jurists and psychologists, performed just as poorly.[14]

In the last quarter of the twentieth century, an avalanche of research would reveal why memory is so treacherous. Memory does not operate like a video camera, which you can later play back and expect a faithful reproduction. Rather, the memory expert Elizabeth Loftus says, we recall parts of events we witness, fill in the gaps with bits and pieces of our experience, and construct what feels like a real memory. "I like to say that memory works a little bit like a Wikipedia page," she says, "because you can go in there and edit it, but so can other people."[15]

Memory can be edited by race: Studies have shown that people are 50 percent more likely to wrongly identify the face of a person of a different race.[16] It can be changed by what people see later, such as a photo in the newspaper or a video on TV.[17] People are apt to see a stranger and believe it is someone they know.[18] Most measurably, people's recollection can be contaminated when they try to identify a criminal in a lineup by unspoken cues from the attending police officer, or by seeing the person in different photos or in a walk-by. One 2008 meta-analysis of ninety-four studies of lineups found that people correctly identified the perpetrator only 46 percent of the time.[19] And yet, we execute people based on evidence with this error rate.

G ladys Oliver and the young men in West Dallas did not need a line-up to pick out Ben Spencer. They knew him. Therefore, three options seem plausible here. First, they saw and correctly identified Ben Spencer as the man in the alley who ran away from Jeffrey Young's car. Second, they believed they saw Spencer and made a mistake. Third, they purposely lied. Let's take them one by one. For simplicity's sake, we will focus on Gladys Oliver, since she watched the scene more attentively and would become the star witness for the prosecution.

First, could Gladys Oliver have correctly identified Ben Spencer on the night of March 22, 1987? That would defy the law of optics, says Geoffrey Loftus, an expert on memory who examined the evidence for Spencer's attorneys in 2019. All visually normal people are equipped with two visual systems: the photopic system during the day (or with electric lighting), and the scotopic system at night, which requires little or no light. On a cloudy, moonless night, Gladys Oliver's scotopic system would likely have kicked in as she peered toward the BMW in the alley. Thanks to the scotopic system, she could see a figure, but in shades of gray: She could not determine the color of the person's clothes or his skin, which accords with her description of Spencer wearing all black. Her ability to see fine detail, such as the collection of features that make up somebody's facial appearance, "would be severely diminished or eliminated," says Loftus, who teaches psychology at the University of Washington (and was once married to Elizabeth Loftus). It would be like seeing a blurry black-and-white photograph.

Moreover, recent research has examined a person's ability to identify another person at a distance.[20] The likelihood of correctly identifying someone sixty-five feet away in low lighting is 11 percent. Gladys Oliver stood nearly twice as far from the car. "Even if a witness was looking at his or her brother," Loftus says, "the chance that they would recognize them was essentially zilch."

Now consider the second option, that Gladys Oliver (and the others) believed they saw Spencer, and made a mistake. Psychological studies show that witnesses are likely to identify a stranger as someone they know, perhaps a neighbor or colleague.[21] This is called "transference error" or unconscious transference. "Confusion between an innocent encounter and a crime scene can turn an innocuous familiarity into inculpating testimony," notes Dan Simon, author of *In Doubt: The Psychology of the Criminal Justice Process* and a professor of law and psychology at the University of Southern California.[22]

This kind of confusion happens all the time. Say you are walking down the street and see a friend. When the person draws closer, you realize you mistook a stranger for your friend. Now consider another scenario: You believe you see your friend, but before you have a chance to correct your error, the person disappears into a store. You go on believing that it was your friend you saw that day. "And in fact," Loftus says, "if your friend happened to have been accused of a crime during that general time in that general vicinity, you would reluctantly have to say, 'Well, I know he was there because I saw him,' even though actually you didn't. So, basically you screwed him."

Given that the lighting and distance made an accurate identification impossible, he says, it's possible that Oliver saw someone who had the shape and build of Ben Spencer, but the person ran away before she could correct her mistake. Later, Oliver might have filled in the blanks when she saw a photo, or Ben Spencer himself, in better lighting and "replaced the original, low-quality memory of the suspect with a clearer image."[23] That clearer image of Ben Spencer would be etched more deeply into her memory every time she discussed her testimony with police and prosecutors, justified it to her neighbors, swapped accounts with the other witnesses, or even thought about it, says Saul Kassin, a professor of psychology at John Jay College of Criminal Justice. "If you imagine something often enough, it starts to feel true and it starts to become a 'memory,'" he says.

"But I don't think that's what happened," Loftus says. "I don't think she misrecognized the perpetrator as Ben Spencer when she was watching him that night. Instead, I think she concluded after the fact that it was Ben Spencer and reconstructed her memory of the actual perpetrator accordingly."

Which leaves the third option: outright lying.

# Chapter 5

# NO EXCUSE

+———+

**I wasn't really scared at first.**

—Benjamine Spencer

On Thursday morning, March 26, Ben Spencer awakened to his relentless, piercing headache. He decided to sleep it off after delivering a sandwich to Debra. As he drove to her office around 11:00 a.m., Spencer saw a Camaro flash its lights at him. The two cars stopped in the middle of the quiet road, facing opposite directions. Charles Stewart, fresh from giving his incriminating statement to the detectives, leaned out his window.

"Man, my girlfriend let me keep her car," Stewart said, "and I was wondering if you could follow me later on this evening so I can take her car back."

"What time?"

"About four o'clock."

"Yeah, I can do that for you," Spencer replied, and continued to Debra's office. She told him she had made an appointment for him to see a doctor about his headache at 3:15 p.m. Driving back, he spotted Stewart in the Camaro, and flashed his lights. Four o'clock won't work, he said, but he can help out earlier. Stewart suggested 2:30 p.m. Spencer said he was going home and to knock on the door when he was ready.

"I go to the house, take a Tylenol, lay down and go to sleep," Spencer recalled. "I wake up to somebody beating on the door. I look at the clock. It's two thirty. I assumed it must be Charles. So I get up. As I'm going to the front door, I can see a bunch of police cars in front of the house. And I think, I wonder what's going on out here? When I open the door, I don't see Charles Stewart. I see all these cops on the porch."

"Do you have any ID?" a detective asked.

Spencer handed him his driver's license.

The detective studied the ID briefly. "Turn around and put your hands on the wall," he ordered. "You're under arrest."

"Under arrest? For what?"

"I'll tell you in a minute," Jesus Briseno replied, and marched Spencer to a police car. Inside the cruiser the detective asked, "You hear about the white guy they found in the street the other day?"

"Yeah, I heard something about it."

"That's what you're under arrest for. His murder."

"*No!* You got the wrong guy."

"No, we have the right guy," Briseno responded. "Some of your neighbors say they saw you the night of the offense walking around, showing off this jambox with the TV on it."

"A jambox? Man, what am I going to do with a jambox?" Spencer asked, then tried to reason with the detective. "Dope fiends steal stuff like jamboxes. Why would I steal a jambox? I got two cars. Both my cars have systems in it. I've got a system in the house. I don't do any walking, so what am I going to do with the jambox?"

"I don't know, but that's what you're under arrest for." Briseno turned to face Spencer. "You mind if we search your house?"

Spencer assented, and Briseno ushered him back into his bedroom and sat him on the bed. Spencer watched as police officers opened drawers and closets looking for a murder weapon, or any of Jeffrey Young's belongings—his Seiko watch, his wedding band, or his jambox. They came across a portable black-and-white TV with a radio on it. "They're like, 'Oh, we got you! We got you!'" Spencer recalled. "I say, 'I don't know what y'all are looking for, but that ain't what y'all are looking for. There's nothing in this house that's stolen. That TV belongs to my mother.' They said, 'Nah, we got you.'"

The television was engraved with his mother's name and driver's license number, and the search turned up nothing suspicious: no blunt instrument, no clothing or jewelry, no jambox or cash, nothing that connected Spencer to the assault. "We're still going to take you downtown," Briseno said. He put Spencer back in the cruiser and drove to Dallas Police headquarters.

About this time, Spencer's sister Janet was driving by his house and saw a half dozen police cars blocking the entrance, lights flashing, uniformed men walking in and out. Debra remembers Janet calling her at work from a phone booth a block away.

"Where is Junebug?" Janet asked, using his family's nickname for her brother.

"He's at home," Debra responded.

"Well, the house is surrounded by police," Janet said. She began to narrate the arrest as it unfolded: Ben's walking out of the house, his hands are cuffed behind his back, they're putting him into the back seat of a cruiser. "They're taking him in."

"Well, maybe he's got some tickets or something," Debra said. "Go see."

"I am not going up there with all those policemen over there," Janet said. "They have guns out and everything."

Janet picked up Debra at the office and drove her home. "It looked like it had been ransacked," Debra recalled, "like they were looking for something. It was just a mess. He was gone."

B riseno ushered Spencer into a windowless interrogation room; in the adjacent room sat Spencer's alleged accomplice, Robert Mitchell. Briseno read Spencer his Miranda rights, and Spencer waived his right to a lawyer, a mistake that ensnares the innocent more than the guilty. Spencer was offered no food or water, but he didn't consider the interview draconian, as it lasted no more than four or five hours. Briseno led the interrogation, accompanied by another detective. In 1987, police interviews were not recorded, and the notes chronicling the interrogation were twelve sentences long. Half of them focused on the last time Spencer had seen Mitchell. Two details were recorded in one sentence: "Spencer was wearing a gold nugget ring and Neiman Marcus watch," confirming Charles Stewart's observation.[1] The notes boil Spencer's alibi down to one sentence: "Spencer used as an alibi that he had been to Christie @ Wendy house on Calypso."[2]

"Wendy" was the nickname for eighteen-year-old Christie Williams. She lived next door to Gladys Oliver and could see Spencer's house from her front porch. The night of the murder, Christie was two months shy of graduating from high school, where her talent in sports—she was ranked one of the top five high-jumpers in Texas—had earned her a full scholarship to Prairie View A&M.

Ben and Debra, who had married ten weeks earlier and were expecting a baby in less time than that, were wholly unprepared for settled life, for the sudden loss of freedom, for the chafing and pointless bickering. Spencer had never cheated on his wife, although young women sought him out, no strings attached. But Christie Williams intrigued him. She was college-bound, athletic, attractive.

As was their custom, Ben and Debra spent Sunday morning, March 22, with her family, and at brunch, Spencer began teasing Debra's older sister. "I'm not a playful kind of person, and I kind of got upset," Debra recalled ruefully. "I was just always so serious about *everything*, and Ben was the opposite. He loved having fun."

They went home and "had words," Debra remembered. "I was like, *Just go away.*" He left the house around 1:00 p.m. Thus began the circuitous journey of a twenty-two-year-old man who had just argued with his wife, yearning to go home and dreading it, trying to find things to do. He blew a few hours with friends at a park and left at five thirty to drive back to West Dallas. He stopped to see another friend, Marlon Oliver, Gladys

Oliver's son. He drove his neighbor and her friends to church. In the car, his neighbor mentioned that her sister, Christie, wanted him to drop by. After picking up some Kentucky Fried Chicken, he parked the car in front of the Olivers' house. He ate the chicken, walked to the side of the Olivers' yard, and threw the bones to the Doberman and German shepherd that were barking furiously at him; that shut them up. And then, about seven o'clock, he knocked on Christie's door for what would become his awkward alibi. What he did not know then was that the most shameful hours of his life would become the ones that would define him, and that the only way to preserve his freedom would be to confess his transgression again and again.

In the living room, Christie turned on the radio and they talked about track, about how nervous and excited she felt about college, about her eagerness to escape West Dallas. "Maybe our conversation was leading to something else," Spencer later wrote to a friend, "but we never engaged in any sex or anything. Maybe a few kisses, but nothing more."[3]

Around 10:00 p.m., Christie's two teenage brothers returned home after a game of basketball. The oldest went to his room, but the fourteen-year-old cooked a burrito and sat in a recliner in the front room with them. "She started hollering at her little brother," Spencer recalled. "His name was Israel. I know his name only because she said it so many times that night. She kept trying to get him to leave the living room, and he wouldn't leave. So I said, 'Well, you want to go for a ride?' She says, 'Sure.'"

Christie changed from shorts to jogging pants, and they drove to North Hampton Park. "We sat at the park for a few hours talking and whatnot," Spencer recalled. "I would say it was about twelve thirty, twelve forty-five, and I said, 'Well, maybe I should take you home.' And she said, 'Yeah, because I got to get up and go to school in the morning.' I said, 'Yeah, I got to get up and take my wife to work.'" Spencer dropped her off, waited until someone let her in, then drove home, where he found Debra lying in the dark, half-asleep and still smoldering from the day's argument.

Spencer told detectives that he never heard an ambulance or a fire truck, never spotted a BMW in the alley, never saw a white man lying in the street. While Jesus Briseno quizzed him, another investigator visited Christie Williams. According to the investigator's notes, the officer showed her photos of both suspects. "She didn't know either one of them," the notes report. "I also showed her mother, Hattie [Walker], the pictures. She didn't know either one of them."

Briseno relayed the news to Spencer. "She said you're not her boy-friend," Briseno stated.

"I never told you I was her boyfriend," Spencer retorted. "I told you I was with her."

"Well, she says she didn't spend the night with a man."

"I didn't say we spent the night. I said we spent several hours together."

"Well, she says she don't know you."

"Well, she has to know me because that's who I was with."

Alibis are a fragile reed on which to hang a defense, and Christie's statement effectively mowed it down. Thirty years later, Christie still viv-idly remembered that visit, as it was her only brush with law enforcement. She said the detective showed her four or five photos, some taken from the front, some from the side. They were blurry, shot too close. "They were like this," she said, holding the palm of her hand a half inch from her face. "You couldn't identify nobody in the pictures."

W hen Spencer's alibi collapsed, he landed in the company of hun-dreds of innocent people in Texas and elsewhere sent to prison for crimes they didn't commit. Alibis are the weapon of last resort for a de-fense attorney and are about as ineffective as a jackknife at a shootout. What's surprising from the little research conducted about alibis is not that police, prosecutors, and juries often doubt them, but that they *always* doubt them and usually dismiss them.

Brandon Garrett, a professor at Duke University School of Law, looked at the first 250 cases of people who were convicted and later definitively exonerated by DNA evidence. He read tens of thousands of pages of trial transcripts, confessions, and judicial opinions to see whether these cases were unfortunate but idiosyncratic goofs or flawed practices baked into the criminal justice system. He concluded that it's the latter. In his book *Convicting the Innocent: Where Criminal Prosecutions Go Wrong*, Garrett found that 68 percent of the accused offered an alibi at trial.[4] Not a single one of them worked, because alibis are often "weak"—that is, uncorroborated by physical evidence. He notes an irony here: A criminal can easily make up an alibi, adorning it with plausible details, because he knows what to reveal and what to hide. But most of us are unlikely to recall where we were or whom we were with three Tuesdays ago at 5:57 p.m. "This is particularly true for an innocent person who did nothing improper on that day and would have no special reason to recall it," Garrett says.[5]

"It's always hard to prove that you did not do something," says Dan Simon from the University of Southern California. "We don't walk around with time stamps and we don't walk around with receipts and tickets to everywhere we go. And we're oftentimes alone, so there's no one to corroborate."

Of the 140 innocent people in Garrett's study who claimed they were elsewhere when the crime occurred, more than 85 percent relied, like Ben Spencer, exclusively on other people to vouch for them.[6] They had no receipts or ticket stubs (although selfies or location data from cell phones might help to cure this problem). A study of US and Canadian alibi cases found the same paucity of physical evidence and pointed to another conundrum: Of the 125 cases studied, only two of the alibis were supported by people other than friends and family.[7]

Friends and family don't hold much weight with jurors, who figure they will lie to protect the defendant. For example, a roomful of friends did nothing to save the "Savannah Three."[8] The three soldiers, who were stationed at Fort Stewart, Georgia, were celebrating at an impromptu bachelor party the night before the wedding of one of the men in 1992. Witnesses confirmed they were at the wedding rehearsal fifty miles away from

Savannah until a few minutes before a fatal shooting there. But the jury discounted those witnesses, and the three men were sentenced to life plus five years. They served twenty-six years before Georgia admitted its error and released them.[9]

Although alibi testimony is intended as "a shield," Simon observes, it can "serve as a weapon" against an innocent defendant."[10] Ronald Cotton was erroneously convicted of rape in North Carolina in 1985, based on the victim's flawed memory. He claimed he was with family that night, asleep on the couch. The abundance of alibi witnesses backfired. "When Ronald Cotton's family got up to testify, they all said the same thing," one juror recalled.[11] They said he was dozing on the couch all evening. "You knew what the next one was going to say after about three or four of them had said that he was on the sofa." They sounded rehearsed. "To me, that would make one think that somebody is guilty."

Even when the suspect could marshal a brigade of compelling evidence that absolved him—strangers who saw him, records and physical evidence, a more plausible suspect, and the laws of nature that still preclude teleporting—he can be convicted. Steven Avery, made famous by the Netflix series *Making a Murderer*, was accused of raping a woman in broad daylight on a beach in Manitowoc County, Wisconsin, on July 29, 1985. He presented sixteen alibi witnesses, all of whom said he was pouring concrete all day with his extended family and friends.[12] At trial, he produced proof of a trip to Green Bay, where he bought paint at a Shopko and introduced a receipt showing he had checked out at 5:13 p.m.

For the state's case to be plausible, Avery would have had just over an hour to assault the victim, leave the beach, load his family into the car—a wife, three young children, and twins less than a week old—drive forty-five miles to Green Bay, troop into Shopko with his brood, grab a can of paint, and check out, drawing the attention of the store manager and clerk (both strangers) who remembered this boisterous family. Still, on the strength of a shaky (and what later turned out to be contaminated) eyewitness account, Avery was convicted of rape and served eighteen years before DNA exonerated him and implicated someone else.[13]

When one compares Ben Spencer's alibi to others, it would surely be found wanting. Spencer claimed *one* alibi witness, a possible romantic interest; he had no receipts, no ticket stubs, no photos or video placing him somewhere other than the crime scene. In the puzzling calculus of reasonable doubt, his alibi amounted to less than zero.

During his first days in jail, "I wasn't really scared at first," Spencer wrote years later. "I knew that they had made an awful mistake when they arrested me and believed that it was just a matter of time before they figured that out." His gut told him that Briseno believed him. "He needed to sort some things out and I was okay with that. I just knew that the truth would eventually prevail in this case."[14]

Those who trust the system often end up in prison, says Saul Kassin, author of *Duped: Why Innocent People Confess—and Why We Believe Their Confessions*. He calls it the "phenomenology of innocence," which is a "generalized belief" in a just world in which people "get what they deserve and deserve what they get." Like Spencer, he says, "innocent people say, 'Wait, I didn't do this. I'm going to go to trial.' Innocent people don't appreciate the peril. They think they're innocent and everything is going to work itself out." Time and again, it does not.

To his credit, Detective Jesus Briseno ran an honest interrogation. It does not appear that he lied to Spencer while questioning him. He could have said that a witness from a nearby office saw the entire assault or that Robert Mitchell had already confessed and identified Spencer as the mastermind. Such lies are legal. But if Briseno avoided a deceptive or coercive interrogation, he succumbed to an error that ensnares the police in virtually every wrongful conviction. As the investigation into Jeffrey Young's murder unfolded, Briseno's sights narrowed on Ben Spencer and Robert Mitchell until they were the only suspects he could see.

*Chapter 6*

# ENTERING THE TUNNEL

+———+

**A stat is a stat is a stat.**

—HOMICIDE DETECTIVE JAMES TRAINUM

After a few days in jail, Ben Spencer's headache abated, replaced by a gnawing worry about his future. Why hadn't he been released? He barely touched the trays of food, and unlike other inmates who passed the day playing checkers or chess, he kept to himself. Finally, on his eleventh day in the tank, around 7:30 Sunday evening, he was escorted to an interrogation room on the lower floor of the Dallas County jail. Detective Briseno was waiting. He told Spencer to sit down. What follows is Spencer's recollection of the exchange, memorialized in interviews and letters to friends, outside investigators, attorneys, and me.

"Did Van Mitchell Spencer commit this offense?" Briseno began.

"I don't know anybody by that name," Spencer replied, "nor do I have any personal knowledge about who committed this offense."

The detective showed Spencer a photograph of Van Mitchell Spencer. Spencer said he did not recognize him.

"Well, you know, he just got out of prison, where he made parole after serving time since 1977 on a life sentence," Briseno observed.

"I told you that I don't know him," Spencer said, becoming agitated. "We didn't move to West Dallas until 1982. I have never met that man in my life."

"Well, you know he's out there walking the streets free, while you're sitting in here facing capital murder."

"So I'm just supposed to lie and say that he did it because he just got out of prison and is now walking the streets free?" Spencer asked. "Why don't you investigate this case, and then the evidence should lead you to the person that's responsible?"

"Why should I have to investigate?" Briseno responded. "I have you charged as a suspect and as far as I am concerned, you're guilty."

"When you finally investigate this case and y'all let me go," Spencer retorted, angry now, "y'all are going to pay me for all of the trouble that you have put me through."

Briseno leaned back in his chair and put down his pen. "I wouldn't worry about suing anybody if I were you," he said, a small smile on his face. "I'm going to personally see to it that you get convicted."

Spencer regrets threatening Briseno; he believes that was the moment that the detective turned against him. Others who have scrutinized Spencer's case have a different view. They believe that Briseno had already made up his mind, and that nothing—no alibi, no evidence exonerating Spencer and implicating another—would alter his course. Briseno, in the experts' view, had already succumbed to the psychological impulse that puts innocent people in prison. Tunnel vision.

E very day, we make decisions based on information, personal preference, gut instinct. Standing in front of the grocery store freezer, you contemplate the frozen dessert section. You may disregard ice cream in favor of frozen yogurt; reject the desserts with mint or fruit and opt for one with chocolate. Or, say you need a new car. Used or new? Rugged like a Jeep or responsible like a hybrid? Black, white, or Sarge Green? You narrow the options until you come to an acceptable, if imperfect, result.

The job of homicide detectives revolves around this winnowing process: Eliminate bad leads and focus on promising ones, like guiding a drone until it locks onto the target. Sooner rather than later, the detective must decide whom he will hold responsible for another's death.

"Cognitive biases help us make decisions in a complex world that would otherwise be so overwhelming we would be unable to maneuver," says Keith Findley, a professor at the University of Wisconsin Law School and cofounder of Wisconsin's Innocence Project. "Without them, the world would be just this unbearable assault of data that we can't deal with." But when the biases send people in the wrong direction, "they can be catastrophic, particularly in a high-stakes game like criminal casework."

The umbrella term for various biases that run amok is "tunnel vision." This happens, for example, when an investigator homes in on one theory or one suspect too soon, to the exclusion of all others. "You have to switch over from an evidence-based to a suspect-based investigation," says the former homicide detective James Trainum, author of *How the Police Generate False Confessions: An Inside Look at the Interrogation Room.* "The danger is when you're not open to anything else but that one suspect—and you begin to tailor the evidence and ignore evidence that doesn't fit your theory."

When you look at the landscape of erroneous convictions, you see recurring contributing factors. Eyewitness identification error. False confessions. Jailhouse informant testimony. Flawed forensic science. Prosecutorial misconduct. "Some cases will have multiples of these, and some will have one," says Findley, who has worked on dozens of wrongful convictions. "All of them, virtually *all* of them, have tunnel vision." The examples are almost limitless, he adds. "Pick virtually any wrongful conviction and you can at least find some features of tunnel vision."[1]

Bias infects every stage of a criminal case and, like venom, spreads through the entire judicial organism. With each stage—investigation, trial, and appeals—the effect of the bias becomes more pronounced and harder to neutralize. It begins with the detective. "We're the ones that get the ball rolling," Trainum says. Police conduct the initial interviews with witnesses and suspects and shape the investigation; they serve as gatekeepers of the evidence that lands on a prosecutor's desk.

"Confirmation bias is contagious, because the prosecutor begins to see the case through our eyes," he says. "And oftentimes they won't critically evaluate what we're bringing them." Once police have a "good enough" suspect, he explains, they usually stop investigating. "Part of that is the fault of the organization, because you're judged on your stats, you're judged on your arrest rate. You're *not* judged if the case is dropped afterward. I mean, that doesn't matter because a stat is a stat is a stat."

The story of Clarence Elkins illustrates how tunnel vision can distort and derail a case from investigation to prosecution to appeal. Early on the morning of June 7, 1998, Judith Johnson was beaten, raped, and killed in her home in Barberton, Ohio. Johnson's six-year-old granddaughter, who was staying with her, was sexually assaulted and left for dead. When the girl regained consciousness, she walked to a neighbor's house. There she was told to wait on the doorstep for forty-five minutes, bloody and traumatized, as the woman made breakfast for her boyfriend. The neighbor then drove the girl home but never called the police. Eventually local police arrived and the girl told them the assailant "looked like Uncle Clarence." Clarence Elkins, who was married to Johnson's daughter, became their sole suspect.

"From that point on," says the former prosecutor Mark Godsey, who represented Elkins in his post-conviction appeal, "there was no going back."

No evidence implicated Elkins. He had an alibi: His wife, the daughter of the slain victim, swore Elkins was at home, asleep. She knew this because she was up and down all night with a sick child. The physical evidence pointed away from him. Two hairs found on the elderly victim did not belong to him. The crime scene was described as a "bloodbath," but police found no blood in Elkins's car, on his clothing, or even in the shower drain. As Godsey notes in his book, *Blind Injustice: A Former Prosecutor Exposes the Psychology and Politics of Wrongful Convictions*, the police were so focused on Elkins that they failed to analyze the grandmother's fingernail scrapings and ignored a bloody lampshade. Nor did they compare DNA, fingerprints, or hair evidence from the crime scene with known sex offenders in the area.

Based only on the child's testimony, a jury convicted Elkins of murder, attempted murder, and rape in 1999. He was sentenced to fifty-five years to life in prison. The appellate court affirmed the jury's decision.

In 2004, the Ohio Innocence Project accepted Elkins's case and sent the DNA evidence from the crime scene to a lab for testing. The tests excluded Clarence Elkins. Elkins's new lawyers appealed for a new trial, but the judge denied the request, ruling that the verdict was based on the girl's testimony and the DNA was irrelevant. Elkins's lawyers approached the prosecutor to support their client's release, but the prosecutor declined. Elkins would stay in prison.

"They came up with all these theories that were just crazy," Godsey recalls. The prosecutors argued that the grandmother had shaken hands with someone and had gotten that person's DNA on her fingers and underneath her fingernails, and then deposited the DNA on herself—what Godsey calls "the masturbating grandmother theory." Prosecutors speculated that the DNA was transferred to the little girl's underwear when the grandmother helped her in the bathroom or folded her underwear. They maintained that Clarence Elkins engaged in a violent murder and rape and managed to leave no DNA trace of himself.

"To me, it was like the prosecutor standing up in court and arguing with great emotion and passion that the moon is made of cheese," Godsey marvels.[2] "Is he evil, trying to keep an innocent man in prison? Or is he just not very smart and truly doesn't understand the DNA test results? Which is it, stupidity or evil?"

It required an outsider to open the aperture and consider more viable possibilities. A private investigator learned that the boyfriend of the neighbor who had left the child waiting on the porch that morning was a registered sex offender. Had police typed Earl Mann's name into the database and tested his DNA at the outset, they would have not only caught the assailant but also prevented more assaults. The phenomenon is called "wrongful liberty." While an innocent person is in custody, the real perpetrator is free to rape and kill. While Elkins was serving time for a crime Mann had committed, Mann raped three girls under ten years old. Under pressure from the Ohio attorney general, and after a second round of testing that again excluded Clarence Elkins, the Summit County prosecutor released him in December 2005.

Tunnel vision often leads to one of the most surprising phenomena in our criminal justice system: false confessions. To be clear, neither Ben Spencer nor Robert Mitchell admitted to robbing and killing Jeffrey Young, and Detective Briseno did not use draconian tactics to elicit a confession. But false confessions allow us to glimpse a secret interaction where police employ a range of questionable tactics and innocent people routinely confess to crimes they did not commit.[3] Confessions trump all other evidence, even DNA. Studies show that nearly half the time people choose to believe an inculpatory confession, even if the DNA points away from the defendant and toward another person.[4]

One out of five innocent people confessed to a murder they didn't commit.[5] How is that possible? Would you admit to murdering someone knowing you could be sentenced to life in prison, or even death? Perhaps you would, if you were under the age of eighteen, or intellectually challenged, which characterizes most false confessors.[6]

It begins in the interrogation room, where tunnel vision is baked into the process. Police possess an astonishing amount of leeway behind closed doors. For example, investigators can lie about the evidence. The US Supreme Court blessed this practice in its 1969 decision, *Frazier v. Cupp*.[7] From then on, the interrogation room became a cauldron of lies, threats, and false promises. Police can say they found a suspect's fingerprints or DNA on the victim, that a video captured him committing the crime,

that witnesses saw him, that his friend and codefendant ratted him out.
They can interrogate a minor without a parent present, as long as the minor has consented. The Supreme Court has banned physical torture but is
fuzzy on psychological torture. The justices last addressed how long a person may be interrogated in 1944, in *Ashcraft v. Tennessee*.[8] In that case,
they ruled that a thirty-six-hour continuous interrogation under the glare
of bright light could render a confession inadmissible. That's the sum total of their guidance.[9]

In the case of the "Norfolk Four," tunnel vision and lax rules led to
results that would make the staunchest police defenders blanch. And yet,
it is typical. On July 7, 1997, eighteen-year-old Michelle Bosko was raped
and killed in her apartment in Norfolk, Virginia. Her husband, a sailor,
found her the next day, after he returned from a stint at sea. Immediately
the detectives zeroed in on twenty-five-year-old Danial Williams, a sailor
who lived next door and who called 911 after her body was discovered.
Norfolk police brought him to an interview room and soon began accusing him of the murder. He denied it and agreed to take a polygraph. The
detectives told Williams that he had failed, when in fact he had passed.
For eleven hours, they escalated their drumbeat of accusations.

"Being in a small room, and you have a person sitting over across the
table from you that's getting in your face, yelling at you, calling you a liar,
poking you in the chest with their finger, and then turns around and says,
'Well, I can help you if you tell me the truth. Tell me what happened.'
And it went on and on and on," Williams told the PBS documentary
show *Frontline*.[10] "He just kept relentlessly going at me throughout the
night to get me to confess. And he got what he wanted. He got me to confess, even though it was a false confession." Williams was arrested and
immediately recanted his confession, but it was too late.

When the DNA results returned, they excluded Williams. The police
rousted Joseph Dick Jr., another sailor who lived nearby and brought
him to the interrogation room. "We can prove you were there. You can
get the death penalty," the detective shouted, Dick told *Frontline*. "I kept
denying it."

He took a polygraph and was told he failed. But the DNA tests excluded Dick as well. The detectives interrogated and polygraphed another sailor, who also confessed; the DNA excluded him. A fourth sailor was polygraphed and interrogated in like manner, and he also confessed. His DNA was excluded like the others. Eventually, the Norfolk police arrested and jailed seven sailors for the crime, even though DNA excluded every one of them.

More than a year and a half after the crime, police learned that Omar Ballard, a convicted rapist, had bragged about the murder. When confronted by police, he quickly confessed. Thus was born a new police theory: The seven sailors had met Ballard, a stranger, in the parking lot, and the eight of them gang-raped and murdered the victim. Ballard insisted he acted alone, and his was the only DNA found at the crime scene. But prosecutors told him that they would ask for the death penalty unless he testified that the four sailors who had confessed had committed the crime with him. The sailors were all convicted and sentenced to life. In 2004, the story of the Norfolk Four began to attract national attention and the pro bono help of three law firms. They were exonerated in 2017, eighteen years after they were convicted and sent to prison.

R esearchers have found that certain types of errors infect certain types of crimes. Mistaken eyewitness identification tends to plague erroneous rape convictions: In the trauma of the moment, the victim misremembers the assailant. Witness tampering distorts child sex abuse cases, because children are so easily influenced by authority figures. Fabricating evidence is rampant in erroneous drug convictions.

Murder attracts a swarm of virulent behavior. "The more serious the crime, the more likely police and prosecutors are to engage in some types of misconduct," says Samuel Gross, a professor emeritus at the University of Michigan Law School. Hiding evidence, putting jailhouse informants and other lying witnesses on the stand, pressuring people to confess, suborning perjury—all the most egregious behavior finds its way to murder convictions. Bad conduct mushrooms in murder cases, Gross says. "It's one thing to let a drug dealer off, but it's another thing to let a murderer off."

Think about the pressure that Detective Jesus Briseno felt in March 1987, his first major homicide involving a white man left to die in the middle of the road in a rough Black neighborhood. Pressure from the police chief, pressure from the prosecutors who were receiving calls and letters from the victim's family—and pressure from the most prosperous man in Dallas. After his interrogation with the detective on April 5, Spencer caught an unexpected glimpse of the forces that would determine his future. He identified the moment only in retrospect. It came as an offhand question from the guard escorting him back to his cell.

"Why has Ross Perot been calling up here asking about you?" the guard asked.

"Who is Ross Perot?" Spencer replied.

"You don't know who Ross Perot is?"

"No."

"He's a billionaire," the guard informed him. "He's been wanting to see if you were in jail."

# Chapter 7

# WITNESSES FOR SALE

+——+

**I would say whatever I need to say to get out of that house.**

—JUANITA SPENCER MCHENRY, *regarding Gladys Oliver*

Before H. Ross Perot ran for president in 1992, the short, wiry self-made billionaire with large ears and a crew cut cast a long shadow in Dallas. "H. Ross Perot was one of the most important figures in Dallas, period," the journalist Bob Ray Sanders says. "He was a very short man, but he talked and walked like he was eight feet tall. And that's how people saw him." He was also stubborn; he demanded and expected results. "Things he wanted to have he usually got—and that would include justice if that's something he wanted."

Perot wanted swift justice for Jeffrey Young's family. The victim's father, Harry, had served as a top executive in Perot's company, Electronic Data Systems (EDS). More than any other civilian in Texas of his time, Perot enjoyed the power to bend the state's criminal justice system to his will, in this case to pressure police to identify the assailants and quickly solve the case. His influence also carried the power to unintentionally distort the truth.

When Jeffrey Young's body was found in West Dallas, Perot set out to find the assailants with his most effective tool: money. He frequently offered rewards through the police department, and sometimes police officials asked him to put up rewards for high-priority cases. According to

police records, at 10:30 a.m. on Thursday, March 26, Jesus Briseno received a call from the head of security at EDS, who asked him to call back.
The cryptic message on the blue "WHILE YOU WERE OUT" slip
read: "(EDS) $25,000." Immediately, notices began to appear across West
Dallas, offering a twenty-five-thousand-dollar reward for the "apprehen-
sion, arrest, and indictment of the person or persons who abducted and
murdered Jeffrey Young." Jesus Briseno's name and number, along with
that of another detective, were listed.

With Perot's contribution, the pot surpassed thirty-five thousand dollars: twenty-five thousand from EDS, ten thousand from Jeffrey Young's
company, and up to one thousand from Crime Stoppers. The largesse created a bundle of problems. At the very least, it could induce some residents of West Dallas to try to frame others. The size of the reward also
suggested the police felt pressure to solve the crime, and the personal intervention by Perot was not lost on the officers of the Dallas Police
Department, who saw the billionaire as their protector.[1]

"If the police knew that Ross Perot had an interest in any case," Sanders says, "they would be out to please H. Ross Perot." Mark Jones, a political scientist at Rice University, notes that the pressure to please can
prompt a rush to judgment. "If you're a police officer or a prosecutor, all of
your incentives were: 'Let's convict this guy,' because the last thing you
want to do is raise doubts about your case if Ross Perot and the family
believed that you found the right guy."

Detective Briseno insisted he felt no pressure and knew nothing about
Perot's reward. When told that his name and phone number were on the
reward poster, he shrugged. "No, no, no. Got nothing to do with that."

If the residents of West Dallas were tempted by the reward, they joined
a line of incentivized witnesses going back at least two thousand years,
when Judas tipped off the Sanhedrin about Jesus for thirty pieces of silver.
Volunteering information about a criminal and risking one's safety surely

merits some compensation. Rewards have always been woven into the fabric of the American criminal justice system, but in 1976, they were given government imprimatur in the form of Crime Stoppers. The organization works with police to provide up to one thousand dollars for anonymous tips—helping to solve, Crime Stoppers claims, some fifteen thousand homicides. And yet, a reward creates a perverse incentive, whether from Crime Stoppers or private individuals and companies, which tend to be more generous. Even a small reward is a bounty for a person who is desperate to pay the electric bill.

When a witness (or, often, a rape victim) misidentifies a suspect, usually she is making an honest mistake: The crime happened in the blink of an eye, it was dark, the witness (or the victim) was too paralyzed with fear to accurately record the memory and later identify the culprit. However, the National Registry of Exonerations has found that in a quarter of these erroneous identifications, the witnesses *knew* they were framing the wrong person.[2] "Misidentifications by strangers are generally mistakes," researchers concluded. "Misidentifications by witnesses who know the suspect are generally lies."[3]

Incentives abound: to protect a friend, to get even with an enemy, to reduce prison time, to land some cash. Tipping off the police incurs no cost and offers a potential windfall for the anonymous witness. Tips usually do not need to be correct for the informant to collect the money. Rules vary from state to state, but in general a tipster receives the money once someone, even an innocent person, is arrested or indicted; indeed, this was the requirement to receive the reward from Ross Perot. In at least forty cases, incentivized witnesses implicated an innocent person for as little as one thousand dollars.

Private rewards, which have no upward limit, have untied many a Gordian knot. A string of robberies, rapes, and a fatal shooting that terrorized New Orleans in 1992 was solved after a tipster identified a nineteen-year-old Black man for ten thousand dollars.[4] Except that it wasn't solved: It would take twenty-one years to prove that the witnesses had lied and that

the prosecutors had withheld exculpatory evidence. In Chicago, a thirty-
five-thousand-dollar reward closed the high-profile case of a Rush University Medical Center student who was raped and murdered.[5] Four Black
teenagers, ages fourteen, sixteen, seventeen, and eighteen were convicted,
based in part on the testimony of the now-flush witness; three of them
received life sentences. DNA exonerated them after thirteen years. The
list continues, a rat-a-tat-tat of testimony corrupted by money.[6]

A reward exceeding thirty-five thousand dollars for information leading to Jeffrey Young's assailants would prove tempting for any
resident of West Dallas in 1987, and in this poor Black neighborhood,
Gladys Oliver ranked among the poorest. She had lived on welfare since
being disabled by polio. To get some cash, she sold her pills for money,
Spencer's sister Juanita recalled, and recruited the kids in the neighborhood to bring her pills from their homes. "She sold those, too. She was
always on the come-up."

When Juanita was a teenager, she and her baby lived with Oliver in the
one-bedroom house along with three other young adults. "They didn't
even have a working bathroom," Juanita recalled. For electricity, Oliver ran
an extension cord from the house next door, which was owned by her stepfather, Leland Banks, known as "Papa Lee." They carried buckets of water
from his house for cooking, and when anyone wanted to take a bath they
went elsewhere. "I think if I were her, I would say whatever I need to say to
get out of the house," Juanita mused. "I have no water. I have no lights. I'd
do whatever I had to do. But it's a shame that she had to take my brother."

Even with signed affidavits from Gladys Oliver and the two other eyewitnesses, Jesus Briseno still had a hole in his case. No one had connected
Ben Spencer or Robert Mitchell to the assault of Jeffrey Young. Even if
they were seen driving in the car—and they both denied that they were—
that did not mean they had beaten Young. They could have simply
found the car abandoned and taken it for a spin.

Briseno needed a witness to the beating.

The voice, abrasive, clanging, unbearably loud, stirred Benjamine Spencer into consciousness. *"Chow time!"* it said. *"Sleep late, lose weight!"*

Spencer winced and looked over to see a young Black man grinning at him. He would later learn that his name was Danny Edwards. Where am I? Spencer wondered, as he took in the thin mattress, the bars around him, the seven other men sitting in the common area of the jail tank eating breakfast. Soon his head cleared: It was March 27, this was the Lew Sterrett Justice Center, and he had been arrested the day before for killing a white man.

Spencer stumbled out of his cell and picked up his breakfast tray. "I didn't have much of an appetite because of everything that was going on," he recalled. "I mean, I'm in jail for *murder*."

"Y'all can eat it," he told Edwards. He returned to his cell, lay down with his back to the world, and went to sleep.

Danny Edwards, in his mid-twenties, was a frequent visitor of jail and knew to hunt for tidbits that could prove helpful in the future. Later, he cornered Spencer and initiated the ice-breaking ritual of every jail tank.

"What are you in for?" Edwards asked.

"I've been charged with capital murder."

"Did you do it?"

*"No!"* Spencer sighed, wary of Edwards, weary with anxiety. "And that," he recalled, "was the extent of the one and only conversation that he and I had."

At eight o'clock on Monday morning, March 30, 1987, Detective Briseno waited for Danny Edwards in a basement room of Lew Sterrett jail. Edwards's record demonstrated that he was a dedicated thief, although not a particularly clever one. He had been convicted five times in the past seven years: three burglaries and two arsons, for which he was sentenced to five years in prison. In January, he had been arrested for his fourth burglary, and on March 17, 1987, while out on bail, he was arrested for

aggravated robbery with a deadly weapon. He had held a .38-caliber pistol
to the victim's head as he unburdened him of his wallet. For this crime,
Edwards was looking at up to twenty-five years in prison.

This was Edwards's predicament as he faced Briseno in the interview
room. No recording or written record of the interview exists, just an affidavit. The five-page affidavit, written in Briseno's meticulous handwriting and signed in Edwards's messy script, reads like a poor imitation of a
Raymond Chandler novel.

"He told me he should have shot the bitch in the head because he had
a gun," Edwards stated, although no gun was ever recovered, and the
medical examiner specified only a blunt instrument, not a gun, as the
weapon. Spencer "grabbed [the victim] by the throat and dragged him
out," Edwards said, and hit him on the back of the head. As the informant warmed to his subject, the details grew more florid—and demon-
strably incorrect. Spencer was angry at his alibi witness, threatening to
burn her house down or, more imaginatively, "He said something about
his uncle getting some of the silver liquid used in a thermometer and injecting the girl with it."

According to Edwards, Spencer and his co-assailant had been "rock-
ing some coke with baking powder"; his friend had been buying coke for
the "white dude" and ripping him off; Spencer "smoked coke for two days
afterward with the girl that he is trying to get to cover for him"; he saw a
"bunch of gold chains" in the car and thought his colleague had taken a
bag that contained some cash and fourteen-karat-gold jewelry. And why
wasn't Spencer worried about a conviction? "Benjamin is sure that the police do not have his prints because he has sanded his fingers to mess up his
prints."

All of this could have been checked. If he had done so, Briseno would
have found that Spencer did not have an uncle in Dallas, available to poi-
son Christie Williams; that Spencer had never been suspected of using
drugs; that Spencer had gone to work the next day and Christie had gone
to school; that the autopsy showed the victim had no drugs in his system;
and that according to the Young family, the victim had very little cash, no

gold chains, and no fourteen-karat-gold jewelry. Finally, Spencer's fingers were intact and his fingerprints pristine.

But Briseno faced a larger problem as he listened to the informant's story. Some crucial details flatly contradicted the other witnesses' testimony. For example, Edwards said Spencer's co-assailant was not Robert Mitchell, but "Vance Mitchell Spencer." Police had considered Van Mitchell Spencer the chief suspect in the assault, identified by several witnesses, until Briseno crossed him off the list. Gladys Oliver insisted Van Mitchell Spencer had nothing to do with the crime. This presented Briseno with an impossible dilemma: The accounts of Gladys Oliver, his star witness, and Danny Edwards, the only witness who connected Spencer to the actual assault, fundamentally conflicted with each other. They could not both be true. He would have to hope that no one noticed.

Even Edwards's account of the car ride differed from the other witnesses' stories. "Benjamin drove the car and Vance kept hitting the white dude as they drove away," eventually deciding "to dump him on Angelina because they thought he was already dead." Inconveniently for Briseno, Gladys Oliver and the two other eyewitnesses all had sworn that Robert Mitchell exited the driver's side and Spencer emerged from the passenger's seat. Also, the victim was found on Puget Street, not Angelina. But Danny Edwards provided the only link between Jeffrey Young's beating and Spencer. Briseno would have to work with it.[7]


The US criminal justice system runs on informants making deals; without them, many violent criminals would never be prosecuted. In many large cities, informants comprise a secret workforce. They compete for the job of informant; they sign contracts with the sheriff's office; they have handlers who guide them, direct their questions, and place them near a suspect whom the prosecutor wants to convict. Informants run like blood through the veins of the jail.

"The entire system is essentially being run as a negotiated market," notes Alexandra Natapoff, a professor at Harvard Law School and the author of *Snitching: Criminal Informants and the Erosion of American Justice*.[8] But the negotiations are friendly, the two sides codependent. "Usually jailhouse informants pop up on our most difficult cases," says former homicide detective Jim Trainum. "We really want to believe what they have to say. We've become very chummy with our informants. And they use the hell out of us."

The employers in this arrangement—the police and prosecutors—need informants to make their cases, especially the weak or circumstantial ones. The informants are paid in the currency of incarceration: privileges like television sets, conjugal visits, leniency in sentencing, even get-out-of-jail-free cards.

"These guys, generally, couldn't care less about the truth," says Scott Sanders, a public defender in Orange County, California, who uncovered a massive snitch-tank scandal there in 2011. "These are guys who are willing to sell their soul and everyone else's so they can get what they want. They're unquestionably the most dangerous witnesses in the system."

No explicit promises are made; if they were, that fact would have to be turned over to the defense attorney, who could use the deal to undercut the informant's credibility. "The deal is structured in such a way that they can testify truthfully that they have received no consideration for their testimony," says Rob Warden, the executive director emeritus of the Center on Wrongful Convictions at Northwestern Pritzker School of Law. The operation rests on the fiction that repeat criminals—armed robbers, drug dealers, kidnappers, rapists, murderers—testify correctly from their moral outrage at the crime at hand. Of course informants receive benefits, Warden says: The agreement may be unspoken, but it's binding, for informants are nothing if not rational actors. "If they provide the testimony and they don't get anything in return, then the whole system collapses."

All this is perfectly legal. The US Supreme Court has enshrined the use of informants, with a few restrictions. The government may direct informants to draw out details of a crime from a targeted suspect, including a confession, before the suspect has hired an attorney or been appointed one. The government can even send an undercover state agent into the jail to nose around and elicit a confession.[9] But once the suspect has a lawyer, the government cannot use an informant to deliberately elicit information from the suspect without his lawyer present; that would violate his Sixth Amendment right to counsel. Fortunately for the government, the justices created a loophole: If an informant gathers information on his own, without directly questioning the suspect—if he just happens to befriend the fellow and learn the (incriminating) details of the crime—he is not considered a state agent, and any information he extracts is fair game.[10]

Yet the appearance of a jailhouse informant is a sign of desperation, an indicator that the prosecution has a particularly weak case. An examination of innocent people who have been convicted based on informant testimony reveals that often these cases are based on circumstantial evidence—not physical evidence like blood or fingerprints, but questionable eyewitness testimony, as in Ben Spencer's case, which then requires an informant to supply the confession and the motive.

"Informants are closers," Scott Sanders says. "They close a gap in the case." This is particularly true in high-profile, gruesome crimes, such as the murder of a white person or a child. Of the more than thirty-four hundred wrongly convicted people profiled by the National Registry of Exonerations, jailhouse informants were employed in less than 1 percent of cases that did not involve murder, but they appeared in 15 percent of murder cases. Jailhouse informants testified in *one out of every four* cases where the defendant was sentenced to death. These defendants were innocent, but a jailhouse informant sent them to death row before they were eventually exonerated. In order to bring someone to justice when they have a "horrible case," Warden notes, "the authorities want to leave no stone unturned."

Whether the root cause is official gullibility or cynical ambition, building a case on jailhouse informants has led to one innocent person after another being sent to prison. Jailhouse informants have helped convict more than 175 innocent people of murder and put 32 innocent people on death row. The system operates in secrecy and is hard to uncover.

"There are no incentives for anyone to come forward," says Harvard's Natapoff. "The snitch has no incentive to come forward. The government has no incentive to disclose this. And the way we officially get to learn about informants is that the defendant actually goes to trial and is entitled to information about the informant in their case. Which happens rarely." If a prisoner is very lucky, a pro bono investigator, an Innocence Project lawyer, a journalist, or his family fights for and wins damning documents.

Sometimes it can be too late. Cameron Todd Willingham was convicted of setting fire to his home in Corsicana, Texas, in 1991, and killing his three daughters, a two-year-old and one-year-old twins.[11] He was convicted based on (disputed) testimony of an arson investigator who said the fire was deliberately set; years later, nine fire experts, including one hired by the Texas Forensic Science Commission, concluded the fire was a tragic accident. The other evidence was a jailhouse informant who testified Willingham confessed to the crime. Before trial, the informant formally recanted his testimony, declaring, "Mr. Willingham is innocent of all charges." The prosecution did not turn over the recantation to the defense. It's unclear whether Willingham set the fire. It's also moot. He was executed in 2004.

A s DNA technology has unearthed just how easily criminal informants condemn the innocent and distort the criminal justice system, some states have put limitations on the use of informants. Texas is among the most progressive, requiring that an informant's testimony be corroborated to get a conviction. California passed a similar law in 2011. But it would be wrong to believe the problem has been fixed. In fact, two months after restrictions on informants were signed into law in California, a massive informant scandal erupted in Orange County.

On October 12, 2011, Scott Dekraai shot and killed eight people in a beauty salon in Seal Beach. His ex-wife, with whom he was waging a custody battle, was one of them.[12] Dekraai immediately confessed, but the Orange County district attorney's office feared he would raise an insanity defense to escape the death penalty. They wanted him dead. The sheriff's department, which runs the jail, moved him to tank 17, which was known informally as a "snitch tank." They placed him next to a Mexican Mafia inmate who moonlighted as a seasoned jailhouse informant. The goal was to elicit statements from Dekraai showing that he was sane and knew what he was doing.

Unfortunately for the prosecution, Dekraai was assigned public defender Scott Sanders. The attorney discovered the informant elicited confessions after Sanders took Dekraai's case, which the Supreme Court has prohibited. He learned the sheriff's office recorded 130 hours of conversations from a microphone in his cell; this, too, was a violation of the Constitution, since the informant was trying to glean information without Dekraai's attorney present.

In the end, Sanders uncovered a systemic and often illegal informant operation run by the Orange County Sheriff's Department—one that violated the rights not just of Dekraai, but of untold numbers of suspects. He unearthed a confidential inmate database that contained detailed information on the movement of informants, tracking where they were assigned and, often, the reasons for the assignment. An eleven-hundred-plus-page "special handling log" described how deputies recruited and used informants, and showed the scale of the cover-up, involving both deputies and prosecutors.

Thomas Goethals, a superior court judge in Orange County, reviewed Sanders's complaint. The judge, a former Orange County prosecutor, at first indicated he believed the mistakes were inadvertent. But as evidence of an extensive, hidden, and illegal snitch network emerged, he reassessed. "Certain aspects of the district attorney's performance in this case might be described as a comedy of errors," Goethals wrote, "but for the fact that it has been so sadly deficient. There is nothing funny about that." He threw the entire district attorney's office off the case.[13] The state's illegal handling of informants led to reversals, new trials, or reduced sentences for more than twenty people, including some convicted of murder or attempted murder.[14]

D anny Edwards was hardly a sophisticated informant, just a small-time thief looking for a break. So how did he glean the information about Jeffrey Young's murder? Some facts were in the newspaper: that Jeffrey Young was working late; that he was beaten; that he was dumped from his BMW. Other details were never released: that Young was discarded in West Dallas; that he had bruises on his neck; that Ben Spencer's alibi was a young woman who had not initially recognized the photos of him.

If Spencer was the killer, he could have provided some specifics, although the fabulous details in Edwards's telling far outnumbered the accurate ones. But if Spencer is to be believed, and he exchanged only a few words with his tank mate, then how did Edwards know that the victim's neck was bruised? How did he know that Christie Williams initially said she did not recognize his photo? How did he know the name Vance [*sic*] Mitchell Spencer? "How could I have told Edwards about someone that I've never heard of?" Spencer asked in a letter to his mother. "It's not possible, so the only explanation for Edwards' claims is that they were devised by Investigator Jesse Briseno."[15]

This is not implausible. The history of wrongful convictions demonstrates that police—intentionally or not—routinely telegraph bits and pieces of evidence to jailhouse informants, who parrot the evidence back in affidavits and court testimony. One wonders if such telegraphy from Briseno to Edwards occurred on that day in Lew Sterrett, even if the transmission was at times garbled.

However Edwards scooped up the information, Detective Briseno could now link Spencer to the assault and murder. On March 30, 1987, Briseno wrote in his notes: "Recommend offense be cleared by the arrest of listed [Spencer and Mitchell] on capital murder warrants." In other words, the murder case was solved.

The investigative notes kept by Briseno and his fellow detectives detail an all-out sprint for four days, until the arrest of Ben Spencer and Robert Mitchell. The detectives continued to interview witnesses after the arrest, but reading the notes, it feels like a cooldown lap. And so when two people identified a far more viable suspect than Ben Spencer—a man with a history of violent robberies—Briseno paid little attention. He had moved on to the next case.

# Chapter 8

# ALTERNATIVELY

+———+

**Mike was like a *crazed* dude.**

—FERRELL SCOTT, *about his friend Michael Hubbard*

For Kelvin Johnson, who had never been arrested before, his arrival at the Dallas County government center jail felt both inevitable and familiar. By age twenty-one, Johnson and his best friend had robbed some twenty restaurants at gunpoint, taking money from the register and gathering jewelry and cash from the diners. He was eventually caught and landed in a holding tank at the county jail, where he reconnected with acquaintances from West Dallas. But seeing Robert Mitchell there was a surprise. Johnson knew him by sight and reputation, enough to know that he did not run in a gang, did not rob people, did not deal drugs.

"What are you in for?" Johnson asked.

"Man, they got me in on this murder that took place in West Dallas," Mitchell replied.

Johnson nodded. Everyone was talking about Jeffrey Young's murder. Then, quietly, Johnson said, "You did not do this. I know who did it." He refused to say more.

Over the next few days, Robert Mitchell spiraled down. "He was constantly crying and praying and reading the Bible," Johnson remembered. The detectives pulled him from the tank and interrogated him repeatedly. On April 11, 1987, Mitchell broke. It was a Saturday, a little more than two weeks after he and Benjamine Spencer had been arrested. "He took a bedsheet and he put it over the rail of the shower in the tank and he put it around his neck," Johnson recalled. When he walked into the restroom, he saw Mitchell swinging but still alive. Johnson, who could squat five hundred pounds, positioned himself under Mitchell's legs and stood up, as if doing a squat at the gym. Johnson held the three-hundred-pound man aloft while other inmates untied him.

When Mitchell was safely down, Johnson begged him to wait it out. "Don't do that, man," he said. "They don't have *nothing* on you. They don't even have y'all's fingerprints."

"Man, why you know so much about it?" Mitchell asked. "Who did it?"

Johnson hesitated, his loyalty battling with his conscience.

"Man, Michael Hubbard did it."

Nothing in Michael Hubbard's background indicated that he was destined to become a killer. His mother was considered a second mother to many of his friends. He and his brothers excelled at sports. His brothers were All-Americans headed for college, and Michael, although only six foot one, dominated the basketball court when playing for Pinkston High School.

"Me and Mike were always on the same team," Johnson said, speaking of high school and beyond, speaking of the old Kelvin Johnson, before he was sent to prison for armed robbery, before he found God there, before he served his time, married, adopted a boy, bought a house, earned consistent promotions at Home Depot, and became a poster child for redemption. Back in 1987, he and Michael Hubbard were inseparable. They went to the same barber and got the same haircut; they spent their leisure hours smoking weed, hanging out at the park, or playing basketball at the gym. Soon they were committing crimes together. "I was the first one who started street hustling," Johnson said. He burglarized stores and eventually enlisted Michael Hubbard.

Ferrell Scott joined them sometime later. After he lost his basketball scholarship at Western Oklahoma State, along with his hopes for a professional career, he returned to West Dallas. Hubbard and Johnson pestered him to hit some stores with them. He resisted. "But every day they came to the park with all these new clothes and shoes. They're egging me on. 'Man, come on. It's easy.'"

Scott finally relented. "I got hooked on it from that day," he said. They would target high-end stores that sold expensive clothes, fur coats, and boots. "We used to find that stuff in the Yellow Pages," he explained. "We would go in the store in the daytime, walk around, see what we wanted, and come back at three or four o'clock in the morning and take what we saw earlier."

"Did you say you'd look in the *Yellow Pages*?" I asked.

"Yeah. That's how we would find stores," he said. "We'd literally rob every boot store in the metroplex, and we never got caught doing it."

The friends began to specialize. Michael Hubbard and Kelvin Johnson robbed restaurants, while Ferrell Scott cleaned out retail stores across Dallas. He also began dealing drugs and developing contacts who would trade drugs for stolen items.

Drugs changed everything, and Michael Hubbard in particular. "When crack cocaine hit the scene, it took him fast," Kelvin Johnson recalled. Ferrell Scott also witnessed the transformation. "Mike stopped playing basketball, stopped taking care of his hygiene, and just wasn't the same dude no more. Mike was like a *crazed* dude."

Michael Hubbard's coke habit fueled a recklessness that disturbed his partners. Now when they burst into a restaurant waving their guns, they worried that Hubbard would actually shoot. In the first three months of 1987, Kelvin Johnson and Michael Hubbard robbed ten restaurants in Dallas. The spree ended a few days after they plundered the upscale restaurant Chez Gerard. According to the prosecution report, the two men entered the kitchen, each wearing red jogging suits and dark ski masks, both holding "large caliber blue steel revolvers."[1] They pointed their guns at the owner, informed him that this was a robbery and that if anyone resisted, he or she would be shot. One employee, who was not present when the two men entered, walked in front of Michael Hubbard. Hubbard "grabbed him and struck him several times across the back of the head with a handgun, knocking him to the floor," the report said. "As a result of the assault, he suffered a one-inch laceration to the back of his head," which required treatment.

After taking the owner's Rolex and nearly fifteen hundred dollars from the register, the armed men walked into the dining room and ordered the patrons to put their jewelry and cash in the center of their tables. While Johnson covered him, Hubbard collected the items and placed them in a black gym bag. They walked out with money and property worth more than two hundred thousand dollars. It was March 28, 1987, six days after Jeffrey Young had been robbed of his cash and jewelry, been struck in the head with a blunt object, and had died.

I n the summer of 1987, a mass of hot air hovered over much of the country, pushing temperatures into record highs for days on end. Dallas baked, with temperatures of around one hundred degrees for most of July and August. From inside Lew Sterrett jail, Ben Spencer looked out the window and watched the cars move down the highway, the heat visibly radiating from the pavement. Inside, the jail's air conditioners blasted frigid air, and even the thermometer measured how different was his new world from the world he had left. During the hottest summer on record, Spencer shivered constantly, and there was no escape.

On July 29, Spencer was transferred to a new holding tank, and happened on Ferrell Scott, fresh off his arrest for possessing cocaine. The two young men knew each other from the neighborhood, but didn't run in the same circles. "As soon as he seen me," Spencer recalled, "Ferrell said this here: 'Ben, what you doing in jail?'"

"Man, you ain't gonna believe me. You know the white guy they found over there on Puget?"

"Yeah."

"That's the offense I'm in here for. They charged me with that offense."

"Man, no!" Scott said. "Man, Hubbard did that."

Over the next few days, Ferrell Scott worked through a complicated moral accounting: Should he remain loyal to Michael Hubbard, or should he tell police what he knew about the murder of Jeffrey Young? Should he sell out his friend for a man he barely knew? As Scott watched Spencer suffer through blinding headaches and a quiet, astonished despair, he decided. "When I get outta here," he told Spencer, "I'm gonna try to help you."

Both Ferrell Scott and Kelvin Johnson were hiding a secret about their friend Michael Hubbard, one that would chafe their consciences until each would excise his guilt. Thirty years later, in separate interviews, the two men recounted the same incident, identical in their details and complementing each other to lay out a wholly different narrative from that of the police.

In late March, Kelvin Johnson, Ferrell Scott, Michael Hubbard, and Michael's brother were sitting around Johnson's apartment, celebrating their successful heist at Chez Gerard's restaurant a couple of days earlier. "We were talking, drinking, getting high," Johnson recounted, "and Michael said—these were his exact words—'The white man who they found dead over at West Dallas?' I said, 'Yep.' He said, 'I did that, man.'"[2]

Hubbard told them that on that Sunday night, he needed money for cocaine and decided to "hit a lick," that is, find a person or a place to rob. He had his eye on Ninfa's, a large restaurant nearby, and tried to recruit some friends hanging out at North Hampton Park. Everyone passed: too much security at Ninfa's. Hubbard left alone, cased the restaurant, and later told Johnson he decided it was "too much for one man to do."[3] As he was returning to West Dallas through the warehouse district, he spotted a white man leaving his office and forced him back into the building. One detail was lodged in Johnson's memory three decades later: "He said the man's phone was ringing inside the place." Who calls an office on a

Sunday night? The white man told him it was the security company.[4] Rushing now, Hubbard said he grabbed a jambox, took twenty-six dollars from the man's wallet, put him into the trunk of his BMW, and drove toward West Dallas, where he lived.

"He was driving the car back and all of the sudden he sees the trunk lid goes up," Ferrell Scott recalled. "And this is his exact words: 'Man, some kind of way this guy open the trunk and try to jump out.'" Johnson continued: "He stopped the car, got out, and saw the dude lying on the street where he was bleeding and shaking." The man had hit his head on the pavement, Scott said, and Hubbard "dumped the car a few hundred yards from where he was." He drove the car into an alley, they both said, and ran away, leaving the motor running. Hubbard told them he was afraid someone had seen him.

Ferrell Scott was still at the park with his friends when Hubbard returned. Hubbard pulled him aside and showed him some of the stolen items.

"Do you recall what he grabbed?" I asked.

"Yeah. A radio, like a jambox."

"Anything else?"

"A wedding band," he said. "And the watch. He had the watch on his arm."

"Do you remember what kind it was?"

"It was a Seiko watch, that kind of looked like a Rolex. But it was a gold Seiko."

They tracked down Scott's fence and showed him the watch. "I sold it for him, to this guy who would buy stuff from us when we went to steal or whatever, or trade it for coke. [He] bought a lot of stuff from us."

In Johnson's apartment a few days later, after Hubbard finished his story, everyone sat very still, wordlessly glancing at each other. "After this, I'm numb," Johnson recalled. "I'm like, 'Michael, keep that to yourself. You shouldn't have told me, you shouldn't have told Ferrell, you shouldn't have even told your brother.'"

Michael Hubbard looked at him, and a small smile crept across his face. He wasn't worried, he said. "They got Ben Spencer and Robert Mitchell."

I n West Dallas, it was common knowledge who killed the white man. Word was, *Hub did it*, but the neighborhood code prevented anyone from alerting the police. For his part, Kelvin Johnson barely knew Spencer and Mitchell, "so I'm cool to keep this information. I'm showing loyalty to Michael." That is, until Hubbard betrayed him. On March 31, Michael Hubbard was arrested for the Chez Gerard robbery, and Johnson bailed him out. Soon after, Johnson was arrested, and Hubbard did nothing. Johnson figured Hubbard had turned on him and was "putting everything on me." After Robert Mitchell's attempted suicide, Johnson decided to trade Michael Hubbard for a reduced sentence.

On April 19, Johnson was handcuffed and driven down to police headquarters for an interview with Detective Briseno. In the affidavit that Johnson dictated to Briseno, he related details about the crime that had not been released to the public: that Hubbard saw "this white dude" locking his office door; that Hubbard told him to get in the trunk of the BMW; that Hubbard heard the office phone ringing, which, the white man explained, was the security company. "Mike had his brother's gun," Johnson stated, although he did not say that he cracked the victim's skull with it. He locked the man in the trunk. "He then drove off in the BMW, and as he was riding around in West Dallas, he looked in the rearview mirror and saw the trunk lid fly open," Johnson continued. "He stopped the car, got out, and saw the dude lying on the street where he was bleeding and shaking." Hubbard parked the car in the alley, ran away, and brought the jambox to a cocaine dealer. All of this dovetailed with the evidence the police had gathered.

But Detective Briseno didn't believe him, Johnson recalled. "He thought I was lying."

"He was trying to save his own ass," Briseno later confirmed.

As Johnson bent over to sign the affidavit, he paused. He pushed the paper away without signing. He has given various reasons: he wanted to talk to his attorney first; he worried that Hubbard would get the death penalty; he fretted about breaking Mrs. Hubbard's heart. He never got a second chance to sign.

Asked if he found Johnson's account at all credible, Briseno said, "Whether he was credible or not, he didn't sign [his statement] and we couldn't use it."

Johnson, then twenty-one years old, took a polygraph. "They was asking me all these questions. I was answering to the best of my knowledge. Understand this here, though. It was frightening." According to Briseno's notes, Johnson failed. Dallas police say the polygraph recording and analysis have been lost. Polygraphs measure the physiological response to the fear of lying; they do not necessarily indicate veracity. This is why polygraph results are barred from the trials, and studies have found that more than 20 percent of innocent people fail their polygraphs.[5]

Sometime in July or September 1987—Ferrell Scott was arrested twice that hot summer—Scott was released from Lew Sterrett jail. He had promised Spencer that he would help him, and he says that after conferring with his older brother, he drove to his attorney's office. Scott told him that Michael Hubbard had confessed to the murder, and his attorney mentioned the twenty-five-thousand-dollar reward offered by Ross Perot.

"He said, 'Ferrell, there could be some money in this for you,'" Scott recalled. "And I was like, I'm not interested in money, I just wanted to let people know that this guy didn't do this, that he was there for something that he didn't do." The attorney handed him the phone; he called Crime Stoppers and made a report.[6] Then they drove to police headquarters, where Scott said two detectives led him into a room—a "Spanish officer" and a "white boy."[7] "They didn't write anything down," he recalled. "They never called me back to question me back about nothing. And after that, I never heard anything else."

Detective Briseno said the meeting never happened.[8] If Scott had come to the station, he insisted, he would have been asked to give a statement. "There is no affidavit by Ferrell Scott in our department file relating to Benjamine Spencer," he stated in an affidavit nearly twenty years after the crime. "Moreover, there are no notes in the file, entered by me or anyone else, regarding Ferrell Scott." Questioned in 2007 about a possible meeting, Scott's attorney testified he could not specifically recall.[9]

B y the summer of 1987, Ben Spencer and Robert Mitchell had been arrested and indicted. The prosecutorial machinery had warmed up, and Briseno would be hard-pressed to reopen the case now, even if he had reservations. This proved excellent news for Michael Hubbard.

"Do you recall if Michael Hubbard had established an alibi?" the private investigator Daryl Parker asked Briseno in 2017.

"I don't know. We never got to talk to him."

"You never talked to him?"

"We made an effort to talk to him," he said. He and another detective visited Lew Sterrett jail to try to interview him. "He was walking down the catwalk. And he saw we were detectives. He was going, 'Fuck you, man.'"

Briseno couldn't coerce Hubbard to talk, and besides, the jailhouse informant had placed Spencer at the scene of the assault. Yet it seemed a casual approach to a potential murder suspect, one identified by two friends who offered details that had never been released publicly.

"Why would they believe a jailhouse snitch but not the guy's two buddies?" the law professor Keith Findley asks rhetorically, then answers in the next breath: "Efficiency." Tunnel vision allows police to solve crimes before they grow cold. It usually works. But when contrary evidence pops up, the investigators experience cognitive dissonance; and if they are to continue down their agreed-upon route, they must quell the nagging questions. In the case of Ben Spencer, Findley says, "they arbitrarily elevated one, the snitch, in reliability, credibility, and significance. And they minimized or disregarded other statements" by Hubbard's friends.

This calculation repeats again and again in wrongful conviction cases.

Police and prosecutors did not pursue, and concealed evidence of, alternative suspects in one out of five murder exonerations, according to a study of twenty-four hundred exonerations between 1989 and 2019.[10] Sometimes, the police lacked the name of an alternate suspect. But time and again, researchers found, when the evidence suggested that police were focusing on the wrong person, they did not change course. When DNA excluded the (innocent) suspect, for example, or when crimes continued with the same modus operandi, even after the (innocent) suspect was in custody, tunnel vision dissuaded police and prosecutors from going back and reassessing the evidence with a new eye.

Often, as in Ben Spencer's case, the detectives actually had the name of a more viable alternative suspect, yet dismissed the inconvenient lead. The Central Park Five ranks among the most famous cases of tunnel vision.[11] The brutal rape of a twenty-eight-year-old female jogger in New York City's Central Park in 1989 triggered outrage and race-based fear across the country. The police rounded up five Black and Hispanic boys, ages fourteen to sixteen, who, they said, had been "wilding" with dozens of others, running through the park and attacking people at random. After long interrogations, police finally elicited confessions that bore little resemblance to the facts and that the boys quickly retracted.

Even before their trials, a DNA analysis of the semen that was found on the victim's sock pointed to only one assailant, and it excluded all the boys. Investigators ignored that red flag, and this one as well: Two days before the assault, another woman had been beaten and raped in Central Park. She remembered that her assailant had fresh stitches on his chin, and using hospital records, a detective tracked down Matias Reyes. But the investigation ended when Reyes, like Michael Hubbard, declined to be interviewed. Over the next few months—while the boys awaited trial in jail—Reyes brutally raped and maimed four more women, one of them in front of her young children; she died later that day. Reyes eventually confessed, thanks to a spiritual conversion, and DNA linked all the crimes to him. The Central Park Five served between five and thirteen years before they were all exonerated.

———

In the weeks following Spencer's arrest, Briseno continued to talk to a few people, but not Michael Hubbard. Cheryl Wattley, a former federal prosecutor who would later represent Ben Spencer in his post-conviction appeal, argued that if the Dallas police and prosecutors had taken an objective look at the evidence before trial, they would have come to different conclusions.

"We have Ben, who has no history of really being involved in any kind of criminal conduct," except for driving a car his friend stole, she said. "And then we've got Michael Hubbard, who's got a gang that's going out and doing major restaurant robberies, holding people up at gunpoint. Let's see, who might be more likely to be involved in jacking up a guy at his office?"

Jim McCloskey, who years later would reinvestigate Spencer's case, understood the rationale, even if he didn't condone it. "You can imagine the pressure on the Dallas Police, especially a rookie investigative detective, to clear this case." All this must have weighed heavily on Briseno as he led his first major homicide investigation. He had three eyewitnesses and a jailhouse confession. "Once all that was developed within a week of the murder," McCloskey said, "the case was cleared, and he was a hero."

*Chapter 9*

# A NOBLE CAUSE

+ —— +

**I didn't want anyone but Ben.**

—DEBRA SPENCER, *on the eve of giving birth to their son*

J ail is a wild card. In this repository for suspects who have been arrested
but not yet tried, you never know who will share your tank: an addict
in withdrawal, a schizophrenic off his meds, a tough guy who refuses to
bathe, a terrified teenager who weeps all night. Unlike prison, where convicted men and women settle into a daily rhythm, jail is loud and bright
and never stops moving, with breakfast carts rolling through at 3:00 a.m.
and inmates rotating in and out, always followed by the shrill clang of the
metal door.

During this chaotic yet empty activity in the spring of 1987, Spencer
found time to reflect on all that he had, and all that he might lose. He
recognized with the piercing wisdom of misfortune that he had been on
the cusp of genuine happiness. "For the first time ever, I opened up my
heart to love a woman," he wrote to Debra.[1] "He realized how much
Debra had altered his trajectory, nosing it upward, persuading him to
sever his ties with his best friend, Ray Lee, who would later die from a
gunshot in the back while stealing a car. "Because of you, I wanted something better out of my life for myself. I knew that so long as I had you on
my side that I would be able to climb to greater heights in life."[2]

Their early marriage—the days when he would bring her lunch and, if the weather was warm, share a sandwich in the park, the evenings when he would draw her bath before he left for work, the miraculous moments when he would place his ear on her belly and feel their baby kick—that intimacy ended abruptly when police arrived at their door.

"I just went into survival mode after he was taken away," Debra remembered. "I had never been through anything like this before and I didn't know what to expect. I just figured he was going to come home pretty soon. Because we had a child on the way. I thought he'd by home by the time B.J. was born."

J effrey Young's murder hit West Dallas like a fire sale at Walmart: With more than thirty-five thousand dollars in reward money, there was a stampede of tips. Van Mitchell Spencer "killed the white dude" and made off with a suitcase of hundred-dollar bills, said one resident. Another claimed that Gloria Faye Childs (no relation to Debra) was "the mastermind." Robert Mitchell was the "wheelman," said another, and Ben Spencer was "the gorilla." One woman told a friend that her brother returned that night with a briefcase full of money and a story about killing a white dude. "If she had known about the reward money," Detective Briseno wrote in his notes, "she would have turned her own brother in to collect the money."[3] Meanwhile, Charles Stewart, the only person who theoretically placed Spencer and Mitchell in the BMW, recanted his statement, then recanted his recantation.

Briseno tried to find order in the rubble, running down some of the leads and finally discarding all except those implicating the two men already in custody. Briseno did not interview Michael Hubbard, he did not talk to Hubbard's friends, he did not inquire about Hubbard's whereabouts that night. When the fingerprint expert asked to examine Hubbard's palm prints to see if they matched the one on the BMW's trunk, Briseno failed to get those prints, even though Hubbard was sitting in jail.

The leads offered by Jeffrey Young's family and friends presented a more delicate problem, revealing an intra-family intrigue. The victim's best friend believed Young was killed after he uncovered an embezzlement scheme at his father-in-law's company in Miami: "He was very scared of retaliation," the investigative notes state.[4] Along the same line, the victim's mother called Briseno to say that her son had been "concerned over a company meeting scheduled for Monday," the morning after he was assaulted.[5] "This meeting involved his father-in-law Jim Coyle," the police notes record. "Family believes that the comp [complainant, Jeffrey Young] might have been murdered as a result of a conspiracy!"[6] For his part, the prosecutor theorized that the "most plausible" theory was that the hit men—i.e., Spencer and Mitchell—blundered. "These guys intended to kill a different person and killed this man by mistake—another who worked in that same building, and it was over a drug deal."[7]

But the surplus of theories could not obscure the paucity of hard evidence. The police had not found the murder weapon. They had not found the stolen items. They had not found physical evidence implicating the two suspects—no hair or blood or clothing fibers to be forensically tested, no cuts or bruises on either suspect's body. As to fingerprints, Briseno had correctly guessed that the expert would come up dry. He reported that not a single print matched Ben Spencer, Robert Mitchell, Michael Hubbard, Ferrell Scott, Kelvin Johnson, or a dozen other people who had blackened their fingers and palms. He ran the prints through the state and federal databases—no hits. The expert did not even find the *victim's* prints in his own car.

"To this day, I am stunned about the complete lack of any physical evidence they had," Bruce Anton, one of Spencer's trial attorneys, said. "The police probably were under pressure, so they just pick somebody out and go after him."

The pressure on Briseno and the district attorney's office escalated each day. Ever since their son was found lying on Puget Street, Harry and Maureen Young had been a constant presence in the investigation. The prosecutor assigned to the case, a woman, briefed Harry Young on the grand jury proceedings, which were secret. Young ferreted out the reputations of various prosecutors and investigators, along with their telephone numbers; he expected, and received, updates. The Youngs expressed dissatisfaction with the female prosecutor and queried why one of the "super chiefs"—the most seasoned assistant district attorneys—was not handling the case.

When the female prosecutor was dumped and another assigned—a man—Mr. and Mrs. Young attended one of his trials, noting in a letter to the district attorney, "We were all favorably and positively impressed. So was the jury, they awarded a life sentence."[8] When it looked likely that Ben Spencer and Robert Mitchell would be tried for "regular murder," not capital murder, the Youngs paid a visit to the district attorney. "The purpose of our meeting was to get the charge back up to capital murder," they memorialized in a letter that summer. "Any comment about us not wanting the death penalty was in the context of wanting to learn the motive. Why was our son beaten to death over an extended period of time? Who was really behind the triple crimes of murder, kidnap, and robbery?"[9]

The Youngs were desperate for anything that might bridge the chasm of grief and provide a measure of comfort. Of course, they were no more desperate than Ben Spencer. "I'm in the county jail charged with capital murder and a bond of $250,000, while investigator Briseno built a case around me," Spencer recalled in a letter to friends years later.[10] Just as the Youngs were helpless to change the past, Spencer was helpless to alter his future.

When the grand jury met on April 21, 1987, to consider the charges against Spencer and Mitchell, Briseno needed to produce something worthy of indictment. He had the three neighbors and the jailhouse informant, but he offered more. On the key issue—the identity of the perpetrators—he indulged in error and overstatement.

"We've got four affidavits from four different people who saw the defendant Robert Nathan Mitchell driving the car and Benjamin Spencer as a passenger," Briseno told the grand jurors. "We've got three other witnesses living right around the area where the vehicle was abandoned."[11]

*Seven witnesses.* That's compelling. Too bad it's wrong. The only person who allegedly saw Mitchell and Spencer driving was Charles Stewart. His affidavit is missing. What does exist—police notes about the interview with him—say nothing about Stewart seeing the two men driving.

Briseno continued: "One of the witnesses saw the defendant—both defendants in the vehicle as they pushed him out in the street."

"So at least one witness saw these two [suspects] with the complainant in the car, and the complainant was pushed out as the car was moving?" the prosecutor asked.

"That's correct," Briseno replied.[12]

The detective was referring to Charles Stewart, whose affidavit has been destroyed. In fact, the only record of Stewart's statements is from the trial: There, under oath, he testified that he could not tell if one or two people were riding in the car, much less the identity of the occupants.[13] But the grand jurors were not privy to that information and indicted the suspects for capital murder.

Maybe Briseno was confused. Maybe he was unfamiliar with the material, even though he had been working the case for a month. Maybe this is a routine part of the process: Indict the suspects to continue the investigation. Or perhaps this reflects a problem endemic among police officers: *testilying*, that is, police officers lying in the courtroom, under oath.

N ew York police officers coined the term "testilying" in the 1990s, and experts say naming the practice did nothing to curb it. By its very nature, the perjury is hidden and rarely uncovered. No one knows how often police lie to cover up constitutional or other embarrassing errors. Former Ninth Circuit chief judge Alex Kozinski noted, "It is an open secret long shared by prosecutors, defense lawyers, and judges that perjury is widespread among law enforcement officers."[14] Legal scholars describe it as a "subcultural norm rather than an individual aberration."[15] *The New York Times* has published several investigative series on testilying.[16] In an unscientific poll, Chicago prosecutors estimated cops lie under oath in one out of five cases.[17] If there's any doubt about law enforcement's complicated relationship with the truth, one need only consider the Minneapolis Police Department's initial description of George Floyd's death in May 2020: Floyd had died after a "medical incident during police interaction," which seems a euphemistic way to characterize a white officer kneeling on a Black man's neck for nine minutes and twenty-nine seconds.[18]

Samuel Gross, at the University of Michigan Law School, looked at nearly thirty-two hundred exonerations between 1989 and mid-2022 and found that police had committed perjury in 13 percent of the trials that led to these convictions.[19] The more serious the crime, the more likely the perjury. Police across the country lied in one of every six murder and death penalty cases. "These are the cases with perjury that we know of," he wrote in an email. "There are others where it has not been spotted, or if it has been, we haven't been told. God knows how many."[20]

When an innocent person is convicted, perjury at trial is like the dessert at the end of a five-course dinner. Long before they testify in court, police engage in a wide array of other bad behavior, including fabricating or hiding evidence, tampering with witnesses, and coercing suspects to give false confessions. In another study, Gross and his researchers analyzed twenty-four hundred wrongful convictions over three decades and found such police misconduct in more than a third of them; together, police and prosecutors crossed the line, ethically and legally, in 54 percent of the cases.[21] Stated more baldly: When innocent people were convicted, more than half the time, misconduct by local and state authorities put them in prison. Again, the higher the stakes, the more likely are police and prosecutors to break or bend the law: They did so in 72 percent of murder cases, versus 32 percent in prosecutions of nonviolent crimes.[22]

Even people in the innocence movement believe that most police officers approach their work with "correct and virtuous" intentions, Sam Gross says. Often, maybe usually, the misconduct springs from an honest desire to protect the public and bring solace to the victims—not from personal or racial animus. Criminologists call this "noble cause corruption."

"Basically, you're doing the wrong thing for what you think is the right reason," the former homicide detective Jim Trainum explains. "We know who the bad guy is. And so therefore we're going to make sure that he doesn't get off because of some fancy lawyer tricks." Rob Warden, at Northwestern Pritzker School of Law, calls it "framing the guilty." The police believe they have the right person, and they just "tweak the evidence a little bit" to assure that the guy doesn't walk. "And so you tend to insulate any information that can be construed as supporting your theory of his guilt, and give short shrift to any information that does not fit your theory of the crime. It's just a human phenomenon. We're all capable of that."

No one can know whether the reasons a police officer illegally influences a witness are noble or cynical. But we do know that witness tampering has sent hundreds of innocent people to prison—and almost one quarter of all innocent people convicted of murder. This is especially true in circumstantial cases with little or no physical evidence, cases that hinge on witness testimony. Imagine the frustration when police "know" who the perpetrator is, but the witnesses won't cooperate. So they apply a little pressure to arrive at the right result.

When Juan Johnson became the prime suspect in a Chicago homicide in 1991, a police officer threatened to charge an eyewitness with murder if he refused to testify against Johnson; the witness capitulated, and Johnson spent thirteen years in prison before being exonerated.[23] Before the 1995 murder trial of Debra Brown in Utah, a witness came forward to say he saw another person leave the house soon after the murder with a gun and cash; the officer told the witness to "let it go, leave it alone . . . if he knew what was good for him." It took eighteen years to exonerate Brown.[24] When a thirteen-year-old rape victim in Lodi, California, told police that the man they suspected, Peter Rose, was not the assailant, the detectives accused her of lying, of being a prostitute and a gang member. The girl submitted to the pressure. Rose was convicted in 1995 based on the girl's identification at trial. Ten years later, DNA exonerated him.[25]

"Synthesized testimony" presents as a more subtle form of witness tampering. Here police ask leading questions and massage the statements of witnesses until they fit with their theory of the case. This is often how jailhouse informants glean details that "only the perpetrator would know." As with other forms of misconduct, there are hundreds of examples to choose from, but the murder conviction of Dewey Jones in Akron, Ohio, in 1995 illustrates the tactic. Police believed that Jones killed a seventy-one-year-old man in his home. They interviewed one witness who had seen the perpetrator at the victim's home around the time of the murder. The witness knew Jones; it wasn't Jones. Police returned a second time with a photo of Dewey Jones and others, and received another unsatisfactory response. They dropped by a third time, and a fourth time, and finally the witness gave them the answer they sought. Another witness received similar "corrections"—he, too, had identified people other than Jones several times, but eventually he, too, succumbed. On the strength of those two witnesses, a jury convicted Dewey Jones, and he languished in prison for nineteen years before DNA exonerated him.[26]

It doesn't take much to alter a witness's testimony. A recent study demonstrated that people (in this case, college students) will accuse another classmate of stealing a professor's phone after thirty minutes of aggressive questioning, even if the student knew the teacher never had a phone in the first place.[27] In another study, two students were left in a room in which a money box containing several twenty-dollar bills was visible. They were told to move behind a cubicle wall, where they could no longer see the money, but they could see or hear each other at all times. After a few minutes, an official came in and told them the money had been stolen. At first 90 percent provided an alibi for the other student; but after being told (falsely) that their colleague had confessed, more than half rescinded their alibi and said they could no longer vouch for the other student.[28] If people change their testimony when the stakes are so low, imagine the temptation to comply with police officers trying to solve a murder case.

Although hiding evidence is more often associated with prosecutors, police indulge in the practice as well: In one third of erroneous convictions, police concealed evidence that would have helped the suspect or undercut the prosecution's witnesses.[29] Sometimes they throw out physical evidence, such as a flashlight with the real perpetrator's blood on it.[30] More often, when testimonial evidence weakens the case, police conceal it.[31]

T o close a case, police navigate through territory in which the boundaries separating the legal, the unethical, and the illegal are not always well marked. Was that interrogation so aggressive that the suspect would say anything to get the police to stop? Did the reward bring out virtuous witnesses or greedy ones? Was the DNA from that cigarette butt at the crime scene exculpatory, or irrelevant? Police make these calls every day, and those decisions determine the fate of the accused.

"There's way too much gray area," says Brendan Cox, a retired police chief in Albany, New York. "Way too much is left up to everybody's interpretation."

Police are judged, demoted, and promoted based on their clearance rate. The clock is merciless: They carry too many cases and never have enough time. Think of Jesus Briseno, a young homicide detective, who, along with a dozen others in the Dallas homicide unit, was trying to solve hundreds of murders in the middle of the crack epidemic. It was like trying to muck out a stall with a teaspoon. What's the harm of stealing a shovel to guarantee the job gets done?

Briseno lied to the grand jury, but that was (as far as one can tell) his only sin of commission. He ran a fairly clean investigation. He didn't coerce Ben Spencer to confess. He didn't plant or hide evidence. It was, rather, his many sins of omission that doomed Ben Spencer. He ran a breathtakingly skimpy investigation. He listened to witnesses who had much to gain from Spencer's indictment—thousands of dollars or fewer years in prison—and discredited more knowledgeable witnesses with nothing to gain. He ignored a far more promising suspect, and failed to question him even though he was sitting right there in a Dallas jail. He closed the case in four days, leaving a trail of loose ends. There's no evidence that Briseno felt particular animus toward Ben Spencer. Rather, as Spencer puts it, "his interest seemed to have been just nailing a suspect, so that he could close this case."[32]

In the end, does it really matter if the corruption is noble or malicious? When police cut corners, dissemble on the stand, or disregard inconvenient evidence or witnesses, the result is the same. An innocent person takes a bus to prison.

E very week beginning in the spring of 1987, Debra Spencer drove to Lew Sterrett jail and stood in line for hours, waiting to snatch a few moments with her new husband. Every week, she grew in size and discomfort—seven, then eight, then nine months pregnant, and eventually she succumbed to sitting on the dirty floor to relieve her aching back. Intensely private, she kept a ferocious silence and never told her colleagues or friends where her husband was. "After Ben was arrested, I was too ashamed to tell anyone," she recalled years later. "I finally had to tell my parents. And my dad said, 'Just come home and I'll take care of you and the baby.'"

On May 14, Debra's water broke. She called her sister, who told her to pack up some clothes, quickly. Her sister drove her to the hospital, intending to see Debra through the birth. No, Debra said, just drop me off. Do I need to call anyone? her sister asked. Ben's mother, perhaps? No, Debra said.

"I just wanted to do this by myself. I was crushed. I didn't want anyone but Ben."

That day, Spencer called and learned that Debra was at the hospital. "You have a little boy and he looks just like you," his father-in-law told him. "You cannot deny this baby."

May 14, 1987, has haunted Spencer for decades. "I should have been there to see you through the remainder of your pregnancy," he wrote his wife. "I should have been there to comfort you when our son was birthed into this old world. I should have been there to drive you home from the hospital with our child. I should have been there to take care of you as a good husband should." He could never redeem the lost moments. "I know that you loved me, but I still feel that I failed you both."

As his trial date approached, Spencer hoped that his son's birth presaged good things, that it might still be possible to wrest himself from this accusation. It is perhaps a mercy, in those early days of fatherhood, that Spencer knew nothing about the history of Dallas's legal system, or the ambitious cadre of prosecutors trained by the most famous district attorney in America. He would find out soon enough.

# Chapter 10

# IN THE SHADOW OF
# HENRY WADE

+———+

**You're looking for tough, mean people.
That's just the way juries were picked.**

—FORMER DALLAS PROSECUTOR ED GRAY

In another time, in another city, Benjamine Spencer could have hoped for a fair fight. Frank Jackson, one of Dallas's most respected defense attorneys, had been appointed to represent him. Jackson believed he had erected an alibi defense that could withstand the prosecutors' fusillade. But what the twenty-two-year-old defendant did not realize as his October 1987 trial date approached was that his battle was not against the prosecutor. It was against the efficient machinery designed by the most famous district attorney in the country at the time: Henry Wade.

Henry Wade had retired as Dallas County district attorney less than three months before Jeffrey Young was killed; the "Chief" would not prosecute Ben Spencer. But his protégés would. Wade had run the district attorney's office for thirty-six years, and it still hummed along with many of the prosecutors he had hired and the culture he had nurtured.

Born in 1914 in Rockwell County, near Dallas, Henry Menasco Wade was the ninth of eleven children, with an early and overarching ambition that set him apart from his crowded family. He attended the University of Texas on a football scholarship, was elected county attorney before graduating from law school, handled espionage cases in J. Edgar Hoover's FBI, served in World War II, and in 1950, at age thirty-six, became Dallas County's district attorney. He liked to win, and he enjoyed occupying the national stage. He was the Wade in *Roe v. Wade*. He personally prosecuted Jack Ruby, the man who murdered President John F. Kennedy's assassin, Lee Harvey Oswald, in 1962, securing the death penalty in the "trial of the century." People gave him standing ovations when he entered a room. He promised law and order, and he delivered.

From the first, Wade waged a fire-and-brimstone style of justice, rolling out the "Wade Plan," which shaped the contours of justice in Dallas for more than a generation. The plan included "swift and sure prosecution of all criminals" and life imprisonment for the "hardened criminal." To achieve that end, he hired alley fighters. "He told me, 'I'm looking for a guy that eats gunpowder for breakfast,'" recalled Ed Gray, who worked for Wade in the 1970s and wrote the only biography of the famed district attorney, *Henry Wade's Tough Justice*. "He wanted somebody with a law degree but who was basically a knuckle fighter."

The Dallas historian Michael Phillips says a joke that was "sort of serious" circulated for years. "They would say: *Anyone can convict a guilty person, but only a really skilled prosecutor could land an innocent person in jail.* And that almost became a macho thing, to just win regardless." Dallas County boasted the highest conviction rate in the country: 93 percent. Local defense attorneys called themselves "the 7 percent club."

Wade's prosecutors competed against each other for everything, including the harshest penalties. They threw a party when someone secured a death penalty. Short of death, they vied for the longest sentences. It began, Ed Gray recalled, sometime in the late 1960s. "One lawyer gets up and tells the jury, 'We don't want just life or ninety-nine years. We want to send the parole board a message that this is a bad guy that should never be paroled. We're asking you to return a sentence of 150 years.'" Game on. One prosecutor won 1,500 years for a dealer selling three capsules of heroin to an undercover cop; another scored 3,000 years for a murder; the winner was 5,005 years for a man who kidnapped and then released, unharmed, the daughter-in-law of a prominent publisher.

"And then we started getting negative press," Gray lamented. "'These DAs are just playing with people's lives,' and things like that." Wade imposed guidelines that capped sentences at ninety-nine years. However, the penalties were not blind to skin color. Blacks were sent to prison for life for robbery. But if a white killed a Black person, prosecutors classified it as a "misdemeanor murder," and would either dismiss it or plead it down to the minimum.

Into this cauldron of manly aggression stepped John Vance, a judge and former prosecutor who succeeded Henry Wade. Vance was a "solid, honest guy," recalled the attorney Bruce Anton, who clerked for him. "He was almost too nice to be DA," remarked Ed Gray. Where Wade was charismatic, Vance was subdued; where Wade was articulate and quick, Vance was tongue-tied and analyzed endlessly before acting or speaking. Henry Wade described him as a "plodder," adding as an afterthought, "but he thinks right."[1] Wade inspired fierce loyalty; Vance earned quiet disdain. "Who wants to be the coach after Tom Landry?" one defense attorney asked, referring to the Dallas Cowboys coach, who led the team to two Super Bowls and twenty consecutive winning seasons.[2]

Not surprisingly, then, Vance failed to transform the office culture and failed to rein in the aggressions. He barely left an impression, except for not being Henry Wade. "It's still the same team of prosecutors and the same culture," the historian Michael Phillips said. "This is Henry Wade's department still." Vance hewed to the same law-and-order approach to justice, noted the longtime journalist Jim Schutze. "Vance was just Henry Wade's errand boy, and an absolute apostle of the Henry Wade philosophy."

I n Lew Sterrett jail, Ben Spencer told himself to trust the system, that truth would prevail. But he worried. He did not know the details of the prosecution's case, did not know the office's win-loss record, had never faced one of the district attorney's armored divisions now barreling his way. But given how little money his attorney was spending on the investigation, and how seldom he visited Spencer in jail, Ben intuited the mismatch. He grew anxious, and angry, and soon he landed in a world of trouble.

He began to vent his anger at the jail's bullies, of which there was no shortage. "And I got into it with every last one of them." He developed a reputation for "running" the jail as the "tank boss." In the fall of 1987, the commander of the jail put him in solitary.

And there, in solitary, Spencer began to feel "a peace of mind." He pondered his behavior, surprised at the trajectory. "I said, Man, I'm going into these different tanks and fighting people. I'm twenty-two years old. I'm a grown man. What am I doing fighting people?" He stopped cursing in that cell. He surrendered his anger, his brokenness, and his future. "I got a closeness to God," Spencer reflected three decades later. "I thank God for that opportunity because it allowed me to connect with who I really am, you know what I'm saying? And who I think, who I *believe* God wants me to be." Ben Spencer's emotional survival, the astonishing absence of bitterness, can be traced to that solitary cell in the fall of 1987.


With his booming voice and deep belly laugh, Henry Wade was a good old boy whose grandfathers, both of them, fought for the Confederacy. But his Black prosecutors never smelled a whiff of racism on Wade personally. "I liked him," said Larry Baraka, who worked for Wade in the 1970s and later became the first Black district judge in Dallas. He met with Wade soon after graduating from law school at the University of Houston. "I had this big Afro and a Van Dyke beard. I wore a black shirt open to the navel with a burgundy blazer because *I'm dressing for success,*" he recalled, laughing. "Mr. Wade looked up at me and asked, 'What can I do for you?' And I said, 'Well, it's not really a question of what you can do for me. It's a question of what *I* can do for *you.*'" Wade hired him on the spot, before Baraka had passed the bar exam. "He spoke with me with respect. And he always kept his word with me," Baraka said, adding, "Obviously, he still had some racist tendencies because he's The Man."

With Wade's blessing, Baraka recruited Black attorneys, including John Creuzot. "I don't know what was in his mind or in his heart," said Creuzot, who is now district attorney of Dallas County. "But I do know that for those of us that worked in this office, he hired women when the law firms weren't hiring women, he hired Black women and men when law firms weren't hiring any of us. And we got promoted and we were treated fairly."

"Let me stop you right there, Barb," said Frank Jackson, when he heard these assessments. "*Everybody* in those days was a racist in Texas." Jackson worked for Henry Wade in the 1970s, and said the district attorney may have treated Black *prosecutors* with respect, but seat a Black man like Ben Spencer at the defense table as a defendant and all comity dissolved. "In those days, Blacks were not viewed equally in courtrooms," he said. A prosecutor trying a case against a Black defendant was starting at the ninety-yard line. The defense attorney had to pray for a miracle. "Racism was infused into just about everything in the criminal justice system at that time." And nowhere was race more dispositive than in jury selection.

I n 1980s Dallas, and almost everywhere across the United States, a trial was often won or lost on the day the jury was selected. One of the first lessons all new Dallas prosecutors were taught was the art of sculpting their jury to eliminate Blacks and other "undesirables." Beginning in the 1960s, they would gather on Saturday mornings for training sessions by seasoned prosecutors, fifty or sixty people in a central jury room. Assistant District Attorney Jon Sparling, who in 1970 landed the first one-thousand-year sentence in US history, would provide a handout on the techniques for jury selection. The eighteen-page handout was "innocuous enough," Ed Gray recalled, but the lecture itself was bracing. "His specific advice was to automatically strike off 'Jews, spics, and dagos.' The exclusion of African Americans was so ingrained that it wasn't even mentioned."

The handout became a chapter in a manual that was required reading for years, called "Jury Selection in a Criminal Case," known better as the Sparling Memorandum. The prosecutor explained the strategic value of peremptory strikes.[3] During jury selection, judges, prosecutors, and defense attorneys may reject any number of candidates from the jury pool for "cause," such as a conflict of interest or obvious bias. Attorneys have a limited number of peremptory challenges, which allow them to reject a juror without stating a reason. In Texas at that time, each side was allowed ten peremptory strikes. To use those strikes wisely, Sparling offered this advice about attitude, appearance, gender, religion, and race:

> You are looking for a strong, stable, individual who believes that Defendants are different from them in kind, rather than degree.
>
> Look for physical afflictions. These people usually sympathize with the accused. Extremely overweight people, especially women and young men, indicates a lack of self-discipline and often times instability. I like the lean and hungry look.
>
> I don't like women jurors because I can't trust them. Young women too often sympathize with the Defendant; old women wearing too much makeup are usually unstable, and therefore are bad State's jurors.
>
> Jewish veniremen generally make poor State's jurors. Jews have a history of oppression and generally empathize with the accused.
>
> You are not looking for any member of a minority group which may subject him to oppression—they almost always empathize with the accused . . . Minority races almost always empathize with the Defendant.

In other words, Ed Gray said, "you're not going to put some Black lady on a jury that goes to church four times a week if you can get some insurance company executives. You're looking for tough, mean people. That's just the way juries were picked."

The perfect jury excluded "pretty much everybody except older white men," Baraka observed. He was appalled by, and ignored, the infamous training. Others, too, dismissed it as unworthy of notice. Yet the racial animus was kneaded like yeast into the culture of the office, where it silently expanded.

In 1986, *The Dallas Morning News* conducted a statistical study of people selected from jury pools in one hundred cases over two years.[4] The racism was staggering. Prosecutors used peremptory challenges to exclude nearly nine out of ten Blacks who were eligible to serve on a jury. If you were a potential juror who was Black, the chance of your being seated on a jury was one in ten; if you were white, it was one in two. If you were a Black defendant, you could not count on a jury of your racial peers. Four out of five Black defendants faced an all-white jury. Of the fifty-four Black male defendants included in the study, fifty-two were tried by juries with not a single Black male juror.[5]

The racial composition of a jury is crucial in a case where there is no physical evidence and rests on circumstantial evidence. The verdict often comes down to gut instinct about the character of the players on the stage before the jurors. Do they trust the white prosecutor or the Black defendant? Do they rule for the state, despite a trickle of inculpatory evidence, or for the defendant, who has presented an avalanche of evidence supporting his innocence? Did unspoken bias doom Lenell Geter?

In 1982, Geter had recently graduated from college, was engaged to be married, and was working as an engineer at a large military defense contractor near Dallas. Based on shaky eyewitness testimony, the twenty-five-year-old Black man was arrested for robbing a Kentucky Fried Chicken fifty miles from his office during his lunch hour, as well as two previous robberies at fast food restaurants. Nine of his colleagues testified he was at work that day, and saw him close to the time of the robbery, making it physically impossible, without, say, a helicopter, to rob the KFC and return to work within the prosecution's time frame.

During jury selection, Dallas prosecutors struck every eligible Black juror. The all-white jury convicted Geter and sentenced him to life in prison. "What they thought was, Geter was just another Black young fellow that was out robbing," his attorney Edwin Sigel told *The Dallas Morning News*.[6] His case drew the attention of *60 Minutes* and the NAACP. His new attorneys discovered that police had lied at trial. They found new alibi witnesses and a likely perpetrator. Confronted with evidence of misconduct and sloppy police work, as well as attention from the national media, Henry Wade's district attorney's office released Geter from prison. "There's no question in my mind that if he were a white engineer, they would not have dealt so harshly with him and they probably would not have found him guilty," Sigel said.

Henry Wade once lamented that the presumption of innocence is something of a bother, but it has its upside. "This safeguard undoubtedly has caused a lot of guilty defendants to be released," he wrote in a 1959 paper for the Institute of Law Enforcement. "But on the other hand, it has caused practically no innocent person to have ever been convicted."[7]

He spoke too soon. During the thirty-six years in which Henry Wade prosecuted supposed criminals, thirty people were wrongly convicted in Dallas and would eventually be exonerated. It's a stunning indictment that, ironically, Wade brought down on himself when he established a world-class crime laboratory. The Southwestern Institute of Forensic Sciences stored evidence for decades, and when DNA began exonerating prisoners in 1989, the evidence that could free countless others was sitting right there in storage in Dallas. Two of the prisoners were awaiting execution when they were declared innocent. Fifteen were serving sentences of life or ninety-nine years. And their race? Nine were white. One was Hispanic. Twenty were Black.

D allas prosecutors were hardly alone in tweaking juries to exclude minorities. Across the South, prosecutors stacked their juries. As US Supreme Court Justice Thurgood Marshall commented in a 1984 case, *Harris v. Texas*: "Prosecutorial abuse of peremptory challenges has grown to epidemic proportions in certain regions of the country."[8]

But two years later, a reckoning came. The case involved James

Batson, a Black man accused of burglary and receiving stolen property in Louisville, Kentucky. During jury selection, prosecutors used their peremptory strikes to dismiss all four Blacks in the jury pool. Batson was convicted by an all-white panel. In *Batson v. Kentucky*, a landmark decision in 1986, the Supreme Court ruled in his favor, opining that peremptory challenges may not be used to exclude jurors solely based on race. "The reality of practice, amply reflected in many state- and federal-court opinions, shows that the challenge may be, and unfortunately at times has been, used to discriminate against black jurors," Justice Lewis Powell wrote for the majority.[9] The court set up a three-step process to winnow out racially discriminatory strikes. First, the defendant raises a challenge. Second, the prosecution provides a "neutral explanation" unrelated to race. Third, the judge decides if the strike constitutes "purposeful discrimination."

*Batson* is a great idea in theory, "except that it doesn't work," says James Coleman, a professor at Duke University School of Law. "The test is almost laughable." Race-neutral pretexts are as varied and numerous as stars in the sky. Many states have cheat sheets on the topic, similar to the Sparling Memorandum, but updated to comply with the court's *Batson* ruling. "You drill and grill these Black prospective jurors and then you find something that will allow you to say, 'Well, this is my race-neutral reason,'" Coleman says. "But it's clear that they're looking for some reason that they can then exclude the person." The judge almost always accepts the explanation, and the defendant can rarely carry his burden to show that it was based on race. "So you lose."

The courts quickly recognized the runaround, but enforcing *Batson* proved nearly impossible. In 1996, the Illinois appellate court called the process a "charade." "Surely, new prosecutors are given a manual, probably titled 'Handy Race-Neutral Explanations' or '20 Time-Tested Race-Neutral Explanations,'" the court opined acerbically, and then cited reasons that prosecutors had used successfully to rid themselves of jurors in recent years: "too old, too young, divorced, 'long, unkempt hair,' free-lance writer, religion, social worker, renter, lack of family contact, attempting to make eye-contact with defendant, 'lived in an area consisting predominantly of apartment complexes,' single, lack of maturity, improper demeanor, unemployed, improper attire, juror lived alone, misspelled place of employment, living with girlfriend, unemployed spouse, spouse employed as school teacher, employment as part-time barber, friendship with city council member, failure to remove hat, lack of community ties, children same 'age bracket' as defendant, deceased father, and prospective juror's aunt receiving psychiatric care."[10]

*Batson* may have prevented some Blacks from being bounced from a jury, but the record to date suggests discrimination thrives to this day. In California, researchers analyzed more than seven hundred cases between 2006 and 2018 and found that prosecutors used their peremptory challenges to strike a Black juror in 72 percent of cases and a Latino juror in about 28 percent of cases. They challenged potential white jurors in 0.5 percent of the cases.[11] Among the successful reasons: for Black jurors, they wore dreadlocks or "blinged out" clothes; for Latino jurors, they favored large earrings or had negative experiences with the US Border Patrol.

Researchers found similar results in Louisiana and Mississippi,[12] but North Carolina claims the title in snubbing *Batson*. A 2018 study found that prosecutors removed nonwhite jurors at about twice the rate as whites.[13] In another study, researchers analyzed more than seventy-four hundred peremptory strikes made by North Carolina prosecutors in 173 death penalty cases tried between 1990 and 2010. The study showed that prosecutors struck 53 percent of eligible Black jurors and only 26 percent of all other eligible jurors.[14] The prosecutor's notes on the jury list can be illuminating. In one 1997 case in Martin County, a prosecutor noted that a white juror was "good" because she would "bring her own rope." But another white juror was marked with a "No" because, according to the prosecutor's notes, she had a child by a "BM," or Black male.[15]

North Carolina's higher courts, which are supposed to referee discriminatory strikes when the trial judge fails, never once found a *Batson* violation against a Black juror in the thirty years since the ruling was handed down. Not in the 114 appeals that came before appellate courts, not in the 74 cases decided by the Supreme Court of North Carolina. At least, they found no fault in striking minorities. Twice, however, North Carolina appellate courts cried foul when the jurors struck were white.

Jury selection matters, because a diverse jury alters both the deliberation in the jury room and the verdict. In one study, researchers split potential jurors into two groups: one panel with six whites, one with four whites and two Blacks. They watched a trial of a Black man accused of sexual assault. Even before they deliberated, members of diverse juries were nearly 10 percent less likely to presume he was guilty than were members of all-white juries. The jury with Blacks evaluated the evidence more thoroughly, deliberated longer (well, eleven minutes longer), discussed more facts about the case, and made fewer factual errors than all-white juries.[16] In another study, diverse juries were less likely to give death sentences.[17] "If you remove people who might be skeptical," James Coleman observes, "you grease the rails to a conviction."[18]

Some jurisdictions are trying to give *Batson* some "teeth," including Washington, Nevada, and Washington, DC, Coleman says. "But most states don't. Most states just simply apply *Batson* the way the Supreme Court announced it. Which means that unless the prosecutor is almost an idiot, they can come up with an explanation that a judge will accept."[19]

B y late October 1987, Texas prosecutors had smoothed out the wrinkles in their case against Benjamine Spencer. Only one task remained. On October 20, Detective Jesus Briseno and prosecutor Jeffrey Hines visited the crime scene. Since their case rested almost entirely on the three witnesses who said they saw Ben Spencer and Robert Mitchell run from the victim's BMW, they needed a map and photographs to show the jury where the car was parked in the alley. If it was parked near the street, Gladys Oliver could see it; if parked farther up, she could not. They made precise measurements, drew a map, took photographs.

But there was a problem, one that the jury would not hear. The detective and the prosecutor had no idea where the BMW had been parked.

The photographs they snapped in late October captured a very different scene from the one seven months earlier. The foliage had changed and some large objects that could have blocked Oliver's line of sight had been removed. In fact, the pair did not even take a photograph from Oliver's window, which would have shown her perspective. Regarding the most important piece of physical evidence—the crime scene—they just guessed.

This was the legal system on which Spencer was pinning his hopes when he walked into the courtroom on October 26, 1987, settled into his chair, and watched his trial open with the selection of his jury.

*Chapter 11*

# THE SHELL GAME

+———+

**Say, what's this? Well, this is important evidence.**

—BRUCE ANTON, *attorney for Benjamine Spencer*

On October 26, 1987, a crowd filled the 283rd District Courtroom in Dallas, the family members, potential jurors, and curious spectators occupying every seat, leaving latecomers to lean against the wall at the back of the room. *The State of Texas v. Benjamin John Spencer* offered several striking plotlines: a Black-on-white murder, a famous billionaire just offstage, a thirty-five-thousand-dollar reward, and an attractive widow with her three young children.

The defendant sat quietly between his two attorneys. On the other side of the aisle, the prosecutor was positioned next to the jury box. The door behind the bench opened and the room hushed as Judge Herbert Line strode to his perch and seated himself. He said a few words of greeting and began voir dire, when attorneys on each side question potential jurors and weed out those whom they believe would vote against them. Jury selection, trial lawyers will tell you, isn't just the most important part of a trial—it's the whole ball game. For the prosecution, it was a math problem: Eliminate as many Blacks and other groups identified in the Sparling memo as possible. For Spencer's defense team, it came down to luck. "You got a Black man accused of killing a white man," Spencer's attorney Bruce Anton reflected. "A *rich* white man and a *poor* Black man. You go in with some trepidation."

There are no notes from the voir dire. There is no record of what questions the lawyers asked; how many peremptory strikes the prosecutor, Jeffrey Hines, used to exclude Blacks; whether Spencer's attorneys objected; how often Judge Line sided with the state and excused a Black man or woman from service. But at the end of the day, eleven whites and one Black would decide Ben Spencer's future.

In fact, the record of the entire trial—the transcripts, the exhibits, rulings from the bench, jury instructions, everything—has inexplicably vanished, despite dogged efforts by defense attorneys, prosecutors, investigators, and journalists to track it down.[1] As a result, the details are fuzzy as to what evidence was presented, what the witnesses said, or how the judge ruled on attorney objections or the admissibility of evidence.

What is not in dispute is that in 1987, minorities faced bleak odds in the courtroom. "If you're Black or brown, you're just guilty, even if the evidence didn't show it," said the former prosecutor Larry Baraka. Judges rarely tapped the brakes when a trial was careening toward a questionable conviction. Almost all judges were former prosecutors, and they gave considerable leeway to the state's attorneys, who generally worked each case in teams of two. "Judges were the third prosecutor," Baraka said.

Spencer worried that with this jury panel—white, well dressed executives and stay-at-home mothers—he had "no chance that they will be fair in reaching their verdict."[2] Then, turning to take in the spectators, he spotted a handful of Blacks, although not his wife or his mother; by court order, they were barred from the courtroom because they might be called as witnesses. (They weren't.) On the whole, Bruce Anton said, the faces were all white—friends of Jeffrey Young or colleagues of his father, Harry Young, at Electronic Data Systems. Ross Perot was not present, but he was keeping tabs. Sitting in the courtroom, still unshackled and theoretically presumed innocent, Spencer sensed that his fate was being sealed, like a character in an Edgar Allan Poe story.[3] With the jury selected, the lead prosecutor had already set the first stone in cement, to be followed by another and another as he bricked up the exit.

"The pressure was on the state to perform in this case," Spencer's lead

attorney, Frank Jackson, recalled. "They wanted the most severe outcome that they could get." And because of that, the prosecution threw all of
its resources into the trial. They planned to call twenty witnesses. The defense would call four. Over the next five days, Spencer watched with dawning dread as prosecutor Jeffrey Hines built his case—the circumstantial
evidence, the distorted facts, the witnesses' untruthful testimony—filling
in the cracks and smoothing the mortar with sure strokes.

From handwritten notes by the prosecutors and Spencer's letters and
interviews, one can glean the contours of the trial. In a circumstantial case like this, where there is no physical evidence and no witness to
the assault, it boils down to who can tell the most compelling story. The
state argued that Spencer needed money and prowled around until he
found a man walking out of his office on a Sunday night; he then stole
the man's watch, his cash, his car, and his wedding ring. To buttress its
arguments, the state presented Spencer's neighbors and a jailhouse informant, who prosecutors said had no reason to lie.

Spencer's defense team argued that he was flush with cash from his tax
refund and his Friday paycheck. Why should he engage in such a risky
venture? Besides, he was with a friend, Christie Williams, the entire evening, and she vouched for him. Spencer's attorneys suggested it was the
*neighbors*, not Spencer, who could profit by helping the state solve the
case: a twenty-five-thousand-dollar reward offered by Ross Perot, and another ten thousand dollars from the victim's company.

If the prosecutor's trial notes are any guide, the state's witnesses told
convincing stories and easily weathered cross-examination. Gladys Oliver
recounted in great detail how she saw Ben Spencer emerge from the victim's BMW and run away. "I know what face I saw," she testified, according to the notes. The jailhouse informant clinched the deal when he
described how Ben Spencer assaulted the victim at his office.

The defense witnesses fared less well. It must have been distressing for
Spencer to hear his key witness, the young woman who provided him

with his alibi, waffling on the stand: First she said that there was "no doubt in my mind" that she was with Spencer at the time of the assault. Later she stated, "I don't know if Spencer had anything to do with it."[4]

Two moments decided Spencer's fate: one during the trial, and one while the jury was deliberating. In preparation for trial, defense attorney Anton had requested any information that would point to Spencer's innocence or impeach the credibility of the state's witnesses, which the prosecutor was ethically bound to provide. Specifically, Anton asked whether any of the neighbors had received reward money—including a reward from Crime Stoppers—in exchange for their information. "Time and time again," Anton said, prosecutor Hines denied having such information. (Hines declined repeated requests for interviews.)

During the trial, Gladys Oliver confirmed this, gaily telling Spencer's lawyer that she would jump at the twenty-five-thousand-dollar reward. "I'll take a piece of that pie. Wouldn't you?" But then she testified, "I haven't collected any or asked for any."[5]

That was the first important moment, the one that punctured Spencer's defense.[6] After deliberating all afternoon and into the evening, the jury reached a verdict. Spencer was fetched from the holding tank. He stood and watched the jurors as they filed in, looking for signs of mercy—sympathy, perhaps—in the set of their faces or in the way they settled themselves in the jury box. He saw none. When the jury foreman declared him guilty of first-degree murder, Spencer felt all the air escape his lungs. "I just couldn't believe it."

Frank Jackson was disappointed but not surprised. "It's hard to overcome a dead white guy who's killed by two Black men in a Black area of Dallas where you dump his body out on the street," he said years later. "It's just hard to overcome that kind of emotional case."

The second pivotal moment occurred after the jury had withdrawn to debate Spencer's sentence. The attorneys waited in the courtroom, expecting a quick decision. Sometime between 9:45 p.m. on October 30 and 12:45 a.m. October 31, Anton glanced over at the prosecutors' table.

"And there's a Crime Stoppers report sitting there," he recalled. Say, what's this? he thought. He picked up the document and examined it. Contrary to her testimony, Gladys Oliver had been promised $580 from Crime Stoppers for her information—not much money, but enough to prove that she was compromised and that she lied under oath. "I thought, Well, this is important evidence," he said. "If somebody had a financial motive to testify, you had to disclose it."


The state generally owns the advantage in criminal trials, having at its disposal public funds to prosecute criminals and a deep bench of detectives and prosecutors to win convictions. The US Supreme Court has long been mindful of this. A prosecutor may try his cases "with earnestness and vigor—indeed, he should do so," Justice George Sutherland wrote in *Berger v. United States* in 1935. "But, while he may strike hard blows, he is not at liberty to strike foul ones."[7]

In 1963, the court attempted to deter foul blows in its landmark decision *Brady v. Maryland*. It ruled that the prosecution may not suppress "material" evidence in its possession that is favorable to the defendant. "Society wins not only when the guilty are convicted, but when criminal trials are fair," William O. Douglas wrote.[8] Nine years later, in *Giglio v. United States*, the court expanded that obligation: The government must also turn over evidence that might undermine the credibility of its own witnesses, including, say, that a jailhouse informant expected a lower sentence for his testimony, or that a witness received or expected a monetary reward.[9]

With *Brady* and *Giglio* in place, a new category of misconduct was born.

Defense attorneys have always known that the government cheats. But only recently could they put any sort of number on it. It turns out that prosecutors hide evidence all the time. A study of more than two thousand exonerations across the country found that police and prosecutors—largely prosecutors—failed to turn over favorable evidence in 61 percent of those erroneous murder convictions.[10] In other words, six out of ten innocent people went to prison for murder because prosecutors did not turn over exculpatory evidence, as was their constitutional duty.

Prosecutors have failed to reveal a range of evidence that defense attorneys would find helpful. Sometimes, police and prosecutors knew that no crime had occurred but prosecuted anyway. In 1996, Kristine Bunch, a pregnant, twenty-two-year-old mother, was convicted of setting fire to her trailer home and killing her three-year-old son in Decatur City, Indiana. The prosecution's arson investigator testified that he found traces of accelerant in the living room and bedroom—evidence of intent, he said. But the actual report, which the prosecutor buried, said otherwise. It showed that investigators found *no* accelerants, only traces of kerosene, which made sense, since the family used a kerosene heater to warm the living room. Kristine Bunch served seventeen years before the report came to light.[11]

When a crime has occurred, tunnel vision, too, can lead investigators and prosecutors to cheat. Consider the case of Michael Morton, who was convicted of murdering his wife, Christine, in Austin and sentenced to life in 1987. Twenty-four years and several court battles would pass before Texas prosecutors turned over the whole file. It showed that neighbors had seen a man casing the Mortons' house several times; that someone had tried to use Christine Morton's credit card after her husband had been taken into custody; and that their three-year-old son had seen the perpetrator and said it was not his father.[12]

Many omissions are far more mundane—a Crime Stoppers report, for instance—and they all slip through a loophole in *Brady v. Maryland*. The Supreme Court ruled that the *prosecutor* chooses what is "material" evidence; that is, the prosecutor decides whether there is a "reasonable probability" that the jury might have returned a different verdict if that evidence had been presented. "It's the fox watching the henhouse," former federal prosecutor Mark Godsey says.

Imagine the interior debate as the state attorneys in these cases mull over the evidence. Did Kristine Bunch's prosecutor read the report that the fire was an accident and not arson, and think: No, that wouldn't help the defense? Did the district attorney prosecuting Michael Morton deem it irrelevant that neighbors identified another man or that the victim's credit card was active while Morton was sitting in jail?

Prosecutors' judgment calls rarely redound to the suspect's benefit. And after they are caught, they have a ready excuse. "Prosecutors say, 'Well, I didn't think it was exculpatory, Judge. I thought it was false,'" Anton says. "'I didn't turn it over because I didn't believe it.'" The state attorneys look at the evidence through the lens of the prosecution, not considering what hay the defense might make with those facts. They consider it "inconsequential," Anton says—a mindset that exists today. "There are still many, many prosecutors who do not understand what exculpatory information is."

Godsey blames "noble cause corruption," rather than simple corruption, for the impulse to bury evidence. "They think that the defendant did something horrendous, and they're actually doing a good thing to cheat and cut the corners to make sure the person doesn't get off," he says. "They're saving the next person—the next little girl this guy would kill."[13]

Federal appeals judge Alex Kozinski opined that prosecutors treat *Brady* like a speed bump, careening over the evidence without being pulled over. In a scathing dissent in a 2013 *Brady*-related case, the Ninth Circuit Court chief judge cited twenty-nine cases in which a prosecutor suppressed evidence. "I wish I could say that the prosecutor's unprofessionalism here is the exception, that his propensity for shortcuts and indifference to his ethical and legal responsibilities is a rare blemish and source of embarrassment to an otherwise diligent and scrupulous corps of attorneys staffing prosecutors' offices around the country," the judge wrote. "But it wouldn't be true. *Brady* violations have reached epidemic proportions in recent years, and the federal and state reporters bear testament to this unsettling trend."[14]

One case Kozinski cites was the capital murder prosecution of John Thompson.[15] In 1985, Thompson was convicted of killing a man in New Orleans during an armed robbery. He was sentenced to death. One month before he was to be executed, Thompson's attorneys discovered that the assistant district attorneys knew the blood evidence excluded Thompson and had intentionally suppressed the lab report. Thompson was released after eighteen years on death row. But what happened next would further enfeeble *Brady*. After Thompson won a fourteen-million-dollar award from the state, in 2011, the US Supreme Court ruled that the district attorney's office could not be held liable for the actions of a "rogue" prosecutor (even though five prosecutors knew of the concealed report).[16] With this ruling, the court enshrined prosecutorial immunity—and removed the consequences for bad behavior.

These are the rare *Brady* violations that we know about. By its nature, this kind of misconduct is stored in closets and locked file cabinets, tucked away from the disinfectant of sunlight, rarely seen and almost never punished. Prosecutorial misconduct is the perfect crime.

"The *Brady* rule is only as good as its enforcement," says Vincent Southerland, at New York University School of Law. "And unfortunately, the enforcement only comes often by dumb luck." Luck, such as glancing over at the prosecutor's table and spotting a Crime Stoppers report; luck, such as stumbling onto evidence that the state's star witness against Ben Spencer had lied, and the prosecutor knew it.

B en Spencer's attorneys filed a motion for a new trial a week after his murder conviction. It was granted. A few days later, Dallas prosecutors reindicted Spencer, this time for aggravated robbery, an easier crime to prove than murder.

The Young family, furious at this turn of events, telegraphed their ire to the district attorney. Within weeks, Assistant District Attorney Jeffrey Hines quit his job for private practice. A new trial date was set for March 21, 1988, almost one year to the day of Jeffrey Young's murder. Spencer returned to jail.

"The first trial, I considered that we won," Spencer's lead attorney, Frank Jackson, said three decades later. "We went to trial, fired our best shot." The jury had given Spencer a much lighter sentence—thirty-five years—than Jackson had expected. A second trial, Jackson told Spencer, is much harder to win than the first. "They know what we're going to do. They know about this young girl that I was using as an alibi witness.

They're going to get to her." The prosecution will tweak their own arguments accordingly. "We're going to go back in with one hand tied behind us because they have had a preview of our case, and their witnesses are rehearsed. They're going to know my cross-examination. They're going to clean up all of that."

In the late 1980s, Texas prisons were so crowded that the federal court had ordered the state to thin out the population. Inmates were serving a fraction of their sentences. On March 18, 1988, the Friday before Spencer's second trial was to begin, the new prosecutor handling the case buttonholed Frank Jackson at the courthouse. He offered a deal: If Spencer would plead guilty to robbery, he would be sentenced to twenty years. In that climate, he could be out in three years. Jackson pulled Spencer out of the tank for a talk. He explained that this was a very good deal, if he would sign for it.

"Sign for it? For what?" Spencer asked. "I didn't do anything."

"Well, you know, if you take it to trial, they're going to try to give you a life sentence, and they're likely to get it," Jackson responded.

"Well, I don't care what they likely to get. I'm not going to plead guilty to something I didn't do."

"If it were me, knowing the parole law at that time, I would have probably taken it and run with it," Jackson said years later. "If I had been Ben, I would have probably said, 'Yeah, okay, I did it and I'm gonna let it go. Go do my time and get out and get on with my life.'"

Back then, as now, the criminal justice system is a little like a game of blackjack. Does the accused stick with his cards, or tap for another and run the risk of losing big? He has to make a calculated decision—a few years in prison with a plea, or possibly life in prison after a jury trial.[17] The house almost always wins.

There is a cost to stubbornly believing that truth will prevail. The "trial penalty" is effectively a tax on the defendant for insisting on a trial that costs money and time for prosecutors, judges, and jurors. "Innocent people are taking their chances," says the psychologist Saul Kassin. "Innocent people are saying, 'Wait, I didn't do this. I'm going to go to trial.'" He calls it the "phenomenology of innocence." "Innocent people don't appreciate the peril. They think they're innocent and everything is going to work itself out."

It usually doesn't. Back then in Dallas, the jury sentences ranged from twice as long to eight times as long as a plea deal for the same crime. A large study conducted in 2018 found that the trial penalty continues to thrive.[18] For example, people who were accused of murder received a sentence of 17.5 years if they pleaded, but 30.7 years if they went to trial. For manslaughter, the penalty was nearly triple for a trial: 5.6 years with a plea, 14.4 years with a guilty verdict.

Frank Jackson understood the risks. Knowing that Spencer had a wife and ten-month-old son, he urged him to talk to Debra. That Friday night, Spencer called his wife and explained the offer.

"Lord, forgive me, but I was like, '*Take it!*'" Debra said years later. "I say, 'You got to come home. I don't want to do this by myself. Take it.'"

"First of all, I didn't commit the offense," Spencer told her. "I just can't see taking time for something I didn't do." And it's not as simple as just accepting the time. He would have to write out an affidavit, spelling out moment by moment how he supposedly robbed and killed Jeffrey Young. "So now I've got to make up a lie to give to the judge in order to receive the sentence that they're offering."

Equally important, a confession of guilt would follow him the rest of his life, making it hard to find work, making him an easy target. "When I get out, I got an X on my back," he told her. "Let's say something else happens, another robbery where they can't figure out who committed the offense. 'Well, you know Spencer, we picked him up the last time, we railroaded him that time. Let's railroad him again!' So now, I'm starting a cycle. Every time they need a scapegoat, who they going to come to? They're going to come to me."

"He did what I expected he would do," Debra reflected. "Take a stand there. He was going to prove his innocence."

Chapter 12

# WHAT THE JURY SAW

†———†

**I don't know whether he did it or not.**

—FRANK JACKSON, *defense attorney for Ben Spencer*

*March 1, 1988*

*Hi Baby Ben,*

*How is my son doing today? I have been watching how big you have been getting lately. Your daddy's little baby is growing up to be a big boy now. They tell me you're getting too big to carry around. I know you've been enjoying yourself and having lots of fun. And daddy can't wait till the time come that you, Mommy, and I can do things as a family together. I want you to take care of your Mommy until I get out there.*

*Your daddy,*
*Benjamine Spencer III*

Three weeks after Ben Spencer penned this letter to his ten-month-old son, he walked into the 283rd District courtroom for a rematch that would chart his future and that of his young family. The odds disfavored Spencer. His shallow bench from the first trial had been whittled down from two lawyers to one, and from three alibi witnesses to two. The state boasted two prosecutors and fifteen witnesses on deck. The district attorney, John Vance, also made a strategic switch. After Jeffrey Hines's abrupt departure, Vance assigned Andy Beach, one of Dallas County's most seasoned and effective prosecutors, to sit first chair on the case.

Blond and lean and handsome, Beach was a force field of charisma. His fellow prosecutors called him "the Beach Boy." He wooed juries, particularly the women, with earnestness and an easy charm. Most of his trials ended in convictions.

Beach was given only ten weeks to prepare for two murder trials—Spencer's trial and that of his codefendant, Robert Mitchell. He did not have the luxury of conducting a new investigation or even vetting the witnesses. "Twelve people have already convicted [Ben Spencer] beyond a reasonable doubt based on these witnesses," Beach recalled. He merely used Hines's playbook, winnowing out the mistakes and the perjury, or so he thought.

The new trial opened on March 21, 1988, under the impatient gaze of Judge Jack Hampton. As with most judges in Dallas, Hampton had started his career as a prosecutor for Henry Wade. He ruled like a man in a hurry, determined to mow through the trials of Spencer and Mitchell, scheduling them back to back. That morning, the judge and attorneys faced a delicate task: to select a jury that did not violate the Supreme Court's *Batson* rule by illegally excluding Blacks. In his notes from jury selection, Judge Hampton placed a capital "B" next to several names, revealing that nine out of eleven Blacks in the venire were rejected. Prosecutors used three of their peremptory challenges to dismiss Black jurors; the defense used none. In the end, the jury consisted of ten whites and two Blacks.

"That's why so many of us get a raw deal—because none of us is on these juries," mused Eddie Clark, a pastor at New Heights Family Church in Garland, Texas, one of the two Black jurors in Spencer's second trial. "And you got people that don't look like us who have already decided, just because of this"—he tapped the dark skin on his forearm—"they got to be guilty." He paused, reflecting. "I think they are being influenced by movies. You know, everybody's a gangster and a drug dealer, whatever. So they've basically already made their mind up."

When the trial opened, Clark, who then worked as a sheet-metal fabricator, resolved to make his fellow jurors keep an open mind. But overcoming Texas racism in the 1980s posed only one challenge. A larger problem involved the prosecution's strategic advantage, before the jury heard a single fact from Ben Spencer's lawyers.

"In the world of psychology, there are things called primacy effects and recency effects," says Valerie Hans, a professor at Cornell Law School and an expert on the psychology of juries. It's good to have the first word, and it's good to have the last; the prosecution generally has both. "The reason primacy is so attractive is that you get a chance to lay everything out. You get to tell your story first." This story will lodge in jurors' minds unless countered—preferably, quickly—by a defense narrative. Spencer's attorney, Frank Jackson, chose to wait until the prosecution had laid out its entire case before his opening statement; researchers today would consider that a strategic blunder, like erecting a mud wall around a sand castle during high tide.

In no small part because of this sequence, the bedrock upon which jury trials rests—the presumption of innocence—is a myth. "There's pretty good empirical data that shows that that's really not how juries approach the case," says Keith Findley, at the University of Wisconsin Law School. If the jurors were presuming innocence, then the defendant would begin at his opponent's goal line, poised to score and be acquitted. But Findley says studies show that when a trial opens, the game begins on the fifty-yard line.[1] "As soon as they start hearing any incriminating evidence—which they hear right off the bat because the prosecution goes first—they pretty much begin operating with an assumption of: *He must have done something. Why would they be putting him on trial if he hadn't done something?*"

In trials with physical, documentary, or forensic evidence, the jury may lean toward an "informational" model, in which the evidence is piled on layer after layer, until finally it arrives at a rational conclusion. But experts say in a case like Spencer's, where no hard evidence exists to connect him to the crime, the verdict hinges on the jury's assessment of the accused, the accusers, and the attorneys. The jurors decide based on whose story they believe and whose they don't, whom they like or whom they dislike. Both sides appeal to gut instincts, emotions, and, often, unconscious biases.

"It's all the subtext," says Professor Dan Simon, of the University of Southern California. The prosecutor will tell you the defendant is a scumbag; he was a horrible father and he was a bully to his neighbors. And the defense attorney will tell you what a great father he is and what hard breaks he got in life. "And none of those has *anything* to do with the guilt in this particular case. They have to do with: Do you like this person and want to let him off? Or do you despise this person and want to see him be sent up the river?"[2]

This is how both sides played *The State of Texas v. Benjamin John Spencer.*

First thing on Tuesday, March 22, 1987, the jury heard the prosecutor's version of events: that Jeffrey Young, a thirty-three-year-old white executive, a husband and father of three, was beaten at his office, placed in the trunk of his BMW, and left to die on a street in the poor Black neighborhood of West Dallas. The perpetrators then drove his BMW to an alley and fled. The medical examiner testified that the assailant had hit the victim's head with "an extraordinary amount of force," cracking his skull in five places and causing his brain to fatally swell. It was a vicious, frenzied attack. Andy Beach conceded that no physical evidence connected Ben Spencer to the crime, and that none of the fingerprints lifted from the office or car matched Spencer's. The lead homicide detective, Jesus Briseno, minimized that glaring defect in the state's case by testifying that it was the "rule, not the exception" to come up empty on forensic evidence.

Then Beach moved to the heart of his circumstantial case: the testimony of the middle-aged neighbor who lived next to the alley. "Gladys Oliver was one of the most effective, believable eyewitnesses that I ever proffered in a felony case," he later recalled, a veteran who prosecuted more than one hundred capital murder cases. "She had a personality, she had a sense of humor, she had a wit, she wasn't going to tolerate silly questions."

Beach vividly remembered his star witness wheeling herself slowly into the courtroom, a forty-three-year-old "pitiful" figure who turned out to be anything but. Crippled by polio, Oliver could not manage the steps to the witness stand, so she sat in her wheelchair, eye level with the jury, her face drawn, a shawl draped over her legs. Not a soul moved as she unspooled her account in her Texas drawl. On the night of March 22, 1987, around ten o'clock, she was trying to sleep with the TV turned on low when she heard the two guard dogs barking next door. "Well, at first I didn't pay attention, but they just kept *rip rip rip*, and I says, 'What is these dogs barking at?'" she told the jury. "And I said, 'Let me get up and see.' And I peeped out, and when I peeped out, I saw this car, I didn't know if it was a BMW, Mercedes, or what, I knew it was a late-model car."[3]

As Oliver peered at the car in the alley, she testified that she saw Ben Spencer jump out of the passenger's side and Robert Mitchell climb out of the driver's side. "When he got out, I said, 'That's Ben!'" she stated, surprised at this turn of events, as Spencer had always seemed a quiet, nice young man. She slipped on a light dress, cracked open the front door, and glimpsed Spencer walking from the alley at the back of her house, up the driveway, and then knocking at Christie Williams's house next door. She had not seen the assault on Jeffrey Young. But with this testimony, she circumstantially identified Spencer as his assailant, for the timing fit and this was not a stranger's unreliable identification: She knew Spencer's face.

Oliver, articulate and believable, provided the cornerstone of the prosecution's case. Thirty years later, the foreman of the jury can still envision the woman in front of him. "She struck me as being very similar to my grandmother, who was kind of the busybody in the neighborhood," Alan Ledbetter recalled. "I still remember her saying"—he adopts a falsetto voice—"'*I peeps out my window* . . .' I mean, it just sounded so much like my grandmother, just keeping an eye on the neighbors. Particularly the neighbors who my grandmother thought were up to no good."

Defense attorney Frank Jackson tried to knock Oliver off her game, but she ducked every punch. During his cross-examination, in an attempt to cast her as an opportunist who lied to the police, Jackson noted that she repeatedly told police she had seen nothing. She kept mum the night of the crime and the next day, until it suited her purposes to come forward.

> Q: You didn't go up to the police officers and tell them what you had seen?
> A: I sure didn't, would you?
> Q: Yes, ma'am, I would have.
> A: Maybe you would have, maybe you would. I didn't.
> Q: And then the next morning, when you had time to sleep on this . . . you didn't call the police either, did you?
> A: No, they came to my house.
> Q: You told them that you didn't see anything, didn't you?
> A: I sure did.
> Q: You were lying to them, weren't you?
> A: I sure was.[4]

"Mr. Jackson was a very effective, competent defense lawyer, a good cross-examiner," Andy Beach recalled, "and he just didn't get anywhere with her." She held her ground, never veering from her story, never intimidated by the white ex–pro football player who was grilling her. This display of backbone can have a profound effect on a jury. Studies show that the more confident a witness is, the more likely the jury is to believe her, even when her account conflicts with the known facts of a case.[5]

Having failed to cast doubt on *what* she saw, Jackson tried to question *why* she eventually came forward—that is, her motivation. Referring to her testimony in the first trial, Jackson implied that Ross Perot's twenty-five-thousand-dollar reward, not her fealty to truth, prompted her to identify Spencer.

Q: Didn't you tell me in a direct response to my question, whether or not you would take any of that reward if it was offered to you, didn't you say, "Yeah, I will take a piece of that pie?"

A: That's what I said. Look at what I'm having to go through with. I didn't know I was going to have to go through all of this, but since I'm going through all of this, yes, sir.

Q: Do you expect to get paid some money?

A: Hell, if they want to give me some, it's fine with me.

Q: You'll take a piece of that pie, wouldn't you?

A: Would you?

THE COURT: Just answer the question.

A: I am not the suspect. I won't be a witness no more either.[6]

Beach breathed a sigh of relief when Jackson concluded his cross-examination. The defense attorney had missed the most important opportunity to derail the prosecution's case: to demonstrate that Gladys Oliver had every reason to lie about wanting the reward money, even if he couldn't prove she had received it. "Gladys is living in a shotgun house out there in West Dallas and selling barbecue on the weekend and has horrible health issues, and grandkids," he said. "She could have used the money." But Jackson never brought that to light.

Nor did the prosecution's other two witnesses from the neighborhood suffer much more than bruises from Jackson's cross-examination. Although they were bit players—"window dressing," Beach called them—they served their purpose: They corroborated Oliver. The jury liked nineteen-year-old Jimmie Cotton. Cotton testified that he was cooking his dinner about 10:00 p.m., after coming home from a game of night basketball, when he looked out the window and saw a BMW pull into the alley and, a few seconds later, Spencer and Mitchell hop out.

"I found his testimony particularly compelling," Alan Ledbetter recalled. "Comes home, nine thirty, ten o'clock, cooking up a mess of eggs, like I can envision a teenager doing at ten on a Sunday evening. And, watching out his window, which had a fairly direct line of sight to the alley where the BMW was abandoned."

The defense attorney pointed out that Cotton could not possibly have identified the men. The light in the kitchen would have made it almost impossible to see into the dark alley; he would see only his reflection. But Jackson could tell that he was getting little traction with the problematic optics.

Through the first day of testimony, Spencer watched in mute helplessness as his neighbors, whom he had liked, erected the wall that would entomb him. "I just couldn't believe what they were saying," he reflected. "I couldn't understand why they were saying it. I mean, none of what they said was true. And to see people that you know, or you think that you know, to take this type of position and virtually set you up to ruin your life . . . I just couldn't believe it."

T he prosecutor dreaded putting Danny Edwards on the stand. The jailhouse informant was an erratic player, but an essential one. No matter how much damage the neighbors' testimony had inflicted on Ben Spencer, the state still needed to connect him to the assault on Jeffrey Young. Beach needed a secondhand confession.

Short, stocky, fast-talking as an auctioneer, Edwards testified that he met Spencer in the jail tank, gave him candy bars and Tylenol, and chatted him up. Over the next day or two, he claimed, Spencer told him his story in bits and pieces. Edwards's extravagant testimony contradicted that of the other witnesses and the state's theory in every meaningful detail. Edwards stated that "Vance Mitchell Spencer," not Robert Mitchell, was Spencer's accomplice. He said they chased the victim into his office, and once inside, Ben Spencer "grabbed him with his tie with one hand and tried to snatch him over the desk with the other," although the victim was wearing athletic clothes, no tie.

Edwards swore that Spencer was driving, contradicting the other witnesses, who said Spencer emerged from the passenger side. He said Spencer kept hitting the victim sitting in the back seat, even though others claimed Jeffrey Young fell out of the trunk. He said Spencer had destroyed his fingerprints by rubbing them off on cement, even though Spencer's fingers were intact. He stated that if "Christine"—wrong name—did not support Spencer's alibi, he planned to inject her with mercury from a thermometer or "put it in her beer."[7] Then, in a line that must have echoed in the ears of the white, middle-class jurors terrorized by the violence of the crack epidemic, Edwards recounted Spencer telling him: "I should have killed the bitch right then and there."[8]

Why would the jury believe Edwards, who was surely angling for a lighter sentence? Perhaps for the same reason that juries have believed the word of informants over innocent defendants in 15 percent of murder cases, and a quarter of all capital cases, in which the defendant was convicted and later exonerated. Edwards admitted he had been facing up to twenty-five years for two first-degree felonies when he landed in jail. Under questioning from the prosecutor, he stated three times that he received no benefit in exchange for his testimony. This is critical, because it means the prosecutor knew, or should have known, that he was allowing Edwards to lie under oath.

With the prosecutor's prompting, Edwards testified that he came forward out of moral outrage, after he allegedly heard Ben threatening his alibi witness over the phone.

"He said he would burn her house down with a little boy with it," Edwards told the jury. "I told him it wasn't right. I told him I had a two-year-old boy, you know, and I said if you got out you'd probably get mad at me . . . and set my house on fire."

"You didn't get anything out of the deal, did you?" Beach queried.

"No sir, just trouble."[9]

With this, Edwards not only placed Spencer at the crime scene and painted him as a child-killing monster, but also undermined his defense in advance. "Whoever it was who orchestrated Danny Edwards's testimony was brilliant," noted Cheryl Wattley, who would join Spencer's legal team years later. By stating that Spencer threatened his alibi witness, Edwards damaged her credibility before the young woman could even get on the witness stand. "It was masterful. Evil, but brilliant."

The jurors were "skeptical" of the jailhouse snitch, foreman Alan Ledbetter said. Still, they concluded that Edwards's testimony largely corroborated the three neighbors' accounts, and gave their stories "a little more credence." The prosecution had plenty of other evidence, and "had that [testimony] been the only thing, I don't know that it would have been particularly persuasive," Ledbetter mused. But the jury reasoned that if the state trusted Edwards's account, then he must be a credible, if greasy, witness. The testimony of the jailhouse informant would later prove the most important evidence in the entire trial.

As a trial moves along, the psychologist Dan Simon says, jurors begin to lean toward one verdict or the other, hugging some details close to their chests and discarding others. "We inflate and deflate," Simon says, "to separate the two choices and enable a fairly confident choice." Jurors will begin to overstate the reasons to support the verdict they favor (guilty), often with irrelevant observations: *Jimmie Cotton must be telling the truth, he graduated from high school with honors.* And they discount the reasons to support the less favored verdict (not guilty): *Danny Edwards may be a criminal, but he has a two-year-old son.*

At this point, the jury had heard nothing to support Ben Spencer's story. Years later, Frank Jackson conceded that the state's evidence was compelling. "There were three eyewitnesses. At least circumstantially, the case was pretty strong." Asked if he thought his client was innocent, Jackson responded: "I have no idea. I don't know whether he did it or not."

# Chapter 13

# THE DEFENSE RESTS

✦———✦

**When we go back into the jury room,
everybody's already decided he's guilty.**

—Juror Eddie Clark

Frank Jackson gestured toward a framed newspaper clipping of a strapping, devilishly handsome twenty-five-year-old man in a Kansas City Chiefs uniform, his hands encircling the ball just before he snatches it from the air. For a time, Jackson held the American Football League's record for touchdown receptions, with four in a single game. Seven years of pro football beginning in 1961—first for the Chiefs, then the Miami Dolphins—have left his body broken, a point of cheerful pride.

"During that time, I accumulated six broken noses," he said. He suffered three fractured vertebrae, a broken fibula, dislocated fingers, separated shoulders, repeated concussions. He would play entire halves, catching touchdown passes, and not remember a thing. Both hips were replaced in 1996. "I'm like a used car. I've got 1996 parts on a 1939 body."

In 1971, Jackson transferred his fierce competitiveness from the football field to the courtroom. His searing cross-examinations were legend, as were his charm and rapport with juries. When he was appointed to defend Ben Spencer in 1987, Jackson was at the top of his game.

"I thought we had a real good shot at a not-guilty verdict," he recalled.

"I felt like we had a substantial defense." But for any number of reasons Frank Jackson, the storied wide receiver, fumbled.

By the time Jackson stood to deliver his opening statement, the prosecution had presented fourteen witnesses, ending with emotional testimony from the victim's father, Harry Young. The state had developed a sizable advantage. Whether it could be surmounted would depend on Ben Spencer and his alibi witness.

Jackson called Spencer to the stand. Soft-spoken, serious, precise, Spencer recounted that he and his wife had an argument on the afternoon of Sunday, March 22, 1987. He left the house, and rather than returning home for dinner with a box of Church's Chicken, as he intended, he drove his friend Ramona to church. On the way, she told him that her sister, Christie, wanted him to drop by the house later. Spencer said he and Christie chatted in her home from a little after 7:00 p.m. to around 10:00 p.m. When her younger brothers returned, the couple drove to the park, talking and listening to music in his wife's red Thunderbird. He dropped her at home just after midnight, waiting until Ramona let her in.

Spencer denied robbing Jeffrey Young, insisting that the hundred-dollar bill he had in his wallet—which the prosecutor claimed was stolen from the victim—came from his paycheck and tax refund. He had told all this to the police detectives who interrogated him. "I kept asking, would they investigate the case? And they would only laugh at me," he testified.[1] Spencer denied having any meaningful conversation with the jailhouse informant, much less confessing to a murder: "He is lying."[2]

When a case lacks hard evidence, jury experts say, jurors' hearts and minds become a "battlefield,"[3] with each side relying on emotional salvos to win the day. Trial attorneys master the art of misdirection, diverting attention from the gaps in evidence to irrelevant facts such as a witness's physical attributes. The cross-examination is the perfect venue. Unlike direct examination, in a cross-examination, a lawyer can embed accusations in his questions and imply that the defendant did something incriminating. The defendant can only offer a denial, which is drowned out by the next round of recrimination. Prosecutor Andy Beach's cross-examination of Spencer was a master class in this breed of persuasion. He treated Spencer's single, nonviolent crime—riding with his friend in a stolen car—as the gateway drug to Jeffrey Young's murder. "Kind of like back on March the twenty-second, 1987," Beach said, "you were in Jeff Young's car without his effective consent, weren't you?"

"No," Spencer said.

"Wouldn't you agree, sir," Beach continued, "it's hard to give somebody consent when they are unconscious and their brain is starting to swell?"[4]

Beach turned to attacking Spencer's character, at one point asking: "Is that when you weren't seeing eighteen-year-old track stars on Sunday nights, you had time to see your wife and son, is that correct?"[5] He implied Spencer's story was "almost too good of an alibi," because it did not rest on family and close friends, but a girl he barely knew. Then, Beach abruptly changed course. "While I am thinking about it," he said to Spencer, "hold both of your hands up for the jury to see. Make a fist. Turn around."[6]

Confused, Spencer stood and made a fist. The jury of ten whites and two Blacks stared at the defendant. The jury foreman, Alan Ledbetter, still recalled that moment thirty years later. He took in Spencer's height, six feet, four inches, and the sheer physicality of the young man. "I remember Spencer's large hands," he told me, and soon surmised the prosecutor's intent. "Since they had not recovered any weapon that had been used to strike Mr. Young, I suspect it was the district attorney's intention to say, *This is a guy that's powerful enough, that whatever he had in that hand, just one mighty blow could be fatal.*"

The other main defense witness, Christie Williams, gave a reluctant performance. She waffled over important details, such as when she and Spencer allegedly drove to the park. "I remember Bruce [Anton] and I had long, long discussions and debates about what to do with Christie, because she was so off," Frank Jackson said.

I n their closing arguments, each side had the chance to speak directly to the jury, remind them of the evidence, and spin an argument that would lure jurors to their respective sides. Once again, the prosecution owned the advantage, for it would have the last word before the jury began to deliberate.

What's striking about Frank Jackson's appeal to the jury is what it leaves out. He barely mentioned the most important fact in Spencer's favor: No physical evidence connected Spencer to the crime. But instead of spotlighting this gaping omission, Jackson nitpicked the character of the state's witnesses. What he failed to produce in evidence, he made up for in scorn. The prosecution witnesses were "slime." Jailhouse informant Danny Edwards was "a one-man crime wave." Charles Stewart, "a self-confessed liar." Jimmie Cotton was sweet but mistaken. Gladys Oliver was lying for the twenty-five-thousand-dollar reward money from Ross Perot. "She's already been paid a little bit and you know what, certainly she hasn't been paid all of it, because Benjamin Spencer hasn't been convicted yet. That's the reason we are here. Her day is coming."[7]

Jackson barely mentioned his client, except to point out that Spencer had a mother, a wife, and a baby. "He ain't rich and he is not white, but by golly, he's a human being too."[8] Jackson challenged the jury to be brave and find reasonable doubt. "Do you have the courage to do that? I don't know. You'll have to search your heart and your conscience when you go back in the jury room and decide if you have got the guts in an American courtroom to do what's right."[9] That should win them over.

While closing arguments are freewheeling compared to the case-in-chief, a prosecutor cannot introduce new facts into evidence or mischaracterize evidence; he can't comment on a defendant's refusal to testify, or mock the defense attorney. Prosecutors regularly blow past the boundaries,[10] but appellate courts rarely reverse a conviction based on this sort of prosecutorial misconduct.[11] More relevant in Ben Spencer's trial, the prosecutor cannot (at any time during the trial) knowingly allow witnesses to perjure themselves, make inflammatory statements that appeal to racism, or cause the jurors to fear for their safety.

The prosecutors' closing arguments checked many of these verboten boxes. Keith Anderson, who served as second chair to Andy Beach, assured the jurors of the credibility of the state's witnesses. He dismissed concerns that Gladys Oliver had testified to qualify for a large reward. "All of this talk about money. Five hundred and eighty dollars, not twenty-five thousand dollars," he said. "Do you think five hundred and something dollars is worth her putting her life on the line and in that neighborhood—lying on someone?"[12] As for the jailhouse informant, Anderson turned Danny Edwards's oily mendacity to his advantage. "If you think the officers are going to get somebody to tell a story, my God, it ain't going to be Danny. They would get somebody with credibility, somebody who hasn't been to the pen twice." Edwards would lie for a lighter sentence and he would lie for money; but in this case he didn't: "Danny's plea bargain was made *before* this even came up and Danny didn't get any twenty-five thousand dollars."[13]

If Anderson appealed to the jurors' minds, Andy Beach appealed to their hearts. Beach asked jurors to trust their gut instincts, their fears, and their eyes when they decided Spencer's fate. "You observed his demeanor up there yesterday, soft-spoken, semi-polite," Andy Beach reminded them. "But you can almost see behind those cold eyes, almost see his brain churning, his brain working the entire time."[14] Remember Spencer's hands, he told them. "You think those hands might be able to impart some damage on someone's neck, to make the deep neck muscles bleed?"[15]

After hearing a description of Beach's closing argument, the psychologist and law professor Dan Simon remarked: "Everything you say smacks of racism to me." The prosecutor was creating an image of "a kind of a bestial human being, which we associate with Black masculinity. Is this a reference, maybe, to an ape? I wouldn't accuse him of racism, but you've got to be afraid, whether intended or not, that it invokes these images."

For the purposes of justice, Simon said, it did not matter that Jeffrey Young was a beloved husband and father, if Ben Spencer did not kill him. Spencer's previous run-in with the law was irrelevant if it could not be connected to this crime. And surely it was immaterial that Spencer had large hands, if those were not the hands that encircled the victim's neck or wielded the instrument that cracked his skull.

On Thursday afternoon, the jurors withdrew to consider the evidence. But in this case, as in many others, the evidence they did *not* hear was arguably more important than what they heard. The jurors did not hear that Gladys Oliver received, or expected to receive, thousands of dollars from Ross Perot, with the approval of the prosecutor. They did not hear about a second alibi witness who placed Spencer far away from the assault. They did not hear about likely alternative suspects, neither Michael Hubbard nor Van Mitchell Spencer. They did not learn about the jailhouse informant's unspoken agreement with the prosecution, or see the written proof that he lied under oath.

Although some of the evidence was hidden by the prosecution, most of it was in plain sight, had Spencer's attorney bothered to look. Indeed, in the trial just three days later, Robert Mitchell's lawyer unearthed a trove of evidence that Spencer's lawyer did not. Royce West, a prominent Black lawyer, called Sandra Brackens, a witness who saw the perpetrator run right by her, and swore it was not Ben Spencer or Robert Mitchell. West offered an alternative suspect: Van Mitchell Spencer, who had been identified by several witnesses as the perpetrator and was the detectives' first suspect before being inexplicably cleared.

West raised multiple problems with Charles Stewart's testimony, and with the conduct of the police. Stewart admitted that he never saw Mitchell driving or Spencer riding in the BMW; it was the *lead detective* who inserted that damning detail into Stewart's affidavit, which Stewart didn't bother to read. "I didn't write that," he stated.[16] Under West's questioning, Stewart stated that he had tried to recant his statement against Spencer and Mitchell, but reverted to his original statement "when they [the police] had me downtown all night."[17] West also called a witness who testified that Stewart told him: "I really don't know anything. I just signed the papers because Gladys told me to sign the papers."[18]

West revealed that the police botched the crime scene, failed to take photographs, and let the BMW stand in the rain before examining it for fingerprints.[19] Finally, he called several witnesses to attest to Mitchell's character. Frank Jackson called no one to vouch for Ben Spencer, a twenty-three-year-old married man and father of a baby boy who once held a steady job.

None of this saved Robert Mitchell: The jury deliberated seventy minutes before convicting him and sentencing him to thirty-five years in prison. Perhaps nothing could rescue a Black man accused of killing a white man in 1980s Dallas. But one wonders if Eddie Clark, the gutsy Black juror at Spencer's trial, had heard this evidence, could he have introduced a slice of reasonable doubt into the deliberations?

Frank Jackson bristles at the questions and what he calls the "bean-counter lawyers" who raise them. They weren't in the courtroom, they didn't know about the pretrial preparation, they didn't know the witnesses he had, they didn't know his client's story. "So it'd be real easy now to do a little Monday morning quarterbacking and say 'I would have.' Well, that's baloney, unless you're there."

When we go back into the jury room, everybody's already decided he's guilty," Eddie Clark recalled. "Everybody's saying, 'Well, I need to go back to work.' And I said, 'We're not going back to work today. We're going to look at the evidence. Because you're talking about a man's life.'"

Clark's attempts to carefully consider the evidence would barely slow the jury on their sprint to convict.[20] Verdicts are almost always determined on the first ballot.[21] Studies show that if more than six jurors favor convicting initially, the jury will convict 94 percent of the time. And if six or more want to acquit, then they will acquit 97 percent of the time.[22]

By the time Spencer's jury sat down to deliberate, the coherence effect had taken root. Coherence resembles tunnel vision, in which jurors, like police and prosecutors, try to make sense of an avalanche of data by emphasizing facts that steer toward a certain conclusion and discarding conflicting facts. "Once you've decided to convict," Dan Simon says, "all the evidence looks more inculpating. If you decided to acquit, all of that ambiguous evidence, the same evidence, will look more exculpating."

To quell the cognitive dissonance that comes from conflicting facts, jurors smooth out the wrinkles. For example, the jury concluded that Spencer's alibi witness, Christie Williams, *and* the state's main accuser, Gladys Oliver, were both telling the truth. "We believed that [Christie Williams] had spent time with Ben. Ben was a handsome guy," Ledbetter remembered. "But we reconciled the timeline. It really squeezed and compressed the amount of time available for perpetrating a crime, but we gave that some thought, and it wasn't strong enough to sway us from the evidence we were receiving or had heard from the eyewitnesses."

In the end, the jurors were presented with only one compelling story: the prosecution's. Eddie Clark blamed Spencer's attorney. Jackson did not offer alternative suspects. He called no witnesses to dispute the neighbors. He barely cross-examined the jailhouse informant. He didn't call a single character witness, or even a family member. "He would just sit there with his legs crossed."

The jurors dutifully considered the evidence for a few hours before breaking for the night. At ten fifteen on Friday morning, after another hour of deliberation, they returned to the courtroom. Alan Ledbetter stood and peered at the verdict sheet in his hands. Spencer watched, still hopeful. "Guilty," the foreman said, and with that, Ben Spencer became #483713, under the purview of Texas's Department of Corrections.

"I'm sorry, Ben, I tried," Frank Jackson whispered, or maybe he didn't. Spencer can't remember.

Spencer was shackled and led out of the courtroom to the jail. The jurors dispersed to their homes for the weekend. On Monday they would reconvene to decide the rest of his future.

*Chapter 14*

# A BRIEF HISTORY
# OF INNOCENCE

+———+

**When the jackal is on the prowl . . .
you better not be where he is.**

—PROSECUTOR ANDY BEACH

He paced the empty holding cell, eight steps lengthwise, six steps across, ten steps diagonally, again and again, as if geometric precision would ward off the peril to come. All four cells, which could each hold fifteen to twenty people, were empty; his footsteps echoed as he circumnavigated his environs, dimly lit by fluorescent lights, no natural light, the natural replaced by the surreal.

"I had a little Gideon pocket Bible, and I was reading from it," Spencer recalled three decades later. He'd pray every few minutes, sing a hymn he learned in church as a child, "just trying to take my mind off of it."

Spencer had been convicted but not yet sentenced, and while he sang and paced, the twelve jurors were debating how long he would be locked in a cell. It was early afternoon on Monday, March 28, 1988. Hours earlier, the penalty phase of Spencer's trial had concluded. It had not gone well.

The penalty phase gave Spencer's defense attorney, Frank Jackson, the opportunity to present mitigating evidence, to describe Spencer's good character and plead for leniency. Jackson had plenty to work with. Spencer doted on his wife and baby boy. He had a job and provided for his family. He fixed ceiling fans for neighbors and gave them rides whenever anyone asked. Yet Jackson mentioned none of that. In a defense presentation as brief as an arctic heat wave, Jackson called Spencer's wife, Debra: "Do you still love Benjamin?" he asked her. "Yes, I do," she responded. He called Spencer's mother, Lucille. "Do you still love Benjamin?" he asked again. "Sure," she said.[1]

Jackson called Spencer to the stand. "I just feel sorry that they feel like I'm lying to them, but I had nothing to do with the death of Jeffrey Young," the condemned man said. "I don't know why—why would anybody want to lie on me, why they want to see me here? I don't know. All I know is I had nothing to do with anything that happened to Jeffrey Young, and I'm just sorry—sorry that I couldn't prove that I was innocent. I'm very sorry."[2]

Andy Beach rose for the cross-examination.

Q: Have you got something in your hand today?
A: Yes, sir, I have a Bible in my hand.
Q: Did you have it in your hand back in March of 1987?
A: No, I did not.
Q: That's all I have.[3]

Jackson's closing argument centered on the battle he had already lost. "There's no question in my mind whatsoever that some of you have got to have a reasonable doubt in your mind as to whether or not Benjamin Spencer did this," he said to the jury. "Please, for God's sake, give that benefit to Benjamin at this phase of the trial, because there's no other chance." Jackson was allotted thirty minutes. He used less than ten.

The prosecutors filled all their time. Keith Anderson told the jury that Ben Spencer's dream is a "nightmare" to any law-abiding citizen. "It's a dream to get something for nothing. It's a dream of a man who's willing to use any force necessary to accomplish that dream." Anderson urged them to sentence Ben Spencer to life in prison, so that he "would not continue to spread his nightmare of death throughout Dallas County."[4]

The final words the jurors heard came from Andy Beach, warning of the imminent and specific danger that Ben Spencer presented. "You know the scariest thing about this case, members of the jury? It's how random it was." Any one of the jurors could be Spencer's next victim, he implied, or their son, or father, or friend. "You see, when the jackal is on the prowl and you've got something he wants, you better not be where he is. It doesn't matter where you are, what part of Dallas County, what time of day it is. If you have the bad fortune of running into Benjamin John Spencer—the family man over there—you're going to end up like Jeff Young."[5]

"They called me a jackal, a robber of dreams," Spencer recalled. "I was like, who are they talking about?"

The jury began deliberating at 10:23 a.m. Alan Ledbetter remembered thinking they had done Spencer a favor by convicting him of aggravated robbery, not murder. "But as it turned out, as we went into the sentencing phase, that favor actually kind of worked against him," he said. "We couldn't think of a worse outcome from an aggravated robbery perspective."

Spencer was escorted back to the courtroom at 2:32 p.m. The jurors took their seats in the jury box. Ledbetter stood and delivered the sentence: life in prison. The judge polled the jury. Twelve jurors raised their hands in agreement. Spencer was handcuffed and escorted back to the holding cell.

"I was the only one in the holdover," Spencer recalled. "And it's cold. And to be honest, I really wanted to die." He wondered if he could commit suicide before the guard took him away, and if so, how. His son had been born, Debra was caring for him by herself, and he would never see them outside the prison walls. How do you envision the other side of a life sentence?

"I just could not see that far down the road. I just felt that I would die before I even had an opportunity to get out again. That's why I wanted to kill myself. Because I just could not see spending the rest of my life, or dying, in prison." He fell silent, reliving the moment in the cold cell. "It was the most devastating night of my life. I mean, it was breathtaking."

But as the minutes alone ticked by, the last quiet minutes he would enjoy for a very long time, Spencer began to reason with himself. I didn't commit this offense, he thought, so the truth will eventually come out. An hour later, a guard returned him to the tank with the other inmates, the likes of whose company he would share for the rest of his life. He called Debra.

"She was hysterical," he recalled. "And I was like, 'You got to have faith, we got to believe in God.'"

"There is no God!" she cried.

"This pain just came over me. I'm like, 'Wait, wait, wait! Don't ever say nothing like that.'"

"There can't be a God," she said, "because, if there was, he wouldn't let this happen to us."

"God did his part," he countered. "The truth came out. The jury just chose not to believe the truth. They believe the lie. That's the way the world is. But we just have to hold on to hope and one day the truth will come out and I'll be home."

Over the years, Spencer has often reflected on the prosecutors' final words. "They said that I've turned people's dreams into nightmares," he said. "In actuality, that's what they did to me. They turned my dream into a nightmare."

How many innocent prisoners share Ben Spencer's nightmare? They literally can't be counted, because no one has any idea how many innocent people have suffered through the wasted days and the meaningless years, the incessant danger and unrelenting tedium of prison. Until recently, the victims of judicial mistakes have been largely invisible, tucked away in large buildings where they don't trouble the free. For most of the life of the United States, this uncomfortable fact remained hidden or denied, until one day in 1932, a young scholar called out the irony of our justice system: We routinely convict the innocent.

"I nnocent men are never convicted," Frederick G. Katzmann stated. "Don't worry about it, it never happens in the world. It is a physical impossibility."

District Attorney Katzmann offered this observation after successfully prosecuting Nicola Sacco and Bartolomeo Vanzetti for robbery and murder in Massachusetts in 1921.[6] He won the convictions and death sentences of the two Italian immigrants, but the trial ignited a fireball of controversy. The ballistics conflicted, witnesses recanted their testimony, and the only certainty seemed to be the anti-Italian, anti-immigrant, anti-anarchist bias in the case. As evidence of the men's innocence emerged, protests erupted in every major city in the United States and Europe, as well as in Japan, Australia, and much of South America. Celebrated writers, artists, and academics pleaded for their pardon or for a new trial. The Harvard Law professor Felix Frankfurter, who would later be appointed to the US Supreme Court, argued for their innocence in a book-length essay in *The Atlantic Monthly*.

Katzmann's "dogmatic statement" had a longer shelf life than the two men he prosecuted, who were executed in 1927. It prompted Edwin Montefiore Borchard, a young Yale Law School professor, to launch the first innocence project. Perhaps for the first time on a large scale, the battle was joined between truth and expediency, fairness and finality in America's trial system.[7]

Borchard hired a team of researchers to pore through newspaper articles and the archives of the Library of Congress, looking for any conviction with the whiff of error. Then, painstakingly, the researchers wrote state pardon boards, defense attorneys, prosecutors, and judges to confirm and flesh out the accounts. Borchard uncovered dozens of wrongful convictions. The result was the 1932 classic *Convicting the Innocent: Sixty-five Actual Errors of Criminal Justice*.[8]

The problems Borchard identified haunt us today: bad eyewitness testimony, lying jailhouse informants, false or coerced confessions,[9] junk science, police and prosecutorial misconduct, suggestive lineups, perjury, unconscious bias, racism—even false memories planted in children.[10] One of his earliest stories, from 1812, recounts the near execution of a man for a murder that never occurred;[11] even today, 40 percent of prisoners who were exonerated had been convicted of "crimes"—such as sexual assault—that were never committed.[12] These flaws have not been uprooted; rather, like an invasive species, they have grown with the population, tamed in some places, out of control in others, but the flaws are so deeply rooted because they are so deeply human.

Borchard tells story after story of people whose lives were derailed by injustice. In "Seventeen Witnesses Identified Him," Borchard relates the plight of Herbert T. Andrews in Boston, Massachusetts, a cashier, who was well liked by his employer, colleagues, and neighbors.[13] On November 1, 1913, Andrews was arrested for forging more than forty checks. At his trial, seventeen witnesses identified him as the man who passed them a bad check. "Andrews later said that police officers took down the testimony of those who identified him," Borchard writes, "and disregarded that of those who said he was not the man," which is as good a description of tunnel vision as one can find. Andrews was sentenced to fourteen months in the Deer Island House of Correction. During his stay, bad checks continued to surface, and police realized the perpetrator was still busy forging. They eventually caught the culprit, sending him off to Deer Island as well. Later, the prosecutor wondered how so many people could have misidentified Andrews: "The two men were as dissimilar in appearance as could be."

Nearly half the examples in Borchard's book involve mistaken identification, which is not surprising, given that some 70 percent of known wrongful convictions have involved mistaken eyewitness testimony.[14] In a prescient foreshadowing of the science of memory developed decades later, Borchard observes that for victims of a crime, or those who witness a crime taking place, "the emotional balance of the victim or eyewitness is so disturbed by his extraordinary experience that his powers of perception become distorted and his identification is frequently most untrustworthy."[15]

Borchard also examines the fragility of alibis, a phenomenon that Ben Spencer experienced. He writes that on August 24, 1924, six bandits made off with ten thousand dollars from the First National Bank of Freeburg, Illinois.[16] A few hours later, policemen in St. Louis, Missouri, picked up Floyd Flood, a painter and chauffeur, because, they said, he fit the description of one of the robbers; and besides, he was a "bad egg," even though he had never been arrested for anything. Two bank employees identified the suspect.[17] At trial, Flood testified that at the time of the robbery, he was driving a cab in St. Louis, more than twenty miles away. His testimony was corroborated by his parents, an aunt, a cousin, neighbors, and several employees of the cab company. He was convicted and sent to prison. When the true culprits were captured and identified, Flood was pardoned and released—two years later. "Notwithstanding the consistent testimony of numerous alibi witnesses," Borchard observes, "the jury preferred to believe the affirmative evidence of [the witnesses] against the overwhelming contradictory evidence."

Borchard offers one of the first accounts of junk science.[18] In 1900, the city recorder of Atlanta received an obscene letter, which he turned over to the federal authorities. He suggested they focus on a particular "negro," Borchard writes, and, along with two other "experts" in handwriting, the recorder testified that the suspect's handwriting shared "incriminating and unmistakable similarities" with the one in the offending letter. The Black man was convicted, sentenced to five years, and was serving his time when another man confessed. The mistake was due to the "impregnable assurance" of the self-described expert, Borchard notes. "Before the apparent certainty, all improbabilities vanished." This story foreshadowed a crisis that would explode a century later. Handwriting—as well as other comparison disciplines, such as hair analysis, fibers, shoe prints, ballistics, blood spatter, bite marks, even fingerprints—is frightfully susceptible to unconscious bias, and the experts, with a trail of letters behind their names, are usually more credible than the truth.

Serendipity rescued all the wrongly convicted people in Borchard's book. Their exoneration would never have occurred "but for the curious concatenation of circumstances," he writes. "The links in the chain which disclosed the truth were as accidental and fortuitous as those which led to the mistaken conviction." Later, Borchard notes that "sheer good luck" was often the moving force in exonerations. "How many unfortunate victims have no such luck, it is impossible to say, but there are probably many."[19] History has proven the chilling accuracy of that observation.

What's arresting about *Convicting the Innocent* is how modern these examples are. Borchard diagnosed the "carelessness and overzealousness" of state officials. "In a very considerable number, the zealousness of the police or private detectives, or the gross negligence of the police in overlooking or even suppressing evidence of innocence, or the prosecution's overzealousness was the operative factor in causing the erroneous conviction." Still, he did not demonize police and prosecutors, nor did he aver that they routinely operated in bad faith. "It is the environment in which they live, with an undiscriminating public clamor for them to stamp out crime and make short shrift of suspects, which often serves to induce them to pin a crime upon a person accused."[20]

B orchard's innocence project was limited in scope and practical impact. His small operation lacked a team of attorneys to fight erroneous convictions in the courts. He simply chronicled the problem. But in doing that, he publicly and methodically refuted the popular conviction articulated by Judge Learned Hand in 1923: "Our procedure has always been haunted by the ghost of the innocent man convicted. It is an unreal dream."[21]

*Convicting the Innocent* softened the ground for one of the first sensational exonerations to play out in the media. In 1933, during Prohibition, two young men in Chicago were convicted of killing a police officer at a speakeasy. Tillie Majczek, the mother of one of the accused, twenty-four-year-old Joseph Majczek, scrubbed floors at night for eleven years until she raised five thousand dollars. Then she ran an advertisement in the *Chicago Times*, offering a reward for anyone who had information about the murder. A young reporter, initially skeptical, gathered more and more evidence of Majczek's innocence, and won Majczek's (and his friend's) freedom. Hollywood snatched up the story, and *Call Northside 777* became a noir classic starring Jimmy Stewart. It's hard to imagine a public appetite for this narrative without Borchard's work.

The sequel to the innocence movement featured the creator of Perry Mason. Erle Stanley Gardner, a former boxer turned lawyer, wrote eighty-two Perry Mason novels, as well as overseeing Perry Mason movies, a Perry Mason radio show, and the iconic television show. In all episodes but three, Mason, the defense lawyer, beats his hapless rival, District Attorney Hamilton Burger. But in reality, Gardner knew the opposite was true. Defendants, both innocent and guilty, nearly always lose.

On a camping trip down the Baja peninsula with his friend Harry Steeger, Gardner began to reflect on the privileges of freedom. "Many times, during those silent watches of the night I lay awake for half or three-quarters of an hour, thinking about the problems inherent in the wise administration of justice," he wrote in his book *The Court of Last Resort.* "And the more I came to revel in my own liberty to go where I wanted to, whenever I wanted to, the more I found myself thinking of innocent men cooped up in cells."[22]

He discovered that Steeger, who published a men's-adventure magazine called *Argosy,* shared his "nagging worry." Steeger told him that if he found a case where he believed that a man had been wrongly convicted, *Argosy* would donate enough space to see that the case was given ample publicity, and "see what the public reaction is."[23]

The two men established a board of experts—including a forensic scientist, a private detective, and a polygraph examiner—people who were already so wealthy or so famous that they needed neither money nor publicity. They called the group "The Court of Last Resort." Beginning in 1948, Gardner wrote up an investigation each month in an *Argosy* column. The cases drew enormous publicity: Thousands of letters from fans, from prisoners, from their friends and families, poured into the *Argosy* offices. Almost always the local prosecutors resisted, offering "official coldness and indifference that at times amounts to behind-the-scenes sabotage,"[24] Gardner wrote. Yet the group won the release of at least four innocent prisoners.

But their success was sui generis: Most of the prisoners were freed because Gardner could walk into a governor's office and ask him to order a reprieve, reopen a case, or issue a pardon. If a prisoner did not attract Gardner's attention, he was out of luck. When Perry Mason's creator retired in the fall of 1958, so did the Court of Last Resort.

Erle Stanley Gardner popularized the radical notion that the state could make mistakes, and injected a trace of doubt about the way we investigate and prosecute crime. The recognition was like a small quake out at sea. The number of innocent people who were cleared and released began to swell, almost imperceptibly at first, growing in height and depth with each passing decade—until the 1990s and the advent of DNA testing, when a tsunami swamped the court system, carrying away the public's confidence in the undertow.

But before 1989, which marked the first year that an American prisoner was exonerated based on DNA, 439 people had been cleared and released—nearly 100 between 1980 and 1988. The exonerations occurred in every state and were not concentrated in the South: California, Massachusetts, New Jersey, New York, Ohio, Florida, and Texas had the most erroneous convictions. However, the numbers deceive, because these states—Texas in particular—saved evidence from trials and were more open to reconsidering problematic convictions.

By the late 1980s, when Ben Spencer was convicted, the movement was catching a tailwind. Emboldened by the accelerating successes, individual attorneys and law firms began challenging in court the convictions of people they believed had been wrongly incarcerated, no longer relying on celebrity pleas to the governor. This began to democratize the innocence movement, but it still had no central organization; it continued to be, in the main, the emanation of an individual lawyer's outrage.

Meanwhile, innocent prisoners became causes célèbres, such as Rubin "Hurricane" Carter, a middleweight boxing star in New Jersey. In 1967, he was convicted of a triple murder at a bar in Paterson, New Jersey. No forensic evidence implicated him; the witness descriptions did not match his appearance; he had an alibi. But a jury convicted him and sentenced him to thirty years to life. A group of celebrities took up Carter's cause, and in 1975, Bob Dylan released the single "Hurricane."[25]

In a show of support, Dylan, Joan Baez, Joni Mitchell, Allen Ginsberg, and Roberta Flack performed at the prison where Carter was incarcerated on December 7, 1975.[26] It would take another decade for the case to finally arrive in federal court. The judge in Carter's case found that local police and prosecutors had suppressed evidence and that the state's key witnesses—two men with long criminal records who aspired to receive a $10,500 reward—had lied at trial. Carter was released, and Denzel Washington played the title role in the 1999 film *Hurricane*.

In the meantime, the media, in particular *60 Minutes*, began to track and uncover wrongful convictions. "Lenell Geter's in Jail," a 1983 exposé by Morley Safer, dissected the case in Dallas, Texas, in which the twenty-five-year-old Black, college-educated engineer was sentenced to life by an all-white jury for allegedly robbing three fast-food restaurants.[27] Millions of Americans watched this soft-spoken, handsome, appealing young man in white prison garb claim that he was innocent, and were confronted with the Kafkaesque nightmare of being Lenell Geter. Eventually, Geter's conviction was overturned and he was exonerated. *60 Minutes* would profile several other prisoners over the next few years. All of them would be released.[28]

Still, this type of justice by anecdote—dependent on the commitment of defense attorneys and the media publicity that shamed officials to revisit and own their errors—was not the recipe for systemic change. It was too unpredictable, too arbitrary. Although Ben Spencer did not yet know it, that system was in the early stages of a tectonic shift.

*Part 2*

# Appeal

+———+

*Chapter 15*

# NO HARM, NO FOUL

✦———✦

**This is the end of Dallas. Last time I'll see it.**

—BEN SPENCER, *on the chain bus to prison*

B lue Bird Corporation produces every kind of bus, from yellow buses
ferrying children to and from school, to chain buses transporting
convicted men and women from jail to prison and back. In late April or
early May of 1988, Benjamine Spencer boarded one of these buses, along
with his new tribe: murderers, rapists, drug traffickers, gang members,
and other ungentle souls. Spencer, like the others, was handcuffed. The
handcuffs were attached to a long chain that ran the length of the bus, the
men tethered like horses to hitching posts. Benches lined either side of
the bus, and running down the middle aisle were two benches nailed
flush together, where men sat back to back, four rows in all. Most of the
prisoners were Black and slept sitting up, shoulder to shoulder, for the
three-hour journey.

"I was awake all the way from Dallas to Huntsville," Spencer said of
his first experience on a chain bus. He gazed out the window, watching
life as he knew it fall away with each mile. As they drove south out of Dallas on I-45, Spencer saw the Overton Road exit as they flew past it. "It was
really kind of tough because that's where I used to get off the freeway to
go home," he said. "And once we got to Simpson Stuart Road, I was like:
This is the end of Dallas. Last time I'll see it. Because I really, I *really*

thought that the world would end before my twenty-year flat would come about," before he would be up for parole.

They arrived at Huntsville, Texas, where several prison buildings dominated the town. For some, the Huntsville Unit is the final destination, as it houses the execution chamber. Texas had wasted little time lethally injecting prisoners after the death penalty was reinstated in 1976: Twenty-seven men had moved from this life to the next by the time Spencer arrived.[1] Texas had abandoned the electric chair, an ostensibly more fraught execution method that could malfunction, with grim consequences. In Florida, for example, six-inch flames shot out of one prisoner's head and twelve-inch flames burst from another's before each was pronounced dead.[2] Of course, we can't truly know if lethal injection is less painful, for the chemicals paralyze the entire body, and the doomed prisoner can't scream out in pain as can a man whose head is on fire.

Spencer stopped briefly at the Huntsville Unit for a battery of physical, intelligence, and psychological assessments, and a few days later, he was chain-bused to his new home: a maximum-security prison called the Coffield Unit. Inside the prison, he was handed a white jumpsuit and escorted to cell Y-205. Prison administrators put the healthy twenty-three-year-old to work immediately. Texas had just opened a new prison nearby, and the Coffield inmates were putting the finishing touches on the project. Spencer was given a job at "Metal Fab," or metal fabrication, where he built bunk beds for the inmates to sleep on, and steel bars for the windows and cell doors to keep them in.

Like all prisoners, Spencer received one automatic appeal, and Texas attorney John D. Nation was appointed to represent him. "I might have spoken to him once," Spencer said. "I just know he was sorry." Sorry as in ineffective, not apologetic. In 1988, Nation had not yet slipped into public ignominy; that would come later, when his law license was suspended twice for neglecting to represent clients in post-conviction pro-

ceedings. (Nation did not respond to multiple visits to his office and letters requesting an interview.) But he did file an appeal with the Court of
Appeals for the Fifth District of Texas. He claimed that the prosecution
did not present sufficient evidence to sustain Spencer's conviction, and he
offered six other reasons the conviction should be overturned.

On May 3, 1989, the appellate court denied them all. The three judges
wrote one half of a sentence about the neighbors' testimony, which was
the heart of the prosecutor's case. They based their opinion entirely on
the testimony of the jailhouse informant, Danny Edwards. They accepted
Edwards's story without reservation. "The evidence clearly supports the
conviction of Spencer as a principal actor," they found, and Spencer had
"conceded" his guilt to Danny Edwards. The record shows, they wrote,
that Spencer, not his accomplice, hit Jeffrey Young on the head with a pistol or handgun and dragged him to the BMW. The record shows that
Spencer, not his accomplice, drove Young's BMW, and intended to take
the car to his uncle's chop shop. "Viewing the evidence in the light most
favorable to the prosecution," the judges wrote, "we determine that the
cumulative effect of all the incriminating circumstances was clearly sufficient for the jury to conclude, beyond a reasonable doubt, that the accused
was guilty as the principal actor."[3]

Then the appellate court turned its attention to the mistakes that the
prosecutor or judge may have made during trial. Here it pulled out its
most versatile counterargument: harmless error. The mistakes were either
insignificant, or they were not mistakes at all.[4] Again, the appellate court
found "no merit" in Spencer's appeal.


Thus began Spencer's journey through the post-conviction world. The
odds of proving his innocence were stacked against him at every
stage of appeal, in both the state courts and the federal courts. Daniel
Medwed, a legal scholar at Northeastern University, likens the justice system then and now to a conveyor belt. "Once a case is on the assembly line,

once it's been produced at trial, once the term 'conviction' is stamped on the side of the case, then everything—the presumptions and inferences and procedures—are all aligned with preserving it and not reopening it," he says. "It's almost like the lid is put on the case rather loosely after a trial, and with each step, it's tightened a little bit more." Rarely does the lid come off, and when it does, scarcely ever do judges or governors—the people who can pull the case off the line because of defects—give it more than a cursory glance.

When Daniel Medwed was a young lawyer, he helped found the Second Look Program, a clinic affiliated with Brooklyn Law School to investigate and litigate innocence claims by inmates in New York prisons. Almost immediately, he recognized that the system is set up to preserve convictions. It makes sense, since at some point the litigation must end or the system would grind to a halt. But in recent decades, the US Supreme Court has erected nearly unscalable barriers to overturning convictions, which can trap innocent people in prison as collateral damage. William Blackstone's famous ideal has been drained of power: "Better that ten guilty persons escape, than that one innocent suffer."[5] The reality is anything but. The labyrinth of state and federal appeals almost always leads to dead ends, even for those with meritorious claims.

"The system is designed to close cases and close them quickly," says Medwed, who authored *Barred: Why the Innocent Can't Get Out of Prison*. "It's procedure over truth."

A conviction transforms everything. During a trial, the defendant is presumed innocent. Every piece of evidence should be viewed in a light favorable to the defendant, and the prosecutor has the burden of proving guilt beyond a reasonable doubt. But once the jury arrives at a guilty verdict, that presumption disappears.

The first stop in the post-conviction journey is the direct appeal in state court, which Ben Spencer lost in 1989. In this appeal, judges look at mistakes that may have taken place in the courtroom during the trial—whether a prosecutor went too far in his closing argument, for example, or a judge improperly excluded some evidence vital to the defense. They cannot consider new evidence or novel legal arguments, nor will they ordinarily look at issues that the defense attorney didn't flag as improper during the trial itself. Prisoners usually lose at this stop. Appellate courts nationally reverse convictions only 7.7 percent of the time.[6] In Texas, it's half that.[7] Of course, a reversal doesn't mean freedom. The prisoner can be tried and convicted again.

In a trial system bulging with convictions and appeals, appellate judges place a premium on "finality," that is, putting cases to bed once and for all. To that end, they rely on legal beacons—such as the doctrines of "deference" and "harmless error"—to steer their way to the correct answer to the question: Was the trial fair or not? Usually the appellate courts navigate to the right outcome by deferring to the judgment of the jury, the trial judge, the defense attorney, and the prosecutor—and by discarding minor errors that had no bearing on the integrity of the trial. But sometimes, these doctrines act more like Charybdis and Scylla, devouring the innocent prisoner who is just trying to paddle to the truth.

Consider, first, the finders of fact, the jurors. The jury has been called "the glory of English law."[8] In the United States, the justice system is based on trusting civic-minded people to employ their common sense and unique backgrounds, sort through the facts, and find the kernel of truth in the pile of conflicting evidence. They are considered the "lie detector in the courtroom."[9] One judge opined that there is something "almost mystical" about juries' ability to find the truth.[10] Appellate judges will almost always defer to the verdict of the people who soaked up the intangibles—nuances that don't come across in a trial transcript, such as the demeanor of the defendant, the credibility of the witnesses, and the weight of the physical evidence.

So revered is the jury that the US Supreme Court has humored jury misbehavior with the shrug of an indulgent parent after the kids throw a keg party. In the 1987 decision *Tanner v. United States*, the court upheld a mail fraud conviction even after two jurors reported that the "jury was one big party."[11] Several jurors drank alcohol at lunch throughout the trial, three smoked marijuana, two used cocaine, and two completed a drug deal with each other. Writing for the majority, Justice Sandra Day O'Connor noted that such misbehavior, if caught, *could* invalidate convictions; "it is not at all clear, however, that the jury system could survive such efforts to perfect it. Allegations of juror misconduct, incompetency, or inattentiveness . . . seriously disrupt the finality of the process."[12] Better to leave well enough alone. The court upheld the conviction.[13] Most jurors, of course, take their civic duty seriously. But it's a measure of the veneration with which juries are held that the high court would not second-guess the judgment emerging from a drunken celebration at a frat house.

The US Supreme Court protects defense attorneys as fiercely as it shelters jurors. In its 1984 decision *Strickland v. Washington*, the majority found that courts should be "highly deferential" to defense attorneys and find them ineffective only if their performance falls below an "objective standard of reasonableness."[14]

It's a low bar, if the case involving George McFarland in Houston, Texas, is any guide. In 1992, McFarland was facing the death penalty for killing a neighborhood grocer. During the trial, McFarland's lawyer dozed "during great portions of the witness testimony," one juror recalled.[15] The lawyer responded that, at seventy-two, he was accustomed to taking an afternoon nap, and anyway, he found the trial "boring." After the defendant received the death sentence, the judge noted that "the Constitution says everyone is entitled to the attorney of their choice. The Constitution doesn't say the lawyer has to be awake."[16] Texas's highest criminal court affirmed the conviction, noting that McFarland "failed to establish that he received ineffective assistance of counsel which deprived him of his Sixth Amendment right to a fair trial."[17] The federal court agreed in 2019, and McFarland remained on death row.

Obviously, Medwed says, most defense lawyers manage to stay awake during their trials. Most cases are not so egregious, but occupy the gray area where it's hard to distinguish an attorney's incompetence from his trial strategy. No matter how poor their performance, defense attorneys appear to get a pass.[18] According to one study, appellate judges found trial lawyers effective in 97 percent of the cases in which defendants claimed their attorney failed to provide an adequate defense.[19]

O n the surface, when appellate judges deny innocent prisoners a reprieve, they are merely following procedures meant to ensure that everyone is treated equally and that the system moves efficiently toward a quick, just, and final resolution. But psychologists will tell you something more fundamental occurs every time judges affirm a conviction—not because they are robotic rule followers, but because they are human. Enter the phenomenon that permeates virtually every wrongful conviction at every stage, from police myopia to prosecutorial single-mindedness to judicial nearsightedness in the appellate court: tunnel vision.

Keith Findley at the University of Wisconsin says that the particular genus that plagues appellate judges is "hindsight bias," also known as the "knew it all along" effect. When you know the end result and review the process that people went through to arrive at it, it's difficult to imagine it turning out any other way. In hindsight, you interpret all the evidence as leading to that conclusion: *Of course* the informant told the truth, he described the assault in great detail; *of course* the alibi witness was lying, she was protecting her friend.

"In hindsight, the conviction will appear more inevitable, a more certain outcome than it actually was going in," Findley says. "And that will make it harder for the judges to fight to reverse the conviction because they're being asked to upset something that looked like it was inevitable all along." They conclude that any mistakes made by the judge or the prosecutor were harmless. "If there was an error, it must have been harmless because: *Look, from the get-go, we've known this looked like a slam dunk.*"

To quell cognitive dissonance, a judge will maximize the power of the prosecutor's arguments and minimize the power of the defendant's, says Dan Simon. "And once you've decided you're not going to overturn the conviction, then none of the [defense] arguments is going to look persuasive."

Even innocence advocates agree that "harmless error" is a necessary evil. In the early days of the republic, any error—the misspelling of a name, for example—could be considered grounds for vacating a conviction. As cases swamped the appellate courts, they threw out cases where the mistake did not lead to a miscarriage of justice.

In its 1967 opinion *Chapman v. California*, the US Supreme Court laid down some rules: If a constitutional violation occurred at trial, then the prosecution must prove the error was harmless beyond a reasonable doubt.[20] Specifically, can the government prove that the error did not "contribute" to the guilty verdict? If it cannot, then toss the conviction. But Medwed says somewhere between *Chapman* and the present day, "the court began to look at whether there was *other* evidence of guilt that would bolster the conviction and dwarf the error. In other words: 'Okay, this error occurred. This closing argument was really bad, but look, there's overwhelming evidence of guilt. He still would've been convicted.'"[21]

"Harmless error" has colonized the legal landscape. It's hard to measure how often innocent people see their convictions affirmed this way. The Innocence Project found that when its clients claimed that prosecutors had made errors at trial, the appellate courts deemed the errors "harmless" 82 percent of the time.[22] These people were later proven innocent by DNA. The National Registry of Exonerations has chronicled nearly three hundred cases of official misconduct that could be identified and flagged at trial; most, if not all, of those convictions were affirmed by appellate courts before the prisoner was exonerated.

The propensity to demote serious mistakes to innocuous slips has robbed innocent people of years of freedom, and sometimes large swaths of their adult lives. Shawn Henning and Ralph "Ricky" Birch were seventeen and eighteen, respectively, when they were arrested for stabbing an elderly man to death in New Milford, Connecticut.[23] The linchpin testimony came from forensic scientist Henry Lee, who would become famous for his role in the O. J. Simpson and JonBenet Ramsey cases. Lee told the jury that the bathroom towels had blood on them, implying that the men had cleaned up the crime scene with them. They were convicted, and lost their appeals. More than two decades later, Centurion Ministries, a nonprofit organization that reinvestigated questionable convictions, took up the case. They retested the towels and found they did not have blood on them. In fact, the towels had never been tested before, in contrast to Dr. Lee's testimony. No forensic evidence connected the men to the crime. But a Connecticut trial judge refused their habeas petition. "The court concludes Dr. Lee was wrong but not lying under oath."[24] It was harmless error.

In a rare acknowledgment of harmful error, the Connecticut Supreme Court overturned the men's convictions in 2019. It ruled that without the towel theory, "the state's entire case . . . could very well have collapsed."[25] The state decided to dismiss charges the next year. It took thirty-one years for the error to be deemed egregious, and for the innocent men—now in their fifties—to be cleared.[26]

The winds that blow appellate judges toward affirming a conviction, even in the face of egregious misconduct by the state, prevail at every stage of the appeal process, up and down the state courts and the federal courts. Ronnie Long suffered through this for forty-four years. Convicted of sexual assault in North Carolina in 1976, his lawyers eventually discovered a bounty of prosecutorial misconduct. The prosecutor withheld evidence, such as fingerprints, hair, and matchbooks found at the scene that had no connection to Long. The rape victim initially described a different assailant; that report was never disclosed to the defense. The lineup was suggestive. The prosecutor eliminated every Black person from the jury pool and ended up with an all-white jury. At trial, the prosecution's experts lied on the stand about the forensic evidence and the chain of custody.

Long's lawyers raised these significant flaws, but he lost his direct appeal in 1977. He lost in the state supreme court eleven years later. His appeal to a federal court was denied in 1990. The first piece of good news arrived in 2005, twenty-nine years after his conviction, when a state court ordered the prosecution to turn over evidence. But in February 2009, Superior Court Judge Donald Bridges denied him a new trial. It was harmless error, he ruled; the suppressed evidence wasn't that helpful to the defense: "The cumulative effect of any items with any value is so minimal that it would have had no impact on the outcome of the trial."

In 2012, Long's next appeal was denied for procedural reasons. In 2016, a federal judge denied his third habeas petition. In 2019, the US Court of Appeals for the Fourth Circuit rejected his appeal, noting that "jurors would consider the impeachment evidence peripheral." In her dissent, Judge Stephanie Thacker wrote that the argument was "nonsensical and offensive," turning the prosecutor's burden of proof "on its head." She concluded: "Appellant must prevail. To hold otherwise would provide incentive for the state to lie, obfuscate, and withhold evidence for a long enough period of time that it can then simply rely on the need for finality. That, I cannot abide."

Long appealed for an en banc hearing before the full, fifteen-member Fourth Circuit Court of Appeals. Lightning struck. Judge Stephanie Thacker was now in the majority. On August 24, 2020, Long won, and his conviction was vacated. Thacker wrote: "A man has been incarcerated for 44 years because, quite simply, the judicial system has failed him." Two state appellate courts and five federal courts had affirmed the conviction of Ronnie Long until, by chance—which is the truly scary part— the composition of the federal appeals court changed, and that court recognized that he had never received a fair trial.[27]

B enjamine Spencer, sitting in cell Y-205 in the Coffield Unit, may not have known just how bleak his odds had become upon his conviction. It was not personal; it was procedural. The machinery of the system was purring along smoothly, indifferent to truth, cool to the touch.

But Spencer did know he needed help on the outside. On November 10, 1989, Spencer picked up a pen and wrote to a wry, balding minister in Princeton, New Jersey, a Vietnam vet who favored Maker's Mark bourbon and could swear with the best of them, a man who was at that moment changing the course of American justice.

*Chapter 16*

# THE PRIEST OF JUSTICE

+————+

**He started a movement. It takes my breath away.**

—KATE GERMOND, *Centurion Ministries*

In Jim McCloskey's recurring dream, he is perched on a riverbank in South Vietnam's Mekong Delta, a place etched into his subconscious from his years serving as a naval officer in the war.[1] A man is standing next to him. A boat chugs by, overflowing with refugees from the North, some clinging to the side of the fragile vessel. Suddenly the boat begins to sink, sucking the men and women and children down into the eye of a liquid tornado, the dark water quickly quieting into a placid surface, concealing the tragedy just beneath.

McCloskey turns to the person standing with him in the dream, panicked, helpless. "There's nothing we can do! Those people are going to drown." Then, out of nowhere, a helicopter flies overhead and drops Navy SEALs into the water. They dive down, deep below the surface, bringing up the people, one by one.

In his dream, the divers save them all. In his waking life, one remains to be rescued.

After eighteen months in Coffield's maximum security unit, Ben Spencer had found refuge in the law library, researching his case. From there he wrote countless letters to anyone who might help him challenge his conviction. His wife, Debra, embarked on the same crusade, with a baby on her hip and a full-time job. They wrote the ACLU, the Martin Luther King Center, lawyers, journalists, and television talk show hosts. "There was just nothing for us," Debra recalled.

One day, a fellow inmate handed Spencer a slip of paper with an address. He said that this place, Centurion Ministries, had declined his case because his sentence was "only" twenty-five years. Centurion focused its efforts on inmates serving sentences of life or death. In a letter dated November 10, 1989, in elegant, precise penmanship, he began: "My name is Benjamine J. Spencer III as I am sure that you noticed by the return address. The reason for which I am contacting you is that I have been suffering from the cause of injustice, for which I have been constantly in search of help."

Over the next ten pages, he laid out his case: the neighbors' allegations, his alibi, the detective's interrogation and threats, the jailhouse informant, the mishaps in the first and second trials. Spencer did not demand or even expect help, acknowledging that Centurion "had its hands full" at this time. "Yet, I am hoping that you may be able to help me whenever there is time and space," he wrote. "May God add blessings to your administration to help it grow because more organizations like yours are needed."

If you had told a twenty-year-old Jim McCloskey that he would save anyone from anything, he might lift a beer in your direction and then return to the serious business of raising hell at Bucknell University. As a member of Phi Gamma Delta, he shed his Presbyterian sensibilities on his way to graduating with a GPA of 2.0. After graduation in 1964, McCloskey enrolled in the navy's officer candidate school and served one year in Vietnam. By the time he returned, safe and whole, he had his life mapped out: He became a management consultant, first for a large Japanese bank in Tokyo and later for the Hay Group in the United States.

But he quickly found the foreign travel "superficial" and his lifestyle "self-centered." In search of meaning, McCloskey turned to romance. He chose poorly. He was torn between a not-yet-divorced woman in Japan and a Times Square prostitute named Brandy, whom he genuinely adored enough to meet her parents. At the same time, he returned to his Presbyterian church in earnest. But—St. Augustine's prayer comes to mind here: *Lord, make me chaste but not yet*—he continued to venture into Times Square.

"I was living a double life. A triple life," McCloskey recalled. "I was very serious about scripture study. But at the same time, I'm up in New York, picking up prostitutes." One night, Brandy being unavailable, he brought another woman to his hotel room. "I fell asleep. And I wake up and she's gone and so is my wallet. I got rolled!" he said, roaring with laughter. He looked in the mirror, and announced to his reflection: "This ain't working."

From these spicy beginnings, the modern innocence movement was born.

In September 1979, a thirty-seven-year-old Jim McCloskey entered Princeton Theological Seminary. For his field-education requirement the following fall, he volunteered to be a student chaplain at Trenton State Prison, which housed the most dangerous inmates in New Jersey.

McCloskey visited the prison each week, and one inmate named Jorge de los Santos stood out as exceptionally stubborn. An admitted heroin addict, "Chiefie" had been convicted of murdering a man in Newark in 1975 and sentenced to life in prison. Week after week, Chiefie insisted that he was innocent. McCloskey was skeptical. He believed that the criminal justice system was "essentially infallible," he said. "Mistakes just were not made. The truth always prevailed."

Chiefie persuaded McCloskey to read the transcripts of his trial over Thanksgiving break. When the seminarian returned to make his rounds, the inmate was waiting.

"Do you believe I'm innocent?" Chiefie asked.

"Yeah," McCloskey responded. "I guess I'm kind of there now."

"Well, what are you going to do to help me?"

"Chiefie, what can I do? I don't know anything about the criminal justice system. I've been a businessman, for God's sake."

"Well, you can't just go back to your safe little dormitory room and pray for me. God works through human beings, and you're the only human being I have."

McCloskey did return to his room to pray, and then he put seminary on hold. From February 1981 to February 1982, McCloskey reinvestigated Chiefie's case, his only weapons being his gut instincts and the chutzpah born of complete inexperience. He shuttled between Princeton and Newark, tracked down new witnesses, confronted informants, pored over police reports, and tried to persuade the prosecutor to consider new evidence. He discovered that Chiefie's conviction rested on the testimony of a drug addict and a jailhouse informant, and both had lied on the stand with the knowledge of the prosecutor.

Before meeting Chiefie, McCloskey mused, "the thought never crossed my mind that police or prosecutors would lie or cheat, or that judges would turn a blind eye to the innocent." Chiefie's case became Jim McCloskey's Road to Damascus moment, the blinding light that led to an astounding insight. "I see that in practically every factual hearing, somebody is more than likely lying." Witnesses lie, jailhouse informants lie, forensic scientists exaggerate, police manufacture evidence and prosecutors hide it. Not always, of course, but surprisingly often. And juries, "with their prejudices and biases and predispositions," typically assume that the person sitting in the dock must be guilty. "Our presumption is guilt, rather than innocence."

McCloskey teamed up with Paul Casteleiro, an attorney who handled the case for free; he would later become McCloskey's legal director. On July 6, 1983, two months after McCloskey received his divinity degree, a federal judge vacated Chiefie's conviction and released him from prison. McCloskey drove him to the housing project where his wife lived. More than a hundred children and adults waited with "Welcome home,

Chiefie!" signs and music blaring from speakers. Chiefie ran to his wife, and as the crowd cheered, the couple embraced for several moments, his face buried in her thick black hair.

That night, McCloskey glimpsed the reward, and the cost, of his success. For the first time in his life, he knew his purpose. "I believed this was destiny, that this was why God put me on earth," he wrote in his memoir, *When Truth Is All You Have.* "Everything that came before, all the ups and downs of my life, was in preparation for this work."[2]

Yet he felt empty. "It was hard to admit it, but I was envious of Chiefie," he confessed. Chiefie was celebrating in the glow of love and home, "and here I was, a forty-one-year-old man, almost broke, living rent-free in the home of an eighty-five-year-old woman." He intuited, correctly, that he would never enjoy family life, his work would permit no competition, and his calling would crowd out any greater affection. Like others in this field, McCloskey was destined to be a priest of justice.

He noticed a pile of papers on his desk, documents from other cases that he had set aside as Chiefie's hearing date approached. He picked them up, poured a glass of bourbon, uncapped a yellow highlighter, and began to read.

Jim McCloskey realized his call was not to the pulpit, but to innocent men and women in prison. With a ten-thousand-dollar gift from his parents, he founded Centurion Ministries in September 1983. The name honors the Roman centurion in the book of Luke, who gazed up at Jesus hanging on the cross and said: "Surely, this one was innocent."

The headquarters for Centurion Ministries was on Library Place in Princeton, specifically, Jim McCloskey's bedroom in the Victorian home of an octogenarian named Elizabeth Yeatman, who allowed McCloskey to live in her mansion in exchange for running errands and helping her with repairs around the house.

After Chiefie's release, McCloskey suffered no shortage of willing clients. One of them, Nathaniel Walker, had been convicted in 1976 of raping a young woman in Elizabeth, New Jersey. He was serving a life sentence plus fifty years. Walker's alibi covered both the timing of the attack and the physical description of the attacker. He claimed he was at the copper factory where he worked. Moreover, the victim told the police the assailant was circumcised, had one testicle, and did not wear glasses; Walker was not circumcised, had two testicles, and was legally blind without glasses. When McCloskey accepted the case, he also found that the rape kit contained untested semen. In 1986, before the precision of DNA testing was available, FBI analysts compared it to Walker's blood type and excluded Walker as the contributor.

On November 5, 1986, Walker's conviction was overturned and the charges against him were dismissed. McCloskey sat in the front row of the courtroom, next to Walker's mother, oblivious to the *New York Times* reporter taking notes a few rows back. The article that ran the next day upended Jim's life and rang the opening bell for the innocence movement.[3] Within days of the *Times* story, Jim McCloskey and Nate Walker had appeared on the *Today* show, in *People* and *Ebony* magazines, and in a slew of outlets across the country. Centurion was the only organization devoted to freeing innocent people in prison. Prisoners took notice.

"Letters started pouring in to Mrs. Yeatman's house," McCloskey recalled decades later. He smiled and began to chuckle quietly. "Here's this woman, eighty-five years old, letters are coming in from convicted murderers, rapists, all over the country," he says, laughing harder now. Letters from San Quentin, Angola, Rikers Island. "And she said, 'Jim, who are these people? Are they going to come and get us? Is there any way you could get an office downtown?'" He took a deep, shuddering breath. "Oh, the poor lady."

On November 6, 1986, when Kate Germond opened up the *Times*, the headline "New Evidence Ends Jersey Man's Life Term" caught her eye. A self-described "raging liberal who marched to stop small-net fishing," Germond instantly knew that freeing the wrongfully convicted fell in her sweet spot. Then she saw the photograph. "Jim was sitting on a wooden chair holding a Princess phone," she recalled, "and he had mail from all over the country unopened on the floor of this one room in this old mansion in Princeton. And I said to myself, 'This man needs my help.'"

Germond and her husband had just moved to New York from California, where she ran a business helping start-ups with logistics. She began commuting from New York to Princeton, helping McCloskey triage the hundreds of requests, figuring out a system to rank the cases, and finding volunteers to answer letters, dig into the prisoners' records and history, and develop the cases that Centurion might want to pursue.

Early on, McCloskey was the sole investigator. "Jim would go interview the person in jail," said Barry Scheck, the cofounder of the Innocence Project. "He'd look at them in the eye, and he would decide in his gut whether they were innocent or not." Then he would camp out in a hotel room while he dug up new evidence. "He was like Truman Capote."

"He was laser focused," Germond agreed. "Fearless." She remembers a conversation with Nate Walker after he was released. McCloskey had invited Walker—who was Black and from Newark—to join him in finding witnesses for a case there. "Nate said, 'He scared the shit out of me,'" Kate recalled. "'He's in this really dangerous neighborhood paying not one bit of attention, this middle-aged white man walking up dark stairwells and knocking on the doors of people who might not want an uninvited guest, never wondering, Hmm, do I need backup?'"

McCloskey had a gift for eliciting the truth. "This friendly, paunchy guy with a sense of humor and a smile on his face walks up with his little clerical collar on, and people just naturally let their guard down," he observed with some wonder. Informants and false witnesses, perpetrators and their families, even some government officials, eventually blurted out their confessions after he encouraged them to "release the guilt of hiding a lie year after year." He added, "My clerical collar didn't hurt."

Nearly a decade before the Innocence Project freed a single prisoner, Jim McCloskey had launched the nation's first organization devoted to reinvestigating wrongful convictions. The reason you may not have heard of McCloskey or Centurion Ministries is that Centurion takes on the cases with no DNA. It conducts painstaking investigations that can only be solved by shoe leather and knocking on doors, without the biological evidence to score a decisive home run.

"To me, Jim McCloskey is the guy to start with," says Robert Norris, author of *Exonerated: The History of the Innocence Movement.* "Without Centurion, there's no organizational foundation for it to become a movement later on." Through the 1960s and '70s, this frat boy turned naval officer hewed to middle-class conservative views: McCloskey dismissed Martin Luther King as a "troublemaker." He thought prosecutors did the work of angels by throwing criminals in jail.

But after his revelatory encounter with Chiefie, "he went in whole hog," Germond said. The spiritual conversion reshaped his politics, his passions, his friendships, his work, how he spent his days and nights. "He just embraced it and fought hard for these people he didn't know at all, and who were out of his world, nothing to do with his world, would never touch his world. But he chose it." Jim's *internal* transformation sparked an *external* revolution. "He started a movement," she said quietly. "It takes my breath away."

By the time Ben Spencer sent his first letter to Centurion, the organization had established a rigorous vetting process. The tiny staff could accept only two or three cases a year out of more than a thousand requests. Securing Centurion's help was like winning a Rhodes Scholarship: Only the most spectacular prisoners with the most compelling and winnable cases won the prize that would transform their lives. "Once we commit," McCloskey noted, "they have us for life."

Unlike other organizations, Centurion responded to every inmate's request, including Spencer's. Within a few days, a volunteer wrote Spencer and asked him to fill out an application. But he also tried to temper Spencer's expectations by explaining that there was no guarantee Centurion would accept his case. Still, Spencer was thrilled. "I kept hoping:

Maybe, maybe, *maybe*," he said. "Anyone who was actually innocent of an offense, I'm sure we all think the same way: that my case is different than everybody else's case. But I kept hoping that there would be something about my case that would make them say, 'Well, hey, maybe *this* case.'"

Immediately after receiving a request, "we put the inmate to work," McCloskey explained. First, they ask the prisoner to write a detailed autobiography. What was his childhood like? How has he used his time in prison—getting in fights, racking up infractions, attending church, earning a GED? Does he have a prior criminal record? "If they have a violent history, they're automatically disqualified," McCloskey noted, because past violence can indicate a propensity for future violence. In the end, he said, the dispositive question has little to do with court filings. "What kind of people are they?" Innocence is not sufficient—many prisoners are innocent—but Centurion must feel confident that if they free a prisoner, he will live a good and productive life, not unleash menace onto the streets. "In a way, we play God."

"I was born on December 20, 1964," begins Spencer's fourteen-page autobiography, penned in small, meticulous handwriting. "I am now twenty-five years of age and have spent the last three years almost locked up for something I didn't do."[4] To read his narrative is to see a young man whose life was suspended, like a snapshot of a high diver just after he launches from the board—his aspirations, his accomplishments frozen in the awkward transition from adolescence to adulthood. Spencer never had time to settle into a career, but moved through a series of jobs: washing cars, light maintenance work, serving at fast food restaurants. "Wendy's is one of the best jobs I've ever had," he recalled; at seventeen, he was named employee of the month. He fell in love, landed a night job loading and unloading trucks, hoped to become a long-haul truck driver, learned his girlfriend was pregnant, and married her. He admitted that he had been arrested for driving with a suspended license, and had pleaded guilty to an unauthorized use of a motor vehicle—that is, joyriding in a car his friend stole—for which he received six years' probation. "I knew that I was guilty of driving the car after knowing that it was stolen, so there was no reason to contest the charge."

The seventeen-page letter accompanying his autobiography, dated December 25, 1989, initiated a duet between Ben Spencer and his Centurion volunteer. This marked another stage in the process, as Matt Camuso asked specific questions about the crime, and Ben returned multipage responses. As part of the protocol, Camuso amassed a written record of the case, gathering the second trial transcript, the legal briefs, the police reports, the affidavits, the court rulings, all with two questions in mind: Is this person innocent? And can they develop new evidence to get before a judge in an evidentiary hearing? Spencer walked Camuso through his case, dividing it into chapters: the day of the murder, the arrest, the neighbors' accusations, the first trial, the second trial, the differences between the trials, witnesses called or not called, and his arrest record, which, fortunately for Spencer, was not violent and thus not disqualifying.

"I wanted them to know everything I knew," Spencer recalled. "And what I didn't know, I wanted them to try to find out." He pointed out errors and inconsistencies in witness testimony. He identified people who could corroborate his alibi—people who were never called, or even tracked down, by his lawyers. At the end of that letter, almost as an afterthought, Spencer provided a lead that would prove pivotal. Another man had been identified as a suspect but never was "checked out" by police: Michael Hubbard.


Jim McCloskey knew nothing of the man sitting in Texas's largest prison. But he knew a great deal about Texas justice. McCloskey had worked on several cases in the convict-rich state of Texas and found startling success. He saved Clarence Brandley from execution, and he was exonerated in 1990.[5] From there McCloskey turned to the case of Joyce Ann Brown, who was accused of robbing a fur store in Dallas, then shooting the furrier and leaving his wife to watch him die. After McCloskey

discovered that the state had hidden evidence and the actual culprit had
confessed, Brown was freed in 1990.[6] But just as he was leaving Texas,
McCloskey learned of another man whose appointment with his maker
had been set by the state. Kerry Max Cook was convicted of raping and
killing a young woman in Tyler, Texas, in 1977. McCloskey found reams
of evidence that witnesses had lied and the state had hidden evidence.
Cook walked out of prison in 1997.[7]

These existential deadlines consumed McCloskey through the 1990s.
Ben Spencer faced no appointed expiration date, just the angst of watching his life disappear, day after day, year after year. But one day, Spencer
sent a personal letter to Jim McCloskey. "I have not given up hope in being exonerated in this case that I've been convicted of committing," the
prisoner wrote in a typed letter.[8] "My endeavors in seeking assistance
[have] been constant and I have no intention of giving up hope."

"You read these letters and your heart is broken," McCloskey said. "If
it's true that they were wrongly convicted, and we have to say 'No,' or
'Come back in a couple of years,' it breaks your heart for them."

But Spencer was playing the long game. "Whether they took my case
or not, this was my lifeline, you know?" he said. "And of course, I didn't
want to cut that lifeline off." He continued to write, and wait, and hope.

Outside Coffield, a scientific revolution was unfolding, shattering assumptions and showing, as McCloskey put it, "what a cruel, mindless,
mean machine the justice system can be."[9] Jim McCloskey knew this. Ben
Spencer knew this. The rest of the world was about to find out.

# Chapter 17

# DOUBLE HELIX

+———+

**What's going on here? Then the penny dropped.**

—SIR ALEC JEFFREYS, *upon discovering DNA fingerprinting*

Dawn Ashworth's parents didn't think twice when their fifteen-year-old daughter left their home in Enderby, a village in Leicestershire, to walk to her friend's house. It was only four thirty in the afternoon, the last day of July in 1986, and the sun would set late over the rural English village. Looking back, those days seem impossibly innocent. The Twin Towers still touched the New York sky. *Top Gun* was setting box office records at movie theaters. Whitney Houston wondered, "How Will I Know?" as she topped the charts. *Murder, She Wrote* and *Family Ties* gathered millions of people each week around their televisions. In 1986, Enderby was a friendly, quiet village, and the Ashworths thought nothing of Dawn's outing—that is, until she failed to come home by nine thirty that night, as she had promised.

Two days later, the body of the teenager was found in a wooded area near a footpath called Ten Pound Lane. She had been beaten, savagely raped, strangled, and left half-naked, covered in twigs and branches. Almost immediately, police suspected this was the handiwork of a serial killer. Two and a half years earlier, in November 1983, fifteen-year-old Lynda Mann had been discovered a few hundred yards away from the place Dawn was found. Lynda, who could have been Dawn's doppel-gänger, also had been left half-naked, raped, and strangled with her own scarf. Police quickly focused on a seventeen-year-old man with learning difficulties who seemed to know more than he should about Dawn's murder. He confessed, then recanted, confessed and recanted, until finally police arrested him. He adamantly denied anything to do with Lynda Mann's murder.

Five miles away, Alec Jeffreys received a call from Detective David Baker of the Leicestershire Police. Jeffreys, a geneticist at the University of Leicester, had gained some fame working with DNA. The detective told the scientist that the investigation had run aground and they needed to quickly solve the two murders. They had a prime suspect who had confessed to Dawn Ashworth's murder, but not to Lynda Mann's. Could Jeffreys test the evidence—the semen from the rape kit from each girl—to conclusively establish that the suspect was guilty, not just of the one murder, but of both murders?

"My initial reaction was, 'Well, yes, we'll try, but don't hold out too much hope,'"[1] Jeffreys replied. "'Nobody's ever attempted this sort of analysis on relatively old, real forensic casework.'"

Alec Jeffreys traces his fascination with science to age eight, when his father gave him a chemistry set. A few years later, while attempting an experiment, he got "a full face of sulfuric acid, which is why I wear this beard now."[2] His relentless curiosity drew him to DNA, the code each of us bears that makes us unique. In the early 1980s, Jeffreys realized that DNA might reveal whether a person is susceptible to inherited diseases, and as a test, he took blood samples of his technician and her parents. He extracted the DNA from the cells, attached the samples to photographic films, and left them in a developing tank. When he retrieved the films, each showed a sequence of bars; all three codes were distinct, and the child's was the composite of the parents'. For the first thirty seconds, he was perplexed. It looked like a "complicated mess," he said. "What's going on here? Then the penny dropped. *Oh, wait a minute.* This is potentially a method for biological-based or DNA-based biological identification."

He was looking at the world's first genetic fingerprint. It was 9:05 a.m. on September 10, 1984. "That was a moment that changed my life."[3]

One could safely say the moment changed the world, or at least any sphere in which identity mattered. DNA could determine paternity and other family relationships. It could be used to identify who left his blood or other biological material at a crime scene. It could be used to identify remains, and indeed, Jeffreys's discovery would later identify a skeleton found in Brazil as that of Dr. Josef Mengele, the Nazi "Angel of Death."

The case that brought Jeffreys onto the world stage involved an immigration controversy. Government officials disputed whether a boy was the son of a British citizen, but Jeffreys' genetic testing confirmed the relationship. It was the first DNA fingerprint case in the world, and it remains Jeffreys's favorite. "Just the look in that mother's eyes!" he later recalled. "She had been fighting the case for two years. That was my golden moment. Without DNA, he could have been deported."[4]

N ow, in the summer of 1987, Jeffreys was being asked to identify the man who murdered two teenaged girls. He agreed, and the police sent over the sample that day. It was a "chilling moment" for an academic more familiar with statistics than strangulation. "Suddenly you've got murder samples in front of you. I remember my blood literally running cold."[5]

He and his team worked overnight. The results surprised him and unsettled the police. The same man had raped and presumably killed both girls; and that man was *not* the suspect in custody. "Either this is a false confession or the science was in fact fundamentally flawed," Jeffreys reasoned. "My instinctive reaction was the second, that there's something horribly wrong with the science because the police were sure they got the right guy. This person had *confessed*."[6] He repeated the tests twice more, with the same results.

"One minute we got the guy," the senior investigating officer muttered, "and the next we've got jack shit."[7]

Without DNA, an innocent young man would likely have been convicted of two murders because he falsely confessed to one—which we know now, but did not know then, happens all the time. Significantly, the first time DNA was used to solve a crime, it did not lead to a conviction, but to an exoneration.

Police released the young suspect and started from scratch. This time, however, they employed the technology that had just thwarted them. They had the DNA profile of the assailant. They were pretty sure he was a local man who knew the roads and footpaths. The police launched a dragnet, sending letters to more than fifty-five hundred men between the ages of sixteen and thirty-three who had lived or worked in the area in recent years. They asked them to submit blood samples, which were then compared with the DNA of the perpetrator. Over the next eight months, 5,511 men showed up at testing centers and gave samples, but no one's DNA matched the assailant's. The investigation halted, until serendipity intervened.

One evening, Ian Kelly was enjoying a pint with his friends at a local pub, and the talk inevitably turned to everyone's obsession: the stalled murder investigation. Kelly mentioned that he had donated his blood for a colleague at the bakery where he worked. The colleague, Colin Pitchfork—twenty-seven years old, married, with two children—had told Kelly that he could not give his blood because he had already been tested once, as a favor to a friend who had been arrested for indecent exposure. Pitchfork then doctored his passport by pasting Kelly's photo into it, and Kelly gave his blood under Pitchfork's name. A woman in the pub overheard the conversation and reported it to the police. Pitchfork was arrested on September 19, 1987. He quickly confessed. According to news reports, a detective asked: "Why Dawn Ashworth?" Pitchfork shrugged and replied: "Opportunity. She was there and I was there."[8] Pitchfork was convicted and sentenced to thirty years in prison.

DNA profiling had passed its first test. But Jeffreys did not foresee the revolution he had sparked. Never in his "wildest dreams," he said years later, did he think his discovery would have the impact that it's ultimately proved to have. "I've been told many times by police that they regard the development of DNA typing as providing them with the most powerful scientific tool in the fight against crime that they've ever had."[9] Apparently, Queen Elizabeth thought so as well: Jeffreys was knighted in 1994.

Jeffreys's discovery moved from scientific journals to the bookstores in 1989, when Joseph Wambaugh published *The Blooding*, his bestselling account of the investigation. To the public, the book told a riveting tale of futuristic science and grisly homicide. To innocent people in prison, and specifically, to Gary Dotson, sitting in a cell in Illinois, the discovery restored something that he had long ago abandoned: hope.

On the night of July 9, 1977, a police officer found sixteen-year-old Cathleen Crowell standing by the side of the road in Homewood, Illinois, a suburb of Chicago.[10] The distraught girl said she had been raped, and the officer took her to the hospital, where an examination found semen, hair, and superficial cuts on her stomach. When shown a mug book, she identified twenty-two-year-old Gary Dotson.

At trial, she was a mesmerizing (and the only) eyewitness, pointing at Dotson and declaring: "There's no mistaking that face." The state's forensic scientist stated that only 10 percent of men could be contributors of the semen, and that the hair found on her body was "microscopically similar" to Dotson's. Neither statement was true. The prosecutor referred to Crowell as a "sixteen-year-old virgin," and branded Dotson's four friends who said he was out drinking with them "liars." The jury convicted Dotson in July 1979. He was sentenced to twenty-five to fifty years in prison.

In fact, no rape had occurred. Cathleen Crowell had invented the story in case she became pregnant by her boyfriend; she lifted the description of the rape scene from the novel *Sweet Savage Love*. She later married another man and moved to New Hampshire, but the lie gnawed at her. In 1985, she confessed to her pastor, adding she had inflicted the superficial cuts on herself to bolster her account. Her attorney told the prosecutors she was recanting her story, but they were uninterested. She confessed publicly in media interviews and offered to stand trial for perjury if the state of Illinois would declare Dotson innocent and free him.

In October 1987, Dotson's attorney read a *Newsweek* article about Alec Jeffreys's genetic fingerprinting, and he petitioned the court to test the rape kit evidence using DNA technology. Nearly a year later, the results returned. The semen had come from the girl's boyfriend, not Gary Dotson. It took another year, until August 1989, before the prosecution finally admitted the error and vacated the conviction. Another fifteen years would pass before Dotson was declared innocent. The state paid him $120,000 in compensation. Gary Dotson had made history of the most tragic kind. He was the first innocent prisoner in the United States to be exonerated by DNA.

I read about Jeffreys in England, hunting for the serial rapist, and I understood immediately what it could do for us and that we could use it," Kate Germond said. Centurion Ministries was helping several prisoners who had been convicted of rape, and she suggested to Jim McCloskey that they try the new technology. "He said, 'Kate, we can't cut corners. You have to do this work, the hard work.'" It's not cheating, she protested, and McCloskey relented. But in the end, Centurion was not destined to launch the DNA revolution in the United States. The small organization stuck to its proven methods, selecting clients based not on cutting-edge science but on instinct, experience, the prisoner's record, and his or her character, listening to an internal voice that this man or woman is innocent.

Jim McCloskey and Kate Germond were a little like Orville and Wilbur Wright, who invented, built, and piloted the world's first motor-operated flying machine. Like the aeronautic visionaries, McCloskey imagined something that had never been attempted: He designed the intellectual blueprint for a movement that would challenge the justice system, proving in case after case that the system was deeply flawed, racist, arbitrary, and unjust. Like the Wright brothers' early planes, Centurion was not built for mass transit. The tiny staff and volunteers shuttled prisoners to freedom one at a time. The role of expanding the number of exonerations would fall to two lawyers in New York City, quick, passionate masterminds who would make "innocence" a household word.

If Centurion Ministries was the pioneer, the Innocence Project was the first organization to mass-deliver prisoners to freedom. The founders, Barry Scheck and Peter Neufeld, were strategic from the start, opting to build a network of clinics at law schools rather than a single, large entity, and litigating the high-profile cases that drew headlines and millions of dollars in support. They had one simple goal, Scheck recalled: "We wanted to transform the entire criminal justice system." And they did.

Both men came from modest families, steeped in Jewish culture, fully invested in liberal causes. Barry Scheck was born in Queens in 1949, one generation removed from poverty. His mother was a sometime journalist and eventual entrepreneur; his father, who did not graduate from high school, became an entertainer. "He learned how to tap-dance from a Black man who was a janitor at a bank," Scheck told an interviewer in 2002, "and he danced Black, as they say."[11] From there, his father opened dancing schools and managed stars like Connie Francis, Mary Wells, and Bobby Darin. His parents were active in the civil rights movement, and Scheck came to see social change as his calling and the law as the engine to execute it. He attended Yale University, followed by law school at the University of California at Berkeley—because he wanted to hang out in the gritty, lefty, "liberated zone," and besides, the tuition was only $435 a semester, "which I actually was able to make playing poker."

Peter Neufeld, a year younger, grew up in Brooklyn, raised by deeply progressive parents. His mother, a homemaker and social activist, served as national president of the American Ethical Union. His father worked in a shoe store, a sideshow to his main passion: civil rights. According to Richard Leo, a law professor at the University of San Francisco who has written a meticulous account of the innocence movement, the Neufelds would drive hundreds of miles to deliver books to "freedom schools" in Black communities,[12] teaching their children about the lingering Jim Crow laws as they wended their way through the South. Neufeld studied history at the University of Wisconsin-Madison—he was suspended twice for staging protests—and returned to his hometown to attend New York University School of Law.

Barry Scheck and Peter Neufeld met in 1976 at the Bronx office of the Legal Aid Society, which provided free legal services to low-income New Yorkers. Their real partnership began a decade later, after Scheck had started a clinic at Cardozo Law School and Neufeld had left for private practice. At the time, neither Scheck nor Neufeld had heard of the DNA fingerprinting that had identified a serial killer in rural England. But once a scientist explained the technology, its precision and its potential, they saw their future unfold before them.

"What we realized," Neufeld said, is that DNA "is a much more robust technology than what they've been using for the last thirty years." They always suspected that evidence like eyewitness identification was not terribly reliable, and now they knew. The double helix provided ground truth, a mathematical absolute so much cleaner than error rates, opinions, and the squishiness of the other evidence on which convictions had previously been won. "Wouldn't it be interesting," Neufeld mused, "to go back and look at some of those convictions with this more powerful technology and see whether or not they got the right man?"[13]

Over the next few years, Scheck and Neufeld mastered the science of DNA. The lawyers learned the microbiology, and they quickly recognized the pitfalls that could distort the results. How was the DNA evidence collected? How could it be contaminated? How was it tested? At what temperature was the evidence stored? How does it degrade? What were the correct statistical probabilities? Neither attorney had a background in science. In fact, they had attended law school to escape the hard sciences.

"The last thing we ever wanted to see as lawyers was any kind of physics or chemical equation," Neufeld said.[14] "But what happens is you have a client whose life and liberty is at stake, and it forces you to learn particular disciplines," such as biology or chemistry, physics or toxicology. "If you don't learn them, then someone may abuse the information and send out an erroneous piece of information to the jury, and your client will suffer as a result."

Kerry Kotler shared that view. Kotler knew his way around police stations by the time he was twenty-two.[15] He had been arrested for car thefts, marijuana possession, possession of stolen property, bribing a witness, assault during a barroom brawl, and two rapes, although the rape charges were dropped. He adamantly denied committing the sexual assault for which he was convicted in New York in 1982. With an IQ of 126, he spent hours in the law library drafting and filing appeals, his hope deflating with each denial. Then, in September 1988, he was sitting in the prison break room watching television when a program about DNA testing began. The implications were obvious. Kotler called his lawyer and asked that the semen from the rape kit be tested.

The results excluded Kotler as the source, but the prosecutor balked at vacating the conviction, arguing that the sample could have been contaminated. In 1992, Barry Scheck and Peter Neufeld took up Kotler's cause, the first DNA exoneration they handled together. Another DNA test, along with proof that the state had suppressed exculpatory evidence, allowed Kotler to walk out of prison on December 1, 1992.[16] Back then, DNA exonerations were still novel, the public was still intrigued, the outrage and perplexity were still fresh, and the press still set up cameras on the courtroom steps.

As he welcomed Kotler to freedom after eleven years, Peter Neufeld made a prediction. "We're going to see dozens more of these cases,"[17] he said. Letters began to arrive—from inmates, their families, and their lawyers—and they piled up, a scene reminiscent of letters pouring through Mrs. Yeatman's mail slot at Library Place, begging for Jim McCloskey's help. Scheck and Neufeld needed a name for this burgeoning organization. They called it the Innocence Project.

To triage the hundreds of requests pouring into the office, they developed three criteria. First, the case had to involve identity as an issue; if it was a murder case and the defense was self-defense, the prisoner might be innocent, but they weren't interested. Second, there must have been biological evidence collected during the initial investigation. And third— what would prove to be the burr under their saddle for years to come— they had to locate the evidence.

They next made a strategic decision to franchise their work. "We organized throughout the law schools," Scheck explained. "In doing it that way, we were able to punch way above our weight, because we were able to train a generation—now, a few generations—of law students who became judges and prosecutors, defense lawyers, you name it, about the problems of wrongful convictions."[18] Initially, the Innocence Project was largely an underground movement. The world did not take notice—that is, until 1995.

The episode that secured the Innocence Project's place in the court-room also nearly discredited its founders. In 1995, Barry Scheck and Peter Neufeld joined O. J. Simpson's defense team. The former football and movie star was accused of stabbing and killing his ex-wife, Nicole Brown Simpson, and her friend Ronald Goldman in her Los Angeles home. It's hard to properly convey the Everest of evidence incriminating the defendant. The victims' blood was detected on O. J. Simpson's socks, inside his white Ford Bronco, and on the bloody leather glove found out-side his home. Simpson's blood was found at his ex-wife's condominium, on the ground and on a back gate. The state's forensic scientists estimated the odds of the blood belonging to anyone but Simpson were one in forty-seven billion.

Enter Scheck and Neufeld. They attacked the Los Angeles Police De-partment, and in brutal cross-examinations they argued that the blood samples the Los Angeles Police Department collected had been contami-nated, degraded, or planted to frame Simpson. Scheck's famous closing argument eviscerated all of the state's forensic evidence. He declared Simpson "an innocent man," entrapped by overzealous police and prosecutors. "There is something terribly wrong about this evidence," he told the jurors. "Somebody manufactured evidence in this case. . . . You must distrust it. You have to distrust it."[19] Along with Johnnie Cochran's statement about the bloody leather glove—"If it doesn't fit, you must acquit"—this created enough reasonable doubt for the jury to acquit Simpson in four hours.

The blowback was swift and fierce. People would stop Scheck and Neufeld on the street and scold, "Shame on you," Neufeld remembered.[20] Scheck was receiving death threats, and employees at the Innocence Project were rattled by the furious callers. "How dare you work for a man that would defend someone [guilty of murder]?" one caller asked. In the media, the lawyers were accused of having "sold their public-interest souls for fame," *The New York Times* reported.[21] Battered women felt betrayed; others accused them of hypocrisy by employing DNA to free poor people in jail, then attacking its legitimacy for a wealthy defendant. "The O. J. case was Scheck's Faustian bargain," wrote *Slate*'s editor, David Plotz, adding: There is "a special corner of hell reserved for O. J. Simpson's lawyers."[22]

On the upside, the world's most famous televised trial shamed police departments and forensic scientists into handling biological evidence with far more care. It introduced the American public to the miraculous power of DNA evidence. And it catapulted Barry Scheck and Peter Neufeld to celebrity status. They became among the most famous defense attorneys in the nation. The number of requests for help quintupled to 250 a month, and Innocence Projects began popping up at law schools across the country.

"I thought that we were really onto something from the beginning with the DNA tests," Scheck told me. He paused, searching for a large enough adjective. "I did think that this would be a very big fucking deal from the very beginning."

As the project began winning victories, prosecutors and lawmakers at the local, state, and federal levels stirred from their complacency. An entirely different arsenal was at hand. And the Innocence Project, with its smooth stone of DNA, proved a surprisingly feisty foe—its size small but its aim accurate, slinging its elegant weapon at the government's tender spot: right between the eyes.

*Chapter 18*

# A PUNITIVE TURN

+———+

**Innocence is not good enough.**

—Legal scholar Daniel Medwed

In the 1990s, DNA set off a chain reaction that unsettled Americans' foundational belief in their system of justice, and unleashed forces that collided in the courts, the legislatures, and the American psyche. Both sides claimed primacy. Truth was pitted against the need for finality, the fear of convicting the innocent against the fear of violent criminals, the impulse to reform the system against the need to protect the public.

As the decade matured, Americans grew familiar with an extraordinary scene: A man in newly pressed clothes strides out of the courthouse, arms raised in triumph, and stands before a bank of television cameras. He beams as he breathes in large drafts of fresh air, turns to hug his mother, picking her up and twirling her around, kisses his wife in a long embrace, awkwardly shakes the hand of his now-grown child, before snatching him up in a bear hug.

In dozens of these moments that repeated themselves throughout the 1990s, the fears of Edwin Borchard and Erle Stanley Gardner were realized. Yet as they piled up, the errors offered fresh insights into what was going wrong with so many trials and how to address the problems. Once you prove an innocent person has been convicted, Peter Neufeld observed, you look at the evidence through a different lens. "You know that there's something wrong with that evidence. Either people were mistaken or people were engaging in misconduct."[1] One could, for the first time, know this "with certainty."

These exonerations were like a full-body scan of the criminal justice system. The patient fell sick or fainted, suffered a heart attack or died. Before CT scans, doctors could see the effect, but not the specific cause. But with imaging technology, they could identify the culprit. See that aneurysm, that cluster of cancerous cells, that blocked artery? See that lying witness, that hidden police report, that flawed ballistics result? DNA showed not only that the system was sick, but how and why. While there were some bad apples—a lazy defense lawyer, a coercive detective, a sneaky prosecutor—the problem had less to do with individuals than with the inner workings of the criminal justice system itself.

As more innocent people walked out of prison into the sunlight, it was evident the technology had the power to correct past injustices. But the success raised a more disturbing question: Can *any* conviction be trusted? What of those cases in which *no* DNA is found? This is hardly a theoretical problem: Police gather DNA evidence at only 10 to 20 percent of crime scenes.[2] If you are an innocent prisoner for whom no DNA evidence exists to be tested, modern forensics affords no help. The exits are closed and there is no way out.

Ada, Oklahoma, had always been a safe, sleepy place, and the residents were horrified when two of its young women were killed within the space of eighteen months.[3] On December 7, 1982, twenty-one-year-old Deborah Sue Carter was found bloodied and strangled in her apartment. Soon, an informant told police he had seen Ronald Williamson with the young woman at the bar where she worked. Eventually, detectives brought him in for questioning. For hours, with a pistol on his hip, the detective "kept walking back and forth like a roaring lion," Williamson told me, "pointing his finger at me, saying he knew I did it."

Williamson kept insisting he wasn't involved, but eventually, desperate, he said he had had a nightmare about the murder.

"I went through a lot of pain over that statement," Williamson told me in an interview for a story on NPR. "It was six words that I used, and they used that as evidence to say that I had confessed to killing Debbie Carter. 'I dreamed I was stabbing her,'" he said, counting the words on his fingers. "*I dreamed I was stabbing her.*'"

Police arrested Williamson and his best friend, Dennis Fritz, and charged them with rape and murder. At trial, the prosecutor presented the dream confession, the initial informant, and a jailhouse snitch who testified to hearing Williamson admit to the murder. A forensic scientist implied that the hairs found on the victim's body matched those of the defendants. We now know that scientists misidentify hair samples more than half the time; it's more accurate to flip a coin. The two men were convicted. Fritz was sentenced to life; Williamson was sentenced to death.

On April 28, 1984, seventeen months after Debbie Sue Carter was murdered, Donna Haraway was seen leaving a convenience store with two men. The newly married college student never came home. Police picked up twenty-three-year-old Tommy Ward, and the same detective who interrogated Williamson now bore down on Ward. For hours, he accused Ward of killing the girl; for hours, Ward denied it. Eventually Ward agreed to take a polygraph. The detective told him he failed.

"And he goes, 'Well, why else would you have flunked the test if you didn't have nothing to do with it?'" Tommy Ward told me during an interview in prison. "And I said, 'Well, I don't know. It could have been my nerves, you know, because I'm a very nervous person. Or it could be anything, or it could have been a dream that I had. He goes, 'Well, what about your dream?'"

Six more hours of interrogation ended with Ward confessing on tape. He said that he and his best friend, Karl Fontenot, abducted Haraway, who was wearing a blouse with little blue roses, then stabbed her and dumped her body in a river west of Ada. They were prosecuted for Haraway's murder. The parallels with the other murder trial were uncanny.

The same detective interviewed the suspects. The same prosecutor tried them. At trial, the same jailhouse informant testified against them. Most improbably, the same sort of "dream confession" doomed them. But one glaring fact distinguished the two murder cases: forensic evidence. Unlike at the trials of Williamson and Fritz, the state presented no physical evidence to condemn Ward and Fontenot. Donna Haraway's body had never been found. Even without a body, the jury convicted both men and sentenced them to life in prison.

In 1999, the Innocence Project asked that the biological evidence from Debbie Sue Carter be tested for DNA. Williamson and Fritz were exonerated and released after eleven years—and five days before Williamson was to be executed. The DNA identified the informant who initially accused them, and he was later convicted.[4]

Ward and Fontenot were not so lucky. Donna Haraway's remains were located a few months after the men were convicted. Her body was not found, as Ward "confessed," in a river west of town, but buried in the woods twenty-six miles east of Ada. She had not been stabbed, but shot in the head. Her shirt did not have little blue roses, but a red-and-white pattern. But her body was so decomposed that there was no biological evidence to test.[5] Without a DNA test, Ward and Fontenot were trapped. Some thirty-four years later, a federal judge vacated Fontenot's conviction, ruling he had not received a fair trial. Tommy Ward remains in prison to this day.[6]

What's most disturbing are not the flaws that DNA revealed in the cases of Ron Williamson and Dennis Fritz. Rather, what haunts people are the *other* convictions, the vast majority of cases where *no* DNA is available for testing. How probable is it that the state of Oklahoma convicted the wrong men in one murder case, but got it right in the other murder case with all the same ingredients, down to the same jailhouse informant? How likely is it that coerced confessions, lying witnesses, hidden evidence, flawed forensics, and all manner of defects pop up only in DNA cases? It's a good bet that innocent people remain in prison for decades, and perhaps the rest of their lives. This is the ice below the waterline.

Wicked people exist. Nothing avails except to set them apart from innocent people," Harvard professor James Q. Wilson wrote in *Thinking About Crime*, his 1975 compendium on crime, punishment, and morality.[7] The forensic advances fifteen years later would challenge Wilson's certainty. "It's really hard to make the argument that you need to separate the wicked from the good if you can't figure out who the wicked actually are," observes criminologist Robert Norris, of George Mason University. And yet in the 1980s and '90s, anxious about the rise in crime triggered by the crack epidemic and ignorant of the rise of wrongful convictions, people stampeded to Wilson's dark views. In this climate, the Innocence Project and other groups could bask in their early victories only briefly before they ran into heavy seas of resistance, not just from politicians, but from the US Supreme Court.

The criminal case that took innocence head-on involved Leonel Herrera, who was convicted of killing two law enforcement officers near Brownsville, Texas. He was sentenced to death in 1982. A mountain of evidence implicated him, but after Herrera had exhausted all his appeals, he compiled evidence that his brother, Raul, shot the officers. Raul, who was no longer alive, had signed an affidavit to that effect and confessed to his attorney, who also signed an affidavit. Raul's son also swore he witnessed his father shoot the officers. The question for the US Supreme Court was: Does the Constitution permit a state to execute an innocent person?

"Let's say you got all the process that you were due," explains Daniel Medwed, of the Northeastern University School of Law. "You got a lawyer. You had a fair trial. You got your appeal. The appeal was relatively fair. You got all these things, but you're still innocent." Is this something that a federal court can look at? In other words, does convicting or executing an innocent person violate the Constitution, and does that person have any recourse?

Apparently not. Writing for the majority in 1993, Chief Justice William Rehnquist held that a claim of actual innocence based on newly

discovered evidence did *not* entitle the prisoner to federal habeas relief—
that is, allow him to go to federal court and ask it to review whether his
trial and incarceration violated the Constitution. He must also show a
constitutional violation—that the prosecutor hid material evidence, for
example, or that his attorney provided inadequate defense. Few rulings,
Justice Rehnquist wrote, "would be more disruptive of our federal system
than to provide for federal habeas review of freestanding claims of actual
innocence."[8] In a concurring opinion, Justice Sandra Day O'Connor
opined that "the execution of a legally and factually innocent person
would be a constitutionally intolerable event."[9] However, she wrote, Herrera could not be "legally and factually innocent" because he "was tried
before a jury of his peers, with the full panoply of protections that our
Constitution affords criminal defendants."[10] In other words, a person
is guilty because he was convicted, and he was convicted because he is
guilty.[11]

The decision was a left hook to the jaw. The federal courts were often
the court of last resort, when prisoners could argue that they did not receive a fair hearing in state court. Federal judges are appointed for life,
and are more immune to political pressure. By contrast, in most states,
judges are elected, and often have a prosecutorial bent, since many came
from a district attorney's office.

"Convicting or even executing an innocent person apparently doesn't
violate the Constitution," Medwed explains. The takeaway from *Herrera*
is that a simple claim of actual innocence is not enough to get a prisoner
to federal court. You need to pair that with a constitutional claim. "Innocence is not good enough."

A few blocks from the US Supreme Court, members of Congress
were in the throes of what became known as the "punitive turn."[12]
One horrific incident seemed to whet the appetite for a law-and-order
crackdown, says Vincent Southerland, of New York University School of
Law: the Central Park jogger assault. Here we learned about "wilding"—

kids rampaging through the park and attacking people for no reason. Here we had a foretaste of "superpredators," the branding of young minority men as "roving packs of wild animals who couldn't be contained and had to be locked away and brought to heel," Southerland says. Social scientists such as John DiIulio Jr., at the University of Pennsylvania, inflamed the fear by predicting a demographic wave of young men who would attack without remorse unless they were incarcerated for a good long time. "Democrats and Republicans alike bought into this moral panic," Southerland says.

Thus, the prospect of reforming the criminal justice system based on the findings of DNA was drowned out by public and political panic. "There was just so much demagoguery going on," Barry Scheck recalled. "Let's get three-strikes laws. Let's get a death penalty here. Let's ratchet up the punishments. Let's run against crime because politically that's popular, particularly in an era when the crime is rising."

In 1992, for example, presidential candidate Bill Clinton chose to leave the campaign trail to witness the execution of a mentally disabled Black man found guilty of murder.[13] Crime was just that good a political issue. The 1990s unfolded a little like a police procedural—a morality play of good versus evil—starring Bill Clinton, with First Lady Hillary Clinton as supporting actor, worrying publicly about "superpredators." The 1994 crime bill, the largest in history, built new prisons and put a hundred thousand new police officers on America's streets. Then-senator Joe Biden captured the mood of the country when he advised: "Lock the S.O.B.s up."[14] Along came Timothy McVeigh and the Oklahoma City bombing in 1995, which killed 168 people, including 15 children at a day-care center in a federal building. In the wake of the worst homegrown act of terrorism ever, Congress acted again in 1996, passing a law and planting a seed that threatened to stifle the innocence movement. It was called the Antiterrorism and Effective Death Penalty Act, known as AEDPA.

"It's blatantly designed to exalt finality and efficiency over justice," Medwed says. The underlying premise was that state courts almost always operate fairly and arrive at the correct verdict—and that guilty people were "capitalizing on loopholes" to secure federal hearings, to wiggle out of punishment, and to flood the courts with frivolous motions "to slow down the wheels of justice."

Congress didn't want justice slowed, it wanted it speeded up, and that's what the 1996 law accomplished. For example, under the new law, a prisoner typically has to file his appeal to the federal court within *one year* of losing in state court. He receives only one chance at federal court, and if he loses there, he must seek permission to appeal—even if he has unearthed new evidence of innocence. In addition, the law requires federal judges to show deference to the state courts, which, Medwed says, "makes it really hard for a habeas judge to even give you a hearing or give you relief, even in an innocence case." The law was not aimed at innocence cases, but it still affected them, because often it takes years to develop evidence of innocence, and by then, the one-year deadline has passed. Before, Medwed says, the federal courts were a lifeline for innocence litigators: Now, "we don't even think a lot about habeas as a realistic option for proving innocence."

"AEDPA allows a federal court to say, 'Yes, the state court's wrong. Yes, this is a wrongful conviction. However, we're not going to interfere with the state court determination,'" says Mark Godsey, head of the Ohio Innocence Project and author of *Blind Injustice*. "It's horrific. It's pure evil. AEDPA is the devil."

D espite these legal and legislative setbacks, disquiet about convicting innocent people had taken root in the public psyche. And in 1993, the cost of mistakes in the courtroom shifted from tragic to existential.

Kirk Bloodsworth, a former marine and a discus champion, was convicted of raping and murdering a nine-year-old girl in Rosedale, Maryland, a suburb of Baltimore. The 1985 conviction relied on five eyewitnesses who said they saw him near the scene of the crime, and some spurious forensic evidence linking his shoe tread to marks on the girl's body. He was sentenced to death.

"When a man knows he is to be hanged in a fortnight, it concentrates his mind wonderfully," Samuel Johnson once said,[15] and it was this sort of urgency that Bloodsworth felt as he filed his appeals. When he wasn't researching law, Bloodsworth worked as the prison librarian, and one day he came across *The Blooding*. "I started reading this thing and I never put it down," he said. Bloodsworth began calling lawyers at various innocence projects, and they told him: "'You've got to find the DNA, Kirk, you've got to find the DNA.' Nobody would touch the case unless there was DNA."

After years of searching, his lawyer found the rape kit in a closet in the judge's chambers. The results pointed to one of Bloodsworth's fellow prisoners as the actual perpetrator. "I screamed it out, I said, 'That son of a bugger! I gave him library books! We lifted weights together!'" he recalled. "And there he was, right underneath everybody's nose. And I think that's what really pisses off the prosecutors and everything. He slid right past them all." Bloodsworth was released and exonerated in 1993. He was the first death row inmate in the nation to be cleared by DNA. With Kirk Bloodsworth's exoneration, a legal debate became visceral. The system had come within a whisker of executing an innocent man.

In September 1998, on the first day of class, a group of journalism students at Northwestern University received their fall assignment: to reinvestigate the case of Anthony Porter, who had been convicted of a double murder on Chicago's South Side and had been awaiting execution for fifteen years.[16] The students found that the conviction rested on perjured testimony and false eyewitness identification. They also tracked down a man who confessed to the crime. In February 1999, Porter was freed and the charges dismissed. Porter's exoneration did not involve DNA, but it turbocharged the central argument that DNA made: The US legal system convicts innocent people.

"I said to my wife, how does that happen in America?" former Illinois governor George Ryan recalled years later.[17] "How do you . . . put somebody in jail for sixteen years of their life and each morning, when they wake up, they have to wonder, 'Today, am I going to get executed or not? . . . And that's when I started to look into things."

Ryan began reviewing the cases of the men on Illinois's death row, taking their files with him "everywhere I went." In 2000, he reached a tipping point. Over the past decade, Illinois had executed twelve people and exonerated thirteen. As Peter Neufeld observed, "Those aren't good numbers."[18]

"So it's kind of like flipping a coin, to live or die, with the death penalty," Ryan recalled. "I decided that I couldn't determine who would live and who would die." He imposed a moratorium on executions in Illinois. Citing the state's "shameful record" of putting innocent people on death row, he said he could not support a system that had proven to be "so fraught with error and has come so close to the ultimate nightmare, the state's taking of innocent life."[19] In his last major act two days before leaving office in January 2003, Ryan commuted the sentences of all 167 Illinois death row prisoners to life without parole.

"I think the 1990s were both good and bad," Medwed reflects. In its attempt to catch criminals and thwart frivolous appeals, Congress and the US Supreme Court blockaded the favored roads leading an innocent person out of prison. "But it was also when the modern innocence movement moved from infancy to toddler and started to get its legs and started to gain momentum," he says. A new civil rights movement seemed in the offing. "I think the 1990s were a tough time for the innocent and the guilty, but there is this kernel of optimism based on the DNA cases."

In Coffield's maximum-security prison, Ben Spencer barely noticed the forensic revolution. There was no DNA in his case, as far as he knew. The 1990s became his chrysalis years, quiet, slow hours spent in the law library, mopping and dusting as a prison janitor, just trying to survive. In that decade, he suffered a traumatic loss, found a surprising ally, and mapped his escape route from prison, one letter at a time.

*Chapter 19*

# A NETWORK OF INNOCENTS

+———+

**He was the good part of me, you know?**
**He was what I aspired to be.**

—WILLIAM EARL JACKSON, *Ben Spencer's best friend*

The Coffield Unit, the largest prison in Texas with more than 5,000 inmates, has two telling epithets. "The House of Pane" is a wordplay on the physical and psychological. Coffield stands four stories tall, a village encased in brick and steel, but mainly glass. "A lot of people endure pain here," Ben Spencer allowed in one of his rare comments on prison life, thirty years into his time there. "It's a horrible place."

The other name also derives from the building's glass walls. The prison has no air conditioning in the Texas summers, which routinely top one hundred degrees for weeks on end. When you walk by people's cells, Richard Miles said, you see inmates lying on the floor in front of their tiny fans. "They've taken the water out of the toilet and put it on the floor to cool their bodies down," he recalled. In his job in the infirmary, Miles saw people die from dehydration and overheating. Prisoners would break the glass to allow the air to circulate. In the winter, the freezing wind whistled through the holes. Then the cells were frigid, the inmates once again miserable, and sick.

"We called it the Glass House," Miles said, who was serving a sixty-year sentence for murder and attempted murder. "And, you know, eventually you're going to become your environment. You're going to either be hard. Or you're going to be broken. So that's what Coffield does."

Often, however, prison does not alter a person's character or personality; it makes him more of what he already is. If you were violent outside, you'd be violent inside; a gang leader outside, you'd run a gang on the inside. If you were dignified or witty or fearful when free, you would carry those qualities with you into your prison cell. Ben Spencer, always mindful of his appearance before, took meticulous care of his white prison uniform, placing it under his mattress to create crisp, clean creases. He avoided fights and stayed to himself, as he had when he lived in West Dallas.

And he nurtured the faith of his childhood. Steven Phillips—forty years for rape—remembered walking one Sunday afternoon into a Church of Christ service on his unit. "There was this tall, eloquent Black guy talking to the congregation of about twelve or fifteen white guys," he said. "That's the first time I saw Ben Spencer." The service moved on to Communion, which Spencer also officiated. As Spencer recited the seven or eight lengthy verses from the New Testament, Phillips said, "I noticed that he wasn't using his Bible. He just knew it. Outright. And I saw through the years that he knew a lot more."

When Spencer was sent away to prison, his wife picked up B.J., their baby, and fled West Dallas, a neighborhood she now loathed, to Oak Cliff, a suburb of Dallas, where her parents lived. "My daddy told me, 'You get that baby and you come straight home,'" Debra said. In Oak Cliff, the schools were better, the streets were safer, and she had a sister, brother, and parents who spread a net under her.

"I still thought Ben was going to come home and take care of me and this child," Debra recalled years later. "That didn't happen, so I started building my own life." The telephone company promoted her to customer sales representative and she began traveling the country to serve large companies. She paid Miss Mable down the street twenty-five dollars a week to look after B.J. She loved her job, loved her son, and loved her husband, but their lives, once parallel, slowly diverged. Her life was too full, his too empty.

Every week at first, then twice a month, Debra would drive the two hours to Coffield Unit with B.J. strapped in his car seat. "Taking a baby to prison, it's nasty," she said, grimacing. As they stood in line to pass through security, her one-year-old squirmed. He needed to be changed, he was hungry, he was fussy, he startled and cried at the cacophonous sounds. Eventually they would enter the visitation room and sit down at a numbered table, bolted to the floor next to a Plexiglas screen reinforced with mesh. Spencer would enter from the back, uncuffed, in his white uniform. They tried to talk, the noise assaulting them, drowning their words.

"You're yelling the whole time," she said. "Everybody is just yelling at their mates or whatever so they can hear." B.J., fascinated by the man on the other side of the glass, would reach out. "He would just stand up on the table and touch the glass. And I'm germophobic. I'm like: *Don't touch that!* It was horrible." Spencer pressed his palm to the glass, and B.J. pressed his, a tiny mirror image, as close as this father and son could get. "I had great hopes of being the best father in the world," he wrote Debra later. "It's not easy to be a good father behind bars."[1]

The two-hour visits felt like a frantic gasp of air to a man drowning in the ocean, a brief reprieve from the inevitable. In mere seconds, or so it seemed, his wife and son were walking out of the visitation room, B.J. glancing over his shoulder and waving. "That's when the depression came," Spencer recalled. "You're up here now," he says, holding his hand above his head, "and then when they walk out of visitation, the excitement runs down," he said, lowering his hand to his waist. "It was a roller coaster."

Two months of marriage isn't long to prepare for a lifetime of separation. "I remember times when he would call, and I would just cry on the

phone," Debra said. "He'd say, 'Don't cry. It's going to be okay.' He'd always tell me, 'I'm here, I want you to live your life. I want you to do what
makes you happy.'"

That wish—for Debra to live her life, to be happy, even without him—
lay deep in the soil of his psyche, until it surfaced sometime in 1992, four
years into his life sentence. Several times Debra drove to Coffield for a
couples retreat. The event started at six o'clock in the evening, putting
Debra back on the road at 9:00 p.m. for the two-hour drive home. For
mile after pitch-black mile, the road from the prison wended its way
through farmland, a country road crossing other country roads, a confusing and potentially dangerous labyrinth before the advent of cell phones
and GPS. "No lights," Debra said, "just the lights on your car." Darker
still was the emotional journey from prison to home. "It just broke my
heart to have to leave him," she said. "I just cry all the way home." Spencer
was always frantic with worry—what if her car broke down?—and there
was no way to check on her.

After one of those nights, Spencer began to think, I need to let her go.


The conversation is pretty fluid in the barbershop," Richard Miles recalled. *Where are you from? What did you do? How much time do you
have?* The twenty-one-year-old had arrived at Coffield only a few hours
earlier and, still dazed, found his way to the barbershop. Ben Spencer, so
fastidious about his hair before prison, had learned from other prison bar-
bers and developed a reputation for stylish cuts. As Spencer trimmed
Miles's hair into a fashionable close cut, the new inmate described his
case. He was innocent, he told the barber; he never killed or tried to kill
anyone. Spencer mentioned his own case but refrained from going into
detail.

Then Spencer put down his scissors. "Man, I have this awesome
organization called Centurion Ministries," he said. "They're the best
that's out there. And if you're really innocent, you need to write them."
That night, Miles sat down and penned a letter. "I had never heard of

Centurion and didn't know there was innocence organizations out here." It would prove the most important letter of his life.

Spencer disclosed another secret: the prison law library. From the moment he arrived at Coffield, Spencer spent hours studying legal doctrine and looking for court precedents that could free him. "I began to have a pretty good grasp of the law, such things like double jeopardy, ineffective counsel, prosecutorial misconduct," he said. "I began to see where a lot of that took place in my case." He also saw the hazards ahead. Spencer realized that Congress had passed a law in 1996 that could blow up his chances of exoneration. The law gave inmates only one bite at the apple to get into federal court. "I never filed anything because I didn't want to mess up that one chance that I had."

But Richard Miles's case was at an earlier stage, and Spencer suggested he start schooling himself in criminal procedure. "He said, when your direct appeal gets denied, you will become your own lawyer," Miles recalled. "You have to file your writ of habeas corpus and so forth. I'm twenty-one years old. I didn't even know how to spell 'writ.'" Over the next few months, Miles learned about *Strickland v. Washington*, the two-pronged test to prove your lawyer was ineffective.[2] He learned how to "Shepardize" cases—that is, to determine whether the legal opinion you want to cite for your appeal is solid precedent. He saw Ben Spencer there every day, and made friends with other legal scholars. In that small room, he discovered a network of innocents.

"You can just kind of tell who is innocent and who's not," said Victor Thomas, who was serving two life sentences for raping a white woman. After watching Spencer settle before the lawbooks every day, Thomas was convinced. "I said, 'Wow, man, he don't even look like he is no robber or raper or murderer or nothing.' Because you can tell. Birds of a feather. They know each other."

The network of innocents encouraged and protected each other, until, one by one, they left Coffield. It turned out that Richard Miles did not kill one person and attempt to kill another. Steven Phillips did not rape eleven women at gunpoint. Victor Thomas did not sexually assault a white woman. Aside from these men, two others who frequented the library with them were also exonerated. As Richard Miles observed: "Coffield Unit was a cesspool for innocent men."

Perhaps it says something about prison culture that Spencer's best friend doubted his innocence at first, and something about prison friendship that it didn't really matter. William Earl Jackson arrived at the Coffield Unit in 1991, and his skill with scissors immediately landed him in the barbershop. Spencer swept up and dusted as a janitor in the front office, and in his downtime, he migrated to the barbershop, a chatty, amiable place. The first time he saw Spencer, Jackson opened the conversation prison style.

"What's you in for, man?"

"For crime I didn't commit."

"Robbery and a murder—you didn't do it?"

"No, I didn't do it."

"I was like, Yeah, right," Jackson said, and he let it go. Over the next few months, the two men became inseparable: Spencer tall, rail thin, with a soft drawl; Jackson, nicknamed Big Earl, tall, wide, with a deep, resonant voice. They lifted weights together; they had long, personal conversations and bouts of belly-shaking laughter. "He was like my blood brother," Jackson said. "It was like he was the good part of me, you know? He was what I aspired to be."

Jackson peppered Spencer with questions about his conviction and alibi, trying to trip him up and find a contradiction in his story. "But every time I done that, he would look at me. He'd say, 'Man, didn't I tell you I was innocent of this crime? The only way I would know something like that is if I was there, and I was not there.'

"I just didn't believe it," Jackson insisted—until the day Spencer mentioned an inmate named Michael Hubbard. "Then it all came back," Jackson said. "It was just like when you rewind a movie or something. I said, 'Ben, you're not going to believe this. I know Michael Hubbard.'"

In the summer of 1987, William Jackson and Michael Hubbard shared a tank at the Dallas County jail. They got to talking, and Hubbard said he was being questioned for a robbery-murder case. "He said, 'I'm not telling them suckers nothing,'" Jackson recalled. "He said, 'I do know that the guy they got, he didn't do it. But that's his tough luck.' That's exactly what he said. 'But that's his tough luck.' That conversation didn't mean anything to me. Until I met Ben."

On February 1, 1995, Kelvin Johnson was finishing the final weeks of his eight-year sentence for the string of restaurant robberies he committed with his friend Michael Hubbard. He wasn't sure whether they were still friends: Johnson had told the police in 1987 that Michael Hubbard, not Ben Spencer, had robbed and killed Jeffrey Young. Maybe Hubbard knew, maybe not; they had lived in different prisons and had never crossed paths.

"Me and some guys, we would go down to the library to get *The Dallas Morning News* and read," Johnson recalled. "And I'm reading this article about this Batman robber," the moniker given to the unknown assailant who had attacked ten men over fourteen weeks in a frenzy of violence. The newspaper published a map and a description:

> Dallas police say one or two men using wood or aluminum baseball bats as their primary weapons are attacking people in the Stemmons Corridor and northwest Dallas. Police describe the attackers as black, 25 to 40 years old, about 6 feet tall and weighing about 180 pounds. One is said to have short hair and a dark complexion; the other has worn dreadlocks and is lighter-skinned.[3]

Johnson remembered that Hubbard was released on parole some two years earlier, in December 1992. He studied the article, looking at the particulars of the attacks. Most took place outside office buildings late at night, early in the morning, or on a holiday. He read about the method of attack: hitting the victims on the head and, in some cases, cracking their skulls. He reflected on the attack on Jeffrey Young in March 1987. "It's the same MO!" he thought. "And the only thing I could think was: He got away with it in 1987, he thought he would get away with it in '95."

Johnson put down the paper and looked at his friends. "Fellows," he said, "that sure sounds like Michael Hubbard."

# Chapter 20

# BATMAN AND ROBBERY

+———+

**Who is behind this smashing of my Jeff's skull?**

—HARRY YOUNG, *in a letter to Benjamine Spencer*

When his car alarm sounded, Ben Carriker glanced at his watch: just after 10:00 p.m. It was Thursday night, January 19, 1995, and all his employees had long left the office in a warehouse district of Dallas. It wasn't unusual for him to work late. He owned the company, and he kept two guns there as protection.

Carriker, fifty-one years old, six foot four, and 220 pounds, opened his desk drawer and grabbed his Smith & Wesson .44-caliber Magnum revolver. He walked outside, into the empty parking lot, then descended the stairs and circled his plum-colored Cadillac Seville. He opened the doors and noticed his coat was missing and that the glove compartment was open. As he straightened up, out of the corner of his eye, he glimpsed someone barreling toward him.

"He had his head down," he said. "He was in a dead run."[1]

Carriker hesitated, reluctant to shoot, and the assailant slammed something—a pipe, a bat, something without edges—just above his left ear.

"Son of a bitch!" Carriker yelled.[2] Seven or eight more blows followed before he managed to wrestle the bat—he now knew it was a bat—into the crook of his arm. Carriker was a former marine, and despite lacerations

to his head and blood pouring down his face, he was a match for the lighter assailant. "At that point, I pulled him against—up against me, belt
buckle to belt buckle. We were stomach to stomach," he told a jury seventeen months later, as the defendant looked on impassively. "I wanted to
see who it was."[3]

Carriker managed to aim his gun and pull the trigger. But he missed—
or so he thought, because the assailant just kept beating him with the bat,
without so much as a twitch to betray that he had just been shot by the
world's most powerful handgun. Carriker tried again, placing his right
hand against the attacker's chest and placing the barrel of the gun under
his chin.

> Q: And then what did you do?
> A: I pulled the trigger.
> Q: And what happened?
> A: It clicked.[4]

"He went wild,"[5] Carriker recalled. The assailant slammed Carriker's
gun arm and hand with his bat again and again. Carriker's hand went
numb. He dropped the gun and fell to the ground. Now the assailant had
both the bat and the gun. He thought: I'm in trouble. I'm in real trouble.

"Then he stood up," Carriker testified. "He walked up to me. He got
down in my face and said, 'I'm gonna kill you, motherfucker.'"

> Q: And then what did he do?
> A: He pulled my gun out of his waistband, stuck it in my right eye. And
>    I said, "Man, don't kill me, 'cause I don't have any money to give you."
> Q: And what did he do?
> A: He pulled the trigger.
> Q: What happened?
> A: It clicked.[6]

Carriker managed to get up, push the assailant away, and run to the
street. He turned around to see his attacker staring at him before he, too,

ran away. Carriker called 911. The man had struck him with the bat seventy times. Carriker suffered deep lacerations on his skull and face, requiring a hundred stitches. More than a year after the attack, he had little sensation in his hand.

This ended the spree of attacks by the so-called "Batman robber," who had injured or nearly killed nine other men between October 1994 and January 1995.[7] The Batman did not experiment with his method, but kept to his script: He crouched in a stairwell or in the shadow of a remote office building and waited for the owner of a late-model car to leave the building. It was always late at night or early morning, on the weekend, or on a holiday, when the victim walked into a vacant parking lot. The attacker swung the aluminum bat like a driver sending a ball down the fairway, yelling "I'm going to kill you, motherfucker!," clubbing his victims again and again, as Detective Stan McNear put it, "not to subdue them but to kill them."[8] The raids were marked more by rage than profit; ten of them, in total, yielded less than $2,000. The assailant broke a jaw, an arm, a wrist, ribs; he lacerated a liver, cracked three skulls, and he left scars on the men's faces and arms from wounds that required stitches.[9]

Michael Hubbard made a strategic blunder when he prepared for what would be his final assault, the attack on the former marine, Ben Carriker. On that night, Hubbard dropped by the house of a coworker at International Marble Collections, where they loaded trucks and operated the forklift. Ivy Anderson was a friend from high school who had already served time for aggravated robbery. Did he want to "go hustling"? Hubbard asked. Anderson declined. One stint in prison for robbery sufficed.

The next day at work, Hubbard could not lift anything and eventually pulled Anderson aside. "He told me last night when he left from my house, he went to jack some guy," Anderson later testified.[10] "He told me he was in this guy's car and the alarm went off, and the guy came out." Hubbard hit the man with the bat and the man pulled out a gun. "And when he hit him with the bat, the gun went off. He told me after he took the gun away from him, he left, and on the way to the house, he felt something sting in his shoulder."[11] Hubbard had been shot and failed to notice.

Hubbard pulled off his shirt to show Anderson an entrance wound the size of a thumb in front of his left shoulder, and an exit wound the size of a grapefruit on his back. Hubbard mentioned that he had thrown the bat on the roof of the warehouse. Anderson was worried that suspicion would fall on him and told his parole officer, his wife, and his supervisor. That is how Detective Stan McNear found the bat, encased in bubble wrap, on the warehouse roof. He tracked down Hubbard in jail in Fort Worth for an unrelated crime. Hubbard confessed to three of the Batman robberies, including Ben Carriker's, and showed the detective his gunshot wound. But the detective had forgotten the police form for a written statement, and he left. The next day, Hubbard refused to leave his cell. McNear shrugged it off. "If he didn't intend to talk to me, I didn't want to go back," he explained.[12]

Hubbard's attorney, Karo Johnson, played his dismal hand as best he could—trying to counter Hubbard's confession, to undermine an informant with no motive to lie and a victim who identified him. His only ace: The DNA found on the bat matched neither Hubbard nor Ben Carriker. But the forensic findings did not sway the jury, which convicted Hubbard on June 27, 1996, and sentenced him to life in prison.

The Batman attacks on ten men in 1994 and 1995 seemed like echoes of the assault on Jeffrey Young in 1987. There is the modus operandi: the off-hours timing of the attacks, the deserted locations, the type of weapon, the types of victims, even the cracked skulls. Both times, Michael Hubbard had a punishing crack habit, according to friends. Both times, Hubbard tried to cajole a friend to help him with the crime, asking Ferrell Scott to "hit a lick" in 1987 and Ivy Anderson to "go hustling" in 1995. And both times, he described the crime to his friends—who then provided the information to the police, directly or indirectly.[13]

Years later, asked about the parallels between the fatal attack on Jeffrey Young and the violent assaults his client was convicted of eight years later, Karo Johnson replied: "My opinion is that Michael Hubbard was the person who likely did that murder." Johnson, who specialized in defending capital murder suspects, added: "He was the most dangerous person I ever represented."

The conviction of Michael Hubbard nurtured Ben Spencer's dream that the state would redirect its sights onto Hubbard. This was wishful thinking, of course. Why would the district attorney's office reopen a successful conviction when the victim's family and the appellate court were both satisfied? Then, one day in November 1996, manna fell from heaven in the form of a letter dropped on Spencer's bunk. The large, sloping block letters were written by an unfamiliar hand.[14]

*7 November 1996*

*Ben Spencer—*
*In March, it will be ten years since our son Jeff was murdered. Our family can never get over it. Your family can visit you and wait for you to get out. We can only go to the cemetery and pretend we are visiting with our son. . . .*
*I would like to come to Coffield to visit with you. Would that be possible?*
*How is your son? He must be getting tall and grown-up as years go by.*
*Enclosed is an envelope so you can write and let me know what you think.*

*Thank you,*
*Harry Young*

Spencer was thrilled beyond words. "I mean, this might be an opportunity," he remembered thinking. "This guy, if he can see that I'm telling the truth, he might be the very person who will dig deep enough to find out the truth, to really find out what's going on." He crafted his response carefully.

*November 15, 1996*

*Dear Mr. Young,*

    *I received your letter in the mail and was very touched that*
*you would write me. I hope that you don't reserve any ill feelings*
*towards me, but in case you do, I suppose that I can understand*
*your reason why. You all have suffered a great loss and I am*
*truly sympathetic to your loss. . . .*

    *You asked about coming to visit me. I think that's a*
*wonderful idea and I hope that you are sincere about coming.*
*I'm certain that you have your reasons for wanting to come and I*
*hope that I can be of some assistance to your need. . . .*

                             *Respectfully submitted,*
                             *Benjamine Spencer*
                             *#483713*

Thus began a nine-month correspondence between a grieving father and the man he believed killed his son. They would exchange fifteen more letters, with Spencer hoping to persuade the father of his innocence, and the father trying to extract from Spencer an explanation for this confounding tragedy.

On December 2, 1996, in a four-page letter, Harry Young inquired about logistics for a visit, and then confessed: *It is difficult for us whenever the holidays approach. We always think about what we had together, and what might have been. It must be difficult for you being away from your family and friends. I can relate to your separation from your son.*

The letter is surprisingly intimate. Harry Young, who served in the marines during World War II, reminisced about friends he had lost in the war, spoke of his Catholic faith, and then confided: *My wife is heartbroken. But we are trying to survive.* He closed by wishing Spencer well for the holidays.

Spencer, eager to keep the communication going, responded immediately: *I have often thought of you and your family down through the years past,* he wrote on December 8. *You are hurting, but now you've begun to reach beyond your pain. I sincerely hope that you will be blessed with the peace which you seek, if you haven't found it already.*

In his next letter, nine pages long and dated December 26, 1996, Harry Young wrote that their lives were haunted by the son not there. *A remarkable thing happens to me almost every night,* he wrote. *I wake up at about 3 a.m. The time my son was pronounced dead was 3:05 a.m.*

Then Harry Young got down to business. *I really do not want to visit to go over a lot of bullstuff. I'm not ready to forgive and forget at this point in time. What I would like to discuss is what really happened on that Sunday night March 22, 1987. I want to know the truth. I have studied the transcriptions of the trials. It is very, very difficult to determine who is telling the truth. I have the blowups of the autopsy photos. When I study them, I don't know what to think. I am devastated.* And perplexed: his son never would have risked his life over a car. *Jeff was such a chicken, he would have given you the keys.*

The elder Young needed to fill the void with explanations and create order out of chaos. And so he let loose some dangerous insinuations, and not for the first time, as he and his wife had voiced these concerns to the police. He wrote that his son's father-in-law had used some of proceeds of Jeffrey Young's insurance to emerge from bankruptcy. *In my heart of hearts, I believe someone, somewhere, put his killers up to it. It may not have been planned and things may have gotten out of control. I may die thinking these thoughts, and there may never be resolution.*

Young figured that Spencer was hired to frighten or injure or kill his son, and he appealed to Spencer's conscience to come clean. *I believe admission and acceptance of your responsibilities is the first and major step before forgiveness can be obtained.*

On January 7, 1997, Spencer acknowledged that he, too, harbored many unanswered questions, and he urged the elder Young to visit him. If only he would come to Coffield, Spencer thought, he could persuade Harry Young of his innocence.

As the correspondence unfolds, Harry Young's letters veer from empathy to accusation, from intimacy to boiling anger. In his letter dated February 14, 1997, he stated that he knew a mastermind plotted the death. *I want to search for the truth, and to find and prosecute the true culprit who is still at large. The enigma is how to do it? Who can fill in the pieces to the puzzle? Who can shed light on what happened? Who can point out who really did it? Most important of all in my mind is, who is behind this smashing of my Jeff's skull?* And then, settling on the simple explanation, he asked: *Why in God's name did you not ask Jeff for his keys if all you wanted was his BMW?*

On April 10, 1997, Spencer set out his case. *I did not commit this offense, therefore I am going to continue to declare my innocence in this case,* he began. Over thirty-two typed pages, Spencer chronicled his childhood, his friendship with Ray Lee and his brushes with the law, the jobs he had held, how he fell in love, married, and eagerly expected his baby. He laid out a minute-by-minute account of his whereabouts on March 22, 1987. He described his arrest, claimed that all the witnesses were lying, that the police barely investigated in their rush for a conviction. He detailed the problems with his first trial, and his second, and finally offered up the names of Michael Hubbard and Van Mitchell Spencer, whom he considered more viable suspects. *You spoke about your son Jeff being a coward and there is nothing wrong with being a coward. You see, if you knew me, you'd know that I am a coward too. I'm scared to take anything from anyone, you couldn't even talk me into going into a store to pick up something without my paying for it. I am not the person that you think I am!*

Spencer closes the letter, not realizing that his words will deeply offend Harry Young. More than a month later, Spencer receives the father's response.

> *I am outraged that you have the gall, the nerve, the insolence, to say that I admitted to you in a letter that my son was a coward (p. 23, line 7). Nothing could be further from the*

*truth. I said he was a chicken when I wrote on 26th December
1996. Do you have any idea of the difference? . . . I am so
outraged that I'm only seeing red, white and blue. If you were
old enough you may have been a protester of the war in Vietnam,
or you may have fled to Canada, or England like our president
did. Talk about lack of guts. Your kind makes me puke.*

*Harry Young*

Ben Spencer wrote three times over the next few weeks, apologizing
for his misstep, asking for forgiveness. In those silent weeks, he felt his
hopes deflate until, *poof,* a possible savior was gone, just like that. Harry
Young wrote a one-page letter on July 15, 1997. He had received Spencer's
letters, he said. *Although your notes are on the back burner for now, they are
still on the stove and percolating. I have not forgotten.*

Harry Young never wrote again. He did not visit the prison before he
died in 2000.

S ometime in the early 1990s, Spencer realized he was, for all practical
purposes, a dead man. He had exhausted all his appeals. A life sentence stretched before him. The only glint of hope was barely visible, years
away, when he would become eligible for parole in 2007. By then his son
would be twenty, and his young wife would have passed through her twenties and thirties alone, shuttling less and less frequently to Coffield, their
relationship like an eclipse, their paths crossing only a few times a year.

"I'm in here, she's out there. Just because my life had been taken from
me, I felt like, she didn't deserve what she was going through," Spencer
reflected. "That wasn't a life for anybody."

On one of Debra's visits, he asked her to divorce him. She refused.

"I really figured he would beat this case," she said. "Something was
bound to happen. And then he would come home soon and we could pick
up where we left off. We had a child to raise."

Debra was her husband's link to the outside world, to lawyers, politicians, investigators, anyone who might take up his defense. She placed money in his commissary account, allowing him to buy soap and toothpaste, paper and envelopes, cans of tuna, tortilla chips, and other special items to make a special dinner, or "spread," on Sunday nights. Month after month, he persisted asking for a divorce and she declined, in a conversational loop that grieved them both.

What changed everything was her father's ride to the laundromat one day in 1993, when he suffered a massive heart attack and died in the car. In the space of an hour, B.J. had lost the most constant man in his life and Debra had lost her emotional ballast. "And that's when the financial stuff really starts setting in," Debra recalled. "I had to help my mom. I had a baby." She had to think about her child's future. She brought divorce papers to Spencer and filed them on October 4, 1993.

"To be honest, it was a relief," Spencer said. "I really didn't want to lose her, but at the same time, I didn't want to hold her back."

Debra's visits dwindled. In late 1996, she met someone and married. She said the man was kind (if overly possessive), and wealthy, and he loved B.J. "I did it because I needed help," she explained. "B.J. wanted clothes, cars, games. He needed stuff for school, and all the activities that I had him in—swimming, karate. And I wanted my child to have everything. I didn't want him to miss a step."

If the divorce was a relief for Spencer, the remarriage was a sucker punch. "I really let her know how I felt," Spencer said decades later. "I said, 'I would've appreciated it if you had told me prior to getting married, because I feel like you just served this to me on a trash can lid.'" He sent all the photographs of Debra back to her; all the photos of the two of them together were mailed to his mother. He kept only the photos that included B.J. "It probably was silly. It's just the way I felt at the time."

Debra's second marriage lasted seventeen months. "I was still thinking about Ben and still wanting Ben to come home. And I knew where my heart was."

But Spencer knew nothing of her feelings or her divorce—only that he had lost his family. He would soon lose his best friend.

One morning in early 1999, William Jackson walked into Coffield's educational department to see what classes were available. He had earned a college degree and was taking every class he could. "Well, you're not going to be here to take any type of classes," the administrator said. "I'm not supposed to tell you this, but you've made parole."

Over the next three months, until his release, Jackson and Spencer spent all their time together, one inmate impatient for the days to pass, the other dreading their end. The day before Jackson was to leave Coffield, they arranged to meet in the gym; they had been working out religiously to whip the larger inmate into shape for the outside world.

"I came in there that day pumped to get my last workout on, because I walk out of here *tomorrow*," Jackson recalled. He looked around. No Spencer anywhere. "I look over into the basketball part of the gym, and he's sitting way over there in the corner on a bench. I go over there. I'm like, 'What's up, man?'" Jackson's voice grew husky in the telling. "He's just looking sad, and still it's not even dawning on me. He says, 'Man, we're not working out today. You go home tomorrow.'"

Jackson sat down beside his friend. "He thanked me for being there for him. Being a person that he could look up to. He thanked *me*. I was like, 'Ben, I thank *you*, man. Never met nobody like you, man.'" Jackson took a shuddering breath. "And we cried and cried and cried just like we were two little boys, two brothers that's gonna be separated. I've likened it to being in slavery. And I was leaving a plantation, I got my freedom and I was leaving him behind. That's the way it was. It was the happiest and saddest day in my life."

The next morning, Spencer was waiting for Jackson in the common area, ready to accompany him as far as he was permitted. After a decade in prison, Jackson carried only a few small personal items. Everything else—a fan for the summer, a stinger to heat water—he had given away, a prison ritual. The two friends walked in silence, slowly, stretching the time. Jackson climbed into the bus and settled by the window. Then the engine hiccupped to life and the Blue Bird bus jerked away. Jackson watched his best friend grow smaller and smaller until the bus turned a corner and he disappeared.

*Chapter 21*

# DOWN TO THE STUDS

+——+

**I walked away thinking, We can't leave this man behind.**

—Jim McCloskey, *after meeting Ben Spencer*

May 20, 2001, was a Sunday, and as usual for a weekend, every seat was taken, more than a dozen people shoulder to shoulder, facing the white-clad inmates on the other side of the Plexiglas divider. The barks of laughter and shouted phrases of affection ricocheted around the room. Eventually, Ben Spencer walked through the door from the prison and settled himself in front of his visitor.

Spencer had been corresponding with Centurion Ministries for a dozen years. He never asked for a commitment; he never complained about the passing years; he answered their questions with detail that suggested copious notes and a photographic memory.

Jim McCloskey, the visitor, inquired about Spencer's prison life, his record at Coffield, his childhood. Spencer peppered McCloskey with questions about Centurion's other clients, some of whom he knew.

"Ben, do you know why I'm here?" McCloskey finally asked.

"Are you here because you want to talk to me about my case?"

"Yes, but *do you know why I'm here?*" he repeated, and perhaps sensing that Spencer could not name a hope that might dissolve, not again, McCloskey said: "Let me tell you why I'm here. From this day forward, you are a client of Centurion Ministries. We're not going to stop fighting for you until you walk out of this place."

As McCloskey remembered it, Spencer barely moved but for the smile that lit up his face. Centurion would hire a lawyer and an investigator, he explained, and they would track down witnesses and any other evidence. Spencer would work with them from prison, providing details and suggesting leads. After an hour, a guard tapped the inmate on the shoulder, and McCloskey watched his new client disappear. "I walked away thinking, We can't leave this man behind."

"For the first time, I began to have hope of one day walking out of prison and being a free man again," Spencer said. For the first time, someone with influence believed him.

T hey became partners, Spencer working his sources on the inside, McCloskey following up on the outside. Together they assembled an alternative narrative, one they believed to be more plausible than the story that had convicted Spencer in 1988.

The task of telling that narrative to a court fell to attorney Cheryl Wattley. A former federal prosecutor, Wattley had worked with McCloskey to win the freedom of Kerry Max Cook, who had come within days of execution before he was finally released. In contrast with the jaw-clenching experience of trying to save an innocent man from execution, Ben Spencer's case would be "straightforward," McCloskey assured her: Run a few fingerprints through the system, talk to a few witnesses, prove that another man had committed the crime, and Bob's your uncle. Decades later, Wattley laughed at her naivete. Still, she understood the system in a visceral way that Jim McCloskey could not.

In the 1950s, Cheryl's parents, Leona and Frank Brown, decided they wanted a little land where they could raise their only child. They found the perfect property in Bethany, outside New Haven, Connecticut. "You won't be happy living there," the realtor suggested after they contacted her. "All the Negroes in this town live over on this other street." For the next several Sundays, Mr. and Mrs. Brown knocked on every door on the street, introduced themselves, and said that they wanted to buy some acreage nearby.

"My mother had more education than all of those people, collectively," Wattley added. Fine with us, the would-be neighbors said. "So they went back to the realtor and said, 'We found no opposition. Sell us the property.'"

They were the first Blacks to move into the neighborhood, and Cheryl Brown was one of the first Blacks to attend an elite preparatory school nearby. After graduating from Smith College, she attended Boston University College of Law, a plan she hatched when she was nine years old, after watching the news one night with her parents. On May 3, 1963, police unleashed dogs on civil rights protesters in Birmingham, Alabama, on the orders of Bull Connor, the state commissioner of public safety. Cheryl noticed a girl about her age standing in the melee, and declared to her parents, "'If she can face that dog for the laws to be changed, then I can make sure everybody knows that the laws have been changed,'" she recalled. "And that has always been the source of my wanting to be a lawyer." Wattley served as an assistant United States attorney in Connecticut and later in Dallas. She was the first Black woman to be nominated for a federal judgeship there. But this was Texas, and she was a Democrat, and she needed to put her daughters through college, so she turned to private practice. Now she teaches at the University of North Texas at Dallas College of Law. Withdrawing from consideration for the federal judiciary was a "blessing in disguise," since she was a free agent when Jim McCloskey came knocking.

Sometime after Debra's fleeting second marriage ended, in 1998, she and Ben struck up a correspondence. It began cautiously, formally, but by 2002, the tone had turned hopeful, and familiar.

*April 24, 2002*

*Hi Love,*
  *God's blessings of love be yours as I address these few lines to you. I hope that all is still well. As for me, still blessed and fortunate to know that God is watching over.*[1]

Ben and Debra reawakened dormant feelings: friendship, surely, and affection—but also, improbably, *love*. In these early, tentative lines, Spencer dared to peek over the prison walls and imagine a life beyond.

> *I'm not trying to pressure you into anything. I just know that*
> *I would like to try to pick up the pieces between us. I still have*
> *mad, crazy love for you and I think that you still love me. If so,*
> *time and space shouldn't mean a thing.*
>
>                               *Love the guy who still wants you!*
>                               *Ben*

Many of Ben's letters to Debra were destroyed in a fire in her mother's garage. All her letters to him were accidentally thrown out at the Dallas jail. The twenty-five hundred existing pages that Spencer sent from prison did not reveal much about life in Coffield. Inmate #483713 refused to write about the food, the gang fights, the indignities of living with five thousand convicts. But these letters did unveil the life inside the mind and heart of Ben Spencer.

B y the time Centurion accepted Spencer's case in 2001, fourteen years had passed since Jeffrey Young was robbed, beaten, and killed. As Wattley and McCloskey began to inspect the evidence against Ben Spencer, they found that the case was held together with little more than duct tape. "It looks like a thorough investigation in the sense that they're talking to a lot of people," Wattley said. "It doesn't look like a thorough investigation when you see what they actually found."

There was no witness to the assault, no physical evidence, just three incentivized witnesses and a jailhouse snitch. With that as their baseline, Spencer's new team embarked on their strategy of demolition and reconstruction. Wattley explained that in Spencer's case, as in every effort to free an innocent prisoner, you have twin goals. "You're challenging the evidence that the government produced, and at the same time you're putting forth evidence that shows that Ben is actually innocent." It's a little like renovating a dilapidated house. They would dismantle the district attorney's case down to the studs and erect a new theory that, they hoped, would identify the true killer.

To that end, they trained their sights on the eyewitnesses, beginning with the prosecution's star witness, Gladys Oliver. On May 1, 2002, Jim McCloskey knocked on her apartment with a bouquet of flowers. "As soon as she saw me, she came wheeling to the door," a three-hundred-pound woman in a wheelchair, according to McCloskey's notes from the interview. "She kept saying, 'I don't want to talk about it, I just don't want to talk about it.' She said she didn't lie." Oliver became upset, complained of having a bad heart and asthma, and popped a pill during their conversation. Finally, McCloskey rose to leave. "Tell Ben, 'I'm sorry that it happened,'" she said.

With Gladys Oliver holding to her story, Spencer's legal team turned to the money trail. They believed that Oliver had lied for twenty-five thousand dollars in reward money and persuaded two teenagers to confirm her account. McCloskey had heard rumors that Oliver had received ten thousand dollars of the reward. "That is like hitting the lottery, especially for somebody in Gladys's station in life economically and socially," he said. If he could track down receipts or bank statements, he could show that Gladys Oliver had lied in court. That would be automatic grounds for a new trial. It would suggest that the prosecutor, Keith Anderson, had also lied in his closing arguments, when he said: "All of this talk about money. Five hundred and eighty dollars, not twenty-five thousand dollars. Do you think five hundred and something dollars is worth her putting her life on the line and in that neighborhood—lying on someone?"

After pursuing every lead, McCloskey could not find records proving that Oliver had received any part of the twenty-five-thousand-dollar reward. But in the course of their investigation, McCloskey said, they stumbled on a critical fact about Oliver: "She was a thief."[2]

Prosecutor Andy Beach had portrayed Oliver as a law-abiding if nosy grandmother when he told the jury: "I'll guarantee you, if . . . Gladys

Oliver had ever been convicted of a crime, you would have found out about that."[3] The prosecutor either knew about her history—a felony conviction for theft, shoplifting, and passing a bad check—and deliberately misled the jury; or he should have known about her record before trial and avoided the misstatement. Similarly, if Spencer's attorney, Frank Jackson, had merely dropped by the Dallas County clerk's office in the courthouse, he would have found Oliver's three convictions. He could have used the information to impugn her credibility before the jury, and offer a motive for her testimony. It was a missed opportunity, one of many.

Failing to find contrition or hard evidence of corruption by Gladys Oliver, Centurion turned to science to challenge the claims of all three neighbors. "It doesn't take a genius to figure out that it was impossible for the witnesses, or any human being, to have seen Ben Spencer and Robert Mitchell exit the victim's car, because of the darkness and distance that night," McCloskey said. "Humanly impossible."

On March 25, 2003, Dr. Paul Michel traveled to West Dallas and studied the crime-scene area between 8:00 p.m. and 11:00 p.m. Michel was a forensic scientist specializing in human vision, and he chose that date and time to most closely mirror the conditions on March 22, 1987. Michel's question: Was it possible for the neighbors to identify *anyone* on that moonless night? He measured from the alley to Gladys Oliver's bedroom window, to Jimmie Cotton's kitchen window, and to Charles Stewart's house. He considered the lighting, the distance, and the fact that the perpetrators were moving fast, all of which would impede the ability to identify a person.

Michel found it "impossible"[4] that Jimmie Cotton could have identified the perpetrators, because the young man was looking at a dark alley from a brightly lit kitchen and would see only his own reflection. Charles Stewart's position nearly a football field away made identification "impossible"[5] as well. Gladys Oliver's house had been razed, so Michel's calculations were inexact. No matter. She could not have identified Spencer, he stated. A person could be no farther than twenty-five feet away to recognize a person on a moonless night. Jimmie Cotton was 93 feet away; Gladys Oliver, at least 113 feet; and Charles Stewart, at least 241 feet away from the alley. The scientist concluded that all three witnesses were lying.[6]

But one witness—known to police and known to Spencer's attorney—did see one of the perpetrators up close. On the evening of March 22, 1987, Sandra Brackens was on the phone with a friend, the long landline cord stretched out to the steps of the front porch. She heard the insistent wailing of sirens until they fell silent a block away. Curious, the fourteen-year-old walked to the intersection to investigate. She noticed an expensive car idling in the alley with the trunk open and the parking lights on. She had barely returned to her porch when a man ran directly in front of her, carrying a silver jambox on his shoulder and another boxlike object in his other hand. She was less than twenty feet away, and the nearby streetlight lit him up like an actor on a stage. He was five foot eleven or six feet tall, a Black man wearing a black leather jacket, pants, and cap.[7]

"I know both Ben Spencer and Robert Mitchell from the neighborhood," she swore in an affidavit, after McCloskey tracked her down.[8] "Although I didn't get a close look at his face, I am certain that the man who ran by my house carrying a silver jambox was neither Robert nor Ben." Mitchell weighed approximately three hundred pounds at the time. The man she saw was slender, but much shorter than Spencer, who is six foot four. She added that Spencer is light-skinned and the man that she saw had a dark complexion.

When the two men were arrested, Brackens stated, she visited Spencer's mother.[9] "I told her I would do whatever I could to help Ben," an offer that Spencer's mother conveyed to his attorney. He dismissed her.

Hi Love, I hope and pray that this letter finds you and B.J. doing fine. I realize that it's getting a little redundant, but I think of you two most all of the time," Spencer's July 19, 2005, letter began. After a few pages of musings, Spencer asked Debra to do him "a huge favor."

> *In the event that anything should happen to me, I don't want*
> *you or B.J. to be consumed with hate or bitterness. I don't want*
> *either of you to demand that justice be served. Bitterness and*
> *hatred are like a cancer, they will eat away at you until they*
> *destroy.*
>    *It's just like my accusers, I don't hold any ill feelings toward*
> *any of them. I hate the fact that they lied on me, but I don't hate*
> *any of them. "Vengeance is mine, and I will repay, says the*
> *Lord." Often times we want to put ourselves in the place of God*
> *and take matters into our own hands; what a shame because*
> *we'll have to give an account for our sins one day. What I want*
> *you to do for me is simple: Be at peace because it is far more*
> *rewarding.*

Once the Centurion team felt confident that they had neutralized the neighbors' accounts, they zeroed in on the jailhouse informant. Danny Edwards had testified at trial that Spencer had confessed to robbing and killing Jeffrey Young. Never mind that virtually every one of Edwards's details conflicted with the state's theory. Never mind that some of his assertions were just plain wacky: that Spencer had rubbed his fingers on the cement sidewalk to erase his fingerprints; that Spencer grabbed the victim by the tie when he was wearing a jogging outfit; that Spencer planned to kill a witness by injecting her with mercury. "The content of Danny Edwards's confession was insane," McCloskey said, "yet they used this."

The jurors believed the jailhouse informant because they thought he had no incentive to lie. Guided by the prosecutor, Edwards testified that he had worked out his deal before meeting Spencer; therefore he received no benefit in exchange for his testimony. "Just trouble," he had said.

"That was an outright, blatant lie," Wattley noted. Edwards did trade his testimony for a lenient sentence. The jail logs showed that Danny Edwards did not have a lawyer when Ben Spencer joined his tank on March 27, 1987, so he could not have cut a deal before they met. Edwards was indeed looking to shave down his sentence when he spoke with Detective Briseno three days later. Not until two weeks after he met Spencer, and ten days after he met the detectives, did Danny Edwards secure his plea agreement. "And he got a sweet deal," McCloskey noted.

Danny Edwards was facing twenty-five years for aggravated robbery, but after talking with the police and the prosecutor, his sentence was reduced to ten years for non-aggravated robbery.[10] In fact, Edwards walked out of jail two months after he testified against Spencer, having served only fifteen months. The documents proved that Edwards had lied under oath, in all likelihood with the prosecutor's knowledge, in exchange for convicting Ben Spencer, McCloskey said. "Danny Edwards bought his freedom with this false testimony."

This matters because Danny Edwards was the only witness to link Ben Spencer to the violent attack on Jeffrey Young. If the jury knew Edwards had an incentive to say what the prosecutor needed him to say, they might have looked more critically at his testimony. Beyond that, Edwards's testimony not only put Spencer in prison but ensured that he would stay there: The Texas appellate court relied exclusively on Edwards's narrative to uphold the conviction.

When Centurion investigators tracked down Danny Edwards, he freely admitted the lie. In a nearly illegible note, he wrote: "Spencer never told me about no murder case. . . . I was set up by the DA, telling me Ben said I'd commit a lot of robbery so I need to get him first. I am very sorry that Ben lost so much of his life because of people like that's don't have no money, and being force to lie on other, or be send to do a lot of time if we've don't cooperate with DA." His affidavit, signed August 7, 2002, was easier on the eye: "When I said that Spencer had never talked to me about having committed any murder, the police officer got upset and went off on me," Edwards began. "Spencer never told me anything about committing a murder. . . . I went along with the Affidavit because I had been threatened and told that the police would see to it that I served even more time in prison."

One of the tragedies of Spencer's conviction, Wattley said, is that all of this evidence was sitting there, had Spencer's attorney Frank Jackson only looked for it. "While we developed and strengthened the evidence, the seeds of the evidence were present in the 1988 trial. They just weren't nurtured and cultivated by the defense team."

Frank Jackson took a dim view of that particular claim. In a letter to Centurion, he pointed out that after his first conviction was vacated, Spencer was given a choice between accepting a deal that would see him released in three or four years, or going to trial.[11] "He chose a new trial, the state hammered him, and now he has questions about my representation. Never fails."

For four years, Spencer's legal team located new witnesses, gathered affidavits, and corralled recantations. They regularly checked in with their client, letting him know every victory they scored. He reveled in this hive of activity, and even Ben Spencer, ever steady and phlegmatic, could not temper his hopes. Giddiness seeped into his letters to his ex-wife. "I feel like a little boy inside when you're around," he wrote on October 21, 2004, after one of her visits to Coffield. "I'm nearly certain that you have some type of a spell on me, but hey, I'm not complaining."

Spencer wrote Debra at 1:00 a.m., at 6:00 a.m., at noon, he wrote every day, he wrote twice a day, he wrote one-page letters but more often five- or ten-page letters. Up, down, unhappy, elated, burdened, faithful, frustrated, grateful—no emotion escaped his pen. He wrote that his case was moving forward nicely and that he hoped he would be out by summer, in time for B.J.'s high school graduation. Mainly, he spoke of love.

"I've never stopped seeing you as my wife," he wrote on November 25, 2004. "Debra, I want us to have the wedding that I really wanted back then. It doesn't have to be big, but I want to be surrounded by family and friends, so that they can witness our love and commitment to each other. Yes, I am asking you, 'Would you marry me?'"

# Chapter 22

# A NEW STORY

+——+

**I'm afraid of dead bodies.
I never murdered anybody.**

—Michael Hubbard

On June 30, 2001, Ben Spencer sent a letter to another inmate in Coffield Unit. Could they meet somewhere to talk privately, perhaps the barbershop, where Spencer worked the afternoon shift? Spencer wrote that he had in his possession the unsigned affidavit that the inmate, Kelvin Johnson, had given to police in 1987, one that implicated Michael Hubbard in the assault on Jeffrey Young. Centurion Ministries had taken on his case, he explained, and was intrigued by Johnson's account.

"After the founder James (Jim) McCloskey read your statement to investigator Briseno, he asked me to talk to you about your statement," Spencer wrote. "I don't wish to make any trouble for you or anything like that. All I desire is to find out the truth regarding this offense and if you can help us do that, I would greatly appreciate that."

Spencer and Johnson talked twice after that in the chow hall, the first time briefly but long enough for Johnson to confirm that Hubbard had told him about the assault. Ten days later, Spencer ran into him in the chow hall again. "Johnson then told me that he has been praying about this since he had talked to me, I told him that I had been doing the same," Spencer wrote in a July 15, 2001, letter to McCloskey. Spencer mentioned that Centurion Ministries was trying to locate copies of the fingerprints that had been lifted from the victim's car and office. "Johnson then stated to me that they're Hubbard's fingerprints, that this was the reason that he kept telling Robert [Mitchell] to chill out, that the truth would come out. I informed him that both me and Robert had hoped that the truth would come out, but that it hadn't"—after fourteen years—"and that's what was bothering us."

Kelvin Johnson did not commit at that time to coming forward or talking to Jim McCloskey, but Spencer had planted the idea.

Having, to their mind, successfully discredited the state's witnesses and razed the prosecution narrative that Ben Spencer killed Jeffrey Young, McCloskey and his colleagues began to construct a new story: The true perpetrator was Michael Hubbard. Hubbard's name never came up in Spencer's criminal trial. The prosecutor had no incentive to introduce an alternative suspect, and Spencer's defense attorney chose to adhere to his simple alibi defense, rather than confusing the jury by mentioning Hubbard's name. It was a puzzling strategy, but Frank Jackson argued that calling a "hoodlum" like Kelvin Johnson to testify about Hubbard's confession could backfire.

Inside the prison, and among some who lived in West Dallas at the time, Michael Hubbard was widely linked with the 1987 killing. In his June 5, 2001, letter to Centurion, Spencer listed several inmates who had told him so.[1] McCloskey and an investigator, Paul Henderson, tracked down every person Spencer mentioned. Most of the men were merely passing on rumors. But one inmate stood out: Ferrell Scott. Scott had not been mentioned at trial or in any of the police reports; he was a completely new witness. Spencer related a conversation the two men had back in 1987. "He stated that Michael Hubbard had committed this offense," Spencer wrote. "He did not go into any specific detail." Perhaps, Spencer hinted, Ferrell Scott might be worth a visit.

McCloskey found Scott in prison in 2001.[2] Discreetly, for visitors and guards were all around, Scott provided new details about the night of March 22, 1987. Together, they drafted an affidavit.[3] Scott said that his close friend Michael Hubbard killed Jeffrey Young, and then described Hubbard's plan to rob Ninfa's, but "things were hot at that time with the police," so they demurred. He described Hubbard's returning several hours later with a Seiko watch, a ring, and "a radio or something like that," and exchanging them for crack. He described the conversation at Kelvin Johnson's apartment, when Hubbard confessed that he had robbed the white man and tried to put him in the trunk of his car. "The dude didn't want to get in the trunk of his BMW so Michael busted him up-side the head." Hubbard discussed driving to West Dallas, and how "somehow the trunk opened and the man got out on the street." Hubbard said he had ditched the car in an alley.

Later, when Spencer told Scott that he had been accused of the murder, Scott was "extremely troubled." He drove to the police station with his lawyer and told the detectives that Spencer and Mitchell "were sitting in jail for something they had not done." They did not ask him to sign an affidavit, nor did they ever follow up. "Knowing Michael as I do, he wasn't bragging or making this up," Scott wrote in the affidavit. "Michael did not brag about things that did not happen."

Informants have short life spans in prison. Both Ferrell Scott and Kelvin Johnson knew they were risking their reputations and their lives by coming forward. Kelvin Johnson waited until he was out on parole before meeting with McCloskey. Ferrell Scott stored an unsigned draft of his affidavit inside his locker, which he planned to sign and execute later. But Michael Hubbard wielded influence within prison, just as he had on the outside. Friends of Hubbard learned of the document, McCloskey said, "and they threatened to kill Ferrell if he executed that affidavit." Scott waited until he made parole, then signed it. "Ferrell Scott and Kelvin Johnson, they're heroes in my mind."

"I think about Ben all the time," Ferrell Scott mused. It was August 16, 2017, and I had reached him at the federal prison in Allenwood, Pennsylvania, where he was serving life for possessing (a lot of) marijuana. In

West Dallas, he said, people felt bad for Ben Spencer. His conviction made no sense. "How do you just go from never doing nothing to murdering somebody? It's a progression. You don't just step off the porch and start killing people."

"How sure are you that Michael Hubbard killed Jeffrey Young?" I asked.

"One hundred and ten percent," he said. "I mean, he did it. It's not like it's a controversy, you know? It's not like, I *think* he did it, or he *may have* did it. He done it. He done it. And he knows he did it. I had nothing against Mike, I didn't want to tell on him, but I didn't want Ben in there for something he didn't do."

"Ferrell, no offense, but why should I believe a convicted felon?"

"I might be a convicted felon, but I'm not a liar," he said. "This is not something that I made up. I'm not saying that I won't lie. I would lie for my family or my kids or my mother, if they were in some kind of trouble. I would lie for them. I'm not gonna lie for Michael Hubbard."


On October 2, 2002, Jim McCloskey visited the Hughes Unit, a maximum-security prison where Michael Hubbard was serving a life sentence for the Batman assaults. According to McCloskey's interview notes, Hubbard almost stood him up. The inmate worried that McCloskey was trying to frame him for Jeffrey Young's murder. "I prayed over it and decided to come out for your visit," he told McCloskey, mentioning he had become a Christian and had a "minister's license."

"It really upset me that my name would ever be mentioned with the Young murder," Hubbard said. "I'm afraid of dead bodies. I never murdered anybody." Hubbard insisted he made the same denial to two detectives who interviewed him for about ten minutes in 1987. (There is no record of that in police files, just as none exists of Ferrell Scott's alleged meeting.) "They asked me if I did it and I said, 'Hell, no!'"

Hubbard asked McCloskey if he thought that he, Hubbard, was involved. "Well, Michael, the thought has occurred to me," McCloskey replied. He noted that there was a "striking similarity" between the brutality of the attack on Jeffrey Young and the Batman victims. He pointed out the modus operandi was nearly identical, with the assailant wielding a blunt instrument like a bat and targeting a particular type of victim: businessmen, working in isolated areas, late at night, with upscale cars parked in front of their offices.

"He was silent for a little bit," McCloskey recalled. "He was thinking. Then he said: 'I'm not the Batman.'"

Asked for his impression of Hubbard, McCloskey laughed: "This is Young's killer. There's no doubt in my mind. *I'm not the Batman.* What kind of defense is that?"

While Spencer's time in Coffield crawled by, life was moving at breakneck speed for his son. Sequestered in a prison two hours away, Spencer became a footnote in B.J.'s life. He had longed to teach his son to swim, to ride a bike, to learn how to rebuild the engine of a car. He urged Debra to let B.J. find his way, even if he made mistakes. "By sheltering him, he may feel that he has missed out on something and the curiosity can lead him down the wrong path."[4]

On those rare occasions when his son visited, Spencer tried to engage in father-son conversations about school and sports, his relationship with girls and with his mother, his plans after high school, maybe college. But these deeper topics never caught. "I really love my dad," B.J. said years later, "and I wish I had a stronger bond with him. But at the same time, I always looked at it like, *I don't want to burden you with my life when you already have a lot of stuff burdening you with your life.* So, it's like, I've never really wanted to make him feel sad."

What B.J. did not say, but Spencer intuited, is that he already had a father in Debra's ex-husband, a man who attended every birthday party, sporting event, and school ceremony. "He'd say, 'How's your dad treating you?'" B.J. recalled. "He didn't ever call him my stepdad. I'd be like, 'He's doing good.' And he'd be like, 'You know *I'm* your real dad, right?' I'm like, 'Yeah, I know you my real dad. I love you. I mean, you made me. There's no comparison to that.'" B.J. tried to avoid discussing his stepfather. "It's like, what you want me to say? He's great and he's doing everything you're supposed to be doing? When I already know that you wish you was here and that you could do stuff that he's doing."

Spencer was left to offering fatherly advice by letter. He warned his son that a life can so easily go off the rails, sometimes through no fault of one's own. He told him that a few wrong choices can be catastrophic for a Black man. "In this place are guys who thought that they had it all figured out, that they could beat the system, but sadly they were wrong," he wrote B.J. "Losing your freedom is a high price to pay and I plead with you my son to stay clear of people and activities that will cost you your liberty."[5]

The fact that he had missed his son's entire childhood overwhelmed him. "Our son is about to step into adulthood and I never had the opportunity to be a real part of his life," Spencer wrote Debra a few days after his son's nineteenth birthday.[6] "I missed everything."

Centurion's investigation gathered new facts plucked from police notes, trial transcripts, autopsy and lab reports, and a blizzard of witness interviews. "I bet we contacted over a hundred people. Easily," McCloskey said. When the team stepped back, the pieces came together like a Georges Seurat painting and coalesced into a firm conclusion: The Dallas police had arrested the wrong men and allowed the killer to slip through its net.

On September 22, 2004, Centurion filed its writ of habeas corpus and asked the court to grant Ben Spencer a new trial. (Robert Mitchell had died in July 2003, two years after he was released on parole.) Its argument was simple: The state's witnesses were lying and the police had failed to identify a more plausible suspect. McCloskey believed the evidence of Spencer's innocence was "compelling and overwhelming." The filing drew extensive coverage in *The Dallas Morning News*, raising Deb's hopes and

Ben's credibility among the guards and inmates. But McCloskey knew the next battle would be trench warfare, where they might gain a few yards of ground, only to be pushed back.

There was cause for optimism from another corner, however. Spencer would be up for parole in March 2007, twenty years after his incarceration. If he persuaded the parole board to release him, Debra hoped, he could fight to clear his name from the outside. They could remarry and become a family again. Once again, the chance of an easy exit was slim— not because of the state's intransigence, but because of Spencer's moral compass.

"Baby, I'm not trying to steal your joy," he wrote her on December 17, 2005. "I want to be out of this place more than anyone else wants me out of here. But it's important that I be very honest with you. There is no telling how much longer I will be in here." To get parole, he said, you must accept responsibility for the crime. "I will never accept responsibility for a crime that I did not commit. I don't want there to be any surprises for you. I know that you want a man who can be there with you and I can understand that. But truth has always meant more to me than my freedom."

Spencer's best prospect resided not with the court or the parole board, but with the district attorney of Dallas County, Bill Hill. In theory, a prosecutor wears the professional equivalent of bifocals. In his downward gaze, the litigator focuses on the fine inculpatory details of his case: that the defendant sitting in the courtroom has brought harm to another with this weapon and that motive, he must be run to ground and removed from society with clinical dispatch. But when the same prosecutor lifts his gaze, he becomes something else entirely: a minister of justice who pursues the truth over a courtroom victory.

It was the latter prosecutor, the truth seeker, that McCloskey and Wattley hoped to meet when they sat down with the district attorney in 2004. Hill had the power to review and reopen Spencer's case, and there was no shame in doing so, since it was his predecessor who had overseen Spencer's trial. The two laid out their case, and they included a polygraph conducted by the most respected expert in Texas, Rick Holden. While polygraphs are not admissible at trial, Dallas police and prosecutors routinely employ them to gauge the credibility of witnesses. Holden had examined Spencer in 2003 and told McCloskey that the score for Ben Spencer's truthfulness was "one of the highest I've ever seen."[7]

The district attorney appeared unimpressed and was inclined to oppose their petition for a new trial. "Here we've got the preeminent polygraph examiner—who you all use—saying that Ben is truthful," Wattley remarked incredulously. "And even that doesn't get your attention, even that doesn't spark an interest?"

Yet Spencer's team felt confident as they ramped up for battle. Confident, that is, until they discovered that the one piece of evidence they needed to decisively win the war to come had been lost by the state.

*Chapter 23*

# LOST IN SPACE

+———+

**It was pure serendipity that the
evidence was located.**

—REBECCA BROWN, *Director of Policy, Innocence Project*

In January 2006, District Attorney Bill Hill formally opposed Ben Spencer's petition for a new trial. In its 138-page rebuttal, accompanied by supporting documents, the state countered each piece of Centurion's evidence. As to the jailhouse informant's statement that he felt pressured to concoct a confession from Spencer, "that statement is false," Detective Jesus Briseno responded in an affidavit. "At no time during the meeting with Danny Edwards . . . did I coerce Danny Edwards to testify falsely against Benjamine Spencer."[1] The neighbors, too, held fast to their accounts. "If I was asked to testify today about what I saw that night, my testimony would be the same as it was when I testified in Benjamine Spencer's trial," Gladys Oliver swore in an affidavit on January 19, 2005. In his affidavit five months later, Jimmie Cotton made the same pledge, literally word for word, suggesting theirs was not the hand that penned the statements.[2] (Charles Stewart had died in a drug deal gone bad before Centurion began its investigation.)[3] Michael Hubbard was not a viable suspect, the state asserted. The friends who identified him were criminals and liars: Kelvin Johnson failed a polygraph (true), and Ferrell Scott never visited the police to accuse Hubbard (disputed).

With their dueling memos and exhibits, the state and Centurion portrayed two irreconcilable views of that March night. What they needed was something that would be immune to the cognitive biases on either side. They needed forensic evidence.

Spencer's case enjoyed an abundance of forensic evidence. Police had lifted fingerprints from Jeffrey Young's checkbook, his driver's license, a chrome railing, and two pieces of paper. They lifted more still from his car: inside the front and back windows on both sides and on the back seat; more promising still, a palm print on the trunk of the car and on the roof on the driver's side. The palm prints did not match those of Ben Spencer or Robert Mitchell, but they had yet to be compared to Michael Hubbard's. The technology used to match fingerprints had galloped ahead in the decade and a half since Young's murder. "Touch DNA" was developed in the early 2000s, and a few skin cells might identify Jeffrey Young's killer. "All we have to do is get the fingerprints that were taken from the car and find out who they match to, and we'll be able to get Ben home," Wattley recalled Jim McCloskey assuring her.[4] "It seemed pretty cut and dried. We were going to have forensic evidence and it was going to be wonderful."

But when she asked the police for the prints, "they couldn't find them. They could never find them again."

The greatest flaw in the prosecution's case—the failure to find physical evidence connecting Ben Spencer to the crime—now haunted the defense. They knew that the evidence had been collected, and according to police records, none of the items with fingerprints or possible DNA had been discarded. They knew the property tag number. They worked up and down the chain of command, pleading with the police to make a good-faith effort to find the physical evidence. Every time, the police claimed the evidence had been misplaced and could not be located. "I just find it interesting that three fourths of what we look for is no longer findable," Wattley observed.

Missing evidence is the single most overlooked and pernicious obstacle to freeing innocent prisoners. It plagues the criminal justice system and traps untold numbers of innocent people in prison. It is especially cruel, because often the prisoner knows that the source of his vindication did exist at one time and perhaps still does, but no one will bother to look.

From the moment Rebecca Brown joined the Innocence Project, lost evidence became her obsession. "I would sit up at night and think to myself, How can we possibly settle these claims of innocence when we have to close *a quarter of our cases* because evidence just simply can't be located?" Barry Scheck said that the Innocence Project could have won "double, triple the number of exonerations" if they had been able to locate the evidence. "Missing evidence is legion," said Mark Godsey, who heads the Ohio Innocence Project. "It's almost like a joke in the innocence world."

The first death-row inmate exonerated by DNA would have died in prison but for the kind of luck that visits very few prisoners. Kirk Bloodsworth, who was convicted of raping and killing a nine-year-old girl near Baltimore, Maryland, in 1985, received a death sentence but won a new trial after his lawyer discovered the prosecution had hidden exculpatory evidence.[5] He was tried again, convicted again, and sentenced to two life terms. In 1989, he learned of the exonerating power of DNA and sought to find the evidence from the crime scene. He knew his DNA would be absent.

His lawyer requested the evidence from the police department, the prosecutor's office, the evidence room at the courthouse, the crime lab. No luck—until the lawyer bumped into the court clerk in the courthouse. "Oh, I know where that is," the clerk said. He explained that the judge in the second trial had been uncomfortable with the verdict and held on to some evidence.

"It was in the judge's chambers, in his closet, in a cardboard box, in a paper bag, sitting on the floor," Bloodsworth recalls. "It was all the DNA—the slides, the swabbing, her underclothes. Everything was there."

But for a judge's discomfort with the verdict and setting aside some evidence for safekeeping, the first death row exoneree would have moldered in prison for the rest of his days.

P robably ninety-nine percent of lost or missing stuff, there was not some conspiracy to get rid of it," says Joe Latta, a former lieutenant in the Burbank, California, Police Department and now the executive director of the International Association for Property & Evidence Inc. Rather, it's the second law of thermodynamics in action: the inevitable decline into disorder. A property room fills up until officers are wedging evidence into every nook they can find.

"It's just chaos," he says. "But nobody says, 'Well, let's get rid of some of it. Let's get rid of the rock from the vandalism case in 1995.' No, they say: 'Let's get a cargo container and put it in the parking lot. Let's put a fenced-in area in the city yard. Let's add another closet. Let's put it in the basement.'" Heaven forbid that the police department moves from one building to another, as it did during the tenure of Ben Spencer's incarceration in Texas. "They just box everything up and move, and they may never get it cataloged in the new location."

For example, Alan Newton had been convicted of sexual assault in the Bronx in 1985, four years before DNA testing began upending convictions. In 1994, he asked that the swabs from the rape kit be tested, but his petition was denied because, the New York Police Department said, the evidence was lost. The Innocence Project petitioned for him in 1997 and 1998, with the same result: The evidence was lost in a fire, one letter said; another reported that it was destroyed by asbestos. Eventually, the Bronx district attorney, who had not been in office during Newton's trial, ordered a physical search of the evidence warehouse in Queens.

"In the end, they found the evidence literally, exactly where it was supposed to be," recalls Rebecca Brown, director of policy at the Innocence

Project. DNA tests excluded Newton, and he was freed in 2006. For twelve years he had petitioned for evidence, and for twelve years, she says, "no one got off their butt. It was pure serendipity that the evidence was located."

Innocence lawyers have learned to work around the inertia of police, says Mark Godsey. They begin by asking for a search, over and over again, until they wear the police down. Failing that—and that usually fails— they insist on a hearing in front of a judge where they put police officers, prosecutors, and crime lab officials under oath and ask them what effort they made to locate the evidence, where they searched, where else they could possibly search. "And a funny thing happens," Godsey says. If the judge agrees to a hearing, "well, they suddenly find the evidence."

The Dixmoor Five learned the power of subpoena only after spending, collectively, ninety-five years in prison. The five boys—three were fourteen and two were sixteen—were convicted of raping and murdering a fourteen-year-old girl in Dixmoor, Illinois, just south of Chicago, in the 1990s. They were tried separately and received sentences ranging from twenty to eighty-five years. They asked for the DNA evidence to be tested, but the Dixmoor police claimed they were unable to locate it. They petitioned again. The police ignored a court subpoena. Finally, in 2009— more than a decade after the final defendant was convicted—a judge ruled that defense counsel could view the storage areas and logbooks themselves. And a funny thing happened: Police conducted another search and found the evidence. It was tested, and all five young men were cleared, having lived out their teens, twenties, and early thirties in prison cells.[6]

You never know where evidence will turn up, in the exceedingly unlikely event it will turn up at all. Maybe it's sitting in the office of a professor in Germany,[7] or in the home of a newspaper reporter in Los Angeles.[8] And you wonder: What if a power outage in St. Louis had not forced the lab techs to empty the storage freezer; would the evidence that cleared a man of rape have ever been found?[9] What if a summer intern at the Clayton County, Georgia, district attorney's office had not noticed the box marked "evidence" next to the dumpster; would the innocent man have served out his life sentence for rape?[10]

And what if Mary Jane Burton had not broken the rules? Where would Marvin Anderson be now? In 1982, Marvin Anderson, an eighteen-year-old Black man, was convicted of sexually assaulting a young white woman in Hanover, Virginia.[11] He was sentenced to 210 years in prison. When DNA testing became widely available, Anderson petitioned for the rape kit to be located and tested. The sheriff's department responded that they had destroyed the evidence after the trial, in compliance with the state's evidence retention policy. Anderson's lawyers at the Innocence Project pleaded with the state laboratory to locate the notebook of the analyst who had performed the serology tests two decades earlier. When they retrieved Mary Jane Burton's notebook from the archives, fortune smiled.

Burton had a defiant habit of retaining evidence from each case she worked, rather than returning all of it to the law enforcement agency. She would tape swabs smeared with blood, semen, and saliva and clippings of hair and clothing, and insert them into their case files. She had retained a semen sample from Marvin Anderson's case. When the laboratory ran the test, the DNA excluded Anderson and identified another man. Over the next few years, the Virginia state lab tested the evidence in all of Burton's files. Twelve other men were exonerated, two of them with life sentences.[12]

"The way I have phrased it to those clients is this," Shawn Armbrust, executive director of the Mid-Atlantic Innocence Project, says: "Amongst a group of extremely unlucky people, you are the lucky ones."

More than thirty-four hundred people have been exonerated since 1989, and many of those exonerations were delayed by years or decades because officials swore the evidence was destroyed or lost when it wasn't. Who knows how many other innocent prisoners have *not* stumbled onto a lucky discovery and instead wither away in prison?

"If you'll forgive me for a moment," said Larry Hammond, an innocence lawyer in Arizona, "but *what the fuck?*! How do we ever feel comfortable having a system in any jurisdiction that allows evidence to disappear? Why don't heads roll? Why aren't cops fired and administrators sanctioned every time we find that evidence has disappeared?"

He knew the answer: the US Supreme Court.

On October 29, 1983, ten-year-old David L. accompanied his mother to a concert sponsored by her church in Tucson, and to his delight, discovered there was a carnival in the parking lot. During the service, he slipped away. He reappeared hours later, traumatized, his clothes inside out. He said a Black man with one bad eye had lured him into his car, driven to the desert, and raped him twice before returning him to church that night. The boy was taken to a hospital, where staff collected semen samples and handed them to the police. But the police failed to refrigerate the samples or the clothing with the biological evidence, and it degraded before a serologist could conduct tests.

Larry Youngblood was Black, known to police for a robbery ten years earlier, and had one bad eye. He was convicted based exclusively on the boy's description. He appealed his conviction, arguing that the destruction of the possibly exculpatory evidence violated his due process rights. The Arizona Court of Appeals agreed and set aside his conviction.

The case made its way to the US Supreme Court. During oral arguments on October 11, 1988, Chief Justice William Rehnquist zeroed in on the fact that the Tucson authorities did not intentionally destroy the evidence. How far must law enforcement officials go to ensure a fair trial, he worried: Must they preserve "every bit of evidence they ever come across,"[13] must they perform all possible scientific tests, follow every lead, no matter how improbable? "How broad is this duty?" he asked. "Is the Constitution going to tell prosecutors how they ought to investigate cases?"[14]

The court issued its decision the following month. By a six-to-three vote, the justices reinstated Youngblood's conviction. "Unless a criminal defendant can show bad faith on the part of the police," Rehnquist wrote, "failure to preserve potentially useful evidence does not constitute a denial of due process of law."[15] In other words, only if a prisoner could prove the state intentionally destroyed or lost evidence could he be afforded a new trial.

Youngblood, who had been released pending the court's decision, returned to prison in 1993. His attorney remained convinced that this was a case of mistaken identity, and in 2000, she requested that the evidence be tested using more advanced DNA technology. The tests showed that Youngblood was innocent; the DNA belonged to a man with two prior convictions for child sexual abuse. The perpetrator was also blind in one eye. Youngblood was freed. He died in 2007 without receiving compensation.

The bad-faith barrier erected by the Supreme Court has proved almost impossible to scale. How do you prove it? "There's not going to be an email from the prosecutor saying: *I am destroying this in bad faith. Ha ha! Gotcha!*" says Somil Trivedi, a staff attorney at the American Civil Liberties Union. "Judges are going to be very hesitant to ascribe bad faith to a prosecutor."[16]

In the three decades since *Youngblood*, according to published opinions, at least 1,675 prisoners have tried to win a new trial by proving the state acted in bad faith when it destroyed or lost evidence. Seven have succeeded.[17]

Youngblood has created an incentive for officials to ignore or mishandle evidence. I discovered this in 2000, when I was covering the Justice Department for NPR. A source passed on a rumor he had heard: Because DNA was overturning so many convictions and embarrassing so many police and prosecutors, the police in Houston were throwing out biological evidence before a prisoner could request that it be tested using the new DNA technology. In other words, innocence lawyers believed the police were sealing in convictions so they could not be challenged in the future.

This alleged spring cleaning occurred after the exoneration of Kevin Byrd. Byrd had been convicted of sexual assault in Houston in 1985, before the advent of DNA testing. The evidence in his case was slated to be destroyed in 1994, but through sheer luck the rape kit was preserved. When Byrd requested the semen be tested three years later, the tests proved that Byrd was not the rapist. Since then, my source told me, he had heard that Houston had destroyed up to three hundred rape kits.

I called the Houston Police Department and talked with the officer who supervised the evidence in criminal cases.

"I've heard that after the Kevin Byrd case, some rape kits were destroyed," I said.

A long pause followed.

"Could be."

Another pause, by me, this time.

"How would that happen?" I finally asked.

"Why would we need to keep them?"

He explained when a person is convicted and has exhausted all his appeals, it's very difficult to get that evidence back into court, so there's no reason to hang on to it. "There's nowhere to put it," he added, referring to rape kits that are a little larger than a shoebox. He declined to say how many the Houston Police Department had destroyed.[18]

As a result of *Youngblood*, "police and prosecutors nationwide now had license to conduct lazy investigations," the legal scholar Daniel Medwed says. "The court had also given them a green light to put perishable biological evidence in a box: ignored, forgotten, and untested."[19]

Between 1999 and 2002, New Orleans officials threw out biological evidence in twenty-five hundred rape cases and fifty-five murders in a mass purge.[20] In 1992, the New York Police Department demolished large quantities of evidence to clear space in its warehouse, and Houston destroyed rape kits throughout the 1990s, citing storage constraints.[21]

"The timing of these purges is important," Medwed argues.[22] In both New York and Houston, the cleanups occurred shortly after the first DNA exonerations.

Many states have tried to counteract the effects of *Youngblood* by passing laws that require police and prosecutors to preserve evidence. But laws can't fix the core problem: chaos. Evidence rooms across the country still look like Dresden after World War II. Joe Latta works with police departments to systematize their evidence rooms, and he has tried to persuade them with the argument that if Walmart knows how many Diet Cokes it has on its shelves, surely the NYPD should know where to find a rape kit when someone's liberty is at stake. This argument seems to catch, until the next robbery or murder. "We chase bad guys," Latta says. "If I'm a police chief, I want more cops on the street. We'll deal with that inventory later."

Some cities have arrived at the twenty-first century, including Las Vegas, Charlotte-Mecklenburg, and Tucson, perhaps smarting from the fiasco involving Larry Youngblood. But Latta says most large cities—New York City, Detroit, Philadelphia, Baltimore, New Orleans—have not. New laws and regulations won't change human nature. Imagine a cop standing in the doorway of a giant warehouse, clutching a request to find a box of evidence from a prisoner's trial, gazing at the chaotic landscape of mattresses and bicycles, shovels and pry bars and thousands of boxes stacked on top of each other, filled with blood samples, rape kits, knives and guns and bags of heroin. Will he or she think: Oh, good, let's do this? Or will the cop say, To hell with it, I'll never find it, and leave?

B en Spencer was becoming a celebrity in prison circles. "I run into guards down here all the time and the first thing that they ask, 'What are they waiting on, why are you still here? Man, they need to go ahead and let you go!'" he wrote Debra on May 29, 2006. He assured her that one day he would walk out of Coffield. "When I think of my future, I always envision you there," he wrote. "I want you to be my future, just as you were my past. You filled me with happiness and joy and I never wanted to lose you and why? Because I never stopped loving you. Whatever becomes of me, I just want you to be there with me."

As 2006 closed, it was game on. Spencer's fate would be decided by a newly elected judge who had barely donned his black robes before a box in his closet changed both of their lives.

*Chapter 24*

# A SECOND BITE AT THE APPLE

+———+

**As the trial progressed, it was very clear
that we had made a tragic mistake.**

—ALAN LEDBETTER, *jury foreman for 1988 trial*

In the winter of 2007, a group of attorneys gathered in Rick Magnis's
chambers. A few weeks earlier, Magnis, a Democrat, had been elected
to preside over the 283rd Judicial District Court in Dallas. The attorneys,
prosecution and defense, wanted to discuss a particular case, one that
Magnis knew nothing about. "One of the attorneys reached down to the
bottom shelf of my bookcase and pulled out this giant box," he recalled.
"It's this case," the attorney said. It was Benjamine Spencer's petition for
an evidentiary hearing.

"I went through the box very thoroughly," Magnis said. Initially he
thought it was just another innocence case filed by a prisoner "who's got
time on his hands. We get a bunch of them." But this one seemed different. "Whenever you're reviewing a conviction from that period of time,
you always think they might be innocent." With each page, Magnis grew
more intrigued. It occurred to him that the case might involve an actual
injustice. "We've got some real issues."

In a rare move, the judge shut down his court for one week to fully
review the evidence. Professionally, Rick Magnis looked at law through a
different lens than the typical Dallas judge. He had never worked as a

prosecutor; rather, he had served as a public defender in Dallas for the previous seventeen years. Philosophically, Magnis was a defendant's dream. "I was raised in the Unitarian Church by liberal parents," he said. "We believe in the inherent worth and dignity of all souls, and I learned from a very early age to treat people with respect and dignity."

He agreed to hold an evidentiary hearing, a mini-trial where he could assess the witnesses and the evidence live. He set the hearing for late July 2007. That a judge would reconsider the conviction bewildered, and angered, the sons of Jeffrey Young. They thought they had buried their father and the judicial combat two decades earlier. "I was like, Really? Is this going to be the rest of my life?" Jay Young, by then in his early thirties, remembered thinking. Ben Spencer had been found guilty in two trials and Robert Mitchell in one. What new evidence could possibly have surfaced? "Three juries, I mean, give me a break. What's new? Why are we doing this again?"

Spencer had the right to challenge his conviction, Jay's younger brother, Jimmy, noted. "But I don't think that a lot of people actually understand the thought process and the emotions that you have to go through." Now they would be forced to endure several days of a court hearing, with its witnesses and crime scene photos, its timelines and dueling experts, as the man convicted of killing their father sat in the courtroom. They would have to relive the worst day of their lives, yet again.

The butterfly effect" is the notion that the tiny perturbations of a butterfly flapping its wings in Australia can cause a tornado in Kansas weeks later. This idea can also describe events in which a singular incident triggers an outsized response, in the way that the death of a Black man named George Floyd sparked nationwide revulsion at racial violence among the police, or the assassination of Austrian archduke Franz Ferdinand triggered World War I.

If you were to look for the butterfly effect in criminal justice, you might point to a conversation between Craig Watkins and Terri Moore in late 2006. Craig Watkins was elected district attorney of Dallas County in November 2006, the first Democrat since Henry Wade, and the first Black ever, to hold the job. Watkins, a defense attorney, had never prosecuted anyone and needed a first assistant to help him navigate these unfamiliar waters. Terri Moore had worked for fourteen years as a federal prosecutor and as an assistant district attorney in Fort Worth.

"I realized that it was very, very important that Craig succeed because he was the first African American Democrat," she recalled years later. "But I had one condition. I would go to work for him only if he would let me implement this idea that I had." Moore envisioned creating a unit within the district attorney's office that would reinvestigate questionable convictions. "I said, 'If you'll let me do this, we'll do it with so much integrity that they'll put it on your tombstone. You'll be a rock star,'" Moore recalled. "And he's like, 'You know what? Let's do it.'"

They created the nation's first Conviction Integrity Unit, which would be replicated in district attorneys' offices around the country. Those units would revolutionize some prosecutors' offices in the same way that DNA revolutionized forensics.[1] Until the Dallas experiment, innocence lawyers depended on the receptiveness of prosecutors, who almost inevitably resisted dredging up embarrassing convictions, or the largesse of local judges who, in Texas at least, were usually former prosecutors and often appeared to ride shotgun with the district attorney's office. But a prosecutor in the Conviction Integrity Unit could simply walk down the hall and collect the evidence, or demand that it be produced, whether it was documents containing exculpatory evidence or a rape kit with the true perpetrator's DNA, just waiting to reveal its secret.

"We looked at DNA cases first because it was science," Craig Watkins said. "You couldn't question that. There's no argument against it." They were playing the long game. "In looking at those cases first, we developed credibility with the Court of Criminal Appeals. So when we brought a case, and we said 'This person is innocent'"—Watkins snapped his fingers—"credibility. Instant credibility."

Watkins and Moore approached the radical idea strategically. "Here is a Black Democrat district attorney doing a white Republican man's job," Moore explained. They needed to bat a thousand, to reassure not just the higher courts but also the citizens of Dallas. "There could not be any question about it, or they'd be like 'Craig's over there letting all these Black people out of prison.' So we had to be right."

The DNA ensured they were right; the crime laboratory ensured they were successful. The crime lab in Dallas, unlike those in Houston and other cities, had stored rape kits and other forensic evidence for decades. Without them, Watkins could not have proven that men and women sitting in prison had been wrongly convicted. With them, the CIU began reconsidering hundreds of convictions, dating back to the era of Henry Wade.

But Ben Spencer's case lacked DNA, and the new district attorney decided to proceed with his predecessor's decision. Watkins would fight Spencer's petition in court.

As Spencer prepared for his first parole hearing in the spring of 2007, his family and friends sent letters of support to the Texas Board of Pardons and Paroles. When he met with one commissioner in March, Spencer told him he felt sympathy for the Young family and was stricken about their loss. But, he said, he didn't kill Jeffrey Young.

"Of course, he didn't believe what I said when I told him I didn't commit the offense," he recalled. In that meeting, Spencer pulled out an article from *The Dallas Morning News* featuring his case and the evidence indicating his innocence. He asked the commissioner if he could put it in his file for review. "He's looking at it, and he says, 'Well, yeah, I can do that.' He's like, 'So you saying you wasn't there?' I said, 'I'm saying I wasn't there,'" knowing that this comment, this lack of remorse, would abort his chances for parole. "It's hard to have remorse for something you didn't do," he observed.

Spencer expected the board to deny him the first time. What he didn't foresee was the influence of the Young family. "Let's just put it this way,"

Jay Young told me. "Spencer has his avenues. We also have avenues. Victims have their avenues, too. So we took advantage."

They drove down to the prison to meet with the parole board members assigned to the case, and organized a writing campaign. They drafted a letter and asked people to sign it—friends, acquaintances, influential businesspeople, and politicians. "Some people said: 'I don't know if I want to get involved,'" Jay Young recalled. "That's fine. Some people were like, 'Nope, I'll sign it.'"

"The reason why we all do that is because we believe in the justice system," Jimmy Young said. "I am not the judge. I am not the jury. But we believe in the justice system and we believe that you should pay for what you did."

In May 2007, Spencer learned that the parole board had not only denied him, but also put off his next review until 2012. "Five years! That's ridiculous, you know?" he wrote to Debra in a letter roiling with uncharacteristic frustration. "Now if I've been down here messing up all the time, catching cases left and right all the time, then and only then could I see them setting parole off for me. I've been a model inmate and I deserve parole now!!!"[2] The reason cited for the denial was "the nature of the offense"—that is, the violence of the assault. "Well that's not anything that can be changed now is it?" he observed. He was right. A spotless prison record would never erase Jeffrey Young's death.

Spencer recognized that the only exit from his life sentence depended on the evidentiary hearing in July. "I believe that this hearing is going to be the turning point in this case," he wrote Debra. "I trust that the truth will not be ignored this time around."

A few days before the hearing, Judge Magnis drove to West Dallas and viewed the crime scene with Spencer's attorney and the Dallas County prosecutor. Magnis knew this was unconventional; indeed, it would be the only time he did so during his years on the bench. He wanted to see it all for himself: the alley where the car had been parked; any obstacles that could block the witnesses' line of sight; the perspectives and distances from which Jimmie Cotton, Gladys Oliver, and Charles Stewart claimed to have seen Spencer exit the car. Standing where it happened, Magnis dismissed Charles Stewart's claim on the spot: From where the young man had stood, more than 220 feet away, "I couldn't have recognized my brother in broad daylight," Magnis observed.

The state, too, was preparing for the hearing. Andy Beach, who had won the conviction against Spencer some two decades earlier, wondered what new evidence the defense could present. And he worried just a little: Had he been wrong to rely on Gladys Oliver?

"All I know is in 1988, I fully believed she saw what she said she saw," Beach said years later. One day, Beach saw his star witness in the courthouse, where she was testifying in the hearing. He pulled her aside. "I looked her right in the eye. 'Gladys, did you tell the truth?'" he pressed. "She goes, 'I absolutely told the truth.' Looked me right in the eye."

The victim's family planned to attend the hearing, and invited friends to help them fill the courtroom. Jay Young had looked forward to the day when he could assess his father's alleged killer: his demeanor, his actions, his responses to the evidence. "I wanted to see him in person, when he was handcuffed."

As for Debra Spencer, never had she felt more keenly the loss of her parents. Her dad had died years before, her mother in 2006, a year before the hearing. "I didn't want to go through it alone," Debra recalled. But she had kept her ex-husband's circumstances secret; there was no confidant she could naturally ask to join her. "I just needed that mother figure," so she called her ex-supervisor, Ann Hallstrom, to sit with her. "She had no idea what I was talking about. I just told her that I needed to go to court, and I needed her with me. She said, 'I'll be there.'"

Inside the 283rd District courtroom, the spectators arranged themselves in stark fashion. "There was a visual racial divide," Cheryl Wattley recalled. On the right-hand side of the courtroom, behind Ben

Spencer, the spectators were predominantly Black. On the left side were Jeffrey Young's family and friends, virtually all white people, including a man intimately involved in Spencer's conviction. The jury foreman from the 1988 trial took a week off from work to attend the hearing. Alan Ledbetter needed answers, and dreaded them. He felt compelled to revisit the evidence against Ben Spencer, a suspect he had judged worthy of life in prison, and he agonized about what he would learn.

One cold Saturday night in October 2002, Ledbetter heard a knock and answered his front door to find a stranger standing on his stoop. Paul Henderson handed him a tattered business card and explained he was looking into Ben Spencer's conviction for a group called Centurion Ministries.

"He says, 'Would you like to hear what really happened on the night of Mr. Young's murder?'" Skeptical but curious, Ledbetter invited him in. Over the next hour, Henderson spelled out what they had investigated. "It was frustrating, realizing that so much of this was in the police records and that we never heard it," Ledbetter said. That conversation left an opening for reasonable doubt and self-reflection. "I wouldn't say I was convinced that he was innocent, but there was certainly a very compelling story now on the table that, frankly, better fit what actually happened than the story that was laid before us fourteen years earlier."

Nearly five years later, the courtroom hushed as Ben Spencer walked through the side from the holding cell, wearing a faded black-and-white-striped jumpsuit and chains on his feet and hands. It was the first time B.J., at age twenty, had seen his father outside of prison. "He looked . . . I wouldn't say *happy*, but he looked like he was satisfied that he was finally getting another day in court to try to tell his side of the story."

Debra showed no expression—the judge had warned against any displays of emotion—and she barely remembers the hearing. "I was numb," she later said. She had to call Ann Hallstrom each night for a debriefing.

Hallstrom remembered everything, especially her first glimpse of Ben Spencer. "I just saw this gorgeous man walk in," she recalled, laughing, "so tall and good looking and friendly. An absolute doll."

Jay Young perceived another man entirely. Spencer was "arrogant," he said, "like he thought he'd win or that he has nothing to lose. I firmly believe the right person is behind bars."

The hearing opened electric with tension. The stakes were existential for each side of the courtroom: Would an innocent man win freedom, or would a killer be unleashed to wreak more havoc on the world? Cheryl Wattley and Jim McCloskey began by attempting to show the state had convicted the wrong man and to offer an alternative suspect. They worked smoothly, Hallstrom recalled, with McCloskey handing Wattley documents just when she needed them. "It was like paper ballet."

Early in the hearing, Ferrell Scott testified that his friend, Michael Hubbard, had returned from his mission to rob someone the night of March 22, 1987, and carried with him a wedding band and a Seiko watch. Hubbard asked his friend to take him to the local drug dealer to make a trade for some crack cocaine.

"Me and Michael was together there when we went there to sell it," Scott stated. Then he shifted his gaze from the prosecutor, who was trying to punch holes in his account, and looked directly at the family of Jeffrey Young sitting in the front row. "I made the deal," he said, addressing them. "I made the deal for the watch."

The room fell quiet as felon and family stared at each other, Wattley recalled. "It was one of the most chilling moments I've ever seen in a courtroom."

During their presentation, Judge Magnis listened closely, leaning in and occasionally interrupting to clarify points. He examined Kelvin Johnson about Hubbard's alleged confession that he had killed the white man, and the judge appeared satisfied that Hubbard had conveyed details that only the real perpetrator could know. As for Sandra Brackens, who testified that she saw a man running away from the BMW and that man was *not* Spencer, the judge listened quietly with few interruptions.

After Brackens was excused, Alan Ledbetter stared at the empty witness stand. By midpoint in the hearing, two of Hubbard's friends and a young woman who saw the perpetrator all insisted that someone other than Ben Spencer was the true culprit. Three witnesses, he thought, tallying up the debits and credits of the trial. Two decades earlier, Ledbetter's jury had relied on three witnesses stating that they had seen Spencer in that alley. Had the defense presented three witnesses insisting on Spencer's innocence, he said, "it would have made it very difficult to convict.

"It was one of those surreal moments," Ledbetter said quietly. He took off his glasses and looked in the middle distance, a soft-spoken man who spends a week each summer running a vacation Bible school for his church. "It's like, okay, this is not supposed to happen. And if it does happen, it's not supposed to take twenty years to correct it." He paused as he fought back tears. "And just that overwhelming sense of, *Poor Ben*. I mean, his life has been taken away from him. And I had played a role in this. There's an element of guilt and grief that I carry for whatever role I may have played in robbing so much of his life from him."

After the break, Ledbetter moved from the victim's side of the courtroom to sit behind Ben Spencer. "I tried to remain unbiased," Ledbetter said. "But as the trial progressed, it was very clear that we had made a tragic mistake."

S pencer's witnesses were necessary but not sufficient to counter the state's eyewitnesses, all of whom were standing by their original testimony. His team needed to show that it was physically impossible for Gladys Oliver and the two teenagers to identify Spencer. Dr. Paul Michel, an optometrist and forensic visual scientist, had testified frequently on behalf of police in police-involved shootings. Judge Magnis had given Michel's report a close reading, and at times took over the witness examination, peppering the scientist with detailed questions. How did he determine where the victim's BMW had been parked? What were the lighting conditions on the night he visited West Dallas? Where was Jimmie Cotton standing in his kitchen, and could he have seen into the dark from a lit room? Would the car's dome light have made a difference, and what about the light at the neighbor's house? What about Charles Stewart, who stood 220 feet away from the BMW?

Later, the scientist stated, "To make facial identification of somebody exiting the car in that area, [a witness] would have to be twenty-five feet or closer." Is it conceivable, the judge asked, that any of the witnesses had such exceptional vision that they could have identified the perpetrator? "No," Michel responded.[3]

Jay Young watched the hearing with growing resignation. He considered it a "circus" with Magnis as the "ringleader." "The way he handled it and the way he asked questions were just kind of a joke to me, and I felt very disrespected," Young recalled. He particularly chafed at Paul Michel's testimony. He once laughed in disbelief, leaving the courtroom after he drew the judge's glare.

When Judge Magnis called a recess, Young headed for the elevator. Waiting at the elevator bank were Cheryl Wattley, Jim McCloskey, "and the lighting expert, the lighting genius, Thomas Edison himself," as Young put it. "And I'm going in my head, Oh, shit." In the elevator, he stood in front of the others, facing the doors. Breaking the agonizing silence, Wattley said, "Hello, Mr. Young." "And I looked up and said, 'How do you know I'm Mr. Young? Is the lighting optimal?' The door opened and I walked out."

Throughout the hearing, Spencer remained quiet and still. At the end of every day, McCloskey reviewed the day's testimony with him, answering questions and assessing witnesses' performance. "We were slowly but surely developing a confidence that things are going our way," McCloskey said. "Things look pretty good, Ben," he would tell him. "They look good. Now, there are no guarantees here, but our case is really holding up very, very well."

When the state began to present its case, Judge Magnis assumed more roles: the director, the choreographer, and the leading man, his doubt playing across his face like ticker tape. This was not the traditional judge that Texas prosecutors had become accustomed to. People in the room recall seeing the judge's reactions—a skeptical incline of the head, an impatient interruption, a snappish retort, such as when Detective Briseno refused to concede that two hundred feet was too far away to identify someone at night: "Do me a favor," the judge said. "Check it out in broad daylight for yourself. Okay?"[4] Anyone could see that it was not going well for the state.

Judge Magnis often politely interrupted Cheryl Wattley when she was cross-examining the state's witnesses. He zeroed in on the squishiness of Jimmie Cotton's story, asking the young man directly if he actually saw Spencer's face. Cotton hedged, saying he didn't see Spencer get out of the car, but spotted him a few minutes later.

> THE COURT: This is very, very important. The question that's been at issue this whole time is whether you identified the man that got out of the car at the time he got out of the car by looking at his face and saying you know he's that person and couldn't be anyone else. You understand my question?
> THE WITNESS: Yeah, I understand.
> THE COURT: Could the person that got out of the car have been some other tall African American male?
> THE WITNESS: Yes, it could.[5]

The judge then turned to Danny Edwards, the jailhouse informant who testified that Ben had confessed to him.[6] After listening to his testimony, Judge Magnis observed that Edwards had offered three different stories: that he heard the confession from Ben's own lips; he heard it from his wife, who made a three-way call for Ben; and he heard it from a cellmate of Ben's.[7]

> THE COURT: Did you ever talk to Mr. Spencer directly?
> THE WITNESS: Directly, no.
> THE COURT: Did he ever confess to you that he committed this crime?
> THE WITNESS: No, sir.

The judge reserved his sharpest examination for Jesus Briseno. He grilled the homicide detective about the thoroughness of his investigation and the acuity of his judgment. Magnis noted that two witnesses had claimed to hear confessions to the assault. He walked the detective through the two stories. There was the informant, Danny Edwards, who gave an account of Ben Spencer's confession involving gold coins and Mafia deals and a drugged-out victim—all of which had no basis in fact. Then he led him through the testimony of Kelvin Johnson, who claimed that his best friend, Michael Hubbard, had confessed to him, and who knew many of the details that were never made public.

"Which one seems more credible under those circumstances?" the judge asked.

"Probably Johnson's," the detective admitted.[8]


Michael Hubbard, by his own account, had converted to Christianity in 1994, claimed to have earned a minister's degree in prison, and carried his Bible wherever he went. It is difficult, then, to reconcile that Michael Hubbard with the one who walked into the courtroom on July 26, 2007.

Hubbard, who was serving a life sentence for the Batman attacks, ambled across the room to the witness stand, despite the shackles on his feet and hands. "He was a big guy. With a bald head, with little beady eyes," Debra Spencer recalled. "He came in and he demanded attention. He wanted to make sure everybody made eye contact with him. He looked at them one at a time, like he was taking a photograph, a picture of everybody. I mean, you could hear a pin drop."

He turned a cold, confident stare to Debra, sitting behind her ex-husband. "I just looked at him back and I was like, 'You're not going to intimidate me.'"

Because Cheryl Wattley had presented evidence that Michael Hubbard, not Ben Spencer, was the actual murderer, Judge Magnis had asked two public defenders to represent him. A gaggle of lawyers crowded around the judge's bench, debating whether Hubbard would claim his Fifth Amendment right against self-incrimination. "While that discussion is going on, Michael Hubbard is sitting in the witness box and he's looking at the Young family," Wattley said. "I obviously have no idea what was going through the Young family's mind, but they knew at that point we were saying 'this is the man who killed your loved one.' And it was a good period, at least fifteen minutes or so, where they were just looking at each other while the attorneys were all up at the bench talking to the judge."

Hubbard declined to testify, citing his right against self-incrimination, and the proceeding ended moments later.

"The hearing exceeded my expectations," Spencer said, smiling at the memory. "I thought that this is it. I'm going home."

# Chapter 25

# JUDGMENT DAY REDUX

+———+

**She was just telling self-serving lies.**

—JUDGE RICK MAGNIS, *regarding Gladys Oliver*

Terri Moore made good on her promise to District Attorney Craig Watkins. By the time Spencer's hearing ended, the Conviction Integrity Unit was ramping up, and soon Watkins was profiled by *60 Minutes*, *The New York Times*, and *The Wall Street Journal*. *Texas Monthly* and *D Magazine* ran him on the cover, and in 2008, *The Dallas Morning News* selected him as Texan of the Year.

If Moore plotted Watkins's path to national prominence, a low-key law professor and defense attorney named Mike Ware executed it. Newly installed as head of the Conviction Integrity Unit, he began with a list of 454 names of prisoners who requested DNA testing in their cases. Texas had passed a statute in 2001 that granted inmates access to DNA tests to prove their innocence, but Ware soon discovered that the prosecutors in district attorneys' offices across the state, including Dallas, would "knee-jerk oppose" any request. "And for stupid reasons," he added.

For example, in 1992, Patrick Waller, a twenty-two-year-old Black man, was accused of abducting two couples, robbing them, and raping the women. All four victims swore there were two assailants, but the police never identified a second man. Waller was convicted of kidnapping and robbery, but not rape, and sentenced to life in prison based on the victims' identification. After the 2001 DNA statute was passed, Waller requested a test of the rape kit. "The DA's office argued, 'No, he wasn't convicted of sexual assault. He was convicted of aggravated robbery, aggravated kidnapping.'" So they denied his petition to test the sexual assault kit. The judge sided with the state, as did the appellate court, and Waller waited helplessly in prison for another six years, until the CIU took an interest. Ware contacted Waller's lawyer and offered to do a test. "Waller was excluded, and they got a clear male profile that they uploaded into the database," he said. "We identified the actual perpetrator, who, long story short, ended up identifying the other perpetrator."

Waller became the CIU's first exoneree, and as the unit accepted more cases, they were dismayed at how easy it was to exonerate prisoners. "It was like getting kicked in the stomach," Terri Moore said. "It's like, 'Oh, my God. And how long has he been in prison?'" Some convictions dated back to 1980, to Henry Wade's era. "It was awful. And it was wonderful," she said. "You just grieve the loss of life for these people that spent their life in prison and the world went by them. And yet it was wonderful to give them their life back."

Dallas became a model that other prosecutors could not ignore. You could dismiss the complaints of an Innocence Project lawyer as so much grousing. But here was one of their own taking shots at the system. In Dallas, Craig Watkins achieved cultlike status among some. Others recoiled. Police referred to his efforts as the "Hug-a-Thug" program. Conservative voters accused him of releasing more people than he convicted. "'How dare he spend his time getting people out of jail?'" Texas journalist Bob Ray Sanders recalls critics complaining. "'We elected him to put people behind bars, not release them.'" But every few weeks or months, another innocent person who had lost decades of his or her life walked out of prison and into people's living rooms on the nightly news. It was hard to argue with televised success.

When Judge Magnis settled down to write his recommendations in Ben Spencer's case, he was mindful of his audience. In Texas, trial judges lack the authority to vacate a conviction and order a new trial. They can only make recommendations to the highest criminal court in the state. It's not an easy sell: The judges on the Court of Criminal Appeals (CCA) are elected; the majority are former prosecutors who run tough-on-crime campaigns. All belong to the Republican Party. However, in part because Texas executes more people than any other state—and more than all but a handful of countries, such as China and Iran—legislators and even the CCA have on occasion proven to be progressive about revisiting questionable convictions. The 2004 execution of Todd Cameron Willingham, who was convicted based on faulty arson science and was very possibly innocent, no doubt helped to open their minds.

Judge Magnis knew his findings must deflect all appellate bullets. He ordered the prosecutors to find another expert on visual science to counter Dr. Michel's findings. They did, but it hardly helped their case: Their expert disagreed that the witnesses needed to be within twenty-five feet to identify a face; one could be as far away as forty feet, he said. "That's okay," Wattley said, laughing, "because Gladys was a hundred twenty-three feet away, so that's three times forty." Even the closest witness, Jimmie Cotton, was more than twice that distance away.

Like everyone else sitting in the courtroom, Spencer thought he might be released soon—maybe a year. In his previous letters to Debra, he described his love, his anxiousness, and his gratitude that he had made it this far. But he never dared describe his dreams, for his future was too fragile a thing on which to rest his hopes. Now, though, he could practically *grasp* freedom, and all the pleasures that entailed, great and small. There was the matter of his wardrobe. He reminded Debra that he liked Polo shirts and he was pleased to hear that 501 jeans were still in style. He sent her his measurements, weight, and shoe size. "I may be a little caught in the past, but I can assure you that I still know how to dress and I will look good in my attire," he wrote on March 4, 2008, with a touch of vanity. "I am about to be free again. I am so ready. I'm more than ready."

He dared to imagine living with Debra and their son in the house she had bought in a middle-class suburb of Dallas. "I want to thank you for giving me a little taste of the family life," he wrote on October 7, 2007. While they were talking on the phone that Sunday morning, Debra had walked into B.J.'s room to rouse him. "Listening to him waking up and being able to tell him to '*get out of that bed*' really touched me. It's strange how the simplest things in life fill me with such joy. I found myself envisioning him laying there in his bed with his big sleepy head." Before, envisioning this domestic scene would have plunged him into sadness for what he had lost; now it filled him with anticipation for what he would find.


O n March 28, 2008, the clerk of the 283rd District Court called Cheryl Wattley, who was preparing for class at her office at the University of Oklahoma College of Law. She screamed so loudly that her assistant ran in to see if she needed to call 911. Wattley called the jail, and the guards brought Spencer to the phone; he absorbed the news with characteristic calm. She then reached Jim McCloskey, who had just returned to Princeton from Los Angeles, where he had secured another exoneration.[1] McCloskey roared with excitement, and then called Debra Spencer with the message she had been waiting for. Debra screamed, B.J. came running out of his room, and they basked in their astonishing new reality.

Judge Rick Magnis had issued his "Findings of Fact and Conclusions of Law." Forty-two pages long, meticulously detailed, it was a grand slam for Ben Spencer. The judge spared the lawyers and investigators from embarrassment and censure. Frank Jackson "zealously advocated" for his client, he wrote, dismissing the claim of ineffective assistance of counsel.[2] He believed Ferrell Scott's lawyer, who testified that he did not remember taking Ferrell to the police station—even though Scott had accurately described the interior and exterior of the lawyer's Cadillac in detail.[3] He stated that Detective Briseno is a "credible person worthy of belief."[4]

Then he dismantled the state's case, piece by piece.

"This Court finds that it was physically impossible for Jimmie Cotton, Charles Stewart, and Gladys Oliver to make any facial identification of a person exiting the BMW on March 22, 1987," he wrote.[5] Charles Stewart was so far from the BMW that even in daylight it would take "super human abilities" to make a facial identification. Jimmie Cotton did not actually see the face of the person exiting the BMW. "Cotton is not a credible witness and is not worthy of belief." Nor was Gladys Oliver "worthy of belief."

"She lied," Judge Magnis said later. "She was just telling self-serving lies and it was clear that she had been motivated by the reward and, very importantly, her fifteen minutes of fame. She was the center of attention, everyone adored her. She was not persuasive. She was not a credible person."

For Magnis, the dispositive evidence was the visual science. "The two experts eliminated the eyewitness testimony. You take away the eyewitness testimony, all you have left is the jailhouse snitch," he said. None of Danny Edwards's testimony was credible, he found; moreover, it was inadmissible hearsay. "Edwards was just a guy in jail trying to make deals to cut some time off of his sentence," he said. "I don't believe that anything he'd said at any point was truthful," including the alleged confession by Ben Spencer. Magnis found that the account given by Kelvin Johnson, who identified Michael Hubbard as the assailant, "is more consistent with the actual facts of the murder and therefore more credible."[6]

Judge Magnis concluded: "The Court recommends that relief be granted on the grounds of actual innocence."[7]

We got real excited. We started planning stuff," Debra said, laughing. She called family and friends, she bought his favorite food, she filled his drawers and closet with slacks, shoes, sweaters, socks, mock turtlenecks; he would be fitted for a suit later. "I thought they was going to keep him in the county [jail] for a couple of days and he'd come home. But that didn't happen. Day after day. It didn't happen."

"I thought Judge Magnis jumped the gun," former district attorney Craig Watkins said. He balked at the judge's conclusion that the state's witnesses all lied and that the lighting experts spoke with godlike omniscience. When Magnis viewed the alley in West Dallas twenty years after the crime, some houses had been torn down, trees had grown, and he couldn't possibly know if the witnesses could see the BMW. The judge should not have so blithely thrown out a jury verdict. "In our estimation, that was not enough for us to make a determination as to whether or not he was innocent."

Jay Young was unsurprised. He had sensed where Magnis was heading during the hearing. His family was once again in limbo. "Sometimes people look at this as winners or losers, based on decisions by public figures, DAs, judges, the Court of Criminal Appeals," Young said. "That's never going to change the fact that *we are the losers here*. We lost our father."

The district attorney's reaction to the judge's conclusions would count against Spencer in the CCA's estimation; but the sheer detail of the ruling—one hundred paragraphs dissecting every part of the conviction—encouraged Spencer's team. "We thought we were on firm ground," McCloskey said. "We didn't see how the Court of Criminal Appeals could not defer to Judge Magnis's findings of fact."

"Now comes the hardest part," Spencer warned Debra three days later: waiting for the CCA to make its ruling. He advised her to keep herself busy. "I know that if I had something else to do besides sit in the day room or look out the window, that time would fly by, before I realized it, the Court will have made their rulings. Don't worry though, I'm going to hang on and remain patient. I'm going to remain steadfast and unmovable, for I know that God is able."[8]

As Spencer continued to wait in Lew Sterrett, one of his close friends arrived at the Dallas jail. Spencer had known Richard Miles since the first day Miles appeared at Coffield prison, and Spencer, as the barber, cut his hair. At the time, Miles was reeling from his conviction and stunned to find himself in a maximum-security prison. After he told Spencer his story, Spencer urged him to write Centurion Ministries. Now, a decade later, Miles had been brought to Dallas for a hearing on his case.

On May 16, 1994, witnesses at a Texaco station in Dallas saw a Black man lean into a car window, pull out a gun, and shoot two men sitting inside, killing one and wounding the other. Within moments, police picked up nineteen-year-old Richard Miles as he was walking home after spending the evening with friends. They put him in the patrol car, drove up to one of the witnesses, and asked if Miles looked like the shooter. Maybe, the witness said, as he viewed the young man in police custody, in handcuffs. Five other witnesses said there was no resemblance. Police corroborated Miles's alibi. Still, he was arrested for murder and attempted murder.

"I don't believe they even thought I did it," Miles speculated years later. "Because I didn't even fit the physical description. The only thing that I can think of is the police wanted to close out a case, and they picked out the first Black male they saw." In 1995, Miles was convicted and sentenced to sixty years in prison.

While Spencer waited for the decision by the Court of Criminal Appeals, his legal team had a little respite. "So we began investigating Richard's case," McCloskey said. They found that police had suppressed key evidence: A woman had told them that her ex-boyfriend had confessed to the murder, and another person had sworn that a different man, not Richard Miles, was the shooter. After McCloskey brought the case to the Conviction Integrity Unit in Dallas, the unit's prosecutors and investigators learned that the ballistics expert had been pressured to testify that she found gun residue on Miles's hands. They tracked down the only eyewitness to identify Miles at trial. The witness said that just before testifying, he told the prosecutor that he didn't remember what the perpetrator looked like. "The prosecutor told him, 'The guy sitting next to the lawyer is the guy you're going to identify,'" McCloskey said. The witness admitted that he had always felt conflicted about the conviction. Centurion quickly won the support of the Conviction Integrity Unit, and Richard Miles was released in October 2009. The CCA declared him innocent three years later.

Wattley visited Spencer to give him a heads-up. "I suppose that they were concerned about how I might feel about this news if I heard it through the news," Spencer wrote Debra on October 4, 2009. "Well, I must admit that I am extremely disappointed in the state for the way that they are handling my case, but I'm also extremely happy for Miles and the way that things are going in his. It's a wonderful thing anytime an innocent person is released from being wrongfully imprisoned."

"Imagine what the heartbreak for him was, where he turned Richard Miles on to us and then Richard gets out," Kate Germond at Centurion reflected. "He never acted out. He just said he was happy for Richard. He's so impressive."


S pencer had remained in the Dallas jail after Magnis's opinion, expecting a quick release. In jail, he had no work to give him purpose, no friends to pass the time with, no church to lift his perspective. He was allowed out of his cell four times a week to go to the recreation yard, but even those breaks taunted him. "I could see people going to work up and down the freeway, and not being able to be a part of that just made it much, much harder," he remembered. "Being so close to freedom but yet not being free is hard, real hard."[9] Once he saw B.J. driving to work across Commerce Street Bridge—"I said, 'There's my son!'"—but the fleeting, one-way connection only saddened him.[10] "I won't lie to you, I am getting very anxious," he wrote Debra a month later. "I'm right here at the door of freedom, but yet it seems so far away."[11]

Little by little, the days strangled Spencer's dreams. "I began to wonder, what's taking the Court of Criminal Appeals so long?" he said. "And so I'm thinking, they must be looking for a way not to grant me relief."

There were compensations to the county jail. Friends and family visited regularly; he could call home easily; he began to build a little library. Debra's visits were the pinnacle. "Once again I must say that you were looking real pretty this morning, your hair was cute and you had on your lil' blue jean outfit," he wrote one Sunday evening.[12] In the end, his faith sustained him. "There were times when I thought that I was at the end of my rope and that I couldn't take no more," he wrote in July 2010, more than two years after Magnis's ruling. "But the Lord would always assure me that I just need to trust in Him. I'm 45 now and despite all that I have been through, I'M LIKE THE ENERGIZER BUNNY, I'M STILL GOING!"[13]

R ichard Miles's exoneration opened a new era for the Conviction Integrity Unit. Before, it accepted only DNA cases, which were straightforward to prove and hard to refute. But prosecutors took a leap into the future with Richard Miles. Wattley hoped this would embolden Watkins to consider joining Spencer's side before the Court of Criminal Appeals, given the parallels: Both relied on eyewitness testimony, which was flawed, and both offered alternative suspects, who were identified by someone close to them.

"I thought that if he were going to look closely at cases of potential innocence, of wrongful incarceration, this is one that screams out for it," she said. "If you're going to say that's what you're about, then here's one that's all teed up and ready to go."

But unlike the evidence in Miles's conviction, which evaporated under close scrutiny, the evidence against Spencer appeared more solid. In Miles's case, the main eyewitness recanted. But when prosecutors queried Spencer's eyewitnesses, they did not back off. "What do you do when the witnesses stay stuck?" Terri Moore asked, when there's no DNA, no silver bullet clearing him? "You have to be able to say, *here's the flaw*. We found the flaw, and the guy didn't do it. But from the work that we did do on [Spencer's case], it just wasn't there."

Watkins concerned himself less with the particulars of Spencer's conviction than the deleterious effect that reopening it might have on future exonerations. "I'm building credibility. I'm not going to take a chance on a person who's been convicted of murder and aggravated robbery, and somebody *died*! I need positive evidence." He dismissed Dr. Michel's visual science as "junk science." Watkins opposed Spencer's petition before the Court of Criminal Appeals.

Here is the conundrum plaguing the DNA revolution. DNA evidence allows investigators to almost always answer this question correctly: Did this suspect assault this victim or not? That's the good news. But when no DNA exists, convictions have proven much more difficult to overturn. The flipside to DNA's light is that its absence plunges the inquiry into darkness, and often, as with Ben Spencer, obscures the path to the exit.

The DNA revolution has had another dramatic effect. DNA is so far superior to all other types of forensic science—hair comparisons, bite marks, ballistics, even fingerprints—that it has eroded confidence in those methods going forward. This is the secret scandal of forensic science, one that we only began to uncover in the twenty-first century: Except for DNA, most forensic science is not science at all.

# Chapter 26

# GROUND TRUTH

+———+

**It's hard to be that wrong.**

—MARK GODSEY, *referring to the FBI's 96 percent*
*error rate in analyzing hair evidence*

hree months after Benjamine Spencer was arrested for killing Jeffrey
Young, another murder in Dallas would lay bare the hidden flaws in
forensic science. True, forensics did not contaminate the investigation
into Jeffrey Young's murder and Spencer's conviction. Forensics failed to
play a part at all. The Dallas police could not match the only physical
evidence—fingerprints—to a single person; then they lost it, eliminating
any chance that the evidence could be tested using newer DNA technology. Still, forensic "science" can be lethal, like a bad strain of influenza,
quietly infecting investigations and felling innocent people, yet barely
registered by the healthy or the unindicted. The story of "junk science"
deserves telling.

On June 20, 1987, John and Sally Sweek were found murdered in their
apartment in Dallas.[1] They were young, twenty-seven and twenty-one respectively, and toiled in the dangerous business of dealing drugs. The
crime scene was an embarrassment of forensic riches: dozens of fingerprints, bloody shoe prints, and notably, a bite mark on John Sweek's left
arm. The prime suspect, Steven Chaney, was a customer of Sweek's, in
arrears of five hundred dollars. Nine alibi witnesses swore they were with

him when the crime occurred. But, like Ben Spencer's alibi defense, Chaney's failed to persuade the police or prosecutors, and he was indicted for murder.

At trial, the defendant watched as forensic scientists testified that Chaney was the only possible culprit. The most dramatic testimony came from two forensic odontologists (dentists) who had much to say about that bite mark. One testified that the wound "matched" the upper and lower arches of Chaney's mouth: "Only one in a million" people could have made that mark. Another dentist testified "to a reasonable degree of dental certainty" that it was Chaney who bit the victim. The prosecution claimed the bite-mark testimony was "better than eyewitness testimony." The jury convicted Chaney and sentenced him to life in prison on December 14, 1987. His conviction was upheld two years later.

Forensic science dates back at least twenty-five hundred years, to the Qin dynasty in China, where handprints were used to solve crimes.[2] Fingerprinting arrived on US shores during the 1904 World's Fair in St. Louis, when experts from Scotland Yard tutored their American counterparts on this remarkable science. Seven years later, Illinois prosecutors convicted a man for murder based on fingerprints left on a freshly painted windowsill. The Illinois Supreme Court affirmed the conviction, ushering in the era of forensic science.[3]

But calling forensics a "science" distorts its genesis and its rigor. Forensic science did not originate in the scientific academy, but in the police department. Its goal is not to find a cure but a culprit, not to solve a scientific mystery but to solve a crime. Unlike other types of science, in which a hypothesis is subjected to rigorous vetting and double-blind studies, open to challenges by other scientists and requiring replication before it can receive a stamp of approval, forensics suffers through none of that.

"There's really no incentive to do the scientific research that would demonstrate that it's reliable," says M. Chris Fabricant, author of *Junk Science and the American Criminal Justice System*. "It's already being used effectively in the only venue for this type of expertise." These techniques aren't venturing into the larger world where they will face peer-reviewed scrutiny. You don't need a ballistics expert or a fingerprint expert in everyday life. Thus, forensic science, rather than being pressed to up its game, was permitted to tread water.

"Nobody pushed back," notes Keith Findley of the University of Wisconsin. "The defense lawyers were afraid of the science and took it at face value. The courts were afraid of the science and took it at face value. And for prosecutors—it worked for them."[4]

By the 1980s, forensic experts were matching all sorts of things to unlucky, innocent suspects. Brandon Garrett, a law professor at Duke University School of Law and author of *Autopsy of a Crime Lab*, pored over thousands of trial transcripts of wrongful convictions. He found that scientists testified with convincing specificity: This bullet casing came from the box of bullets found in the suspect's closet. This wire was cut with the suspect's pliers. This bloody shoe tread came from the suspect's boot. This piece of masking tape came from the suspect's roll. They matched fibers, human hair, animal hair, bloodstains, shards of glass, bite marks. Their conclusions were delivered with calm authority. In one case, an FBI "image analyst" looked at the black-and-white surveillance photos of a bank robbery and declared that the robber was wearing the same shirt found in the suspect's closet, even though the shirt was mass produced. The expert was asked the odds of another person's shirt matching the one in the surveillance photo. Only one in 650 billion, he responded, "give or take a few billion."[5]

"Examiners said all kinds of amped-up things," Garrett notes. "They get to come in and reach very detailed, precise opinions that can answer key questions in a case. And unfortunately, courts have often just let stuff in, saying, 'I don't know—blood spatter? *Maybe* that person's an expert. They *say* they're an expert.'"

As a result, no one knows precisely how many innocent people have been convicted based on flawed forensic science. The National Registry of Exonerations has found more than 750 cases—nearly a fourth of all the wrongful convictions they've confirmed. When DNA demonstrated that the wrong person had been convicted, faulty or misleading forensics was involved nearly half the time. "There was just a blizzard of error in these known wrongful conviction cases," Garrett says. DNA freed prisoners, but only after traditional forensics put them in prison in the first place.

In the right hands, forensic science can provide strong evidence of a suspect's guilt. But in the wrong hands, and for the unlucky, it captures innocent people in a vise of pseudo-inerrancy. This is the frightening secret of our criminal justice system: We condemn people with sketchy science, performed by biased technicians, working in a broken system.

As a trace analyst for Ohio's Bureau of Criminal Investigations (BCI) from 1977 to 2009, G. Michele Yezzo specialized in hair, fiber, glass, footwear, tire marks, and blood spatter, but she claimed she could analyze virtually anything. In one case, she was able to look at a photograph of a tire mark in a snowbank and connect it to a tire on a suspect's car; she didn't examine the actual tire, but she looked at a brochure for that type of tire.[6] Based on her testimony in an otherwise circumstantial case, the (Black) defendant was given the death sentence. In another case, Yezzo reassembled more than twenty pieces of a broken windowpane and claimed that she found tread marks matching the suspect's shoes.

One exceptional effort bears examining. On February 12, 1981, Barbara Parsons was bludgeoned to death in her bed in the small town of Norwalk, Ohio. Blood coated the walls and floor, and soaked into the bedsheet and nightgown covering the body. In all this blood, the prosecutor would later claim, lurked a clue.

The police interviewed the victim's husband, James Parsons, who offered an alibi. He had left home when his wife was still asleep, had gone to the coffee shop and then to his auto-repair shop, where he saw customers all day. No forensic evidence connected him to the crime. The case went cold for nearly a decade, until a young detective began nosing around the town's most famous murder. He wondered if he could connect the bedsheets and nightgown to what he believed was the murder weapon: James Parsons's Craftsman breaker bar, which he used to cut off bolts at his garage.

The detective turned to Michele Yezzo, who would later coauthor a textbook called *Bloodstain Patterns.* Yezzo sprayed a chemical on the bedsheet and nightgown to enhance the bloodstains. As she watched, she later said, the letters "S" and "N" rose to the surface—consistent with the letters on the Craftsman breaker bar. But Yezzo failed to photograph these impressions, and they dissolved in a few minutes. The evidence was ruined and could not be replicated or retested by the defense.

In 1993, twelve years after the crime, James Parsons was charged with murdering his wife. At trial, Michele Yezzo, a seasoned witness, chose her words carefully. She conceded that millions of other Craftsman tools were imprinted with the same logo. But, she testified, "my opinion is that there is nothing that makes it inconsistent with this bar. There are individualizing characteristics that are consistent with this bar."[7]

Even back then, jurors had come to expect some magic from their forensic experts, and Yezzo did not disappoint. Mike Donnelly, a justice on the Ohio Supreme Court, told me that no testimony is more compelling to a jury than that of a forensic scientist, who presents as clinical and unbiased, and trails a raft of credentials after his or her name. He watched the process in hundreds of cases when he was a trial judge. "I sat there for fourteen years," he said, "and when forensics experts and trace-evidence experts testified, the jury hung on their every word. *The jury hung on their every word.*"

The jury deliberated for less than five hours before finding Parsons guilty. He was sentenced to fifteen years to life.

In 2013, the Ohio Innocence Project accepted Parsons's case. Donald Caster, Parsons's attorney, decided to request Yezzo's personnel file. "It was really just a Hail Mary." On February 23, 2015, a package of 449 pages arrived. The records showed that Yezzo had failed basic tests several times, and seemed to tilt her analyses in favor of the prosecution. "Her findings and conclusions regarding evidence may be suspect," the assistant superintendent of BCI wrote in a memo on May 11, 1989. "She will stretch the truth to satisfy a department."[8] Two days before she was to testify in James Parsons's trial in 1993, handwritten notes from an internal investigation stated that Yezzo had a "reputation of giving dept. answer [it] wants if stroke her."[9]

"My jaw dropped," Caster recalled, and then he filed a motion for a new trial. None of these concerns had been revealed to the defense attorneys. In April 2016, after hearing this evidence of bias, a state court vacated Parsons's conviction. The judge declared the guilty verdict "unworthy of confidence." Parsons was released, twenty-three years after his conviction, a fragile man suffering from heart disease, cancer, and dementia. He died ten months later, at age seventy-nine.[10]

For her part, Yezzo declined to discuss this or any case she worked on, but she insisted she never skewed her findings. "I am not the one to say, 'That person did it,'" she said. "I can say: 'This is what I have from the physical evidence.' That being the case, I'm not judge and jury, and never will be, and never have been."

There is nothing in the thousands of pages of court documents, personnel files, and other records to indicate that Michele Yezzo is malicious, deceptive, or particularly incompetent. She's not like the chemist in the Massachusetts state crime laboratory, who boosted her productivity by falsifying reports and "dry-labbing"—that is, reporting results without actually conducting any tests. In one trial, she testified that a man was caught with a rock of crack cocaine, when it was actually a piece of *cashew*. The man served fifteen months before the state admitted its error. Since then, the state has reversed convictions in twenty thousand of her cases.[11]

Nor is Yezzo like the supervisor of the serology division at West Virginia's state police crime laboratory, who faked evidence in several cases in which an innocent person was convicted of murder or sexual assault—two resulting in life sentences.[12] A review of thirty-six of his cases found that he had lied about, made up, or manipulated evidence to win a conviction in every single case.[13] Another, larger review concluded that "any testimony or documentary evidence offered by [the serologist] at any time should be deemed invalid, unreliable and inadmissible."[14]

No one knows how many corrupt scientists work at labs; presumably it's not something they brag about.[15] "The bad apples are not the problem," Mark Godsey says. "The problem is the good apples."

When a technique requires judgment calls, as most forensic techniques do, analysts do not notice the invisible toxin that invades their reasoning and infects their results. Cognitive bias afflicts even good, ethical scientists—including the top fingerprint experts at the FBI[16]—and study after study demonstrates its power. Itiel Dror, a cognitive neuroscientist at University College London, has shown that contextual information influences experts in a range of forensic disciplines. For example, fingerprint examiners found a match if they were told the suspect confessed—and excluded him if told he had an alibi.[17] Forensic anthropologists were far more likely to wrongly conclude that a male femur came from a female when they were shown staged images of a recovery scene containing a bra.[18] Polygraphers,[19] and even those interpreting DNA mixtures[20]—which involve the genetic code of more than one person—bungled their conclusions when they heard a suspect had confessed.

Cognitive bias can affect anyone, in any circumstance. But it's particularly dangerous in criminal investigations. The incentives for bias are built into the structure of forensic science: With few exceptions, the forensic analyst works for the state, hand in glove with police and prosecutors, creating a motivation to support their views. "Forensic experts get to know the prosecutors and they get to know the police," says Justice Donnelly, who started his career as a prosecutor in Cleveland. "It becomes a team effort. You're all part of 'Team Ohio.'"


The drumbeat of exonerations and subsequent bad press grew louder as the 1990s gave way to the 2000s, in every state and in virtually every forensic discipline. A teenager was convicted of murder and rape in upstate New York based on a trifecta of squishy science: hair, a year-old soil sample, and a photograph matching the suspect's clothing to the crime scene. He served twenty years before DNA exonerated him.[21] In

Arizona, a man was convicted of burning his trailer home with his wife and toddler inside based on discredited arson "science." He served ten years before DNA exonerated him.[22] A hair expert persuaded a jury to convict a young man in North Carolina of raping an eighty-three-year-old woman, concluding there was one-in-a-thousand chance the two hairs found in her house were anyone else's. He served twenty-five years before DNA freed him.[23]

Finally in 2009, the National Academy of Sciences published a scathing report, "Strengthening Forensic Science in the United States: A Path Forward." It concluded that the science of forensics is not, on the whole, scientific. For several years, experts from all sides—forensic scientists, prosecutors, police, medical examiners, defense attorneys, judges— examined disciplines ranging from fingerprints and ballistics to bite marks and blood spatter. They drilled down on the question: How good is forensic science at matching a suspect, or any piece of evidence, to a particular crime scene? The answer: There's DNA, and then there's everything else. Only DNA can definitively connect a person to any place or any thing. "With the exception of nuclear DNA analysis," the report states, "no forensic method has been rigorously shown to have the capacity to consistently, and with a high degree of certainty, demonstrate a connection between evidence and a specific individual or source."[24]

Some types of science, such as serology, toxicology, chemical analysis, and of course DNA, rest on solid scientific foundations, although the results can be swayed by unconscious bias. The larger problem involves pattern analysis, which demands judgment calls: figuring out if this bullet came from that gun, if that tire created the tread at the muddy crime scene, if this fiber found in the suspect's car matches the victim's sweater. "It's just comparison," Mark Godsey says. "It's just eyeballing it."

Fingerprint experts incorrectly match two prints less than 1 percent of the time. But experts in almost any other type of comparison science routinely fail. For years, forensic dentists claimed they could match a suspect's teeth to the bite marks on a victim's body with "virtual certainty," despite the fact that skin is elastic and bite marks change over time, or that dental experts often could not agree whether a mark came from a human's teeth or an animal's.[25] Studies found that forensic dentists get it wrong 15 percent of the time; one study showed the error rate to be as high as 63 percent.[26] Blood spatter experts, who look at patterns of blood to detect how the wounds were inflicted—by, say, a six-foot, right-handed man with a hammer standing over the victim—fare little better than the dentists. In a recent study, experts were shown photographs of a crime scene, where the authors conducting the study knew the "ground truth," that is, how the bloody patterns were created. The scientists botched the test 11 percent of the time.[27]

The prize for error, however, must go to microscopic hair evidence. This technique has now been largely superseded by DNA analysis, but it helped put untold numbers of people in prison and dozens on death row. By 2015, the FBI had reviewed hundreds of criminal cases in which its examiners had testified that hair found at a crime scene incriminated a suspect. The FBI concluded that its experts had provided scientifically invalid testimony in 96 percent of the cases—including thirty-three of the thirty-five death penalty cases.[28]

"It's hard to be that wrong," Godsey observes.

Imagine if the pathologist analyzing your biopsy failed to detect cancer cells 96 percent of the time. What if 15 percent of the packages you ordered never arrived? If 11 percent of your internet searches yielded incorrect information, would you trust the search engine? But in criminal cases, where the testimony of a forensic scientist can persuade a jury to take away someone's freedom or his life, these error rates will do. According to the National Academy of Sciences, it's worse than that: Aside from a handful of studies mentioned above, there are almost no rigorous reviews of any discipline of forensic science. We have no idea how accurate they are, or whether they're valid at all. It's like playing darts without a board. You can claim a perfect throw, but who really knows if the dart hit the bull's-eye—or went wildly off course?

The cauldron for these mistakes is the crime laboratory. Even today, labs present a "crisis of national proportions," says Sandra Guerra Thompson, author of *Cops in Lab Coats: Curbing Wrongful Convictions Through Independent Forensic Laboratories*. "It's like whack-a-mole. You improve a situation one place and then there's a new crisis somewhere else."

Duke University's Brandon Garrett keeps a running tab of scandals at crime laboratories. He says that hardly a month goes by when he doesn't add another lab to the list, whether in specific cities (Cleveland, New York, San Francisco, Detroit) or in entire states (West Virginia, Montana, Connecticut). Some crime labs, notably in Washington, DC, have been shut down and their work outsourced elsewhere.[29]

In this bleak landscape, one laboratory stands out, for both bad and good: the Houston Police Department Crime Laboratory. It's safe to say that March 11, 2003, was not a banner day for the Houston lab. "Worst Crime Lab in the Country," the headline in *The New York Times* announced, with the subhead: "Or Is Houston Typical?"[30] Houston drew mortifying attention because it was so large, its analyses had so many errors in them, and its mistakes were so existential: Houston executes more people than any other city, and often the convictions were based on the testimony of its lab's forensic scientists.[31]

Two cases brought the crisis from simmer to boil. In one sexual assault investigation, laboratory experts identified hair and blood in a rape kit as belonging to George Rodriguez and excluded another suspect. In 2004, seventeen years later, retesting found that Rodriguez was not a contributor and the other suspect was.[32] In a second case, seventeen-year-old Josiah Sutton was convicted of committing rape in 1999, based on the crime lab expert's analysis of DNA in the rape kit. When the DNA tests came back, Sutton told his attorney that the results were impossible. "There's no way on God's green earth," he said. The attorney responded: "Well, I'm sorry, man, but that's what they came up with."[33] Sutton was exonerated five years later, in 2004, after the DNA was retested.

Chastened, Houston ordered a top-to-bottom review of the lab, which revealed that it was something of a house of horrors. For six years, the roof over the evidence storage room had leaked, contaminating the evidence. The head of the DNA unit had no experience with DNA. Technicians were poorly trained, kept shoddy records, misinterpreted data, or made reports on evidence they didn't bother to test (again, known as "dry-labbing"). Some two hundred convictions based on the Houston lab's work were called into question. The experts botched 20 percent of the tests on blood-evidence samples. Nearly a third of the DNA samples had "major problems"—including those for a quarter of the death penalty cases.[34]

"Houston was a hot, stinking mess," recalls Peter Stout, who took over as president of the laboratory in 2017. "One thing that set Houston apart is that level of ugly, bad notoriety. There's actually a real strength in that. It got bad enough that everybody said, 'Okay, we've got to do something different.'"

Legislators shuttered the laboratory, metaphorically burning it to the ground, and from the ashes rose the Houston Forensic Science Center in 2012. No longer part of the police department, it is now a "local government corporation" with a board of directors that includes defense attorneys and an exoneree. It analyzes evidence for both defense and prosecution, and hands over test results to any defense attorney who asks. Stout says the laboratory steers clear of sketchier disciplines, such as hair and bite marks (which he calls "black magic") and blood spatter ("close to black magic").

But the innovative jewel in Houston's crown is blind testing. Periodically, the lab's managers slip a sample into the stream of evidence where they know the truth in advance—this sample is cocaine; the owner of this latent print is in the database; this DNA mixture involves these three people. In this way, the lab can confirm whether its analysts are arriving at the correct answer. "We've never fired anybody for the mistake," Stout says. "We have certainly fired people for the lie about the mistake." Early studies, published and unpublished, suggest that their error rates are far lower than the national average. Stout says he's lucky. Houston had the money and shocking history to reinvent itself. Most laboratories do not. Now Houston is considered the finest crime laboratory in the nation.

B ecause of its record number of executions and its record of mistakes, Texas has confronted its demons and emerged with a new vision. It has put in place more protections to prevent future mistakes and greater restitution for past ones than any state in the country. It created a new, independent forensic laboratory. Texas passed a "junk science law" in 2013, the first state to do so, which allows a prisoner to return to court for a chance to overturn a conviction based on discredited forensic science. Only a handful of states have followed suit.[35]

Most remarkably, the Texas legislature created the Texas Forensic Sciences Commission, with the mission of investigating complaints from prisoners, their families, laboratories, and advocacy groups such as the Innocence Project. The commission asks questions like: Is this technique based on reliable science, or individual judgment? Did, or do, the experts overstate their findings?[36]

An early watershed moment occurred in the case of Steven Chaney. Recall that Chaney was convicted of the double murder of the Sweeks and sentenced to life, based largely on bite-mark evidence. The national Innocence Project, led by Chris Fabricant, director of strategic litigation, lodged a complaint with the commission. On September 16, 2015, Chaney was transferred from prison to a Dallas courtroom to watch the dentists and the lawyers debate his case. Three dentists, looking uncomfortable, defended their work, noting it had been accepted in courts since 1975. "The problem is whether or not the science *works*," observed Lynn Robitaille Garcia, the commission's general counsel. "It can't be just because the judge says it's okay."

The commission did its homework, examining the science, cognizant that some three dozen people who had been convicted based on bite marks had been exonerated. "What we saw in looking at the research is that dentists aren't any better at matching that marking to a human than anybody else," Garcia said. "There is no agreement within the community about whether the pattern of injury left on skin is even a human bite mark—never mind did Steven Chaney bite that person?" A month after the meeting, Chaney's conviction was vacated, and the commission set out to write a report on bite-mark evidence. The commissioners concluded that it was unreliable science.[37]

Commissioners can't make law, but they can influence it: They recommended a moratorium on bite-mark evidence. Later, the Texas Court of Criminal Appeals, in finding Chaney innocent, wrote a seminal decision that discredited the technique—an opinion that has been embraced by many courts around the country. The commission has other sciences in its sights, including hair analysis and DNA mixtures.

Asked how he would rate the Texas Forensic Science Commission, Chris Fabricant says, "I don't think it really can be measured. They're so important because it's one of the very few places where science is really the only issue."


By early 2010, Spencer had languished in the Dallas jail for more than two years. Finally, in August 2010, he chose to return to Coffield Unit, where he could work and exercise and gather at church with other believers, where he could live the settled life of a convicted criminal. There, in his maximum-security prison, he waited with mounting anxiety for the Texas Court of Criminal Appeals to decide his future.

*Chapter 27*

# NO WAY OUT

+———+

**I hope we reached the right opinion.**

—Lawrence Meyers,
*judge on the Court of Criminal Appeals*

For the first part of 2011, Spencer's days followed their usual routine: in bed by 7:30 p.m. and rising at 1:30 a.m., reading the Bible, working as a prison janitor, worshipping at church, and making his beloved "spreads" on Sunday nights. He wrote letters, stayed out of trouble, and hoped that his time in prison would end soon.

Spencer *almost* persuaded himself that soon he would leave Coffield for good. Judge Rick Magnis had eviscerated the prosecution's case. The Court of Criminal Appeals would surely follow his recommendation. In his mind, Spencer hoped. In his heart, he worried.

On the afternoon of April 21, rumors raced around Coffield Unit. An inmate stopped Spencer in the hallway. "Man, you're going home," he said, "I just heard that on the news." Spencer waited, but no order came for him to board the chain bus to Dallas. He called Debra, who had been waiting by the phone, dreading his call. "Has anyone told you?" she asked. "No, nothing," he said. "The court ruled against us," she said. In the stillness that followed, Debra could hear inmates yelling, a television blaring, doors slamming. Eventually he said in a quiet voice, "Okay."

In a unanimous decision, the Court of Criminal Appeals rejected Judge Magnis's findings that Spencer deserved a new trial based on actual innocence. At the time, Texas was one of only five states to consider an innocence claim without a constitutional violation; not even the US Supreme Court had done that.[1] But the court, loath to overturn a jury verdict, set the bar so high that the judges called it a "Herculean task."[2] Spencer had to prove that he and his team had found "newly discovered evidence" that was not available at trial. Usually that meant DNA, but it included other evidence: when police find a videotape of the crime that definitively excludes the prisoner, for example, or when a victim of sexual assault recants, or when a forensic technique on which the conviction rests (such as bite marks) is discredited. Beyond that, the evidence must be so compelling that a jury would find the prisoner "unquestionably innocent."[3]

Judge Magnis believed Spencer had met the Herculean burden. But the eight elected judges on the Court of Criminal Appeals—all Republicans, five of them former prosecutors—dismissed Spencer's arguments.[4] (One judge on the nine-member court had recently retired.) The evidence pointing to Michael Hubbard was speculative at best, they found. Danny Edwards—the jailhouse informant who admitted that Spencer had not confessed to him, who claimed Spencer sanded off his fingerprints—was more credible than Hubbard's friend Kelvin Johnson. The judges gave "little weight" to the scientist who challenged the eyewitnesses' ability to identify Ben Spencer. He could not replicate the crime scene, they concluded, because too much had changed since 1987. The scientist's "assumptions" could not "overcome the testimony of witnesses who said they had enough light to see."[5] Even if the eyewitnesses could not identify Ben Spencer, that "does not affirmatively establish his innocence."[6]

"It's unfortunate for him," District Attorney Craig Watkins remarked afterward, "but I think it's great for our criminal justice system that we're not going to get bogged down."[7] The Young family felt vindicated. "We live in a system that you're innocent until proven guilty," Jay Young said, "and he's been proven guilty twice."

P aradoxically, Ben Spencer was trapped by the *absence* of physical evidence against him. DNA was unavailable to implicate him or exonerate him. "We can eliminate all evidence of guilt, but as long as we don't have that scintilla of affirmative evidence of innocence, he's going to sit there in prison," Judge Magnis said later. How could any person affirmatively establish his innocence without DNA, which is absent in the vast majority of crimes? "How can you prove that you didn't do something? How can I prove to you that I really didn't have oatmeal this morning? It's just ridiculous. It's a ridiculous standard." Magnis paused, still frustrated a decade later. "I believe the Court of Criminal Appeals has placed greater value on having a consistent ruling, on finality, than the truth."

In her office at the University of Oklahoma, Cheryl Wattley broke down in tears. "Is there something else I should have done?" she wondered. "Where did I go wrong with the Court of Criminal Appeals?" Worse, she and Jim McCloskey had fanned Spencer's hopes because Judge Magnis had stated he was innocent. "And then you get hit with a sledgehammer," McCloskey said. "An unexpected ambush, a sledgehammer by the Court of Criminal Appeals. And you know that you have *no other legal recourse* once they make their decision."

Not only had the court uprooted Spencer's immediate hopes, but it had also eradicated his future legal options. Spencer's team had explored appealing to the federal court, but they were too late for that.[8]

"So the only thing left was to try to find new evidence, try to figure out what did we miss, what did we overlook?" Wattley recalled. "What more investigation can be done?"

Centurion had already spent several years and some $250,000, and had unearthed plenty of material: new forensic evidence, a more viable perpetrator, proof of perjury by the prosecution's key witnesses. How could they possibly find more persuasive evidence twenty-four years after the crime? April 20, 2011, was a professional nadir for Wattley. Still, she observed, "whatever struggle we may have, it is nonexistent in comparison to the fact that Spencer is still sitting in a cell wearing that white jumpsuit."

"I don't want you to worry about me, but I'm really struggling right now," Spencer wrote in a letter to Debra a month after the decision. "On the outside, I appear to be holding up quite well, but then on the inside, I'm torn up. I'm battling with all types of things: who I am as a person; what does the future hold for me? You name it, I'm probably troubled with it. I keep wondering, is prison the life that my future holds for me? I don't want to spend the rest of my life here, but I wonder, will they ever do the right thing in this case?"

The problem here is, we can't retry the case," Judge Lawrence Meyers explained. It was late August 2017. Judge Meyers, now retired from the Court of Criminal Appeals, smiled at me affably, a balding man with a cherubic face wearing pressed jeans and a polo shirt. We were settled in his kitchen, where his three Labrador retrievers were snoring softly as he skimmed his twenty-one-page opinion that had denied Ben Spencer a new trial.

It was a valid jury conviction, he said, one that could be overturned only with conclusive proof of innocence. He conceded that their "Herculean burden" might keep innocent people in prison, but the judges' hands were tied. "We can't grant relief based upon the way the system is set up," he said.

"But if you are Ben Spencer and you are innocent, where does that leave you?" I wondered aloud.

"Oh, I don't know," he sighed. "Mr. Spencer has been in jail for a long time. Mr. Spencer may be eligible for parole."

"Do you feel that you all reached the right opinion here?" I asked, gesturing toward the opinion.

"I hope we reached the right opinion," Judge Meyers said. "You can't

ever say with absolute certainty. You don't want anybody in jail who is innocent." He hesitated, casting about for words. "I don't know if 'confidence' is the right word. I feel like it was the best we could do based upon
what was brought to us at that particular time. I hope Mr. Spencer—I'm
not saying I hope he's innocent—I'm just saying that if he is, I'm just hoping that we did the right thing in this particular case, is what I'm hoping.
And that Mr. Spencer has hopefully been rehabilitated."

For nearly a quarter century, Spencer searched for an escape from the
labyrinth of Texas law. One by one, the exits slammed shut, and
Spencer was forced to pin his hopes on the sympathy of the Texas Board
of Pardons and Paroles.

The Texas parole board is not a sympathetic group. It denied parole to
Spencer the first time in 2007, when he reached his twentieth anniversary
in prison. Cheryl Wattley suspected that the well-connected Young family was opposing Spencer's release, so in 2011, she hired an attorney, Gary
Cohen.

Cohen specialized in helping prisoners win parole, and he knew his
way around the system. "They're all tough," he observed. "You don't find
any goddamn liberal Democrats on the parole board. But they're all reasonable people." Mostly, they're overwhelmed. The fifteen commissioners
receive eighty thousand to ninety thousand parole petitions a year, moving through cases at a rate of three to five minutes per petition. They give
particular weight to "victim protests," in this case, the objections by Jeffrey Young's family, friends, politicians, and others the family persuaded
to object to Ben Spencer's release. The personnel file is confidential, and
a prisoner cannot see the material submitted by the victim's family, the
prosecutor, the sentencing judge, or corrections officers. "We're shooting
in the dark; we're not able to check for factual errors, hearsay, bald-face
accusations, or stuff that's accusatory but without basis in fact," Cohen
said. Since most of the materials in an offender's file are generated by police, prosecutors, or corrections officers, the nature of information the

board relies on is "slanted." Prisoners can submit letters and briefs, of course, but "it's a really one-sided process."

On June 6, 2012, Wattley and Cohen met with two parole commissioners at the regional board office in Palestine, Texas. That's what hiring a lawyer buys you: time with the commissioners. She argued that Spencer was innocent, that a judge had concurred with that conclusion. She said that Spencer could not accept responsibility for a crime he did not commit. But look at his character and his record: He's had only three infractions in twenty-five years, he attends church, he has a responsible job in the prison's education department, he's earned an associate's degree, he doesn't even have a tattoo. She assured them that he had a job lined up and a place to live. "It was a forty-five-minute monologue," Wattley recalled. "They said, 'Thank you for your presentation.' I asked: 'Any questions?' They said, 'No, ma'am, we're just required to allow you the opportunity to make a presentation.' It was the most useless procedure I've ever seen."

All through the 2010s, the Young family and Spencer's supporters waged a battle of letters. The thrust and parry grew particularly intense in 2014–2015, when Spencer's team rallied all his supporters and the Youngs recruited influential people to beat them back. Dozens of Spencer's family, friends, and other exonerees sent in impassioned pleas, along with some powerful supporters. Judge Rick Magnis wrote that he closed down his court for a full week to review the evidence and then presided over a hearing. "It remains my judicial opinion," he wrote, "that Benjamine Spencer is actually innocent of the crime for which he has been convicted."[9] Alan Ledbetter, the foreman of the jury that sentenced Spencer to life in prison, wrote that he was the only person to sit through both the trial and the evidentiary hearing. "I was convinced beyond any reasonable doubt that Ben was innocent," he wrote, and implored them to allow Spencer "an alternate ending that puts this extreme miscarriage of justice in the annals of history."[10]

Bruce Anton, Spencer's original attorney, wrote that he remained struck by the shoddy police investigation and lack of physical evidence. "I am still appalled that another suspect, and probably the killer, was not properly investigated. In hindsight, it seems that the police had tunnel vision."[11] Rafael Anchia, a member of the Texas House of Representatives, wrote that enough is enough: "Mr. Spencer has lost much of his life behind bars; it is only just that he be pardoned and released so that he might enjoy what life he has left."[12]

And finally, after opposing him at every turn, District Attorney Craig Watkins switched sides. Watkins wrote that he now believed Ben Spencer was innocent. "Interviews have been conducted. Nighttime visits to the scene were made. Based on those activities, it is my position that Mr. Spencer should be granted a pardon based on actual innocence." The date of the letter was November 21, 2014, a few days after he had lost his re-election bid. When Watkins could have helped, he didn't. Now, defeated and powerless, he had nothing to lose.

The "victim protests" from the Young family and their supporters are confidential. However, through a public information request, certain letters from prosecutors in the district attorney's office were made available. Andy Beach, who prosecuted Spencer in the second trial, sent his first opposition letter in 1989. Writing on official stationery, Beach said that Ben Spencer "savagely" beat Jeffrey Young and will "forever be a violent threat"; he had cost the Young family incalculable pain. "I have never seen a victim's family so permanently and unalterably [devastated] by this horrible crime."[13] In 2006, when Spencer was coming up for parole the first time, Beach wrote that since the time of his arrest, "Ben Spencer has been trying to escape the consequences of his horrific crime." The victim had missed twenty years of birthdays, anniversaries, graduations, and weddings. "Jeff's dad went to a way too early grave with the cause being, quite simply, a broken heart."[14] Beach's opposition as a private citizen in 2013 was briefer, but chilling: "They waited and they pounced. Minutes later Jeff Young was discarded on a dark Dallas street like a bag of garbage."[15]

Karen Wise, an appellate lawyer in the district attorney's office who served as second chair during the 2007 hearing, seemed even more determined. She wrote the board four times between 2012 and 2015. She had spent many hours with the victim's family, and they were "still devastated by Spencer's heinous act," she wrote in a 2013 letter. "Ben Spencer clearly has no empathy or sympathy for the family of the man he so callously murdered." She concluded: "Spencer will not hesitate to use violence to get what he wants, no matter [whom] he harms in the process."[16]

Every year, Spencer received the same letter from the parole board. He was denied for two reasons: his "criminal history"—namely, that he had been convicted of a violent crime—and "the nature of the offense."

"Well, that's never going to change," Jim McCloskey observed, echoing Spencer. "What happened to Jeffrey Young, as tragic and as brutal as it was, will never change. So, I just hope and pray that someday the parole board will get tired of denying him and will eventually let him go home."

Spencer was perplexed. "I mean, you do all that you can to stay out of trouble and do things to increase your chances to be released on parole, but none of it seemed to matter at all," he wrote to Debra a few days after he was denied parole again, on December 9, 2015. "Well, I'm not going to allow their decision to defeat me. I'm going to press on." He closed by thanking her for putting money into his commissary account, allowing him some small prison pleasures: corn chips, salty peanuts, vanilla wafers, cereal, M&M's, and chicken soup.

During that decade, Spencer clung to two ideas: that he was innocent, and that God was running the universe according to his inscrutable plan. As the days turned into years, as fall gave way to winter and spring to summer, he never loosened his grip on those twin beliefs. His letters expressed the range of emotions, yet they were surface feelings, swaying this way and that like aquatic plants, but rooted in the bedrock of his faith.

And so Spencer became a wry observer of prison life. "Since returning to Coffield, I have learned one important lesson," he wrote Debra. "There is nothing on TV nowadays."[17] Later, Spencer was transferred to the education department, where inmates who were about to be released on parole took classes to help them adjust to the free world. "Where I work is like a circus because it's full of clowns," he wrote Debra. "They're supposed to be in school trying to get a GED, but they're too busy trying to holler at their homeboy. Walking around with their pants below their butts. If they put as much effort into getting their GEDs as they put into hanging out in the halls and restrooms, they would have a college degree by now."[18] He watched them leave prison, these inmates who had killed or raped, distributed crack or robbed at gunpoint, and he braced himself for another year and another denial.

Spencer also despaired. Fighting his rebellious heart, he released Debra from her commitment to him. "You have waited long enough for this to end," he wrote her in 2014.[19] "I would like for you to have what I cannot provide you. Be happy so that I can be happy for you." But Debra stayed, and he let his mind wander. "Just think, you and I would nearly have 30 years in together," he wrote in 2016. "Could you imagine waking up with me lying next to you this morning?"[20]

But Spencer never questioned God. Even McCloskey, a minister, wondered about the yawning chasm between God's promises and Spencer's life. "Jesus said at one point, in John: 'The truth shall set you free,'" McCloskey said. "Well, we know what the truth is. The truth is that Ben Spencer had nothing to do with this crime. And it has not set him free. And the *prospects* of the truth for setting him free do not look strong."

But through force of will or strength of faith, Spencer never dived very deeply into existential doubt. The price was too steep. And so, from behind the prison walls, he steadied himself and he steadied Debra. "I started out being angry, and Ben talked me out of my anger," Debra said. "I'd say, 'How you feel?' He'd say, 'I'm okay, and we'll keep fighting this. I still have hope, and God is going to turn it around. I need you to be strong. I need you to keep B.J. strong. I need you to hold up and just be there for me.' That's what I did."

Outside prison, Spencer was gaining a following. Supporters held several rallies for him on the courthouse steps. They showed up every time the district attorney released another exoneree, wearing T-shirts with the words: "I am Ben Spencer." *The Dallas Morning News* wrote articles and editorials. Southern Methodist University held a symposium devoted to Spencer's case. His fame seeped into prison, to both guards and inmates.

"A constant question that I am asked by both, 'Man, when are they going to let you go?'" Spencer wrote to Ann Hallstrom in 2016. "My response is usually, 'That's a good question, considering the fact that I never should have been convicted in the first place.'" They also observe that Texas will have to pay him once he's out. "I inform them: 'There's not enough money in the world that can make up for the years that I've missed out on.'"[21]

After Ann Hallstrom sat with Debra through the evidentiary hearing in 2007, she and Spencer became lively pen pals. Indeed, Spencer kept up a correspondence with an array of people who came to believe in his innocence. Dr. Jerry Lancourt and his wife, Jinna, who learned about his case at the SMU symposium, began writing and visiting regularly, a fact Spencer remarked upon in every letter. "With the exception of my family, I've been alone and on my own," he wrote as he neared his twenty-sixth year of incarceration. "To now have others on board and supportive of me in this case means a great deal to me. For the record, I need all the friends that I can gather, so thanks for being my newest friend."[22]

He corresponded regularly with many others, including jury foreman Alan Ledbetter. Spencer spent much of his money on stationery, cards, and stamps; he never missed a holiday, birthday, anniversary, or Valentine's Day. He followed the Lancourts' RV trips, inquired after doctor's appointments. He never ceased to ask about Ann Hallstrom's work or her grandson and his obsession with Spider-Man. He played down his disappointment after another parole rejection. "I was really anxious to get out too, so that I could get that Church's Chicken that you promised me," he wrote to Hallstrom on August 19, 2012, after he received a letter rejecting his parole once again. As he approached his fiftieth birthday and Christmas in 2014, he confessed to the Lancourts that holidays were especially hard, then added: "It's that time of year and I want to have my pity party, I suppose."[23]

On rare occasions, he let his friends see his struggles. "Being here in this prison is just a state of existence," he wrote Hallstrom in 2016.[24] "I'm alive, but barely. It's like being in a coma, from which I've yet to come out of. The only difference probably is that I am conscious of my surroundings, making for a more miserable existence." But in the next paragraph he regrouped. "I give all the praise to our God and Creator. Not only does He provide me with the strength and faith to continue on, He's also blessed me to encounter some very amazing folks. God is good."

The Lancourts gave him a typewriter in 2015—"THANK YOU, THANK YOU, THANK YOU!!!"—and his "new toy" changed his life.[25] Together, he and Jerry Lancourt labored over a public statement, sending drafts back and forth until Spencer scrapped them all and wrote from his heart. It was called "The Falsely Accused: In the Words of Ben Spencer."[26] "I must admit that I am not quite sure where to begin with the details of this case, but I can assure you that wherever I start, that it will be the truth," he wrote. "The proverbial problem for me has been trying to figure out, what's significant and what's insignificant? My fervent prayer is that I will not fail in my objective in pointing out the serious wrong that has been imposed upon me, my family, and the family of the victim Jeffrey Young."

The support buoyed him, and he returned to the law library. "Well I'm sure that by now you've heard the good news," he wrote to the Lancourts on June 16, 2013. Referring to a recent US Supreme Court ruling, he told them that until now, the law had limited the time that prisoners could bring new claims of innocence to one year. But a few days previously, he explained, "The Supreme Court ruled that an actual innocence claim is not time-barred if they can show through a preponderance of the new evidence that no jury would have convicted him if they had this evidence to consider."[27] He said that meant that Cheryl Wattley could file his case in federal court.

He wrote Wattley long letters with legal and investigative strategies. In one particularly detailed letter in 2012, Spencer urged her to find a crucial witness: "While she might very well still be a 'drug addict,' she is key to this case." He suggested hiring a certain investigator. He urged her to file in federal court. He cited nine Texas appellate court cases showing the state cannot incarcerate a person with "no evidence." He quoted law journal articles on post-conviction remedies, and he outlined potential *Brady* claims and evidence of ineffective assistance of counsel. "Have you reviewed the case *Finley v. Johnson*?"[28] he queried. "I ask because I was reading it over this morning and it seems to have some merits that might be helpful to us." He goes on to give the legal citation and quote relevant sections of the decision.

Then, on February 13, 2017, two new names appeared in a letter to Debra. One was Faith Johnson, a Black Republican who had been appointed district attorney in Dallas to finish the term when the previous district attorney resigned for mental health reasons.[29] "Faith Johnson claims that she wants to exonerate the innocent, and this case will certainly provide her with the opportunity to do just that," Spencer noted. The second was a private investigator named Daryl Parker, who wrote Spencer out of the blue. "In his letter he said that he believes that this case deserves to be reinvestigated and that he would like to do that for me."

Spencer's story was about to take a turn.

*Part 3*

# Darkness and Light

+——+

*Chapter 28*

# THE SURGE

+——+

**Short of an absolute, unforeseen miracle,
there's not much daylight.**

—Jim McCloskey

It was just past 10:00 p.m. on June 23, 2017, as Cheryl Wattley, Daryl Parker, and I unpacked our tools: a one-hundred-foot measuring tape, a camera, and recording equipment. A block away, a half dozen teenagers were hanging around a stoop playing a game of dominoes. If we had been here some thirty years ago, we might well have seen another group of young men playing dominoes on the stoop. We might have watched a light gray BMW creep along Hartson Street and pull into the alley in front of us. We might even have seen who climbed out of the car and ran away.

"Daryl, go stand under that streetlight," Wattley said, pointing to the light near the alley where the BMW was parked that night. The private investigator strode over to the single lamp on the block and turned to face us.

"What do you see?" she asked me.

"A shape," I said. "I can't tell if he's Black or white."

"You can see a silhouette of a man," Wattley observed.

"How far do you think that is?" I asked.

Wattley walked to the alley and returned, noisily unspooling her hundred-foot tape measure.

"This is only forty feet, and you can't even see his face."

On March 22, 1987, three neighbors claimed to have seen Benjamine Spencer and Robert Mitchell park the car and run away from the alley. The closest neighbor stood more than twice that distance away.

I surveyed the neighborhood, now in the throes of gentrification, and recognized that this was a fool's errand. How could we replicate the physical crime scene, or coax wary neighbors to tell us their secrets, or find new alibi witnesses—much less discover new evidence three decades after Jeffrey Young was killed? How could I, a journalist without subpoena power, with no weapons but curiosity and a tape recorder, reinvestigate a settled conviction?

Still, I knew that every now and again, the passage of time offers up surprises. Earlier that day, I had arrived in Dallas on assignment for *The Atlantic* and National Public Radio, the former where I was a contributing writer, the latter where I had, until recently, worked for nearly twenty years. I assumed Spencer's story would arrive at a predictable conclusion: that without DNA, a wrongly convicted prisoner cannot demonstrate his innocence. This had been McCloskey's frustrating insight when he told me that Spencer's case still haunted him, that a day did not go by when he did not think about Spencer, a man declared innocent by a Dallas judge yet denied relief by the district attorney and Texas's highest criminal court. "We've got no place to go," McCloskey said. "We've exhausted all of our appeals."

Although McCloskey had officially retired from Centurion Ministries, he remained immersed in Spencer's life. It was his last unsolved case after forty years of investigations and several dozen exonerations. Every other Saturday morning, he waited for Spencer's call from prison and tried to radiate whatever optimism he could muster. Without avenues for him to pursue, he could only hope for a lightning strike of luck.

"The only option that I can see is that eventually, at some point, they will finally grant him parole. There's no other way, unless miraculously, out of nowhere, new evidence emerges." Maybe the real perpetrator would suffer a pang of conscience and confess to the crime, he said. Maybe some lost evidence would resurface—evidence that could be tested for DNA. "But short of an absolute, unforeseen miracle, there's not much daylight."

Every day for several weeks that summer of 2017, Daryl Parker and I waged an intense investigatory campaign that Parker called "the surge." From eight in the morning until ten at night, we knocked on doors all around Dallas, almost always running into dead ends or feeling the whoosh of air as doors closed in our faces. When not canvassing Dallas with Parker, I interviewed prosecutors, defense attorneys, the victim's sons, and Spencer's family, and met Spencer for the first time in prison.

In the end, we found two dozen people who knew details about the crime, a surprising tally in a case that was three decades old. I also discovered a fundamental principle of cold cases: Time is both the enemy of truth and its friend. Memories fade. Witnesses die. Evidence degrades or disappears. And yet time can reveal truth just as a Polaroid snapshot slowly reveals the details of the scene it captured. Relationships change. Old loyalties dissolve. Conscience eats away at one's sleep. A person no longer has a reason to lie. And so Parker and I began to build a case.

Clean cut with his Marine Corps flattop, direct but respectful, Parker had a knack for persuading people to reveal past crimes, telephone numbers, and stories they'd never told anyone else. Parker joined the marines at seventeen—he needed his parents' signatures—and served for two decades in twenty-eight countries in the Middle East and South America. After retiring from the military, he joined the police in Allen and then McKinney, Texas, taught at the northern Texas police academy, and became a criminal investigator.

"I began to see that you cannot win against the police," he told me during one of our interminable drives to find a witness north of Dallas. The system is supposed to be balanced, but even as a patrol officer, "I could go out and I can make anything stick on anyone." He left the force to become a private investigator and began doing pro bono exoneration work on the side. He realized that Innocence Projects may have great lawyers to argue in court, but to get before a judge, you need to find new evidence. You need to go out and interview witnesses from ten, twenty, thirty years ago, reconstruct the crime scene, and figure out that it couldn't have happened the way the prosecution claimed. "So the hard investigative work, somebody has to do that kind of stuff," he said. He started a nonprofit, Actual Innocence Review, to fill that gap.

Spencer's case offered an abundance of possibilities, since the prosecution left so many questions unanswered. "This case lacks so many things," Parker observed. "It lacks a murder weapon, it lacks a witness to the assault, it lacks the victim's stolen property. It lacks any forensic evidence: no fingerprints, no blood, nothing. The only thing that puts this case on Ben Spencer is eyewitness testimony." Today, he said, in the world of DNA and skeptical juries, such a paucity of evidence would never fly.

On our second day, we drove to the meticulously landscaped home of Jesus Briseno, the retired detective who headed the murder investigation into Jeffrey Young's death. Parker called such uninvited visits "manhunting," and they result in many more strikes than hits, and far more anger than affirmation. This was precisely the reception we received from the detective outside his home: a cold stare, followed by stomping away into the house.

Briseno's rejection notwithstanding, we set out to answer the most pivotal question: Who ran away from the victim's BMW on the night of the murder? The official answer had been determined at the beginning of the investigation, when the detectives made choices as to whom to believe and whom to discount. Investigators chose to believe some neighbors and ignore others; they chose to credit the jailhouse informant who implicated Ben Spencer and discount two other criminals who identified Michael Hubbard.

Early Sunday morning, June 25, we tracked down one of Spencer's neighbors, whom both the police and Spencer's attorney had disregarded. Sandra Brackens, now forty-four years old, agreed to meet us at her childhood home in West Dallas, a tiny place that housed three generations of the Brackens family and abutted the alley where the BMW had been abandoned. She arrived late, having spent the night helping her daughter suffer through early labor pains. Soft-spoken, articulate, with an astonishing memory for details thirty years in the past, Brackens worked two jobs, the day shift at Verizon, the night shift at UPS. But she shrugged off her exhaustion as she described the night of March 22, 1987. "Whatever y'all need me to do, I'm here to do it."

A fourteen-year-old Sandra Brackens was sitting on her front porch, talking on the phone, when suddenly a dark-skinned man, between five foot eight and six feet tall, cut across her yard and sprinted in front of her, fifteen to twenty feet away. He wore all black—baseball cap, jacket, pants, and what sounded like "church shoes" from the way they slapped on the pavement. He carried a silver jambox on his shoulder. She couldn't see his face, but as he passed under the street light, she could see his skin tone. Unlike Ben, whom she knew, he had a dark complexion.

"He didn't appear to be as tall as Ben. He didn't appear to be as thin as Ben. This wasn't Ben."

"You're sure?" I asked.

"Positive. Thousand percent positive. It was not Ben."[1]

We told her that the perpetrator had cracked the victim's skull in five places. She gasped. "I've never known [Ben Spencer] to have a disagreement with anybody." She held a dimmer view of one of his accusers, Charles Stewart, who claimed to have seen Spencer that night. He had since died in a drug-related shootout, but soon after the arrest, Brackens confronted Stewart. "I asked him, 'Why y'all lie on them people?' He was like, 'Man, we was trying to come up,' so basically, for reward money," Brackens explained. "I was like, 'That's somebody's lives that y'all ruining—for a few dollars? Really? That's disgusting.'"

Early in the investigation, Brackens told Detective Briseno what she had seen. Briseno said he didn't believe her, speculating privately to Parker that she might have been "one of those crack whores." As we sat on the porch, she wondered aloud why the detective had never followed up, and, a little embarrassed, I repeated Briseno's comment. Brackens looked shocked, then gazed down at her hands for several seconds. She seemed on the verge of tears.

"I have never in my life used a drug, never. I don't even like Tylenol," she whispered, almost to herself. "I was fourteen years old. Wow." She looked up, fiery now. "Tell Detective Briseno, I have the IQ of a genius. At fourteen years old, I was taking high school classes. Tell him *that's* what I was doing at fourteen."

More puzzling was that Frank Jackson, Spencer's defense attorney, never called Brackens as a defense witness. He said that she was too equivocal. "If I didn't put her on, it's simply because I felt like she would hurt us more than she would help us," Frank Jackson had explained. "And you never put a hostile witness on the stand. That's just the kiss of death to trial strategy."

"The statement is quite surprising to me," Brackens responded. After all, *she* approached Spencer's mother and offered to testify, and she testified in Robert Mitchell's trial. "I was always ready to testify on behalf of Benjamine Spencer."

Brackens led us into the alley and stopped by a tree. This is where Jeffrey Young's BMW was abandoned, she said. There had been a trailer and a chicken coop between Gladys Oliver's house and the alley, which blocked her view. As Parker began measuring the distance from the tree to the alley and the street, he grew visibly excited. He explained that according to Brackens, the BMW had been parked much farther into the alley than we had been led to believe. It would have been difficult for Jimmie Cotton to see the car from his kitchen window, and the angle would have made Gladys Oliver's view nearly impossible, even without the trailer and the chicken coop. This was speculation, of course. The police took no crime-scene photos that night. But it was also potential new evidence, since Brackens had never been asked for this information before. She agreed to sign an affidavit. "If I thought for one second that either of those two could be capable of something like that, I wouldn't be talking to y'all," Brackens said. "In this case, I will always say they did not do this." She paused, still reeling from the assault's brutality. "Oh, man. Man, five places?"

Our next witness would be less forthcoming.

G ladys Oliver, now in her early seventies, had never strayed from her testimony implicating Spencer and Mitchell. She was an enigmatic and divisive character. Most of her neighbors believed she had lied to receive the twenty-five-thousand-dollar reward, but there was never hard evidence that she did. Ostracized, she left West Dallas for a friendlier neighborhood and disappeared, popping up occasionally to confirm her story in affidavits or in court for prosecutors. Her consistency impressed prosecutor Andy Beach.

"This isn't a case of mistaken identity," Beach remarked when we met up in a jury room in the Dallas Courthouse. Now in his sixties, he wore his blond hair long and wavy, and was trim and stylish in his blazer and jeans. He spoke earnestly, candidly, as if taking the listener—the juror—into his confidence. One can see why Beach won so many trials. "Either she's a monster that just picked out two completely innocent human beings—she said this is their unlucky day, and I want that twenty-five thousand dollars—or she saw what she saw. Okay? No in between."

I wondered which Gladys Oliver I would meet as Parker and I drove to her apartment complex. Parker had visited Oliver already, but she had grown upset and asked him to leave. Perhaps, I hoped, someone less imposing, like a short, middle-aged woman, would have better luck. I knocked and a teenage girl opened the door to an apartment as dark as night. I peered in to see Gladys Oliver in a recliner, a rug over her lap on this sweltering day, her motorized wheelchair within reach. She was shrunken, nearly blind. A plate of chicken bones sat on the table next to her.

"Who are you, ma'am?" Oliver asked, as the girl settled down on the seat next to the door, barring my entrance. I stood in the doorframe and explained that I was a journalist from Washington and hoped to talk with her for a few minutes. What about? she asked. About a case where she had been the star witness, I said. She started hyperventilating, trying to hoist herself out of the recliner, as if to flee, but her body trapped her. "Oh, no, oh, no," she whimpered. "Don't talk to me. I don't know anything," she said.

"You sure? Just for a couple of minutes?" I ventured, a little worried; a possible heart attack crossed my mind.

"Oh, no, oh, no. No, ma'am. Please don't knock on my door, please."

"I'm sorry," I said, not budging.

"I had a stroke and my thinking... I'm kind of messed up in the head. And I don't see out of one of my eyes. The sugar ate up one of my eyes," she added, referencing diabetes. "I'm just not together."

Seeing as she was unlikely to blurt out a confession, I said goodbye. I left, saddened. Gladys Oliver seemed tormented. Was she haunted by the consequences of her truthful testimony? After the trial, she received threats from people who suspected her of sacrificing Spencer for reward money. "I know my mother's not a liar," her son, Marlon, told us later. "If my mom said he did it, trust me, he did."

Or perhaps she was afflicted for telling a lie, her conscience burdened for the past thirty years? I would never know. Her daughter told me she suffered from Alzheimer's disease. The pivotal story in the case against Ben Spencer is forever lost in the fog of dementia.

There's a third option. What if Oliver's lie became her reality? Dr. Geoffrey Loftus, the memory expert, suggested that Oliver could have believed the perpetrator looked like Spencer and because he ran away, she never had a chance to correct the mistake. It's possible, he said, that she created a memory of Spencer in the alley—and later, after revisiting that memory time and again, had etched it into mind; it's possible she honestly believed Spencer was the perpetrator.

"Let's imagine that, having discovered the reward, she thinks, *Huh?* Wow, who might that have been?" he explained. If she's going to avail herself of the reward, she must come up with a name. "That she said, 'Okay, I'm going to make somebody up. How about Ben Spencer? He's a reasonable candidate. Let me think: What does Ben Spencer look like? Oh, yeah, he could have been the guy that I saw.'" The more she thought about it, the more she rehearsed this memory of Ben Spencer as the perpetrator, the stronger and more "confidence-evoking" the memory became. "And so even though it begins with a lie, it could wind up a strong, convincing memory to her."

This memory distortion happens to everyone. One night in July 1984, Jennifer Thompson was twenty-two, aiming to graduate with a perfect 4.0 from Elon University in Burlington, North Carolina, when she was awakened at around 3:00 a.m. to find a man towering over her. She decided if she was going to be raped, she would put the bastard behind bars. "I willed myself to note the details," she later recalled.[2] She studied his face: the hairline, the mouth, did he have scars or tattoos? She imprinted in her memory his high, broad cheekbones; small, almond-shaped eyes; a faint shadow on his upper lip. Later, at the police station, she reeled off what she remembered. They asked her to do a composite sketch, and she happily complied. "You want to help the police," she told me thirty-five years later. "You want this person apprehended. You want this person taken off the streets because what you don't want is other people to be harmed."

The police soon caught Ronald Cotton, a Black man whom Thompson tentatively identified in the first photo lineup. But with each viewing, with each conversation, her certainty flowered. In 1985, Cotton was convicted largely on the strength of her testimony, and given life in prison plus fifty-four years. But Ronald Cotton did not assault the young woman. Ten years later, DNA showed that a man named Bobby Poole was her assailant. Yet when Thompson confronted the real rapist, she failed to recognize him.

"My memory was completely contaminated," she recalled. "There was no memory of Bobby Poole up there. Instead, it was Ronald Cotton raping me."

This contamination occurs time and again in criminal trials. What's unusual here is that Thompson and Cotton became friends and wrote a book together, *Picking Cotton*, about the fallibility of eyewitness testimony. If this intelligent, determined woman who memorized every detail of her assailant's face can get his identity wrong, anyone can.

At 4:00 p.m. on a sweltering Sunday afternoon, Daryl Parker and I arrived at the childhood home of Christie Williams, Spencer's alibi witness. In 1987, the small, tidy home was next door to Gladys Oliver's, and their yards abutted. Hattie Walker, Christie's mother, opened the door, then turned around and walked inside, leaving it ajar. We followed her into a small dining room. She sat down at the table, gesturing toward two chairs laden with boxes and old magazines. She looked at us expectantly, and we realized she didn't know why we were there.

"We're supposed to meet your daughter here," Parker told her. She nodded. "We want to talk to her about Ben Spencer." At the mention of the neighborhood's most famous murder, she perked up. "Ben didn't do it," she said emphatically. "In my heart and in my soul, Ben didn't do that." Oliver had lied for the reward money, she insisted. Besides, she said, it was physically impossible for her neighbor to look out her back window and identify Spencer.

"Couldn't nobody see out that back room where they said she saw that boy at," Mrs. Walker said. "Now, you see my house like it is now," she said, waving airily around the dining room. The table was covered with papers, shopping bags, a toaster, a broken lamp, not a square inch open. All around the room, stacks of boxes and garbage bags full of clothes were piled to the ceiling. She nodded with satisfaction. Gladys Oliver's house was just as crammed with stuff, and anyway, Gladys Oliver was short, maybe five foot one, and obese, not nimble or quick on her feet. "If you got clutter and boxes up to your windows, how can you—that short—get up there?" she asked rhetorically. "And she was crippled. How can you get up there and see out your back window? You can't do that. That's my point about it. You couldn't see back there."

Eventually, Christie arrived. In 1987, her speed in track won her a full scholarship to Prairie View A&M. Now nearing fifty, she had maintained her athletic build. She worked two jobs: at the phone company during the day, then as a home-care nurse in the evening. She was bone-tired, she said, but she laid out what she could remember.

She and Spencer had been together between around 8:00 p.m. and midnight. He could not have robbed and murdered Jeffrey Young. "Not in the time frame that they are saying, because I know for a fact that we were together at that time that they were saying that it happened," she said. "So I'm like: Nope. It couldn't have happened."

Then, almost as an aside, she mentioned evidence that the jury never heard: a new alibi witness. "My brothers came in, and my baby brother came up here because he wanted to watch TV." She didn't recall the precise time, 9:00 or 10:00 p.m., around the time Jeffrey Young was being assaulted miles away. So persistent was her brother that Spencer suggested they drive to the park for some privacy. Hattie Walker confirmed this account. "When I came home about eleven or something, my boys was up. They'd usually be in bed and they were up and they were sitting on the couch, I said 'What y'all doing sitting up on this couch?'" They told her Christie was out, with Ben Spencer. "So how did all that happen in that frame time and they at the park, and I'm here at eleven?" she asked. "It just wasn't right. They railroaded that boy."

"Could we talk to your sons?" I ventured.

"I don't know, I'll ask them," Walker replied.

B y the time I walked into Jimmy Young's town house that evening, I was worried about tunnel vision. Nearly everything I had read and almost everyone I had interviewed persuaded me that Ben Spencer had been framed. I had to fight the same instincts that had, possibly, sent two innocent men to prison when the Dallas police had succumbed to tunnel vision in 1987. Jay and Jimmy Young, the victim's sons, provided an emotional antidote, if not a factual one. We talked for more than two hours in the airy, modern, meticulously decorated living room, reviewing what they recalled of their father's death. They would not discuss the trial or the attempts to exonerate Ben Spencer, except to say they were weary of fighting for the convicted killer of their father to serve out his life sentence.

"It's a lot of work," Jimmy commented. "There's a lot of mental steps that you have to take to get yourself in the right frame of mind. There's a lot of margaritas consumed. Sometimes there's a lot of people involved. There's a lot of conversation. There's a lot of different opinions. I'm really tired of this. It's been thirty years. It's difficult."

His older brother, Jay, pointed out that there are many opinions—from defense attorneys, prosecutors, investigators, journalists, and judges—but only one incontestable fact. They lost their father. Jay's children never met their grandfather; Jay was never able to play a round of golf with his dad; he could never ask his advice about how to deal with an errant child or how to resolve a thorny business problem. His father lost his life; it's only right that Spencer should lose his freedom. "Do I think he should get parole?" Jay asked. "No. And if he did get parole, I'd be very upset. My dad won't come back. My dad's not getting parole."

"Have you ever considered whether Mr. Spencer might be innocent and spending his life in prison for a crime someone else committed?" I asked.

"No," Jimmy replied immediately. "Nothing has changed my mind. I believe in our justice system. There's nothing that has come out to make me think any other way."

Over the years, prosecutors in the Dallas County district attorney's office have assured the family, the court, and themselves that Jeffrey Young's true assailants had been convicted. Spencer is guilty, period, and every time a writ is filed or a journalist writes a story, it questions the integrity of the system and threatens the emotional health of the family. This certainty washes through the criminal justice system in virtually every jurisdiction. Sometimes it's called "belief persistence," sometimes it's called "escalation of commitment," but whatever it is called, the result is the same: No amount of evidence will change their minds.

*Chapter 29*

# INNOCENCE DENIERS

+————+

**We love Magnis, but he's wrong.**

—District Attorney Faith Johnson

District Attorney Faith Johnson swept into the room, trailed by three prosecutors and a media relations manager, and settled herself at the head of the table. She was pure Texan: larger than life, television ready, a tall, attractive woman with long wavy hair and wearing a string of pearls. Judge Johnson, as she was called—a reference to her previous job—was the first Black woman to serve as district attorney of Dallas County, having been appointed by the Republican governor to finish a term vacated by the previous occupant.

It was June 27, 2017, my fifth day in Dallas, and she opened what felt like a board meeting by introducing her acting head of the Conviction Integrity Unit, a young, quiet woman named Cynthia Garza. Garza explained the process of reinvestigating convictions, and acknowledged that the low-hanging fruit—the DNA cases—had been all but plucked, and that the rest, like Ben Spencer's, were exponentially harder. "They take years and years to investigate," she said. "We're working hard, and we're working strong, and we're keeping the wheels turning."

Johnson, who had never been involved in Spencer's case, laid out her confirmed view of Spencer's guilt with a surprising command of detail. The conviction was "solid," she said. Referring to his neighbors, she pointed out, "These people were not strangers. They were friends and they knew him. *Three* of them knew him, not just one. That's why we believed in our conviction, and that's why we have fought to uphold this conviction all of these years." She beamed. "Guess what? The Court of Criminal Appeals agrees with us."

I pointed out that the neighbors did not see the assault; the only person to connect Spencer to the robbery and murder was the jailhouse snitch, Danny Edwards, and his testimony was wrong in practically every detail.

"We can talk all day long about the jailhouse snitch," she responded. "We can just say: So what? He got confused. But he was consistent with one point and that is that the defendant Spencer admitted to committing [the crime]. He never changed that point regarding his testimony."

What about Judge Magnis's finding that witnesses were lying for the reward, that the jailhouse snitch admitted he never heard a confession directly, that the evidence pointed to another perpetrator, Michael Hubbard, and that Spencer was actually innocent?

"We knew he was wrong!" she exclaimed, laughing. "This wasn't our first rodeo. We've been going at this since, what, 1987? We've had two trials. We've had a writ hearing. We've had the Court of Criminal Appeals. This decision has been upheld for so long. For one man to say he should get a new trial, well, he was wrong! I mean, we love Magnis, but he's wrong."

"It's not as though we just said, okay, we're done. We got him convicted twice, and that's it," Lori Ordiway added. Ordiway headed the appellate section of the district attorney's office at the time. She said when Centurion filed a petition with new evidence in 2004, her unit interviewed some thirty witnesses before concluding that Spencer was guilty. What she didn't say was that the Conviction Integrity Unit has always been part of the appellate section. The unit could not make a move without Ordiway's consent. The appellate section's mission was to preserve convictions, not unravel them. "We want to protect our system," Ordiway said. "It's a wonderful system where every person is innocent, including Mr. Spencer, until proven guilty by the jury of their peers. That's why, when someone comes in sixteen or seventeen years later and files an application for a writ of habeas corpus, it is a heavy, heavy burden."

Spencer needed newly discovered evidence, the district attorney said, and this provided an opening. I had filed a public information request with Dallas's crime laboratory, the Southwestern Institute of Forensic Sciences, to determine if it had retained any biological evidence that could be tested for DNA. The lab had responded that as of the last request in 2011, it had kept the fingernail clippings of the victim's right hand. Since the perpetrators may have struggled with Jeffrey Young as they dragged him toward the BMW and placed him in the trunk, it was possible—a long shot, but possible—that he had scratched the assailants and snagged a bit of their DNA with his fingernails. I asked Judge Johnson, with tape rolling, whether she would allow any biological evidence to be tested for DNA.

"If there's some possible newly discovered evidence that could lead to the exoneration of Mr. Spencer, yes, we would support looking at it," she responded. "Because we don't want any innocent person to be in prison."

With this agreement, I concluded the interview. I had enjoyed my conversation with Judge Johnson, even as I sensed I was being played. McCloskey held no such warm views. Since the early 2000s, he said, he and Wattley had approached four district attorneys and begged them to look into the case, the latest being Faith Johnson. "We never got a response," McCloskey said. "They just listened to us. They just did nothing. We were infuriated. We were disgusted."


I handed Andy Beach the jail logs from March and April 1987, the ones pertaining to Danny Edwards. Oddly, the man who prosecuted Ben Spencer in 1988 and won a life sentence seemed more open to reconsidering the case than Faith Johnson, who had nothing to do with the original trial. Perhaps Beach figured he had nothing to hide. He had an impeccable reputation as a prosecutor who always won but never cheated, who did not believe that every person the police hauled in was guilty. In fact, in recent years, he had switched sides to represent people facing execution as the chief of the new Capital Defender Division within the Dallas County public defender's office.

As Beach scrutinized the jail log, I explained the context as best I could. The evidence from the jailhouse snitch achieved gold status when Edwards swore that he received no benefit for his testimony. He swore that he had reached his deal with prosecutors before he even met Ben Spencer, and thus had no incentive to make up a story that Spencer had confessed to him.

But the jail log told a different story. It showed that Danny Edwards made a deal *after* meeting Ben Spencer: When Edwards entered the meeting with the police, he was facing twenty-five years in prison, and when he (and his lawyer) were done negotiating, he faced a maximum of ten years in prison. In fact, I reminded Beach, Edwards walked out of prison two months after he testified in Spencer's second trial.[1]

At trial, the informant told the jury that he was coming forward because it was the right thing to do, casting himself as a credible witness, not a slippery and desperate criminal. Given Edwards's insouciance toward the truth, I observed, who knows what else he lied about on the stand?

Beach stared at the log for several seconds, as if hoping he'd find a flaw in the math. "I really can't make any sense of what happened," he said quietly. No prosecutor would have been assigned to the case that early on, so who approved the deal? I wondered aloud if Danny Edwards's perjury might have tainted the process. Not at all, Beach insisted.

"Danny Edwards, to my way of thinking, did not influence the jury's decision in this case, and probably hurt us more than it helped us," he said.[2]

We moved on, but for the rest of the interview, Beach appeared rattled. I asked if he thought the state had possibly prosecuted the wrong man. "I cannot sit here and tell you today, one hundred percent, Ben Spencer's guilty," Beach said. "I sure hope he is. I sure hope he didn't have to do one day without his freedom for a crime he did not commit. That's a prosecutor's worst nightmare."

Edwards's deal, and perjury, sufficiently troubled Beach that he sent me an email a few days later.[3] "I was not involved in whatever 'deal' Edwards got way before first trial happened," he wrote. "So Detective Briseno and/or (snitch) Edwards's lawyer went to the DA and/or the first assistant and cut whatever deal they made," he wrote, concluding, "Really strange."

I tried to find who was responsible for the deal, and why they made it. But anyone who could know the answer either had died or refused to speak with me. My request for the prosecutor's records was turned down. Edwards's deal remains a mystery. The devastating effect of it does not.

L ara Bazelon calls them "innocence deniers." They are prosecutors who refuse to seriously entertain even the most blatant evidence of a wrongful conviction. Bazelon's first brush with such denial occurred when she headed the innocence project at Loyola University Law School in Los Angeles. In 2012, she inherited the post-conviction case of Kash Register, a man who had been convicted of murder some thirty-three years earlier. Register's new lawyers had discovered that the prosecutors had suppressed key evidence. They knew that all the witnesses had either lied or had said that Register was *not* the killer. Bazelon laid out her case before a group of prosecutors in the district attorney's office. "At the end of this hour-long presentation, they basically told us to go fuck ourselves," she recalled.

They went to court, and during the evidentiary hearing, Bazelon eviscerated the prosecution's original case. "At one point, the judge called us up to the bench and said off the record to the prosecutor, 'Do you honestly think at this point that Mr. Register is guilty?' He said, 'It doesn't matter what I think, Your Honor. The point is that in 1979, twelve people came back and said that he was guilty.'" The judge said, "I just have no idea what we're doing here," and vacated the conviction.

"What is this mentality about?" Bazelon wondered. She has written extensively about prosecutorial resistance to righting old mistakes.[4] "It doesn't align with their ethical obligations," she noted. "They're supposed to be ministers of justice, and they leave that by the wayside, because they're so fixated on winning."

In 1935, the US Supreme Court laid out the role of the prosecutor in *Berger v. United States*. A prosecutor is not an ordinary party to a case but represents the "sovereign" who has an obligation to govern impartially. A prosecutor's ultimate interest, the court declared, "is not that it shall win a case, but that justice shall be done." Thus the prosecutor "is in a peculiar and very definite sense the servant of the law, the twofold aim of which is that guilt shall not escape or innocence suffer."[5]

A wealth of research suggests that once people reach a belief based on some information, they will retain that belief, even when the basis for it has been debunked.[6] In order to reduce the cognitive dissonance—that is, the psychological discomfort of seeing one's beliefs collide with new information—prosecutors will work much harder to support their beliefs than to modify them. Criminologists call it "belief perseverance" or "belief persistence."

Belief persistence pops up time and again in sexual assault convictions. Here's how it works: A man is convicted of rape. Years later, DNA comes along and excludes the convicted prisoner. Rationally, the current prosecutor might say, "Wow, we made a terrible mistake, it's not this guy, let's let him go and charge the real perpetrator." Many prosecutors do just that. But others "prop up their preexisting beliefs by constructing new hypotheses that are consistent with the evidence," Keith Findley at the University of Wisconsin says. "Hence, the unindicted co-ejaculator. 'Oh, it's not his semen? Oh, well, then he must have had an accomplice who also raped her and happened to leave his semen,'" even though no evidence was presented in the original trial that there had been two people.

The roll of exonerations is filled with such accounts. Typical is the case of Juan Rivera, an intellectually disabled teenager who was convicted in 1993 of raping and murdering an eleven-year-old girl in Waukegan, Illinois. His conviction was vacated because of a surplus of errors; he was tried and convicted again. Twelve years later, DNA tests excluded Rivera as the rapist, and his conviction was vacated. The prosecutor tried Rivera again in 2009 with a new theory: that the eleven-year-old girl had consensual sex with someone else prior to being killed by Rivera. He was again convicted. Eventually the appellate court reversed the conviction, saying it was "unjustified and cannot stand." He had served twenty years. The prosecutor opted to forgo a fourth trial.[7]

In another case, not even a confession from and DNA match to an infamous serial rapist-murderer persuaded prosecutors that two teenage boys were innocent of murder. In 1985, Rolando Cruz and Alejandro Hernandez were convicted and sentenced to death for abducting, raping, and murdering a ten-year-old girl in Naperville, Illinois, in 1983. After their convictions were reversed on appeal, they were convicted again in 1989. By then a serial murderer named Brian Dugan had confessed to committing the crime alone. Cruz and Hernandez were retried again in 1995, after DNA had proved Dugan was the rapist. This time, the prosecution claimed the two men had committed the crime with Dugan. After Cruz was acquitted, prosecutors dismissed the charges against Hernandez.[8]

"That's belief persistence in action," Findley observes.


G iving up a win is very hard for the prosecution," says Dan Simon, author of *In Doubt*. "It's to admit that they screwed up. It's to say that their techniques and methodologies are faulty, which they're going to use tomorrow, and the next day, and the next day."

To avoid the "huge emotional, internal cost" of such admissions, Simon notes that prosecutors have on occasion gone to astonishing lengths. For example, former New Orleans district attorney Leon Cannizzaro sometimes fought exoneration cases for years until the prisoner had run out of appeals. When backed into a corner, he favored gangster-like tactics to preserve the conviction. In one case, it came to light that the two eyewitnesses had been pressured by police to identify the wrong person.[9]

When they recanted their testimony, his office threatened them with perjury.

"Their theory was, 'Judge, either they lied at the initial trial or they're lying now, but either way, at some point they lied,'" says Lara Bazelon. "'One way or another, you should convict them of perjury,' which is, of course, a felony." Cannizzaro's office did prosecute the witnesses, and a judge acquitted them.

Most prosecutors try to do the right thing, Simon notes. But what they don't realize is that just below the conscious level, another psychological process is working, unnoticed, like software, called "escalation of commitment." The more wedded a prosecutor is to an outcome, and the higher the cost of reversal, the less likely he or she is to correct what might be a mistake.

"When you're a tailor and you cut someone's sleeve too short, it's a fifty-buck mistake. We'll sort it out," Simon explains. "But if you send someone to prison for fifty years, you've crushed their lives. So, ironically, the more grave the mistake, the less likely you are to at least try and remedy it."

Instead, you batten down the hatches and plow ahead. Ben Spencer had weathered these headwinds for thirty years. All he could hope was that new evidence would steer his life, little by little, one degree at a time, out of the wind and toward a safe harbor.

*Chapter 30*

# NO JUSTICE FOR SOME

+———+

**He say I did it. I say he did it. The best liar wins.**

—Jailhouse informant Danny Edwards

Sometimes I lose my voice, which is inconvenient for a radio reporter. I have partially paralyzed vocal cords, and whenever I get a cold, my voice disappears, sometimes for a day or two, sometimes for a week, once for a month. When that happens, each day is a torture of helplessness. I hear conversations but can't participate. I observe, but can't persuade, or question, or laugh out loud. I have to simply surrender my will and my self-expression—and there is nothing, *nothing*, I can do about it. This may not be so bad—probably a mercy for my family—but then there is the chronic pain, the unrelenting, throbbing ache that invites thoughts of suicide, not in the immediate future but eventually, for the prospect of feeling this pain for a lifetime is more than I want to bear. I survive with a series of questions: Can I endure this for a day? No. For an hour? No. For thirty seconds? Yes, I can bear this for thirty seconds. The most surprising fact of chronic pain is there is no relief, for how do you escape your own body? How do you flee from yourself?[1]

I was thinking about this as I passed through the front gates of the H. H. Coffield Unit to meet Ben Spencer for the first time. I reflected on how I boil over in frustration when my voice silences me for more than a few days, how I melt in despair as my vocal cords throb. Please don't get me wrong: I am not equating my affliction with Spencer's life. I have medication to dull the pain; Spencer has no such numbing agent. Still, my body offers a sliver of understanding. What would it be like to be helpless and effectively mute, unable to control your future—not for thirty seconds, or one hour, or one day—but for more than thirty years? What would it be like to be Inmate #483713, sitting across from me behind a Plexiglas window?

June 26, 2017, marked the first of many times Spencer and I would talk. I strained to hear his soft drawl over the couple yelling to each other a few seats down in the narrow visiting room. Spencer was fifty-two, having just passed his thirtieth anniversary of incarceration. His hair was flecked with gray and deep lines were etched across his forehead. He was six foot four, lanky, and still handsome. He looked like a cover model in his prison uniform; even the prison-order glasses were stylish on his face. But the man who once favored snakeskin boots and Perry Ellis shirts was consigned to prison whites.

"This is as sharp as I get now, this white uniform," he said, chuckling grimly. "You know, some of these guys, they press their own clothes. They put water on them, put them under the mattress." Spencer ended this practice years ago. "I don't even care. I'm just at a point where . . . I'm still hopeful, but at the same time, it's like I'm stuck in a system."

Spencer's days unfolded in military order. At 1:30 or 2:00 a.m. every day, he slipped out of his nine-foot-by-four-foot cubicle, spacious enough for a bunk bed and a table. He dressed silently in his white uniform before tiptoeing past the 110 sleeping men in his dorm room to fix some weak coffee. He would open the locker under his bed, where all his possessions reside: a Bible, a fan, a radio and headphones, stationery, a John Grisham novel, and most prized, photos and letters from his family and friends. Sometimes he would start a letter, sometimes not, before he reported to his job between 3:00 and 4:00 a.m. in the prison's education department. He generally put in twelve hours each day, particularly in the summer, for the building was an air-conditioned reprieve from the stifling residential section.

His last good friend, William Jackson, was paroled eighteen years ear-lier. He had "acquaintances" among the prisoners, but he considered the civilians in the education department his friends. "The people I work for, they're pretty good people," he remarked. "They've read about my case. They're always asking me, 'When are they going to let you go?'"

He had watched the world, and his family, barrel into the future, leav-ing him planted in the 1980s. "I listen to old-school music, and whenever I hear music from the eighties, it shoots me to a time and place," he said. "And I think, Man, why am I here? When can I get a break? And to have all these obstacles—not just the courts but now the parole board. When does the truth have meaning?" He was quiet for a few seconds. "You know, there seems to be no justice for some."

Ben Spencer lived in the past, because he had no present and he did not trust the future. He no longer worked out at the prison gym. "If I'm not getting out, what's the purpose of it? I'm going to die anyway in this place," he said. He no longer visited the law library. He no longer attended church.

But even as he noted these changes, I recognized that Spencer was not giving up. Rather, he was anchoring his hope over and beyond the prison walls of his human life, into the eternal, a time beyond death. He no longer counted on witness recantations or biological evidence, the fickle stuff of humanity, but looked to the evidence of things not seen, which is, after all, the New Testament definition of faith. And so, he still believed in God. He still prayed. "I just kind of embraced the fact that hey, I might be here the rest of my life. What I believe and what matters most is that I know that I have faith in God. What anyone else thought or believed didn't matter anymore."

It's not that hope is gone; it's just that hope is painful. Still, Debra Spen-cer said there is one emotion she has never seen. "Ben never got bitter," she said. "If it were me, I would be angry. Why am I here? *Why why why why why?* But to be bitter or to say something bad, I have never heard it."

We were sitting in Debra's tidy television room just off the kitchen. The breakfast table was set for two; the linen napkins were ironed and the coffee cups were positioned above the mats. She never ate there; she was waiting for Ben, has been, for three decades. It occurred to me, not then but later, that her house reflected her personality, and it offered a clue as to how she coped with the past thirty years: All the blinds were drawn, for she is intensely private, keeping all but a handful of friends at arm's length, never revealing her secrets or her feelings, never letting anyone see inside. Every pillow and every photo was in its place, for she has coped with a life defined by unpredictability by controlling whatever she can.

Debra rarely smiled, as if carrying the weight of Ben's confinement. When she did, her smile was blindingly beautiful, an unexpected bright explosion of life, like lightning, or fireworks. But now, in the summer of 2017, she was not smiling. She was staring uncomfortably at my tape recorder as I began the delicate process of excavating her life. We talked about her childhood, falling in love with Spencer, her disbelief when he was arrested, her despair when he was convicted and sentenced to life. Why she didn't cut Spencer loose long ago, why did she remain in his orbit?

"After all that went down, I'd think, 'I'll probably never find another guy like Ben,'" she recalled. "People used to always tell me, 'You're so picky.' I'm not picky. I just know what I want. And he does exist because he existed before."

"If he gets out, would you ever remarry him?"

"No, I don't think so," she said. "Too much has passed. I've changed a lot. I don't think I will remarry him, but I am on his team forever." He's more than welcome to stay with her if he's released, she added—an important gesture, as the court would insist that Spencer return to a stable environment, preferably not West Dallas. "I'll do whatever I can to help him get back up on his feet."

Unlike Spencer, she had harbored a slow, burning anger at God.

"It got real spiritual," she said, laughing at her chutzpah. "A few weeks ago, I just fell on the ground crying and I was like, 'God, if you want me to believe that there is a God, you're going to have to show up." I remember Ben calling me that night and I told him what I had done and he was like: 'Listen,' he said, 'God is still here. God is doing his part.' I said, 'Well, I don't see how he could let an innocent man rot in jail the way he has.'"

She took a deep breath. She didn't really believe God had abandoned them, but the Almighty has been mum about the purpose of all this loss. "I know He's right here with us. But the blessing that He's given us out of this? I just don't see it yet."

As I prepared to leave, Debra leaned forward, urgent. "I know there's something out there that they can find to free him. There has to be *something*. I believe they know what it is, there's something they know and they're not saying. I just feel it deep in my heart."

D aryl Parker positioned himself just to the right of the door. It was June 27, 2017, and behind us, the rain poured down in sheets, cascading from the roof of the two-story apartment complex. It was designed like a Days Inn, metal doors spaced twenty feet apart. Parker, a former police officer, raised his hand to knock, then noticed I was standing directly in front of the door. He silently nudged me to the side.

"Sometimes they shoot through the door," he whispered, and in my thirty-five years as a journalist, I had never considered the possibility that someone would shoot me as I lingered outside an apartment. Over the next few weeks, I would learn a few tricks of investigative work. Knock, don't ring the bell. If no one is home, talk to the neighbors. Always be polite (easy) and often be direct (hard). Don't call ahead. Just screw up your courage and show up at their home.

We waited. We heard someone shuffling into the hallway. "Who is it?" a woman yelled.

"Ma'am, it's Daryl Parker," he called out, as if that clarified anything.

We had visited every address listed for Jimmie Cotton in Parker's private-investigator database. This one, his mother's apartment, was the last. I tried to slow my heartbeat. Parker lifted his hand to knock again when the voice, closer now, asked, "What do you want?"

"Ma'am, we're looking for Jimmie Cotton."

The door opened, and the elusive witness, Jimmie Cotton, six foot five, rail thin, dressed in a yellow T-shirt and jeans, was standing before us.

Cotton seemed a little nervous as I pulled out my recorder. The blinds were drawn, the room lit by a single lamp casting a faint yellow glow. In the back, I heard his mother's television, abandoned when she came out to eavesdrop on the conversation. I didn't want to spook him, and I had mapped out a cautious route for this interview, allowing Cotton to unspool his story slowly.

What do you remember about that night? I began.

As if he's been waiting for this question for a decade, Cotton blurted out: "I ain't going to say it was him, I ain't going to say it ain't him. Because it was dark." With that, the interview became a confessional, as he dismantled his testimony from thirty years back. He saw only one man, not two, he said—corroborating the account that witnesses gave to the police that night and contrary to his testimony that he saw Robert Mitchell emerge from the driver's side and Ben Spencer from the passenger's side. The man was rushing away from him, he said. He never actually saw his face. He just assumed it could be Spencer from the tall, lanky build. In fact, the detectives told him as much.

"They tell me it was Benjamine," he recalled. "The police was saying that Benjamine was under investigation for this murder. I said, 'It looked like him. Maybe it was him.' And they went on from there."

"Did you feel pressure?" Parker inquired.

"Uh-huh. Because I was young then. I was scared. I was still in school."

"What are the chances that it was Benjamine that you saw?" Parker asked. "Do you think it's like a fifty percent chance? Or a ninety-nine percent chance?"

"I'd say forty-five percent chance."

Parker and I exchanged suppressed smiles. Cotton agreed to meet with Spencer's lawyer and sign an affidavit detailing his story. He'd take a polygraph as well. I circled back to Parker's question, just to confirm: What chance was it that the man you saw was Ben Spencer?

"I'd say about thirty percent chance."

Parker and I fell quiet, wondering if he was just saying what he presumed his guests wanted to hear.

"Jimmie, are you feeling pressure from us?" I asked.

"Naw," he said. "I feel bad about this. If he didn't do it, he needs to be out." He shook his head. "That's a long time. Thirty years."

W e rolled to a stop across from the hot-pink house, its girlish ostentation at odds with the frenetic drug activity that dominated the neighborhood. This was the last known address of Danny Edwards, the jailhouse informant. We knocked on the door, and a young man answered. He said eight families live in the 2,100-square-foot house, and he's never heard of Danny Edwards. We walked back to Parker's Jeep and were about to leave when we saw a petite woman with long brown hair waving us over.

"Do you want to talk to Danny?" she asked. "I'm his fiancée."

She told us he worked at night as a repo man, but he'd be here tomorrow morning. Then, incredibly, she gave us his cell number. We called and made an appointment with the only person who connected Ben Spencer to the death of Jeffrey Young.

The next morning, Danny Edwards greeted us gregariously, gently setting down his puppy, a Labrador–pit bull named Queenie, before shaking our hands. He was recently released from prison, after serving time for the latest in a series of convictions that made prison his home for half his life. He spoke in a rapid-fire murmur, and I tried to make sense of what he was saying, asking him to repeat things more slowly. When he did, he recanted his entire testimony.

"Where it started at is the he say–he say," he began. According to

Edwards, he met Spencer in Lew Sterrett jail, and three days later, the police called him into an interview room. They showed him a document purportedly signed by Spencer, which Edwards said he did not read. They told him that Spencer had accused him of killing Jeffrey Young. *No*, Edwards said. *Spencer* confessed to *me*. "He say I did it. I say he did it. The best liar wins."

Edwards told us that Spencer never confessed to killing Jeffrey Young. "He didn't say that. He said they was *accusing* him of doing it. He didn't even know the guy. He ain't ever been over there." Nor had Spencer threatened the alibi witness, Christie Williams, as he swore at trial, thus sabotaging Spencer's alibi defense. "He ain't said nothing, threatened nobody." Edwards explained that accusing cellmates of a crime in exchange for a reduced sentence is simply how the game is played in jail. "When I realized he didn't do it and I saw the seriousness of it, I checked, but it was too late. It was already out there. They get me on falsifying and lying to the court, all that shit." He held to his story rather than risk perjury charges.

We told him that Spencer never accused him of murder, and pointed out that many details in his trial testimony were flat-out wrong, such as what the victim was wearing, who Spencer's partner was, and how Spencer had rubbed off his fingerprints to evade detection.

"'Cause he never said it! I'm going on what they [the police] say."

"So you were just kind of making up details?" I asked.

"Yeah, making up what they throw out to me," he said, referring to the police. "You can say anything: I can take it and make it better than what you said."

"Mr. Edwards, you've lied in the past," I said. "Can I ask why we should believe you now?"

"Frankly, I don't care, ma'am," Edwards replied. "I don't got any reason to lie to you. I pay my own bills. I do my own thing. It was different when I was young," when he was facing a long prison term if he didn't testify against Ben Spencer, and a perjury charge if he changed his mind. "But that shit is over with. It won't hurt me now." The statute of limitations for perjury in Texas is two years.

"How is Ben, anyway?" he asked.

"Ben Spencer's been in prison for thirty years," I said.

"I thought he was out."

"No. He's in for life."

He peered at us, the silence stretching.

"How does that make you feel?" Parker asked.

"Like shit," he whispered, drawing out the expletive.

We thanked him, and before we left, we asked if he would write out an affidavit. He agreed. "Ben didn't do it. In my heart he didn't do it. He lied on me and I lied on him. That's what it is."

As we drove to Jesus Briseno's house the next afternoon, we tallied up our work so far. Of the four people whose testimony put Spencer in prison, only one, Gladys Oliver, had stuck to her story. On the other side of the ledger, two witnesses—Jimmie Cotton and Danny Edwards—had recanted on tape. Charles Stewart was dead, but two people swore that Stewart had told them that he never saw Spencer and lied at trial.[2] Beyond that, Sandra Brackens insisted that she saw a perpetrator who was not Ben Spencer, and then proceeded to show us where the BMW was parked in the alley. If she was correct, neither Gladys Oliver nor Jimmie Cotton could have seen the BMW parked in the alley from their vantage points.

Still, this is a world of malleable truth. The "truth" can bend under pressure from police and prosecutors, private investigators and reporters. Perhaps Jimmie Cotton was not suffering pangs of guilt; perhaps he looked at Daryl Parker with his military haircut and me with my microphone and felt corralled into giving a false recantation. Or Danny Edwards, who spins lies as easily as he breathes—maybe he was just messing with us. We needed to run all this by the detective who led the investigation. Fortunately, Jesus Briseno had grudgingly agreed to meet us at his home at three o'clock.

Briseno was standing on his porch, legs apart in a shooting stance. Sensing we had a short window before he walked into the house, we zeroed in on the witnesses—those he had credited and those he had ignored. We started with Michael Hubbard, an alternative suspect whom Briseno had dismissed. Briseno insisted that he tried to interview Hubbard, who was in jail at the time, but Hubbard demurred. "Once he says he don't want to talk to you, that's all you can do. Unfortunately, that's the way the law is."

"Presumably, you've had suspects before who said they didn't want to talk to you," I countered.

"Oh, sure, they do it all the time. That's nothing unusual." But, he added, "you can't coerce them, that's the way the system works."

Two days ago, I told the detective, Cotton admitted that he couldn't confidently identify the person running from the car.

"Well, it's their conscience, not mine," he said, referring to all three neighbors. "I did my case under the belief that those people who come forward were being honest. I can only do so much. I was not the one that put him [Spencer] in there."

Parker informed Briseno that Danny Edwards had also recanted his entire testimony and admitted that Spencer never confessed to him, but that he made up the confession to win a lighter sentence.

"Yeah, but why you going to believe him now?" Briseno asked, which is a reasonable question.

"I think the answer to that is back then, he thought he had something to gain by lying," Parker said. "What does he have to gain now by lying? He's out. He's free."

Briseno laughed.

"It's too bad when you can't read a person's mind and know he's lying right off the bat."

"Danny Edwards and Jimmie Cotton said that the police had given them the information and they just signed the affidavit," I continued, tiptoeing into the land of police misconduct.

"No, we don't work that way," Briseno said, upset. "There you go again, the lies. It's lies! We don't give them the information. We ask them for the information."

Briseno was done with us. We thanked him for revisiting the case, which has plagued him for thirty years. "It is a nightmare," he observed. "If those people lied, what can I say? We asked them, are you being honest? Is this true? And blah blah blah. So what else can you do?"


We had one piece of unfinished business before I left Texas for home in Washington, DC: finding Hattie Walker's sons. The men, who were teenagers on March 22, 1987, reportedly saw Spencer with their sister Christie at around 10 p.m., the time Jeffrey Young was being assaulted miles away. All week, we kept circling back to Walker's house, each time politely asking for her sons' addresses. She repeatedly told us they didn't remember anything and that they didn't want to talk to us. We weren't sure we believed her.

On the morning of August 23, 2017, at eight o'clock sharp, we knocked on her door. Hattie Walker answered, stone-faced. I apologized for pestering her, but we would just like to talk to the boys ourselves, please?

"I asked them," she insisted, "and they said, 'Mama, we don't know Ben. We don't know nothing about that.' So they grown men now, I can't make them, you know?"

After a few more minutes of unsuccessful pleading, we relented and walked toward our cars. We had probably crossed the line into harassment already, but a minute later, we turned toward the house and noticed a red Bronco parked in the driveway. Simi, the older brother, had just arrived and gone inside.

"Daryl, we've got to go back," I said.

"Yep. And this will probably get us kicked off the property for good," Parker predicted.

We knocked again. "He's in the bathroom," Walker reported when she opened the door. "He'll be right out."

Simi stepped onto the porch. He told us he remembered that night only vaguely but gave us the address of his brother, Israel. Ridiculously exhilarated, we drove across town, turned into Israel's gated community, and knocked on his door. An imposing man, easily three hundred pounds, smoking a cigar, bellowed behind us: "Can I help you?" We told him we wanted to talk about Benjamine Spencer. "Yeah," he said, laughing, "my mom just called to warn me."

He invited us in and settled into a chair, a huge aquarium providing the only light in the living room. He smiled. He remembered Spencer well. "He was a good older dude when I was growing up." Spencer taught Israel how to swim and play football. He tried to teach him how to read, with limited success.

Israel also remembered the night of March 22, 1987. He and his brother played street football against the kids in the projects a few blocks over. Before they left for the game, they saw Spencer and his sister sitting on the couch, talking. When they came back—he doesn't recall the exact time, but it was dark—they saw Debra Spencer's red Thunderbird parked in front of the house.

"We said, 'Damn, Pretty Boy's here!'" They burst into the house. His brother walked straight to the bedroom, but Israel fixed himself four burritos—"Don't tell Mama!"—and sat down in the living room. He pestered the couple for ten or fifteen minutes. They finally left.

We explained that Spencer was accused of killing Jeffrey Young at around 10 p.m. Israel shook his head. "He didn't do that, man. That man was in the house. I saw him." He paused. "What's he doing now?"

"He's still in prison," I replied.

"Shit, man, *thirty years*?!"

Parker asked if he'd go to court and tell his recollections under oath. "I'd do anything to get him out," Israel said. "I wouldn't lie for him. But I saw him, me and my brother, we saw him. I probably can't remember the little things. But I know one thing. I saw him there."

We thanked him and walked to the Jeep. We closed the doors and burst out laughing. "We'll run it past the attorneys and see what they think," Daryl said, grinning, "but I think that's the nail in the coffin."

Of course, Israel Williams's story fell short of the appellate court's

Herculean burden. It was not newly discovered, incontrovertible evidence of Spencer's innocence. Israel was just another witness corroborating Spencer's alibi; his account may not carry any weight at all. Still, he was a *new* witness. He was another grain of sand tipping the scales of justice.

A fter the article I wrote about Ben Spencer's case was published in *The Atlantic* in January 2018,[3] the magazine received a letter to the editor from inmate #768545 with the improbable name of John Quincy Adams. "I spent 12 years on the Coffield unit with Spencer, and I'll never forget the first time I saw him," the letter began. "Another prisoner pointed him out: 'That's Spencer, the barber, he's innocent.' An outsider wouldn't understand how extraordinary those words were, a guy claiming innocence is such a bloated cliché that it's beneath contempt. Even after 21 years of incarceration, Spencer remains the only one I've ever known to be exempt from this general skepticism."

A month later, in February, the Texas Board of Pardons and Paroles once again denied Spencer's release. More crushing still, in September 2018, Dallas County's crime lab, the Southwestern Institute of Forensic Sciences, reported that it could not find the fingernail clippings of Jeffrey Young's right hand, from which, Spencer's legal team had hoped, they could extract and test some DNA. Officials at the crime laboratory stated that the evidence had been lost, thrown out, or returned to the police department when the lab moved in 2011 to a larger building in Dallas. Just like that, the hope of a perfect answer evaporated.

I found myself wondering once again about the elusive nature of truth. Either Ben Spencer killed Jeffrey Young or he didn't. But without DNA or other irrefutable evidence, the answer remains just beyond reach. On both sides, there are prosecutors, judges, jurors, witnesses, family members, and friends who would swear by their position. It's possible we will never know the truth, and this uncertainty comes at a cost, not only to Ben Spencer and his family, but to Jeffrey Young's family, who are the only verifiable victims. Even if we can settle on some version of the truth, it might not matter. In a court of law, sometimes truth is irrelevant. Sometimes the truth does not set you free.

But serendipity might help. And on November 6, 2018, Election Day, serendipity delivered.

*Chapter 31*

# FRESH EYES

**The only thing I think about is whether those witnesses were lying.**

—Detective Jesus Briseno,
*thirty-two years after the conviction*

I was very interested in European existentialism as a philosophy and as literature," John Creuzot said. "When you talk about existentialism, you talk about people who are in a crisis, some shape, form, or fashion. And that's what this business is. Everybody's in crisis. It doesn't get here unless there's a crisis."

I was surprised at the turn in the conversation. The last time I was in this conference room, on the eleventh floor of the Frank Crowley Courts Building, then–district attorney Faith Johnson did not discuss Dostoyevsky as a window into the human condition. She did not engage in a two-hour conversation about her childhood and her philosophy of criminal justice. And she did not appear to be wrestling with a murder that occurred three decades earlier.

But on this December day in 2020, the new district attorney of Dallas County, in a light blue shirt, gray slacks, and no tie, strode into the room with no entourage except a press officer. He settled himself across the table and snapped the lavalier microphone onto his shirt. Creuzot hummed with energy, a handsome, almost entirely bald, light-skinned Black man with a runner's build. Even his N95 mask, a fixture during the pandemic, could not conceal his expressions—surprise, delight, soberness, caution—or his extravagant laugh.

John Creuzot was the first district attorney in more than thirty years to take a serious look at Ben Spencer's conviction. The two men shared a similar point of origin, before one life was derailed and the other thundered ahead. Creuzot was born in New Orleans in 1957, where his father worked at the Chevrolet dealership. "My dad could sell all the cars he wanted, but he was not allowed to put a foot on the showroom floor." His mother, with her uncanny eye for fast horses, won enough at the racetrack to pay the electricity bill. He and his brother tagged along, scanning for discarded winning tickets. "I would scoop up tickets off the ground, go through them, and cash them in." This proved remarkably profitable, since many New Orleans gamblers cared less about the winnings than about the party afterward.

In 1969, the family opened a small fast-food restaurant in Houston, where they had moved. Frenchy's initially offered po'boy sandwiches, but it was the Cajun fried chicken that put them on the map—and, in a fortuitous stroke of geography, between Texas Southern University and the University of Houston. Every night at ten thirty, teenage John and his cousin loaded up boxes of chicken and drove to the dorms housing the universities' athletes. A PA system announced their arrival. They would sell out in minutes. "I remember the first day we made ten dollars, and I remember when we made twenty-five dollars," Creuzot recalled. "I remember when we made fifty dollars. And now it's a multimillion-dollar business."

Nearing graduation from North Texas State University (now the University of North Texas) in 1987, Creuzot realized his philosophy degree would not wow prospective employers. "There's not much you can do with a philosophy degree except go to grad school and get some more degrees in philosophy." He attended Southern Methodist University's Dedman School of Law. He discovered that he liked the law; he relished the battle of criminal litigation, and upon graduation he went to work for Henry Wade at the Dallas County district attorney's office.

It was there, in 1988, that he watched one of the most publicized examples of a wrongful conviction: the case of Randall Dale Adams, made infamous by Errol Morris's documentary *The Thin Blue Line*. The filmmaker systematically disassembled the Dallas prosecution's case, which had landed a luckless Adams on death row in 1977 for allegedly killing a Dallas police officer. Skeptical that Adams was guilty, Morris set out to interview on camera everyone connected to the crime. When the documentary opened in April 1988, the Dallas justice system was the one on trial: Morris's reporting revealed that witnesses lied, prosecutors suborned perjury and hid evidence, and police opted not to arrest the more likely killer, David Harris, because he was under eighteen and ineligible for the death penalty.

John Creuzot, then a young prosecutor, sat in the packed courtroom during Randall Adams's appeal. There he began to reassess the integrity of the system. "Mr. Adams, he hadn't done a damn thing, except he's in the car with the wrong person. So I knew back then the system can go haywire."

The Adams case was a reckoning. "Is this how we do things here?" Creuzot wondered. "I lost faith in a lot of things. I lost faith in prosecutors who I thought I admired to actually put on a good case and try it straight up." He found the covering-up and defensiveness of the prosecutors in the face of their obvious misdeeds "disappointing and disillusioning." He despaired that an innocent man came within three days of execution while the real perpetrator was free to kill again, which he did.[1] After Adams won and his conviction was thrown out, the Dallas County district attorney, John Vance, considered retrying Adams for murder.

"So that's when I quit," Creuzot said. He set up shop as a defense attorney. Creuzot's defense practice was barely a year old when he was tapped to fill a vacancy as a judge on one of Dallas's trial courts, a position he held for twenty-one years. On the bench, he earned his reputation for creating a drug treatment program that reduced recidivism by a third and probation revocations by two thirds. He understood these kids, he knew their unspoken fears and their gnawing pressures. He had watched people cycle through his court year after year whose crime was addiction and whose punishment was to be fed into the maw of the criminal justice system.[2] Such experiences prepared him "maybe more so than the average lawyer down here to be attuned to the human condition," he observed.

Creuzot decided he wanted to change the prosecutor's office from within. He ran for Dallas County district attorney in 2018 and trounced Faith Johnson. On his first day in office, Creuzot made one change to the organizational chart that would transform the lives of prisoners like Ben Spencer. He moved the Conviction Integrity Unit—a small group of prosecutors and investigators who reexamined questionable convictions— out from under the umbrella of the appellate division. "The way they look at it in Appellate, their job is to affirm the conviction," he said. "He's guilty, he's guilty, he's guilty. It became obvious to me that the mindset was to affirm convictions and not get to the truth."

On Creuzot's watch, the CIU's mandate became locating the truth by deconstructing the case—the investigation, the evidence, and the trial— and determining what, if anything, went wrong. Then it would reconstruct the case from the ground up, building an accurate story based on facts and evidence. Cynthia Garza began reporting directly to the district attorney. "Cynthia didn't have any restrictions on her, not from me or anybody else in this office," Creuzot said. "And it's not just Ben Spencer's case. Any case. I've seen too many people convicted that shouldn't have been convicted."

On February 21, 2019, Cheryl Wattley and a lawyer named Gary Udashen arrived at the district attorney's office and made their pitch to the new district attorney and the head of the Conviction Integrity Unity, handing out documents and running through their Power-Point presentation. This was the fifth time Wattley had laid out the case for Spencer's innocence, a deflating exercise that had always ended with a polite thank-you and an eventual rejection.

John Creuzot harbored serious doubts. For the moment, he was not concerned with the underlying question: Did Ben Spencer kill Jeffrey Young? The actual innocence question would come later. Rather, he was skeptical that there existed enough new evidence to get the petition into court in the first place.

"This case is problematic because it's been up and down a ladder so many times," he said. "You start running out of things to litigate." He did not want to be reversed by the Court of Criminal Appeals. He did not want to face a public flogging by conservative rivals, who would claim he was soft on crime. And he did not want to needlessly drag the victim's family through their worst nightmare once again. Ninety-five percent certainty was not good enough. "It needs to be rock solid."

Yet for the first time, Cheryl Wattley was not facing enemy lines. Creuzot and Garza seemed genuinely intrigued as they listened to the arguments. The case had gained considerable notoriety over the years, and Spencer had gained a loyal following. Over the past two years, Daryl Parker and I had unearthed new evidence: Jimmie Cotton had recanted, as had the jailhouse informant Danny Edwards. A new alibi witness, Christie Williams's brother Israel, had sworn in an affidavit that Spencer had been in his house with him at the time of the crime.

But Wattley's most effective weapon was Gary Udashen. Affable and low key, Udashen was considered one of the most effective innocence lawyers in Texas, and he had just joined Spencer's case pro bono. He brought fresh legs to an exhausted defense team. "It's been a long battle," Wattley noted. "Gary is the new steamroller."

Udashen would manage the case, prodding the Dallas district attorney's office to view it with fresh eyes. He and Creuzot had known each other since law school and enjoyed a warm friendship. He had also mentored Cynthia Garza, and had invited her to join the law firm he founded with his brother, Robert. They worked together for several years before Garza landed a job in the Conviction Integrity Unit and began to upend bad convictions.

A trim, balding white man with a genteel drawl, conservative in dress and manner, Udashen is one of the few defense attorneys who routinely praises the Court of Criminal Appeals. After graduating from SMU law school in 1980, he opened a defense practice with his brother, hoping to defend the innocent and to change the system. He quickly found that most of his clients were "some shade of guilty." He took on his first innocent client in 2001, winning his exoneration in 2008, and since then he has been involved in more than two dozen exonerations. Udashen spent half his time on this pro bono work, and a full quarter of his time on Spencer's litigation. "I was making enough money that I could take the time," he said. "Just like the Spencer case. I would rather spend all day today working on the Spencer case than any other case I have. It's satisfying. It's interesting. And it's the reason why I wanted to be a lawyer."

Ben Spencer's saga had attracted attention in Dallas, but that's not why he said yes when Wattley and McCloskey called. "Jim McCloskey is really the father of the innocence movement," Udashen explained. "If he believes Ben is innocent, then I believe Ben is innocent, because Jim knows how to analyze these cases."

Minutes into his review of the file, Udashen understood McCloskey's point. On the night of the crime, the witnesses at the scene told police that they had seen *one* man hop out of the BMW and jump into a sports car; the police neglected to jot down their names. Three days later, Gladys Oliver and two teenage boys said they had seen *two* men, Spencer and Mitchell, leave the BMW. "Both stories can't be true," Udashen observed, adding that the bystanders had no reason to lie, whereas the neighbors had plenty of reasons. Had a jury heard both accounts, he believed they never would have convicted Ben Spencer or Robert Mitchell. "That's what really from the very beginning convinced me that Ben was innocent."

But Udashen realized that arguing innocence was a losing strategy. Wattley and McCloskey had tried that before, and the Court of Criminal Appeals had rejected their case. The evidentiary bar was nearly impossible to clear without DNA. This time, they decided to argue that Spencer did not receive a fair trial, which required only a preponderance of the evidence—that is, 51 percent. They felt they had ample evidence to prove that all four witnesses lied on the stand. Just get him out of prison, they figured; we'll worry about exonerating him later.

Udashen and Wattley presented this less ambitious plan to John Creuzot and Cynthia Garza in February 2019. As Udashen wrote in an email to McCloskey and Wattley a few weeks later, "What Creuzot really wants from Cynthia is for her to find something else to add to what we have already put together." Reading between the lines, he wrote, "because of the history of this case, and the position previous DAs have taken, he [Creuzot] feels compelled to be extremely cautious."[3]

Spencer's team had taken the case as far as they could. They had found all the evidence they could from the outside. Only someone inside the district attorney's office could demand that police and prosecutors turn over their files and actually get a response.

After Spencer's lawyers left the meeting that afternoon in February 2019, the two prosecutors sat in Creuzot's office and considered the political and legal risks. Then they smiled. "I said, 'I don't want to just stick my toe in the water. I'm going to go all the way in,'" Garza recalled. "And he's like, 'Okay, go ahead. You have my blessing to do whatever you need to do.' And that's how it started."

The first time I met Garza, in the 2017 meeting with then–district attorney Faith Johnson, she had barely spoken a word. Now working for Creuzot and free to follow her instincts, she displayed an insatiable appetite for answers. This curiosity, coupled with an apparent indifference to the politic answer, had emerged early in her life. When she was a child, her parents called her "l'abogada," the lawyer, because she always defended the littler kids on the playground. As a teenager, she thought she might join the FBI or perhaps become a forensic psychologist. As immigrants from Mexico, she said, her parents provided a modest upbringing but they also prioritized education, and there was no question that all their children would attend college.

Garza put herself through Southern Methodist University in three years. For her distinction project as a psychology major, she explored the inherent flaws of eyewitness memory—research that would come to haunt and help her. She forsook psychology and opted for SMU's law school, where she met her husband. Upon graduation, she applied to several district attorneys' offices, a rite of passage for serious lawyers in Texas. She never got past the first interview.

"I have the qualifications. I don't see what the problem is," she lamented to her mentors, Robert and Gary Udashen. "They said, 'You know what the problem is? This thing that's on your résumé.'" They pointed to her research on eyewitness memory. She realized that in her interviews, the prosecutors always asked her to describe her project. "I told them that I thought that eyewitness memory can be flawed. Did I tell them that you could still try a case with an eyewitness? Yes, you can, but you've got to be really careful." It was a disastrous mindset for a prosecutor who was bent on convictions. But it was a perfect mindset for a prosecutor who would challenge bad convictions in the Conviction Integrity Unit. For Ben Spencer, whose conviction rested on eyewitness testimony, Cynthia Garza was a godsend.

After meeting with Spencer's lawyers, Garza immediately began to gather the available evidence. Tens of thousands of documents awaited her: every witness statement, every police note, every record from the crime laboratory and from every hearing, the transcripts for the trials of Ben Spencer and Robert Mitchell, the appellate briefs, the appellate decisions, the avalanche of new evidence unearthed by Centurion Ministries and later by Daryl Parker and me, the barrage of filings traded between the prosecutors and Spencer's team in the 2000s, the nine boxes of documents from the district attorney's office that had never been turned over to Spencer's lawyers—internal memos, parole letters, attorney notes, page after page after page. The whole ordeal was like harvesting a cornfield with a pair of scissors.

J immie Cotton fidgeted continuously. He leaned forward with his el-
bows on his knees, rubbed his eyes, leaned back, stretched his long legs
in front of him, clasped his hands. The camera recorded it all, with the
date stamped on the video: July 31, 2019. Cotton had recanted his trial
testimony three times since 2017: first with Parker and me, then with
Parker alone, and finally with Spencer's lawyer, Cheryl Wattley, who
asked him to sign an affidavit. Each time, he peeled off another layer of
his testimony. On this day, Rick Holden would try to determine the
truth.

Holden, who ran Behavioral Measures & Forensic Services Southwest,
Inc., was one of the state's most respected polygraphers. In his chatty
Texas twang, he asked Cotton where and when he was born. "I have socks
older than you!" he joked, although Cotton was fifty, divorced with three
children, living with his mother, and working a cash job building fences.

"This is not about getting you in any trouble," Holden said, explaining
that Spencer's lawyers, who hired him, merely needed to know what Cotton could recall about the night of March 22, 1987.

Cotton leaped to respond. He had been washing dishes when he noticed a car pull into the alley. "I seen somebody get out of the car, but it
wasn't Ben Spencer because he was too short," he said. One man, not two,
he affirmed. "I didn't see Benjamine get out of the car," he repeated.
Later—he was fuzzy on the precise timing—he told Gladys Oliver that he
had seen the car. The next day, she pulled him aside.

"She told me she told the police that she saw Ben get out of the car,
hop the fence, and cut through her yard." She said that if the police came
to him, "stick to the story that Benjamine jumped my fence. Every time I
go down there, she'd tell me the same thing. 'Stick to the story, stick to
the story.'"

After nearly an hour of conversation, Holden walked around his desk
carrying his polygraph equipment. He fastened straps around Cotton's
chest and stomach, a cuff around his left upper arm, and a sensor on
his right middle finger. He explained that the instruments detect skin

resistance (sweat), heart rate, breathing patterns, blood volume, pulse rates, and oxygen levels.

"There's a lie pattern that's in your brain," Holden said. The first time you lied about taking a cookie from the jar, with all those incriminating crumbs on your face and hands, you learned that lying had unpleasant consequences, or, as he put it: "You got your butt busted." You developed a physiological response to lying.

"And when the brain identifies something that can cause you a problem or get you in trouble," he explained, "that causes the internal organs through the body to respond immediately." It was Cotton's "internal fingerprint." Holden spent a few minutes determining a baseline physiological response, then began asking questions, mixing relevant questions in with irrelevant ones.

*Is it true that you did not see Benjamine Spencer get out of that car that night?*

*Yes.*

*Is it true that Ms. Gladys told you to say you saw Benjamine Spencer get out of that car?*

*Yes.*

*Is it true that Ms. Gladys told you to stick to the same story she told the police?*

*Yes.*

Those were the questions that counted. Holden ran through the series three times, and they were done. Four days later, he submitted his analysis.

*Test Results: NO DECEPTION INDICATED.*

*Professional Opinion: The examinee's answers to the relevant test questions are considered: TRUTHFUL.*


John Creuzot and Cynthia Garza already believed Jimmie Cotton had perjured himself at Spencer's trial, even before they saw the polygraph video. A subsequent conversation with and affidavit from him in January 2020 confirmed their view. Likewise, they quickly dismissed another neighbor, Charles Stewart, who had testified he could identify Spencer from a football field away. There was hearsay evidence—he told at least two people that he had lied for the reward money. Also, Garza interviewed two prosecutors who admitted that Stewart's testimony defied credulity: They had visited the alley and seen for themselves that no one could identify someone at that distance, especially at night. They signed affidavits to that effect.[4]

With two out of four witnesses discarded, Garza began a new search. Determined not to succumb to the tunnel vision that had hobbled the original investigators, she tracked down witnesses barely mentioned in the police reports, culled ancillary police records, and interviewed every prosecutor involved in the case. She located boxes of untested fingerprints, only to find they were for another case. She found records showing that a gold Seiko watch had been found among the stolen goods of Michael Hubbard's drug dealer—only to learn the watch was not Jeffrey Young's. She investigated whether Jeffrey Young's father-in-law might be involved, as Harry Young had charged, and came up with nothing concrete. She spent hours trying to track down bank records and other documents showing that Gladys Oliver had received the twenty-five-thousand-dollar reward in exchange for her testimony and came up dry.

In July 2020, Garza hit paydirt. A decade earlier, in July 2010, Gladys Oliver had casually mentioned to two Dallas prosecutors that she had received five or ten thousand dollars in reward money for identifying Spencer and later testifying in his trial. If true, that fact would destroy the credibility of the state's star witness, the only one who had not recanted. The timing was critical. In 2010, the Court of Criminal Appeals was still considering the case, and this evidence could have swayed the court in Spencer's favor. Year after year, Cheryl Wattley and Jim McCloskey had pleaded with the prosecutors to give them the paperwork corroborating Oliver's admission. None came.

But as head of the Conviction Integrity Unit, Garza possessed powers that defense lawyers did not. When she demanded records from police or prosecutors they had to comply, particularly as she had the district attorney's backing. She asked for records of that pivotal meeting, and there, in a file cabinet, were five pages of handwritten notes that would unravel Gladys Oliver's testimony and integrity.

On July 2, 2010, Jena Parker drove with two prosecutors, Mike Ware and Terri Moore, to Gladys Oliver's apartment. Moore had created the Conviction Integrity Unit, Ware headed it, and Parker served as its paralegal. According to Parker's notes, Oliver talked about her family and neighbors—*Spencer nice and quiet, no grudge with family*—and the events of that night. *She didn't see Spencer hurt anyone. Saw him get out of car and the other guy. Dogs barkey. Gladys nosey.* And then, the middle of the conversation: *Gladys got 5000 or 10000 after trial but before next trial—Ross Perot check.*

In other words, Oliver had lied at Spencer's second trial when she denied receiving any money except for $580 from Crime Stoppers.

It was not a recantation. But given that Oliver never budged from her accusation, proof that she perjured herself was the next best thing. In the view of Spencer's legal team, Oliver's admission clinched the deal. The prosecution had, wittingly or unwittingly, presented false testimony with *all four* of its witnesses, in a case resting entirely on those witnesses. Spencer's trial attorney in 1988 never knew about their incentives, much less their fabrications. The witnesses had denied, under oath, that they were seeking money or, in the case of the jailhouse informant, a lighter sentence. For nearly twenty years, McCloskey and Wattley had been hunting for the missing piece of evidence that would impeach Gladys Oliver, while the prosecutors had had it in their pockets the whole time.

But Garza and Creuzot did not consider Jena Parker's note to be a home run. They wanted other corroborating evidence, such as bank statements, or the admission directly from Oliver herself. Three weeks later, on August 12, 2020, the two prosecutors and two investigators drove to the last known address of Gladys Oliver. She lived in a new, treeless neighborhood of tightly spaced McMansions in Forney, twenty miles east of Dallas. A late-model white Mercedes sedan was parked in the driveway. They knocked.

Eventually the door was opened by a young woman, Oliver's grand-daughter and caretaker, Glaevettea Oliver. They inquired after Oliver. The young woman said Oliver was unavailable. The district attorney of Dallas County introduced himself and explained why they were there, stressing that it was important that they speak to her. "Glaevettea again said that Oliver was unavailable and that she would get back with us with Oliver's availability," investigator Seancory Patton swore in an affidavit. They never heard back.[5]

Spencer's team was done waiting. Three weeks later, on September 1, 2020, Udashen and Wattley filed a writ of habeas corpus, asking the court to reconsider Spencer's case. They presented four grounds, or reasons, why his 1988 trial was unfair. Three grounds involved witnesses: They claimed that Gladys Oliver, Jimmie Cotton, and Danny Edwards had provided false testimony. (They could not challenge Charles Stewart's testimony because he was dead.) The fourth ground stated that advances in visual science proved the neighbors had "zero" ability to identify the men in the alley.[6] The team knew that Creuzot remained unpersuaded, and Garza continued to hunt down witnesses, but they wanted to start the clock. Spencer was trapped in prison as a coronavirus was killing inmates all around him.

A few weeks later, I drove the five hours from Dallas to Kerrville, Texas, and met up with Detective Jesus Briseno at his favorite fish shack, on the Guadalupe River. He was still a slim man, with thick white hair and a stylish goatee. His features were neat, his chin pointed; he was a man who controlled what he ate, worked out, and retired in this flat expanse nearly three hundred miles southwest of Dallas. It was December 3, 2020, and we chatted uncomfortably about the case, the long silences filled with the tinny sound of country-western Christmas carols coming through the speakers.

I filled him in on the recantations and the evidence that even Gladys Oliver was lying. He sipped his club soda, staring sightlessly at the slow-moving river. I asked him if he ever thought about Ben Spencer's conviction. "The only thing I think about is whether those witnesses were lying," he said, then looked at me. "Sorry I could not read their mind, but I could not. I had to go by what they were saying. They got up on the stand and swore that they were being truthful. There's nothing else I can do about that."

When Spencer's attorneys filed his petition in court, the starting gun fired and the race began. The district attorney had twenty days to make his initial response, although the true deadline was six months away, when a judge was required to decide whether to support Spencer's petition or not.

Until then, Garza would investigate at a furious pace. The next six months would determine whether Ben Spencer would die an old man in prison—that is, if the coronavirus did not kill him first. In the meantime, Garza had picked up the scent of something more troubling than lying witnesses. She suspected the state had cheated.

*Chapter 32*

# AND THEN THERE WERE NONE

+———+

**We're like, "Come again? What do you
know about this reward money?"**

—Assistant District Attorney Cynthia Garza

I have doubts about whether or not Ben Spencer did it," Andy Beach said, unprompted, a few seconds after I turned on the recorder at the outset of our conversation. It was an unexpected revelation coming from the prosecutor who put Spencer behind bars for life.

"Three things give me pause," Beach continued, as we sat in a jury room on December 9, 2020. He counted them out on his fingers. Number one: Spencer had passed a polygraph; but of course, Beach has known criminals who can pass a polygraph. Number two was more troubling: A famous exoneree named Michael Morton, "who is by all accounts just a stand-up, incredible human being," believed in Spencer's innocence. And number three: "If Ben Spencer had admitted his guilt fifteen years ago, he probably would have gotten paroled. The fact that year after year after year he comes up and refuses to admit it, that gives me a lot of pause."

The last time we met, in 2017, Beach had insisted that Spencer's original trial had been fair and the right man had been convicted. He said that he had looked his star witness in the eye, and Gladys Oliver promised that she had told the truth at trial. Now, paradoxically, Beach believed "with

80 to 90 percent" certainty that Gladys Oliver saw Ben Spencer leave the victim's car—*and* he harbored doubts about Ben Spencer's guilt.

"I can't reconcile it," he admitted. "All I can tell you is that I'm a different person now than I was thirty-three years ago. I have a lot better understanding of the sin nature of man than I did. I was naive. I thought people, when they looked me in the eye and talked to me back then, they were probably telling me the truth. I didn't think a human being would deliberately frame two completely innocent human beings for money. Here we are thirty-three years later, and I know there's a Satan, and I know people are tempted, a lot more than I did back then."

Beach added that he had reread the trial transcripts for both Ben Spencer and Robert Mitchell in preparation for our conversation. "I walk away going, How in the hell did I get a conviction in either one?" he said, shaking his head in wonder. "*Absolutely*, there's reasonable doubt." Spencer had put in more than three decades in the penitentiary, he said, "and I'm going to tell you right now, I try guys a lot worse than Ben Spencer that did a lot less time than thirty-three years. He's done his time. He needs to be out."

It was not clear what prompted Andy Beach's ruminations. Evidently, something had come to light that had caused him to reassess the verdict all these years later. In the fall of 2020, I was not privy to the details of the district attorney's reinvestigation; I had not yet read through the memos, affidavits, and letters about the case, much less understood their effect.

Nor had I seen the private letters from Ben to Debra. Those handwritten missives told of a rich emotional history, offering a glimpse into their personal drama and testimony to the toll that incarceration had inflicted on them and their son, on their family and friends, on their faith in God and in the state. One bright December day in 2020, I dropped by Debra's house to check a few facts, and found treasure.

"Ben and I have been talking," she said, after we had finished our work. She looked at me levelly. "If you want to see his letters to me, you can."

"Is that a question?" I asked. "*Yes, I want to see his letters.*" She led me to the guest room, opened the closet door, and tugged out a thirty-five-gallon storage bin, nearly three feet long and two feet wide, containing hundreds of white envelopes.

"He's a very faithful writer, isn't he?" I observed.

"He is," she agreed. "They could come two or three times a day."

I rushed back to my rented apartment and placed the letters in chronological order on the living room floor. I stood back. Spencer's letters to Debra provided a visual barometer of their relationship. Those from 2001–2003 combined to create a small stack of obligatory dispatches. In 2004, 2005, and 2006, his letters arrived at a faster clip. During those years, Centurion's investigation was gaining momentum; those were the years when Ben and Debra dared to rekindle their romance for the first time in nearly two decades. By 2007, the year of Judge Rick Magnis's evidentiary hearing, the letters were thick and abundant, hundreds of pages written in Spencer's minuscule, neat handwriting. Sometimes Spencer lamented the court delays and foot-dragging by prosecutors, but mostly he dreamed about their new life together, a family of three.

They began to shrink in 2011, after the Court of Criminal Appeals ruled against him, and by 2019, the correspondence had dwindled to two letters and four cards. True, Ben and Debra were talking on the phone at that time, accounting for some of the sad trajectory. But Debra's later emails to Spencer, which she shared with me, seemed equally deflated.

Then, in September 2020, after his lawyers filed the writ of habeas corpus, the mood lifted. "I wish you were here holding me and me holding you," Debra wrote in a September 27, 2020 email. "I really need you." She prayed that he would be free, and soon: "I want a fair chance at being married to my husband and just living a normal and faithful life together. LORD PLEASE HEAR MY CRY." She wrote in closing, "I love you, Ben, and I need you to know it. Not only do I love you, but I want to be in love with you like we used to be. I truly believe you are the love of my life."

A few weeks later, Debra marveled at their recent conversations. "I love that we have both dropped our guard and spoke love into existence," she wrote. "For so many years, I felt totally useless and unworthy of this life. I have felt that our lives were destroyed and would never come together again. I had almost lost hope. Thanks be to God that I have that HOPE again." She told him they would fight "this injustice" together. "Thanks for caring and loving me the way you do," she continued. "You have no idea what you have given me. You gave me a new life when you married me. And then you gave me our big, precious baby boy. Now, even from behind bars, you've given me the best friendship ever. I love you dearly." She attached two photographs of "a woman who's in love with you."[1]

I witnessed a similar metamorphosis in Spencer. From 2018 to the summer of 2020, Spencer called me every few weeks. For two years, we would spend all of our thirty-minute conversations discussing the minute details of his case, speculating about the new district attorney, and discussing new leads to chase down. In March 2020, our conversations shifted from legal strategy to personal safety when Covid-19 seeped into the Coffield Unit. He remained a master of stoicism—*I'm doing all right so far* was the usual refrain. But it's hard to practice social distancing in a dorm room with 110 men, he observed, when the cubicles are four feet apart. He reported that thirty men in his dorm were quarantined with fevers over one hundred degrees. The two men on either side of him contracted Covid. He wore his mask all the time, even when asleep. He washed his hands whenever he could and wiped down the phone with a rag from a bucket next to the phone. "I mean, when I start hearing about guys dying, that scares me," he told me on the phone one night in July 2020. "I'm like, Man, I don't want to die here."

Then, in the fall of 2020, the topic abruptly changed. Debra became the topic. The two had started talking a couple of times a week, he told me. "I mean, feelings that I had suppressed for a long time have surfaced, and I think it has for her as well. I really would like to remarry her."

He knew he needed to rein in his optimism. "I have to chill out because I don't want to overdo it," he said. He laughed softly. "But, you know, *this girl is in my head.*"

During the fall of 2020, Cynthia Garza was navigating the complexities of the case, uncovering erroneous testimony and prosecutorial misconduct. The accounts of Jimmie Cotton and Charles Stewart had already been dismantled. The testimonies of Danny Edwards and Gladys Oliver were damaged but still lethal. The question for Garza was: Were the accounts of Oliver and Edwards sound enough that a jury might still believe them? That was John Creuzot's standard: Before disrupting a jury verdict, the evidence needed to be "rock solid."

There was no dispute that Danny Edwards, who had testified that Spencer confessed to the crime when they shared a jail cell, was a serial liar and a deeply flawed witness. But Edwards's shifting recantations fell short of the district attorney's standard. How could prosecutors be confident that Edwards's final, complete recantation was the truth, when lying was the refrain of his life? Here Gary Udashen helped the district attorney's office maneuver to the finish line. The question is not whether we should believe Edwards now, Udashen argued in an email. The question is whether a jury, hearing all of Danny Edwards's stories, would find his *initial* claim at trial to be credible. "That is really not even a close question," he wrote. "Obviously no jury would find Edwards' trial testimony worthy of belief."[2]

But Creuzot wanted more, and Garza hunted for outside corroboration. She started at the beginning. "It was always a mystery to me how Danny Edwards even popped up on the radar," she told me. She examined police and prosecutor files, searching for a clue. She found it in a "WHILE YOU WERE OUT" message. On March 29, 1987, at 12:30 p.m., Leilani Edwards telephoned Lieutenant Ron Waldrop of the Dallas Police Department. Waldrop's name and number had been printed on the Electronic Data Systems (EDS) reward poster offering twenty-five thousand dollars for information leading to the arrest and indictment of Jeffrey Young's killers. On the blue note, in different writing, someone had scrawled: "Danny Edwards, 8:00 a.m. 3/30/87," and listed Edwards's cell number.

Of the many versions of the story Danny Edwards had offered, one involved his wife, Leilani. He admitted to Judge Magnis in 2007 that Spencer did not confess directly to him, but indirectly through his wife. He said Leilani had facilitated a three-way call between Spencer and his alibi witness, Christie Williams; he said she overheard Spencer talking about the murder and threatening to hurt Christie Williams and her child if she didn't back him up. (Williams was childless.) No one ever spoke with Edwards's wife to confirm his story. It took some sleuthing—she had changed her name—but eventually, Garza and her investigator paid Leilani Edwards a visit. Did she remember Ben Spencer talking about a murder?

"She said, 'I've never heard that name before,'" Garza recalled. The prosecutor then asked if she ever made three-way calls for Danny Edwards.

"Oh, yeah, I did that," Leilani told Garza. "But, you know, I never overheard anybody saying anything like that. I would have remembered that. I mean, that's a crime." She signed a statement to that effect.[3]

This independent corroboration satisfied Garza, and with Edwards's testimony dismantled, she turned to the final, heretofore unsinkable witness.

Gladys Oliver had never strayed from her testimony, and now she was "unavailable" for an interview. True, she had undermined her credibility when she told prosecutors that she had received at least five to ten thousand dollars in reward money. But maybe she was confused; maybe, as the Young family insisted, she was suffering from dementia when she made that statement. Garza returned to her files again. A police report of a burglary at Jeffrey Young's business three months prior to the robbery piqued her curiosity. The report stated that the thief broke through the wall of the office and stole only one item: a briefcase.

"What was in the briefcase?" she recalled wondering. "Hello? Who can tell us anything about this?"

The witness listed in the robbery case was Leroy Perry, who worked with Jeffrey Young. Garza and her investigator tracked him down. In that interview, as an aside, Leroy Perry mentioned the reward offered by Ross Perot's company, EDS.

"We're like, 'Come again? What do you know about this reward money?'" He told them that he had gone to the courthouse to watch Ben Spencer's second trial in March 1988. During a break in the trial, he happened to sit on a bench next to Harry Young, the victim's father, who worked for EDS, which had offered the twenty-five-thousand-dollar reward. They struck up a conversation. "Harry told him that the reward money had been paid off to this woman whose name he didn't know," Garza said. Harry Young mentioned the woman was a neighbor who identified Spencer and Mitchell running from his son's car. "She got the money, and in his mind, it was ten thousand dollars."[4]

The serendipitous conversation delivered two revelations. First, it meant that Oliver had lied at Spencer's second trial when she claimed that she received no money except for $580 from Crime Stoppers. Second, Leroy Perry provided unimpeachable corroboration: He had no incentive to allege Oliver received money when she didn't.

"That was for us very significant," Garza explained, "because outside of what Gladys had said, we didn't have anything else to support her receiving this amount of money."

"I think finding Leroy Perry was the single most important thing that was done on the reinvestigation of this case," Gary Udashen said. "She found Leroy Perry! Nobody, *nobody*, ever thought until Cynthia did, 'Maybe we ought to talk to Leroy Perry.'"

For Garza, all the new evidence fell on one side of the scale. "Once you start knocking down witnesses one by one, by one, by one, then this case that was built on eyewitness evidence is more of a house of cards," she said. But a question gnawed at her: How could the district attorney have put on such shoddy witnesses in the first place? Did prosecutors know they were presenting false testimony to send a possibly innocent man to prison for life—and simply not care?

H ey, a few things I want to discuss with you," Debra emailed Spencer on October 31, 2020. "You really need to slow down and please stop telling people our plans and thoughts. You will seriously run me back into shutdown mode. Think about it. I don't like attention on me. And attention will cause me to shut down really fast. Ball is now in your court. But I've given you FAIR WARNING ♥"

Spencer had seen this coming: *I have to chill out because I don't want to overdo it*, he had told me. Now the lovestruck Debra had exited left and the private Debra occupied center stage. Their dream had gained mass and momentum, and the reality made her skittish. More worrisome, Ben and Debra had been married only two months before he was incarcerated. They had not settled into an emotional rhythm. She had mastered her profession, climbed into the middle class, and singlehandedly raised a boy to manhood. She was not the twenty-two-year-old Debra he had married. But Spencer had lived in a time warp, and the chasm troubled her.

"I know he's institutionalized," Debra told me one rainy day, as B.J. listened on the couch. "He's used to guards telling him what to do, when to eat and when to wake, when you can move and when you can't move." She had heard the stories of men who came home docile and uncertain, and the prospect of seeing Spencer emasculated disturbed her. "I don't want him to be in his room and don't come out because no one has told him to come out." She didn't want him to ask permission to fix a snack, go to the store, take a walk.

"I'm just as institutionalized," she admitted. "I'm not used to anyone being in the house with me," not for years, ever since her son moved out.

The past haunted B.J. as well. At thirty-three, B.J. possessed a large build and soft manner. His career had been nomadic—working security, laying down cable for corporations—and during the pandemic slowdown he spent much of his time rebuilding his grandmother Lucille's home in West Dallas, which had burned down five years earlier. I asked him if it has been tough, growing up without a father—one in prison, no less.

"I always had a stepdad," B.J. responded. "My stepdad was always there, like at every function. I mean, I'd never introduce him like, 'Hey, this is my stepdad.' It was just like, 'This is my dad.' And so everybody thought he was my dad."

Ben Spencer had recently told me that his son had not visited for nearly a decade, ever since the Court of Criminal Appeals refused to release him in 2011. It was the only time I have heard Spencer choke up. But B.J.'s avoidance seemed less a rejection than an act of emotional survival for a young man who had been devastated too often. And how could Spencer compete with a man who attended every birthday party and school ceremony; how can an idea compete with flesh and blood?

I t was past 6:00 p.m., and dark, and the cold December rain soaked into my jacket. I was squatting in the mud in front of a clothes dryer that had been pulled out of the shell of Lucille Spencer's house and was sitting in her front yard. It looked like an appliance factory had exploded here: A refrigerator, dishwasher, washing machine, furnace, window air conditioner, and an assortment of smaller appliances decorated her yard, now rusty after three years in the rain and heat. Lucille had "stored" some of Ben's documents in her dryer, her grandson, B.J., told me. My mind was racing: Maybe I would find the transcript from Ben's first trial, or witness affidavits that had gone missing, or the wayward police reports about the fingerprints in the victim's car.

I pulled open the door of the dryer. A three-inch lizard leaped out from the dark onto my chest, and I reared back in primal terror. The creature jumped off and darted away. I eyed the dryer warily. B.J. handed me his work gloves. With my cell phone flashlight, I peered inside the dryer to find mounds of moldy documents, black with water damage. It smelled of decay: What might have been gold had turned into dust.

Fortunately, there were a few folders with readable documents. Back in my apartment, I cleared space on the floor for my new treasures, carefully pushing Ben Spencer's letters to the side. The pages were stuck together, and I thought, What the hell? and placed them in the oven at two hundred degrees. I was pleased with the outcome: The corners browned nicely and the centers were pristine. I teased them apart with the help of my hair dryer.

There was no one crucial document, no smoking gun that cleared Ben Spencer and implicated another. What I had was both more mundane and more profound. There were police reports, legal briefs, and judges' decisions. There were Spencer's extensive notes from his three court proceedings. There was an annotated log of his phone conversations with Wattley and McCloskey; journal entries describing encounters with his accusers and with Michael Hubbard; drafts of letters to friends, to his legal team, to Harry Young. There was a list of his favorite bands. There were lengthy, handwritten pages of Spencer's legal musings, titled "Thoughts that crossed my mind regarding this case" or "Notes of importance to self." Most were written after he had lost at the Court of Criminal Appeals. He had exhausted his appeals, and yet here he was, continuing to analyze his case, to offer leads and theories, and to make queries about court rulings that might favor him. Page after page, year after year.

Surrounded by these slightly charred documents, I thought: No guilty person would do this. Spencer was unrelenting, meticulous, agonized, and driven to prove he did not murder Jeffrey Young. And there, in my little living room, at 2:13 a.m., I just *knew*. Ben Spencer was innocent.

W e in the CIU community, we joke that we're the island of misfit toys," Cynthia Garza said. "No one wants to be with us." She laughed ruefully. Some prosecutors have told her she's nothing but a defense attorney with a badge. They resist her queries: *Why are you looking over my shoulder?* they ask. *Why are you checking my work?* Police officers place her in a category akin to internal affairs; they consider her a "traitor." Defense attorneys bristle at the implication that they botched the trial, and offer grudging help at best. "You have no friends," she observed.

Garza was, by all accounts, a gracious person. But in gathering evidence, she was as instinctual, relentless, and unstoppable as a great white shark.[5] Pity the prosecutor who caught Garza's unblinking eye.[6] Pity Andy Beach.

If Gladys Oliver had received a monetary reward before the second trial, and Andy Beach had put her on the stand without telling Spencer's lawyers, that would be considered a violation of due process and grounds for a new trial.[7] Spencer's trial attorneys could have used the information to demonstrate that the state's star witness had a motive to accuse Spencer; they could have damaged her credibility with the jury. Beach told me that Oliver had not received any money before the trial. He would never suborn perjury. "I'm just not that stupid. I valued my bar card. I wasn't going to jeopardize it over this crazy case I inherited from another prosecutor."

It was entirely possible that EDS gave Oliver the money without Beach's knowledge. But under a new interpretation of the law, it did not matter whether Beach knew Oliver was lying; it was still grounds for relief.[8]

Of course, Beach could not be blamed for what he did not know. But as he talked to Garza, he wandered into the quicksand of prosecutorial misconduct. He insisted that Oliver did *not* receive any money until *after* the second trial. He made sure of it, he said: He called EDS after the trial and told them that Oliver's testimony had convicted Spencer, and she should be entitled to the reward.[9]

"When Andy said that, I was completely shocked," Garza recalled. "I said, 'Andy, do you realize what this is?' There have been cases that have been overturned because a witness is testifying with a certain expectation of getting something in return, and it's not divulged" to the defense. The US Supreme Court has ruled that a prosecutor must turn over so-called impeachment evidence—in this case, evidence about Oliver's motives that could undermine her credibility—and failing to do that is considered prosecutorial misconduct.

"I didn't talk to the defense about that," Beach responded. "I mean, why would I? They knew about Gladys and her wanting this money because she said she wanted 'a piece of the pie.'"

"Andy, this is not good. This is not good," Garza said.

"Well, it is what it is."

"I know it is what it is. And we're going to have to do something."

"That was difficult," Garza reflected. "I like Andy. He was someone that everybody looked up to. And lots of people hold him in high regard. I still do."

Spencer's trial attorney, Frank Jackson was less charitable. By dangling a reward in front of their star witness, "it gives them a chance to grade her paper," he said. "The implication is [her testimony] has got to be favorable to the prosecution or she's not going to get the money. As a matter of fact, it's pretty clear. Andy's saying almost emphatically that she has to testify first and *then* we'll make a decision whether or not we help her get the twenty-five thousand dollars."

But, I countered, Andy Beach assumed that you knew she expected the reward, because she had said "I'll take a piece of that pie."

"*I'll take a piece of that pie?*" he repeated, incredulous. "That tells me that there's more money floating around out there that she has an expectation of getting? I don't think so. I don't go into the courtroom with a Ouija board. *Jesus.*"

In December, Garza reported her findings to the district attorney, who had been monitoring the investigation closely. "This case was coming apart at the seams," Creuzot said. "And so all of a sudden, it became very easy to see that Mr. Spencer didn't get a fair trial." What surprised and disturbed him most was that every problem with the prosecution had been right there, in their files. "We've had it all along. We just weren't honest about it."

*Chapter 33*

# REPRIEVE

+———+

**This is what my life should have been,
and now I'm living it.**

—Benjamine Spencer

On January 21, 2021, Benjamine Spencer became one of the rare prisoners in America who persuaded a prosecutor to take a second look at his conviction. In this, he was the luckiest of the unlucky: Having served decades for a crime he likely did not commit, he was on the verge of at least partial vindication, if not exoneration.

In his filing with the court, District Attorney John Creuzot laid out five reasons why Spencer's original trial was unfair. Counts one and two stated that two witnesses—Jimmie Cotton and Danny Edwards—lied on the stand when they swore that they saw Ben Spencer running from the crime scene (Cotton) or heard Ben Spencer confess to the crime (Edwards). Third, Gladys Oliver lied when she testified that she had received only $580 reward from Crime Stoppers, when in fact she had received $5,000 to $10,000 from Ross Perot's company. Fourth, Oliver lied when she stated she had not been promised, or did not expect to receive, a monetary reward after Spencer's trial was over. And finally, the district attorney stated that the prosecutor, Andy Beach, suppressed evidence that Oliver was lying, which was a *Brady* violation.

Five grounds. Spencer only needed one for a new trial. It was a devastating indictment of the Dallas justice system.

The family of Jeffrey Young could only watch as the battle turned against them. When news of the Dallas district attorney's filing became public, I reached out to ask them for comment. The family members either ignored my request or told me never to contact them again.

"There was nothing I could tell them that was going to make it okay," Beach recalled. "There was nothing I could tell them other than we did our job back in 1988 and that I understood their bitterness and their anger at the system." Beach, who had remained in close touch with the family for thirty years, said they felt victimized again, this time by the judicial system and the media that, they believed, had pressed for Spencer's release.

Beach was also stung by the accusation that he had hidden information from the defense. "I worked thirty-six years to make my reputation and to preserve it," he said. Ending his career with a black mark bothered him. Anyway, he said, he did not suppress evidence: Gladys Oliver's motives were apparent to all. "You would have to be a Martian to not understand Gladys hoped she would get the reward," he wrote me. "I didn't disclose Gladys expected the sun to rise from the east the day after she testified, so guess I should have done that."

Within days of Creuzot's filing, Spencer boarded the chain bus from Coffield prison to Lew Sterrett jail in Dallas to await his release. He tried to keep his euphoria in check. After all, he had been in this same jail awaiting release thirteen years earlier, only to be sent back to prison. But this time felt different. Even the guards believed him, he told me during one phone call in January 2021. "They said, 'Man, you've always said you was innocent. Man, you actually *are*!'" Spencer said he would miss some of his coworkers, but he fantasized about biting into his first Whopper at Burger King, getting his driver's license, finding a pair of round-toe ostrich boots, earning a paycheck. He wanted to rebuild a car with his son. But mainly he longed to spend time with Debra, to sit on the couch and watch a movie, to invite friends over for barbecue, to mow the grass and then enjoy a tall glass of iced tea. He craved autonomy. "I just know I want to be able to step outside and get some fresh air."

O n Friday, January 29, Debra drove to Cedar Creek Lake with her friend Laurie Foster. Debra's six closest friends rented a house there for one weekend every January. The two argued the entire way. "I was like, 'Okay, we're not going to do this,'" Debra recalled. "And Laurie's like, 'Yes, you need to tell them.'"

Only three friends in the world knew of Spencer's existence. But as it was likely that Debra's intensely private life would soon turn into a media circus, she needed to disclose her thirty-four-year secret. Telling her friends would provide a preview for the larger, public reveal, since all six friends were white and had little exposure to the legal system.

The morning after they arrived at the lake house, Laurie pulled out the most recent *Atlantic* article that I had written about Ben Spencer's case.[1] She began to read it aloud. The group listened, puzzled by the story of Ben and Debra Spencer—they knew her as Dee Dee—and the conviction that left an innocent Black man in prison and a young mother to raise her child alone.

"Why is Laurie being so dramatic?" Paul Patterson thought.

"We were here on holiday," Rick Pineda recalled. "We're having a good time. And just out of the blue, Laurie decides to read the story, which on the surface is not a real happy story."

Laurie finished the article. The group was silent. Kathy Pineda began talking about a man she knew in prison and Laurie said: "Stop. Does Ben and Debra Spencer not ring a bell?"

They just looked at her. Laurie said: "It's Dee Dee!"

Rick turned to Debra: "Is your daddy in prison?"

"No, my daddy isn't in prison," Debra said, laughing.

"It's her ex-husband," Laurie said.

They looked at their friend for a long moment, then jumped out of their chairs and embraced her. They returned to their seats, silent now, as the weight of her secret settled on them. "We just got a whole lifetime of burden," Rick said later. "It was pretty overwhelming. This wasn't just a onetime thing. This is something she's been living for all those years."

"I've told Dee Dee that I want to meet Ben when he's ready," said Karen Comeaux, who had known about Spencer for a year. "I know it will be an adjustment for him." Adjustment on both of their parts, Laurie added. "Dee Dee is used to living alone and living the Dee Dee life in her Dee Dee world," she teased. "So, yeah, it is always going to be a big adjustment for both of them. But I can't wait for him to get out. I can't wait for him to become part of our group."

"They found your story to be unbelievable / believable, hurtful, racist, prejudiced, unjust, and downright wrong," Debra wrote Spencer in an email after the weekend. "They feel that you are a man of integrity, hero, brave, forgiving. And the list goes on and on. They can't wait to meet you."[2] She added in a postscript: "Oooh people want to know if you have a sense of humor like mine. And I told them, 'Well, maybe a little one. He laughs, but not like me.' So I need you to learn to laugh when you come home. And not just when I'm mad at you."

Day after day, a crowd gathered outside the Dallas County courthouse, waiting for Judge Lela Mays to sign off on Spencer's release. Usually this was a formality, but for reasons she did not disclose, she took her time. Spencer's mother, his siblings, and several dozen supporters bundled up in the cold for eight-hour stretches during the once-in-a-century polar vortex that reached Texas. Debra waited at home, bringing in a half dozen care packages a day from family and friends and stacking them in Ben's room.

He called from jail every evening, cheerfully reporting on the day's privations. Prison officials had not allowed him to bring anything from Coffield, and now the Lew Sterrett commissary was closed indefinitely.

He had no toothpaste, soap, deodorant, nothing to read, nothing to write with, nothing to do but look through the bars. The guards kept him locked in his cell 24/7. They had suspended recreation because at one degree Fahrenheit, it was too cold outside. With Covid rampant, he was grateful to be in a single cell, but he wished he had a winter coat in the frigid jail.

Debra tried to hide her anxiety in small talk. *What did they serve for dinner?* she queried when he called one evening while I happened to be visiting.[3] Meat-and-potato goulash, he said. *What did he want to eat when he got home?* T-bone steak. *Grilled with gas or charcoal?* Charcoal. *Which restaurant did he want to visit first?*

"I haven't been to very many restaurants," he observed.

"Really?" Debra said, in mock surprise. "Where you been?"

"Locked up. I can only remember one restaurant I went to."

"Can you remember Pizza Hut?"

"The one on Clark?"

"The one where you met that girl."

"How could I ever forget it? The start of my life."

The call ended. Despite her light tone, Debra was troubled. "I don't know what's taking so long," she said. "I have a bad feeling."

Every day, Spencer's family, friends, and legal team waited, puzzled by the delay. The judge was out of town; the judge asked for an extension; then another; the judge refused to sign the findings or hold a hearing. The judge let the deadline pass, allowing the case to be transferred to the Texas high court without her endorsement—a move that could delay Spencer's release for months or kill his chances altogether. District Attorney John Creuzot worried that the judge would deny the request. "I knew this case could slip like an egg on olive oil."

To the family of Jeffrey Young, the state of Texas had sided with a killer and betrayed the real victims of the assault on March 22, 1987. With a signature, the district attorney had rewritten their history. They fumed.

Every victim responds differently, explains Jennifer Thompson, who wrongly accused an innocent man of raping her in the 1980s. Thompson has worked with countless victims and perpetrators through her non-profit group, Healing Justice. She understands the dual assaults on the victims—first by the perpetrator, then by the state.

"We're asking these victims—who have been traumatized, retraumatized, traumatized, retraumatized over and over and over again for decades—to believe that the system now is getting it right," she says. "For thirty years, the system said, 'No, we gave you justice. We know this is the person who did it.' Then, all of a sudden, one day they're like, 'Oh, well, actually, we're not really sure, and this person is going to walk.'"

The reversal threatens to dismantle the emotional scaffolding that comforted the victim's family all these years: the feeling of security and righteous retribution, their trust in the justice system—indeed, in the very notion of justice.

"One of our deepest motives is to believe the world is fair and that people get their just desserts," says the psychologist Carol Tavris. "Now you're going to rip that away from me?" Tavris is the coauthor, with Elliot Aronson, of *Mistakes Were Made (But Not by* Me*): Why We Justify Foolish Beliefs, Bad Decisions, and Hurtful Acts.* She sees in the Young family's behavior the classic signs of cognitive dissonance—that is, the discomfort of trying to hold two conflicting beliefs simultaneously: that Ben Spencer killed their loved one, and that the evidence against Ben Spencer has fallen apart. This unconscious discomfort is as visceral as hunger or thirst, and a person will go to great lengths to alleviate it.

"What are their choices?" Tavris asks. "To open up all that pain, adding to it fury at incompetent prosecutors and corrupt witnesses," along with the possibility that the real killer went free? "Or to deny the evidence?"

In situations like this, Tavris says, the "default resolution" is to trivialize or dismiss the new evidence. For example, the Youngs' central argument is that two separate juries found Ben Spencer guilty in 1987 and

1988. They dismiss the new evidence that all the witnesses had incentives to lie. Dissonance theory bets they won't change their mind. "The greater the investment in a belief—in time, emotional conviction, money, harm inflicted, whatever the deep 'cost'—the greater the motivation to hold on to that belief," Tavris says. The Young family invested heavily in Spencer's guilt. They pressured the district attorney's office to solve the crime, by both letter and appointment. They opposed Centurion's investigation in the 2000s and sat through the evidentiary hearing in 2007. They waged letter-writing campaigns to ensure that Spencer was denied parole. And they petitioned every consecutive district attorney to refrain from reopening the case. Rare is the victim who accepts the new evidence, Tavris says. "The Youngs' behavior is completely the norm."

Jennifer Thompson has a different perspective: "It's not necessarily cognitive dissonance. It's trust." Thompson knows all about cognitive dissonance. When she was a college student, she had confidently identified her assailant, and her testimony sent him to prison. When DNA identified another perpetrator, she had to reconcile her strongly held belief with the truth. We think these victims are trying to "willfully disregard" the new evidence, "and it's not fair," she says. "It's not because they're bad people. It's not because they don't want to know the truth." But when the state substitutes one "truth" for another, why should they believe it? Particularly for the Young family: Why should they believe the district attorney now, since his investigation turned up no hard evidence such as DNA to irrefutably exonerate Ben Spencer?

"It is a terrible thing to be wrongfully convicted. It is an awful, awful thing," Thompson notes. "But it's not the worst thing." The worst thing is to lose your husband or child or mother. A victim of wrongful conviction can see visitors in prison, write letters, talk on the phone, fall in love, maybe one day start a new life outside. The family of a victim can see their loved one's grave. And after the exoneration, the public chooses sides, giving the wronged man the headline and consigning the dead man to obscurity.

I began to understand Jay Young's anger. The whole system is set up to erase the victim. Jeffrey Young's name isn't even on the case: It's *State of Texas v. Benjamin John Spencer.* Now, with Spencer on the cusp of being freed, if not exonerated, Jeffrey Young and the cavernous hole his murder created would be eclipsed.

"He has a right to be angry because now the story isn't about his father," Thompson observes. "The story is about this soon-to-be-exonerated man. What we fail to remember is that this family will never have their father again. They're never going to have this person at Christmas and at Thanksgiving." She pauses, then says pointedly, "Listen. They don't owe the exoneree, the media, or anybody anything. *Anything.*"

On March 12, 2021, the judge unexpectedly scheduled a bond hearing for three o'clock that afternoon. Sitting in Lew Sterrett jail, Spencer was unaware of this. He called his son for a chat, who blurted: "Dad, are you getting out? Mama said they signed the papers." Spencer called Jim McCloskey. "It's happening. It's happening. You're going home." As he was relaying the news to Debra, a guard approached. "Come on, Spencer. You need to go sign some papers. They're trying to get you out of here."

"I get up there to the floor where the court is, and the bailiff come out there," Spencer recalled. "He's like, 'Okay, this is what's going to happen, man. We're going to have a Zoom conference with the judge, and we're going to try to get everything situated and get you out of here today.' I said, 'Okay, if that happen, hey, man, I'm all for it.'"

Outside the 283rd District courtroom, the room where Spencer had been convicted twice before, four dozen or so supporters were milling around. Judge Mays had banned the media and spectators from the room and was holding the hearing on her court's YouTube channel. At 3:10 p.m., the court hearing was convened on Zoom, with the judge at her home; John Creuzot and Cynthia Garza at the district attorney's office; Spencer, wearing a faded gray-and-white jumpsuit, in the front row of the court-room, flanked by his attorneys, Cheryl Wattley and Gary Udashen; and Debra, Lucille, and B.J. seated one row back. People in the hallway hud-dled in clusters, peering into their phones.

Wattley assured the judge that Spencer was not a flight risk and should be released immediately. The district attorney had no objections.

"After reviewing all of the information, I am going to grant a PR bond to Mr. Spencer," the judge concluded, releasing him, without bail, on his personal recognizance. Piercing screams—*he's getting out, he's getting out*—drowned out her next words. The supporters, most of whom didn't know Ben Spencer, danced, hugged, clapped, and cried. Many were not even born when Spencer was convicted. Yet to them Spencer had become a symbol of the calcification of the criminal justice system, and his release a small victory.

Outside the jail, a dozen cameramen jockeyed for position in front of the podium. The crowd had grown to two hundred, and, against proto-col, the guards opened the doors to the lobby of the jail. People surged in, laughing, high-fiving. Ben and Debra appeared from the corridor and halted, dumbstruck, as people started cheering. They moved forward slowly, holding hands, Debra smiling uncomfortably, Ben beaming.

When Ben Spencer walked out the jail door into the bright, warm eve-ning, John Creuzot strode over and pumped his hand. The two Black men sized each other up and grinned.

"Hey! How you doing? How you doing?" the district attorney asked.

"I'm all right," Spencer said happily, surveying the crowd.

"Good, you're looking good."

"Thank you. Yeah, you are, too."

"They haven't run me out of town yet," Creuzot said with a laugh. He stepped to the podium and spoke into the cluster of microphones. "We agreed with the conclusion that Mr. Spencer did not get a fair trial. He deserves a trial, a *fair* trial." The district attorney said he doubted that his office would try him again. "There's really substantively not much left as far as evidence is concerned." His office would keep an "open mind that somebody else did this," and would continue to investigate other suspects.

You're saying the killer may still be out there? a journalist yelled.

"That's correct," Cynthia Garza said.

"We're looking into that," Creuzot echoed.

Spencer spoke for less than a minute. He thanked his legal team, his family, the people who supported him all these years. "I am just excited. I'm going to try to reconnect with my family. I appreciate you all," he said.

An hour later, throngs of people were streaming through Debra's home, reporters and photographers with their notepads and cameras trailing this intensely private woman as she presented Spencer's room, his closet brimming with new clothes, packages stacked up on his bed. The Spencers were on public view now. It was the price of freedom. Eventually the reporters left, and friends gathered around Spencer in the living room. His words bubbled out, his gold tooth flashing, his voice raised in excitement. "I didn't think I'd get out tonight, but then the guards were like, 'Yeah, man, you're getting out! Hurry up, man!' And I didn't even have time to put my tie on! I just threw it in my bag."

Aside from being stymied by the kitchen faucet, Ben slid seamlessly into the present. He showed no hesitation, no befuddlement or shyness. He had leapfrogged three decades. When he was last free, he had never heard of email; now he held an iPhone in his hand, a gift from Daryl Parker.

As Parker and I left around 9:00 p.m., Debra's six best friends were sitting along one side of the dining room table. Spencer was standing on the other side, addressing them as if he were a college professor. He looked every bit the part: tall, lanky, bespectacled, speaking softly, telling stories about prison, describing his friends there, explaining why he wasn't bitter, praising Debra, and crediting his faith. We walked outside into the soft, warm night air, free—something I had always taken for granted until this moment.

The next morning found Debra rushing around the house, making coffee, texting people about the lunch celebration later in the day, asking a friend to pick up as many copies of *The Dallas Morning News* as possible. Spencer's story led the paper, and a photograph of him hugging his mother took up most of the page above the fold. He was a minor celebrity. "It's been on all TV news programs," he commented, a little bedazzled. "Fox, ABC, NBC, I haven't seen CBS yet."

Debra threaded the cuff links through the cuffs of his new tailored blue shirt. He had chosen his wardrobe carefully, in the middle of the night. "The bed was too soft for me," and the adrenaline was too great, he admitted. He slept an hour. "I'm just lying in the bed like, '*Man*,' you know." Enlivened by the silence after years of sharing a dorm with 110 snoring men, he finally gave up on sleep and started looking through his new clothes, trying to decide, for the first time in three decades, what to wear.

We walked out the front door and stood on the step, breathing in the early spring air. We could hear lawn mowers in the distance. He gazed up and down the street. "It feels natural," he said. "It feels like I've always been here. Because I should have been here. This is what my life should have been, and now I'm living it."

My phone rang. "Hey, just calling to make sure you got everything you needed," the district attorney said.

I did, I told him, and then mentioned a rumor that he had teared up when he met Spencer. He didn't answer right away. "He's spent thirty-four years in prison. Every witness who accused him lied. The case fell apart and he sat there year after year," Creuzot said. "I mean, he's walked out of custody into a world he does not know. Half his life gone. *Of course* you feel emotional."

"Are you going to try to prove his innocence?" I asked.

He sighed. "I don't know if we can do that. Gladys is still there, saying she saw him. If she were to testify today, it's still possible that twelve people would convict." But, he added, "we're still investigating. We're moving in the direction of not just 'he didn't get a fair trial,' but 'he may be innocent.' We're not there yet, we have more work to do. But, you know, that's kind of where I see it."


We had been at the Urban Arts Center for three hours, and the celebratory luncheon was supposed to be winding down. The impatient looks of the caterers, however, were lost on the guests at the far end of the room, positioned under a huge royal blue banner that read "In Truth There Is Freedom—Ben Spencer." Around the head table were Ben and Debra and seven men, some standing, some sitting. Every few seconds they erupted in laughter, happily shouting over each other, piling one story on top of another. This was the prisoners' table, and most of these men had been wrongly convicted and later exonerated. They had so many years and memories to catch up on—the good warden; the bad guards; the riot when they hit them with tear gas; who started that fight, anyway? Spencer occasionally jumped in with a story, but mainly he smiled.

They began to swap stories about their early days of freedom. One said when he went out for his first meal, "I didn't know what I wanted to eat because I had never had that many choices." Not just the food but the cutlery: Sporks—spoons with prongs like a fork—were the only utensils in prison. "When we went to sit down, I didn't know how to actually use the fork to cut the food."

"I went to the grocery store," another said. "I was trying to work the self-service thing, and I couldn't figure it out. My biggest thing was these people behind me thinking how stupid I am." He turned to Spencer: "You're going to feel inadequate a whole lot, bro. Just take your time." Turning to Debra, he said: "What did I ask you to do with him?"

"Have patience," she said.

"He's going to mess it up," another said. "I done lost so much stuff, money and everything, because I wasn't going to ask for nobody's help. He's going to need some help."

For a short time, maybe some months, maybe a couple of years, Ben Spencer could revel in his new life. But soon, he would have to turn his thoughts to the Court of Criminal Appeals, the court that had sent him back to prison once before. Every Wednesday morning at 9:00 a.m., the judges issue their decisions. Any given Wednesday, Spencer could be returned to prison for life.

# Chapter 34

# LIMBO

+———+

**I can't just go say, "We think he's innocent."
That's not how it works.**

—District Attorney John Creuzot

S tatistically, exoneration is rarer than climbing Mount Everest. More than six thousand people have scaled the world's highest peak; only about thirty-four hundred US prisoners have been declared innocent to date. In asking the Texas Court of Criminal Appeals to vacate his conviction but not explicitly exonerate him, Ben Spencer was more like one of the thirty thousand people who climb Mount Kilimanjaro in any given year, with the help of eighty thousand guides and supply bearers. Spencer must merely persuade the court that he was convicted in an unfair trial—legally speaking, a relative foothill, especially since the district attorney joined his petition.

"It's going to sail right through," Gary Udashen predicted while they awaited the court's decision.

In that state of suspension, Spencer was still considered a convicted criminal responsible for the death of another person. Because of his legal status, in the months after his release in March 2021, Spencer was rejected by every company to which he applied for a job. He was finally hired as a facilities engineer at the Hall Arts Hotel, only because the Dallas billionaire Craig Hall, who owns the property, had followed Spencer's story and believed he was innocent.

On May 15, 2024, the Texas Court of Criminal Appeals ruled seven to two to vacate Ben Spencer's conviction. The ruling leaves Spencer in legal limbo, considered a defendant who has been indicted but not yet tried in court. Now the district attorney must make a decision: whether to prosecute Spencer again and bring his case to trial; dismiss the charges "in the interest of justice"; or dismiss them based on innocence.

The district attorney has sole, unreviewable discretion over Spencer's fate. Creuzot told me he would not retry Spencer; he lacks the evidence to bring a case. This leaves the two types of dismissals. He could dismiss the charges "in the interest of justice," deciding the district attorney's office does not have enough evidence either to convict *or* to exonerate Spencer. Spencer would be free but tainted, without compensation or redemption. Spencer and his team are hoping that the prosecutor will take the third route and dismiss the charges based on *innocence*. This would clear Spencer's name and automatically grant him more than $2.7 million in compensation from the state.

The district attorney doesn't need to meet a "Herculean burden," Udashen explained. "The standard is: Can you say that no rational jury in light of the new evidence would find this person guilty?"

Creuzot balked at this analysis. "I can't just go say, 'We think he's innocent.' That's not how it works." He said he needs compelling evidence of actual innocence to exonerate Spencer and satisfy himself, his critics, and ultimately the voters.

"I think we can all agree that he would not have been convicted," Garza said. "But is it enough to prove that he's innocent? I don't know yet." She has "personal beliefs, based on evidence," that Spencer did not kill Jeffrey Young. But she has yet to amass dispositive evidence. "That's why the investigation continues."

To that end, in the months after Spencer's release, Garza was following every lead. She looked into a similar murder in which a white man was left to die on a street in West Dallas, on a day when Spencer already was in custody. She explored why the detectives so quickly dropped several other potential suspects. But the most direct line of investigation centered on Gladys Oliver and Michael Hubbard. Each of them could exonerate Spencer with a few words under oath.

If Oliver recanted, Creuzot told me, the case against Spencer would collapse. "Then everybody has backed off. That, in my opinion, would be very strong evidence for actual innocence." But there was proof only that she is a serial liar, not that she lied about seeing Spencer that night. "Does that mean that you could get twelve people who are going to absolutely, unequivocally find him not guilty? No, it doesn't mean that at all," Creuzot said.

Anyway, Gladys Oliver had disappeared. After she contracted Covid in 2021, she spent some weeks in the hospital and was released. By the time I knocked on her door again, her family had been evicted.

Michael Hubbard proved easier to locate: he was in the Mark W. Stiles Unit in Beaumont, Texas. Hubbard was serving a life sentence for his nighttime "Batman" attacks. One rainy Saturday afternoon, I came across a letter on the Texas Department of Corrections website to Judge Robert Francis from "Field Minister Michael E. Hubbard." It was sent August 8, 2017.

"I would like to share with you Sir, on the progress in which God has blessed me to obtain," Hubbard began. "It's been a marvelous journey, in which I would not change for all the world." He lamented his past actions, but noted that Jesus had forgiven, changed, and redeemed him, and now he was calling him to ministry, or, as Hubbard put it, "teaching biblical truths to the brothers in white." He listed twenty-five Christian courses he had completed, including Anger Management (*Facing the Fire Within*). Now he serves as a field minister, or inmate chaplain, in his unit. "My life is now on the right track and I thank the Lord Jesus Christ for using You as a vessel to push me in the right direction." The right direction was, unsurprisingly, out of prison. "My greatest desire, would be a chance to re-entry [*sic*] society and become the man God has called me to be." He asked the judge to help him reduce his sentence and allow him to leave before he was up for parole in 2026. The judge filed the letter on June 5, 2018, with the note: "No action to be taken."

I made several requests to interview Hubbard, which he officially declined. Aware that Garza was investigating his possible role, I showed her a copy of his letter.

"Field Minister Michael E. Hubbard," she said, laying down the letter. "A changed man."

"He's still declined my interview requests."

"So, not that much."

The district attorney told me he would consider granting Hubbard immunity if he would tell what he knew about the night of the murder. But Hubbard was coming up for parole in 2026, and Creuzot and Garza doubted that he would risk confessing. "There's no incentive," Garza said. "Absolutely no incentive."

The lights dimmed in the three-thousand-seat sanctuary. With a sudden flourish, the orchestra launched into an upbeat praise hymn. First Baptist Church of Dallas boasts a world-class orchestra and choir, and as the worship leader began to sing, the choir, 150 strong, appeared on the jumbo screens. I spotted Debra's face several times; she was, as far as I could tell, the only Black vocalist.

"Worthy, worthy, worthy is your name," the congregation sang. I glanced at Spencer, standing next to me, singing gustily. He touched his eyes every now and again, and finally removed his glasses and wiped the back of his hand across both eyes. Here is a man who survived three decades in a maximum-security prison, where he worshipped in a windowless room with a small group of convicts. Now, standing in this predominantly white megachurch, he wept—in relief that his long nightmare had ended (for now); in gratitude for his new home, new friends, and new life; in grief for all the years he had lost.

After the service, we stood outside the sanctuary. Debra seemed to know everyone and greeted them all. Spencer waited quietly, but time and again, people approached him. A staff member of the church shook his hand; a middle-aged woman was praying for him. People advanced shyly, as if they didn't want to embarrass or disturb him.

"What's been the biggest surprise since you've come out?" I asked him.

"How many people have embraced me," he said.

A few weeks earlier, as Spencer waited for Debra to finish choir rehearsal, a man walked up and handed Spencer an envelope with a hundred dollars. One Sunday a woman gave Debra a thank-you card with a check for three hundred dollars inside. A GoFundMe campaign raised twenty thousand dollars in a matter of days; almost all the contributors were strangers who had heard about his case by word of mouth.

But it did not stop with money. The owner of a steak house learned of Spencer's story and special-ordered some ribs. When the Spencers arrived for their reservation at the restaurant with friends, the owner served the couple himself, not letting on that he owned the place. At the end of the meal, he refused their money. The owner of a car dealership, Laura Hunter, invited Spencer to look for a car. He fell hard for a 2016 Dodge Durango, which cost twenty-three thousand dollars, three thousand more than the amount raised by the GoFundMe campaign. Hunter put up ten thousand dollars toward the car, and set Spencer up with a line of credit.

Then there was the matter of Spencer's gold front tooth, which Debra wanted swapped for porcelain. She found a dentist named Jonathan Clemetson through church, who replaced the tooth and performed Spencer's first real dental exam in thirty-four years. At the end of the appointment, the dentist asked if Spencer had any questions.

"Well, I guess, just how much all this is going to cost?" Spencer wondered.

"Ben, you don't owe me a thing," the dentist said. "It's been a privilege. And if you have a problem," he added, "don't hesitate to call, day or night."

To many, Ben Spencer had become a symbol, a repository for generosity, a chance for people to heed the better angels of their nature. In the era of George Floyd and the attack on the Capitol on January 6, in the middle of a nation riven by politics, people found in Spencer some common ground. With the possible exception of Texas appellate judges, it turns out that neither Republicans nor Democrats support imprisoning an innocent person.

D uring those giddy early days, Ben would often call me from the car, roaming around with his son, eating a Whopper from the Burger King drive-through. "Life is wonderful!" he crowed one day in April 2021. "I woke up, and I was free, and I spent the day with Debra and B.J. And I'm just grateful to be out."

"It's just like I'm living a dream or something," Debra marveled a few days later. "One time I pinched him. He goes, 'Why did you pinch me?' I say, 'I just cannot believe you're home.'" She laughed. "Ben walks so lightly, I turn around and suddenly he's there. I told him, 'I'm thinking about getting a cowbell to put around your neck. Or a rattle.'"

The worry that both Debra and Ben had quietly harbored never materialized. Father and son picked up as if the years that consumed the entirety of B.J.'s life and half of Ben's were simply restored, the clock set back. "It's like B.J. is five and Ben is thirty," Debra said. "They're best friends. They talk every day. They love each other. It's the best thing ever."

Yet as they settled into daily life together, tension in the house began to rise. Ben felt both free and confined: free, after sharing a room with 110 other men, and confined when he awkwardly bumped into the former wife he barely knew. For Debra, Ben's presence felt like an occupying force invading her sanctuary.

One day in early May 2021, I met Spencer for lunch at the Hall Arts building, where he worked as a parking attendant. We sat outside on a bench at the back of the building. Ben's uniform hung loosely on him. He was losing weight. He ate his panini slowly, and I handed him half of my chicken salad sandwich, which he stored in his bag for later. We chatted about new developments in the district attorney's investigation. He nodded, preoccupied.

"What's up, Ben?" I asked.

"I've been trying to get out of Debra's hair," he said. "She doesn't talk to me a lot. We sometimes just drive around in silence. I think Debra's having a hard time with the fact that I was with someone else the night that this offense happened."

"That was thirty-four years ago."

"But here's the thing. I broke her trust. I deeply care for her, but when she looks at me, it's a reminder of that."

The betrayal still bothered Debra, a little. Every couple has their list of aggravations and hurts, and betrayal figured in theirs. What was unique to Debra and Ben is this: Everything was conspiring against their survival. Time, experience, accomplishment, all created a canyon-sized distance between them. "It didn't turn out like the fairy tale," Debra admitted one day. "I wasn't prepared for the stumbling blocks. I wasn't prepared for his attachment to me. There's a lot, mentally, that I didn't know would happen."

Everyone had been expecting a Hollywood ending, but their emotional adjustment has proved anything but smooth. They had been thrown together and expected to blend as the world watched. Their personalities always clashed from the moment they met, but they never had the time to smooth out their differences, to navigate young adulthood and weave their lives together, to seal a partnership. Time and circumstance had sharpened the contrast, from sepia to black and white. Debra was always independent, feisty, tightly wound, and confident, and has grown more so in the past three decades. Ben was always quiet, easygoing, a loner who had chosen to make few close friends, but when he did, his fierce loyalty left his heart vulnerable. Prison reinforced this behavior, teaching him to keep his head down and his thoughts to himself.

"He's adjusting well," Debra said. "But he has a twenty-two-year-old mentality in a fifty-six-year-old body." She said this not as criticism, but as fact. In March 1987, Debra and Ben had stood side by side, about to launch into adulthood and family life together. Thirty-four years later, Debra had raised a child alone, succeeded in a largely white corporate world, traveled the country for work, ascended to the middle class, bought a house and cars, and built a community of trusted friends. Ben had stood on the sidelines, watching it all rush by.

S pencer was immensely proud of all her accomplishments, but he was not smitten by them. "I tell her, 'That's not why I want to be around you. I don't care about those things. I care about you.'" Prison cured him of the desire for frivolous acquisition. All he needed was freedom, and Debra. "I've told her over and over again that I just want to grow old with her."

After his release, Debra and Ben were living underneath a sword of Damocles. The Court of Criminal Appeals could deny his appeal at any time and he would be physically erased from her life forever. How could Debra make plans and commit her heart when Ben could be yanked away anytime?

Perhaps that corrosive fear speeded their undoing, for as April yielded to May and May to June, their relationship nearly unraveled. In early June, Debra asked Ben to pack up and move in with his family. "To be honest, I'm not in a good place with Ben right now," she texted when I reached out. "I still need to slow down but I have to work because I have extra bills now."

When one's life is snatched away and then returned thirty-four years later, every day of freedom multiplies in value. Getting upset, storming off, all the *drama*, it made no sense to Spencer. "It might be our last day together. God never promised us tomorrow," he commented one day while we were eating sandwiches on his lunch break. "In fact, I told her the other day, 'You have to lighten up a little bit, enjoy life. We don't know what tomorrow going to bring, so let's just enjoy today. Let's not be upset. Let's not be offended.' Debra has always been wound tight, and I'm not. I'm just relaxed and easygoing, because life is a breeze, so why not blow with the wind?"

Debra relented, and Spencer did not move out. Over time, Spencer's constancy, which irritated Debra in the early days of his release, became her emotional ballast in the chaos of their public lives. Her affections shifted. It presented in the most mundane ways. One midsummer day, she was napping and bolted awake when she felt him touch her feet. "I was about ready to rip him one," she said, giggling. "*Do not touch my feet.* Then I just looked at him and he was praying. I was like: Aw, that's love." She never doubted his love, not from the first day home. "My thing was how we going to get my love and his love in sync. I didn't know if I could fall deep in love with him. I knew I loved him and would do anything for him, but falling in love was different."

*Chapter 35*

# STATE OF PLAY

+———+

**Your fate does not depend upon
the righteousness of your case.**

—CHERYL WATTLEY

The double helix has sparked a revolution previously unseen in the history of criminal justice. It has changed the way we discover truth, revealed the deep flaws in our justice system, and triggered a public reckoning. Happily, the soul searching has led to some reforms.

The pioneer of the reform movement is not a blue state, not California or New York or Washington, but deep-red Texas. Over the past quarter century, its courts and its legislature have put in place rules to not only prevent *future* wrongful convictions, but also to correct their *past* mistakes and free the innocent. "After we led the nation in false convictions and prosecutorial misconduct and killing everybody, it's time we did a one-eighty," says John Creuzot, "or at least turn that ship around, slow it down, and veer it in another direction."

To avoid convicting an innocent person in the first place, Texas passed the "Michael Morton Act,"[1] requiring prosecutors to open their files and provide all their evidence to defendants, rather than choose which (exculpatory) files to disclose. Today, even if the prosecutor did not know he was failing to turn over information helpful to the defense, it is still considered a *Brady* violation and grounds for vacating a conviction.

The legislature has rewritten its laws about how jailhouse informants are used at trial. The state now must track, and disclose, any previous testimony that the informant provided in other trials, and the benefits they received in exchange for their testimony;[2] nor can prosecutors use jailhouse informant testimony unless they can corroborate the allegations.[3] Beginning in 2017, all police interrogations are recorded, which has minimized the number of false confessions.[4] Texas has changed procedures for police lineups to prevent eyewitness misidentification. It leads the way in forensic science, having built a world-class laboratory in Houston and created the best forensic science commission in the country.

If a prisoner claims he has been wrongly convicted in the past, Texas has paved broad paths, relative to other states, to give him a chance to prove it. A prisoner can return to court at any time and present new evidence of innocence. Dallas launched the first Conviction Integrity Unit to reinvestigate questionable convictions in 2007; since then, Houston, San Antonio, Austin, and Fort Worth have started their own units. Together, according to the National Registry of Exonerations, those CIUs have exonerated more than two hundred people, far and away the most of any state.[5] The Texas legislature passed a broad "junk science law" in 2013, which allows a conviction to be reconsidered and overturned if new scientific evidence is developed that contradicts the findings of the original trial.[6] Finally, Texas offers the most generous compensation for exonerees: an initial lump sum of eighty thousand dollars per year served, and then eighty thousand dollars annually for every year they were incarcerated.[7]

Most states have erected some guardrails to prevent the conviction of innocent defendants, as well as opportunities for prisoners to prove their innocence. Of course, not every state can be as progressive as Texas. When it comes to handling evidence, for example, only a handful of states have opted for the open discovery laws that Texas has enacted—that is, turning over all the evidence in the prosecutor's files. The rest follow the US Supreme Court's ruling in *Brady v. Maryland*. *Brady* requires only that they hand over evidence that is material to someone's innocence—and prosecutors are the ones making that call.

As for DNA, biological evidence can be a silver bullet, but only if you can get your hands on it. All states allow post-conviction testing, but some states only allow testing for certain crimes, such as sexual assault or capital murder. Some states throw out the evidence after a year or two, unless a prisoner specifically petitions for it to be retained, which requires a level of legal savvy that many prisoners lack. Some states prohibit a person from testing the DNA after he's served his time—a problem for convicted sex offenders who want to clear their name and remove themselves from the sex offender registration list. Some bar a prisoner from DNA testing if he's pleaded guilty, which seems reasonable until you consider that one out of ten of the prisoners exonerated by DNA had pleaded guilty.[8]

If the proper handling of documents and physical evidence is tricky, the proper handling of witnesses is exponentially more complex. The single largest contributor to wrongful convictions is eyewitness testimony; nearly half the time, eyewitnesses misidentify an innocent person as the perpetrator. Police can further contaminate that memory, and to avoid that, half the states have reformed their lineup procedures.[9] Slightly more states are recording police interrogations, which can help prevent, or at least rein in, the kinds of bullying, false promises, or lying that lead to false accusations and confessions. Yet every state continues to allow police to lie about their evidence—telling a suspect that his friend ratted him out, for example, or that his DNA was found on the murder weapon. The only exception is lying to minors: Currently, two states, Illinois and Oregon, prohibit it. "It's a nice first step," says the interrogation expert Saul Kassin. "But it's not just juveniles we have to worry about. This is a tactic that works on everybody."

Jailhouse informants are beginning to draw skeptical glances. Informants testified and lied in 15 percent of the murder cases in which the convicted person was exonerated. Now some states require prosecutors to disclose what benefits the informant expects in exchange for his testimony, or to corroborate the informant's account before putting him on the stand.[10] Informants continue to testify freely in the vast majority of states, but these rules are better than nothing. "Ten, fifteen years ago, this was not on the agenda," says Alexandra Natapoff, author of *Snitching: Criminal Informants and the Erosion of American Justice*. "The criminal justice *Titanic* moves slowly."

In a culture steeped in shows like CSI and the magic of forensics, almost nothing has been done to curb the abuse of "junk science," which has helped send some eight hundred innocent people to prison. By 2023 only seven states had passed laws that explicitly allow a prisoner to return to court to challenge discredited forensic science.[11] Most states have taken little notice of the fact that the top scientists in the United States have deemed much of forensic "science" useless at best and dangerous at worst. The states appear unconcerned or unaware that almost any comparison technique, from hair evidence and ballistics to blood spatter and boot prints, aids little in identifying a perpetrator. And they ignore the science showing that forensic experts easily succumb to cognitive bias and unwittingly give the police and prosecutors the answer they crave.

The states generally write the rules governing the fate of those accused and convicted of crimes, through the statutes passed by legislatures and rulings handed down by state courts. But for some basic constitutional rights, the US Supreme Court has the final word: the right to a fair play by the state; the right to a racially unbiased jury and trial; perhaps most important, the right to have one's claims heard in federal court.

Since the late 1980s, the court has acted like a cosmetic surgeon, nipping prisoner rights here, tucking them there, until the face of criminal jurisprudence is, if not unrecognizable, then drastically altered. It ruled that even if the state lost or destroyed evidence that could prove a prisoner's innocence, unless the prisoner could show that the state did so intentionally, he was stuck in prison.[12] It ruled that prosecutors could cheat and suppress evidence, and never pay a personal price.[13] The court effectively baked racism into the criminal justice system when it ruled that even overwhelming statistical evidence of racism in death penalty cases was immaterial: The prisoner must show evidence of discrimination in his specific case.[14] And beginning in the 1990s, the Court has blocked innocent prisoners from the one safe harbor: the federal courts.[15] Federal judges, who are not elected, used to be fair umpires for the wrongly convicted. Now they are spectators. Today innocence lawyers don't even consider the federal court as a viable option.

In 2022, the US Supreme Court, reshaped by the Trump presidency, crossed an existential threshold. In *Shinn v. Ramirez,* the court ruled that a prisoner on death row could not provide compelling evidence of his innocence.[16] The justices considered a pair of cases in Arizona, one involving Barry Jones, whose lawyer failed to investigate and find proof that Jones could not have committed the murder for which he was convicted. After an evidentiary hearing, a federal judge vacated the conviction, and an appellate court affirmed the decision. But the US Supreme Court disagreed. Justice Clarence Thomas called the federal judge's intervention an intrusion on state sovereignty, adding that "serial relitigation of final convictions undermines the finality that is essential to both the retributive and deterrent functions of criminal law."[17] In a scathing dissent, Justice Sonia Sotomayor wrote, "Two men whose trial attorneys did not provide even the bare minimum level of representation required by the Constitution may be executed because forces outside of their control prevented them from vindicating their constitutional right to counsel."[18]

Faced with the prospect of executing an innocent man, Arizona's attorney general freed Barry Jones the next year. His life was spared despite, not because of, the Supreme Court. Others may not enjoy Jones's luck. The court's ruling leaves the fate of prisoners to the politics of the state that prosecuted them in the first place.[19]

"This Supreme Court has been a disaster," Barry Scheck says.

I f DNA jump-started the innocence revolution, and innocence lawyers
drove it forward, then it's the local prosecutors who are moving it into
the future. New laws and court rulings cannot ensure that an innocent
prisoner will be treated fairly. Detectives and prosecutors can always justify finding a way around the rules. But since the Dallas County district
attorney's office established the first Conviction Integrity Unit in 2007,
some prosecutors have used their clout, their access to internal records,
and their power to compel testimony to redress erroneous convictions. In
recent years, these offices have freed more than seven hundred prisoners
by working with, rather than opposing, innocence lawyers.

"It is far more successful than anybody ever thought it was going to
be," says Patricia Cummings, who headed CIUs in Dallas and Philadelphia, "and it's had far more impact than anybody thought it was going to."

But the commitment to this counterintuitive endeavor depends, in
the end, on the chutzpah of individual prosecutors. Some district attorneys, such as John Creuzot, have set their teams loose to reinvestigate and
correct wrongful convictions. But of the nearly one hundred CIUs nationwide, just six offices account for 75 percent of the exonerations.[20]
Most district attorneys simply promise to set up units during their campaigns, then forget about them, says Terri Moore, who started the first
CIU in Dallas. "For the most part, I think it's Conviction Integrity Units
in name only. I don't think they're doing anything." More than half of the
units have not brought about a single exoneration, including in large cities
such as San Francisco, Phoenix, Washington, DC, Memphis, and Denver.

In other words, the luck of the draw determines a prisoner's fate. As
proof, one need look no further than Ben Spencer's case. His legal team
presented evidence to four district attorneys before they enjoyed any traction with John Creuzot. When Cynthia Garza headed the unit under
Faith Johnson, she was not allowed to investigate; when Creuzot ran the
office, she was allowed to turn over every rock to find evidence of Spencer's innocence.

This throws an element of capriciousness into what should be a system that treats all people the same way. "The fact that it's contingent on who is sitting in the district attorney's office, while heartwarming for Ben's current circumstances, is very troubling for someone else," Cheryl Wattley says. "Your fate does not depend upon the righteousness of your case, but on the willingness of the person to look into your case."

Happenstance determines all manner of decisions that chart a person's future. Will the detective dig down into the case, or close it with a cursory investigation? Will the trial judge keep the physical evidence in his closet, or toss it? Will the forensic scientist return all the evidence to the police, or retain a small sample for each case that can be tested later? Will the police chief or the head of the crime lab make one more search for evidence that could clear a prisoner? Sometimes the answer is no: the Dallas Police Chief comes to mind. And sometimes the answer is yes.

On July 23, 2021, I dropped off a letter at the Southwestern Institute of Forensic Sciences, Dallas's crime laboratory. I had heard that Dr. Jeffrey Barnard, who heads the lab, liked to solve cold cases from the 1980s and '90s, largely through advanced DNA testing. In my letter, I described Ben Spencer's case and noted that the lab had possessed the fingernail clippings of the victim's right hand as recently as 2011, before it moved to another location. The perpetrator might have left his DNA there during a struggle. Spencer's lawyers and I had requested four searches so far, but they had come up empty.

I asked him to take a "personal interest" in the search. "I am hoping that this search won't merely duplicate the previous ones, but will be a *de novo,* top-to-bottom search for that evidence," I wrote, suggesting that this fit into his area of passion—discovering the truth in old cases.

Seven weeks later, the lab located the evidence.

Barnard met me in the lobby of the crime lab in his cowboy boots, blue jeans, and a purple checked shirt. After we settled in a deposition room, he described the discovery of Jeffrey Young's fingernail clippings. "I didn't know anything about the case," he said. "But it's like, well, someone's taken the time to write the letter. It didn't seem like it should be that big a deal for me to put pressure on them to say, 'Let's go one more time.' And then sure enough, they find this whole area that they hadn't checked before. And that's where it was." Not just DNA evidence from the fingernails of the victim's right hand, as had been previously reported, but also from the left.

Tim Sliter, chief of the lab's physical evidence section, headed the search and recruited a half dozen scientists to help him. One section of the room contained boxes with evidence from the previous lab, including some specifically labeled "Dr. Barnard's special projects."

"I'll fess up," Sliter said. "I saw these boxes when I searched the area, and I did not think to open them, because they were so clearly labeled." He and his colleagues wrapped up their search and were ready to release the report declaring defeat when Barnard forwarded my letter to Sliter. "That kind of kicked it into a higher gear."

They returned to the room and eventually someone opened a box for Dr. Barnard's special projects. There were the fingernail clippings—along with evidence from several other cases. Someone had dumped the evidence there for the move and never got around to sorting it later. "It was serendipity," Sliter said. He warned me that the fingernail clippings were unlikely to clear Spencer. They probably only contained the victim's DNA. Still, maybe Spencer's new luck would hold.

In this story of generosity, you can see more indicia of a troubling pattern: Ben Spencer's freedom hinges almost entirely on individual people taking an interest; if he is exonerated, the credit goes to a person's character, not to the law. Jeffrey Barnard was more interested in truth than regulations. "That's why I go back and work on these old cases," he said. "I don't want somebody to be forgotten."

W ith all due respect to Edith Wharton," Daniel Medwed observes, "the age of innocence may be over." The innocence movement that officially began when the first American prisoner was exonerated by

DNA in 1989 has enjoyed a terrific run and freed several thousand innocent men and women. But in recent years, the number of DNA exonerations has been falling, and now it is dropping precipitously. The wrongly
imprisoned men and women are dying, or are dead. "If you were thirty
years old and convicted in 1960, I hope you're still alive, and we can free
you," Medwed says. But eventually, all the cases with untested DNA will
run out. "Time is an enemy."

Fine, you might be thinking, now the state tests the blood, semen, and
other biological evidence right away; investigators will catch the true perpetrator before trial. But consider this: In the majority of violent crimes,
no DNA is gathered at the crime scene—not in drive-by shootings, armed
robbery, well-planned murders, or even some sexual assault cases (because
condoms were used). In other words, the majority of cases in the future
will be tried without the benefit of DNA, and if the wrong person is convicted, he will have no silver bullet—no untested DNA as in previous
decades—to later annihilate the conviction.

"Overturning a wrongful conviction, even with DNA evidence, is extremely difficult," says Rebecca Brown at the Innocence Project. "But
when you don't have the benefit of DNA, it's so much harder." Without
the ground truth of DNA, how does a prisoner persuade a judge that his
confession was coerced, that the blood-spatter evidence was junk science,
that the prosecutor should have turned over evidence about the jailhouse
informant?

"It comes down to, really, serendipity," Brown says. "That's what
makes this so difficult. We should not be having to depend on luck."

On a practical level, there will be few easy post-conviction cases. All the
cases will look like Ben Spencer's. Old-style gumshoe investigators like
Jim McCloskey and Daryl Parker will spend countless hours knocking on
doors, tracking down witnesses, begging for evidence from reluctant
prosecutors and police. Lawyers will file petition after petition, argue in
court, win, lose, and file more petitions as the blameless person sits on his
cot in prison. Twenty-two years passed from the time Centurion accepted
Spencer's case to his tentative release, and he has not been exonerated.

Daniel Medwed has another worry. What will the public think when DNA exonerations disappear from the headlines? "Almost inevitably, there'll be a perception that it's no longer a problem because we fixed the underlying flaws," he says. But we haven't, because we haven't fixed the human problems, the biases and greed, the genuine mistakes and malpractice that still warp the process. "The same things that cause a wrongful conviction in a DNA case—mistaken eyewitness identification, police misconduct, false confessions, bad forensic evidence—all of those same factors presumably apply in the non-DNA realm," he says. Perhaps a memory of wrongful convictions will linger in our minds, an anachronism, like Model Ts or rotary telephones. What worries many people is that with time we'll forget that innocent people are still convicted every single day.

# Chapter 36

# A PARTIAL JUSTICE

+——+

**I opened my eyes on this side of
eternity and there you were.**

—BENJAMINE SPENCER

For the moment, Ben Spencer is the luckiest of the unlucky. Of the
tens of thousands of innocent men and women who have been convicted and will not leave prison until their sentence, or their life, ends,
Spencer has beaten the odds. He has defied a criminal justice system that
routinely makes mistakes and fights tooth and nail to preserve them. At
the beginning, he possessed no resources, no weapons, nothing but his
word, which seemed as likely to prevail as a tent in a tornado.

It took three decades for his luck to turn from bad to good, and in the
meantime, the state stole the prime of his adult life. He had expected to
raise a family with the woman who captured his heart, to teach his son to
drive and change the spark plugs in his Gran Torino. He could not grab a
beer with a friend, cook up some ribs in the backyard, spend a weekend
with his dad in the country as he grew old. The state stole all his choices:
Would he and Debra have a little girl to dote on? Would he tire of driving
long-haul trucks and become a pastor after all? Maybe he didn't feel like a
BLT today but wanted a turkey on rye. It didn't matter. All his choices, all

his moments, were dictated by a system that brooked no disagreement, not from a convicted criminal like Benjamine Spencer.

And yet, if his luck holds—if he's not sent back to prison by the court—he may live the remainder of his life in freedom. What shade of freedom has yet to be determined. But DNA testing is where Spencer's luck seems to have run out. The biological evidence has not solved the crime; it has not identified the killer, or conclusively cleared Spencer's name. A laboratory has tested the victim's fingernail clippings and found the DNA does *not* belong to Ben Spencer. But the scientists have been unable to determine if the DNA belongs to Jeffrey Young or to someone else. The tests suggest that the DNA is Young's,[1] meaning that the killer did not leave his genetic evidence. The prosecutors and Spencer's attorneys concluded they can go no further, a disappointing but predictable result that ends the search to identify the killer.

For months, Spencer has been leaving Post-it notes on Debra's refrigerator each morning. One Saturday morning in January 2022, I read through a few at random, these three-inch-by-three-inch love letters, and noticed the common themes. He is grateful that he is free and confident that God has a purpose for their suffering and a plan to redeem their lost years; mainly, he is astonished that she has returned to his life. "Another blessing from the Lord this morning," he wrote in his precise, microscopic handwriting. "I opened my eyes on this side of eternity and there you were." "There were many days that I did not know if I could ever be free again, nor whether we would ever reconnect," he wrote on another day. "But look at me now! I am free and we're about to be remarried." And on December 21, 2021: "There's just 20 days left before we become Mrs. and Mr. Spencer again."

Debra, who guarded her heart from disappointment for so many years, had been won over.

"He wore me down with love," she said. "That was something I had never experienced. He wore me down with love."

re you angry at anyone?" I ask, as the camera rolls. It is two days before the wedding. Spencer wears a pressed white shirt, dress pants,
and dress shoes, and with his high cheekbones and even features, he could
be an actor portraying Ben Spencer in a feature film; he's just that handsome. A film company, Anchor Worldwide, is gathering video for a possible documentary. Debra sits on a stool just off camera, in a red cable-knit
sweater and red Texas baseball cap, listening intently.

"No, I'm not angry," Spencer says.

"Not even at Gladys Oliver?"

"No. I have no place in my heart for hatred. I don't believe that is con-
ducive to anything positive."

"I'm trying to get my head around this," the camerawoman, Leslie
Bumgarner, says. "I can't help but think about what I would do in that
situation, or how you would even deal with that."

"Well, I've always felt either I'm going to live for the world or I'm going
to live for God," he says, not in the way of an evangelist but of a rational
actor explaining Pascal's wager. "If I'm going to live for God, I just didn't
feel that I could be bottled up with this hate or envy or jealousy, wrath, or
malice. I just couldn't allow myself to be filled with those things."

I recalled the observation by Kate Germond at Centurion, who had
worked with countless exonerees. "You and I would be whining endlessly," she said. "They don't complain. They just put one foot in front of
the other. *They're just better than we are.*"

Spencer wants to be fully exonerated so he can get a job and begin life
anew, he says. But the compensation that comes with exoneration is beside the point. "I mean, there's thirty-four years that have been taken from
me; there is not enough money in the world to pay for that. I would have
preferred to have been here with Debra, raising my own son." What can
he teach B.J. now, when he's thirty-five? "In my way of thinking, my faith,
our reward is not what we receive here. It's what we hope to attain when
we leave this world. I simply want to make it to heaven. If I can make it
there, then everything else is irrelevant."

But on this side of death? He looks down, hesitant to voice his outrageous hope. "I know that my greatest wish may never come true—that one day the Young family could just come to accept that I'm innocent." His voice cracks. "I see them as I see myself. We're all victims of a lie. Of course, they're victims of their loss of their father, brother, husband. But they're a victim of lies as well, because they have been fed a lie, and they've bought into it."

No one in this scenario has received justice. On this, Jay Young and Ben Spencer agree. Jeffrey Young's death will dog them both the rest of their lives.

"For me," Jay Young says, "it'll never be over until my last breath."

Since Ben Spencer's release, District Attorney John Creuzot has once again vanquished his opponent, Faith Johnson, in the 2022 election. He and Cynthia Garza have continued to exonerate innocent prisoners. Garza has gained nationwide recognition for her work, and in 2023 was given a Distinguished Alumni Award by the SMU Dedham School of Law. Spencer's newest attorney, Gary Udashen, has been involved in at least three more exonerations since then. Cheryl Wattley, who still runs an innocence clinic at her law school, was named Trial Lawyer of the Year by the Dallas Bar Association in 2021 and received the Legacy Award from her alma mater, Smith College, in 2024. Daryl Parker's investigative firm tripled in size during Covid; between running the firm and his all-night surveillance gigs, he reinvestigates cases through his nonprofit, Actual Innocence Review. Gladys Oliver, the state's star witness, died in April 2023, having never recanted her testimony.

Then there is Jim McCloskey, the man who felt called by God four decades ago to spend his life freeing innocent prisoners. One day in the spring of 2021, I drove to Princeton to collect McCloskey's files on Michael Hubbard. I was sitting on the couch going through two big boxes we had carried up from his basement, pulling out files, chattering away with a grin on my face, astounded at his research.

"Jim," I said, "I just don't know how you did all this work. I mean, the man-hours that were involved in this."

He was slumped in his wingback chair, his legs stretched in front of him, looking at me. "Barb, I was just thinking I could never do that today. I am done. I am empty. I've given everything I have." He shook his head in wonder. "It's just so hard. Once they're convicted, it's a Gordian knot. It's almost impossible getting them un-convicted."

McCloskey said that he has never, not for one second, doubted his call. But he has doubted God. "There are many moments over these last almost forty years, I question, Does God really exist? And if God is real, then *why?* What's the purpose, what's the redeeming value of all this unjust suffering?" He added that no theologian has answered that question to his satisfaction. For now, he pushes through, his faith bent but not broken, because an embattled faith is better than none.

As evening approached, we began talking about that ignominious night when he hired a Times Square prostitute, only to find his wallet gone when he awakened. Shaken at finding himself at a spiritual nadir, he enrolled in Princeton Theological Seminary, and launched a revolution that would transform how Americans see guilt and innocence.

"You're not going to like this, because you don't like compliments," I said. "But Jim, you've changed the world."

"Oh, come on, Barb! Jeez and Christmas, man!"

"It's true, Jim," I insisted. "No one was doing this work. If you were in prison, you were never getting out. That's how it was. You've changed the world. Do you ever think about that?"

"No, I never do. That's too big a concept to comprehend for me."

"But you did it one step at a time. It's not like you set out to do it."

"No, no, not at all. Just one case after another. Just head down. I've been in a tunnel for forty years. No, that thought has never entered my mind."

"So you're going to get a mansion in heaven," I mused. "And I just want to know, when I have a fourth-story walk-up . . ."

"Yeah?"

"Can I come over for dinner?"

"Absolutely!" he bellowed. "Just don't roll me!"

McCloskey erred in at least one prediction. He was not done. He soon realized he was not wired for retirement. When the bestselling author John Grisham asked him to write a book with him, McCloskey accepted.

O n January 10, 2022, exactly thirty-five years after their first wedding, Ben and Debra arrive at church, accompanied by a small village of people in the wedding party. More than four hundred friends settle quietly in the hauntingly beautiful Truett Chapel, darkened but for soft lighting and scores of white candles glowing at the altar.

In the bridesmaids' room, as a dozen women chat and perfect their makeup, Debra sits stiffly in front of the mirror while her friend Laurie braids her hair. Even now, in the giddiest of moments, she can never forget that her future hangs on one word from a court of nine Republican judges: Relief is GRANTED, or relief is DENIED.

Spencer, in a room down the hall, seems untroubled by the legal sword dangling above them; he merely smiles as his groomsmen tell stories. "I'm just ready for the vows to be made and get on with life."

The ceremony begins at five o'clock, and for all the singing by Debra's friends in the choir, for all the magical lighting, for the moving sermon by a minister Debra considers her spiritual father—for all of that, one image lingers. As the wedding party stretches across the stage, five ex-convicts, including Spencer, stand solemnly on the platform. Of those five men, four had been convicted of a crime they did not commit. Those tuxedo-clad men had wasted, among them, more than one hundred years in prison.

Ben Spencer's story is not over. His redemption is partial, just as the innocence revolution is partial. It remains mired in procedures that preserve erroneous results at the expense of the truth; yet it is infinitely fairer than the defective system of thirty-five years ago.

Ben Spencer is the luckiest of the unlucky. He's lucky because a nonprofit organization named Centurion Ministries spent $250,000 reinvestigating his case. He's lucky because two of Dallas's most prominent lawyers and a private investigator donated their time to litigate his case. He's lucky because *The Atlantic* and NPR, among other media outlets, brought his case to the public. He's astronomically lucky because an open-minded district attorney and a tenacious prosecutor reopened his case, even though there was no easy DNA fruit to be plucked. How many innocent prisoners—particularly those with no DNA in their files—draw this sort of legal and media firepower?

Yes, for now, Ben Spencer is lucky. But in America, should one's freedom depend on luck?

## AUTHOR'S NOTE

+———+

Often, I replay a conversation I had with Jeffrey Goldberg in March of 2014. Jeff, a friend and writer (now editor in chief) at *The Atlantic*, had been taping an interview at NPR and learned that I was leaving the network after nineteen years, chiefly for health reasons: A paralyzed vocal cord had derailed my ability to do on-air radio reporting. Perceiving this might present something of an existential crisis, he called to reassure me. This isn't a close call, he said. I was now free to engage in ideas in a larger way, not driven by the news or confined to a few minutes on the radio. And let me tell you how it's going to play out, he continued. Your thoughts will drift to your area of keenest interest. You'll think about a story you covered five years ago, or ten, and you will realize that you're obsessed by it. You're going to follow your obsession.

Three years later, I stumbled onto Ben Spencer's case, and published a story about it in *The Atlantic* in January 2018. The article changed nothing external. Ben remained incarcerated. He had exhausted his appeals and, barring a miracle, he would die in prison an old man. Yet, his story felt like a mystery novel whose last pages had been lost in a fire. I became, like Jim McCloskey, haunted by the unfinished business.

For several months during 2020 and 2021, I lived in Dallas, trying to uncover new evidence and solve the murder of Jeffrey Young. In the process, I conducted more than two hundred hours of interviews with Ben Spencer, his family, his friends, his investigators, and his lawyers. The district attorney in Dallas County and the head of the Conviction Integrity Unit spoke with me repeatedly. Former prosecutors and detectives, some reluctantly, fit me into their schedules. I read some twenty-five hundred pages of Ben's handwritten letters from prison, and pored over more than ten thousand pages of court documents, investigative notes, and other records. With the help of a private investigator, I tracked down old witnesses who recanted and new alibi witnesses who attested to Ben's innocence. Unless otherwise stated, every quote from a person, letter, or document was conveyed directly to me. I followed my obsession.

I said my reporting changed nothing external. But internally, it brought about a wholesale renovation. We all know of the "observer effect," in which the act of looking at something changes it, whether that be atoms or people, politics or law. The phenomenon pervades journalism, and in fact is often its raison d'être: Nothing brings down a politician, or a movie producer, or a secret policy of housing immigrant children in cages, like a story in *The New York Times*.

But, sometimes, there is a *reverse* observer effect, and that was the case for me. Ben Spencer's story transformed my reporting, and not just by supplying some new tricks of the trade. I was thrust from the safe media landscape of Washington, DC, into the streets of Dallas, where the facts reside. People yelled at me, slammed doors in my face, threatened me, and evicted me from their apartments. I was never really in physical danger, except perhaps when I ventured into some neighborhoods of Dallas alone. The larger danger was psychological. For decades, I had hidden behind the manufactured neutrality that shelters journalists from charges of bias and lawsuits. But sometimes, the "on-the-one-hand, on-the-other-hand" paradigm distorts the truth, because the pound of facts on one side so obviously outweighs the ounce of facts on the other. And so, for the first time in my career, I have blown through the boundaries of my craft and am stating my opinion: The justice system is broken, and Ben Spencer is innocent.

More personally, and profoundly, Ben's story transformed my faith. This came as a surprise. I had thought deeply about my Christian beliefs for more than two decades. I wrote a book about the science of spirituality, to answer my own questions: *Is there more than this material world? Can an educated person believe in God?* For a decade, I reported on religion for NPR, covering the fights over homosexuality, the inerrancy of the Bible, priest sexual abuse, the politics of the Christian Right, and religious fanaticism in every faith. And the schisms! Watching such deeply religious people fighting over shrinking pieces of ecclesiastical real estate—well, it was enough to make anyone an atheist. I suffered a crisis of church.

But after watching Jim McCloskey live out his call, despite his haunting doubts, these doctrinal battles seemed as irrelevant to me as trigonometry is to a third grader. One day, I thought: Why don't I try to master addition before tackling the Pythagorean theorem? Faith is pretty simple if you'll only dip into the Old Testament prophets. *What doth the Lord require of thee, but to do justly, and to love mercy, and to walk humbly with thy God?* This was the lean faith that drove Jim McCloskey, Ben and Debra Spencer, and almost every person working on Ben's behalf. Ultimately, I found my own faith, one that did not depend on doctrinal accuracy or unexplained miracles, but on action: Feed the hungry, clothe the naked, heal the sick, give refuge to the immigrants, *visit the prisoner—* visible behavior infused with invisible power that some would call God.

On October 18, 2023, I set out for a bike ride and was sideswiped by a car passing at upward of thirty miles an hour. A broken hip and collarbone, both requiring surgery, and three broken ribs now seem like a bargain: Change the position or dynamics by a fraction—had we collided a second earlier, had I been an inch farther to the left—and the outcome could have been existentially worse. In the hospital, I began to reflect on this very real possibility: *What if I had died?* I'll spare you the cliché of recounting the gratitude for my extraordinary family and my close friends, whom I don't deserve. But when I contemplated my career, my overriding reaction was: *I cannot believe my luck.* Had I died, *Bringing Ben Home* would have been my last story, the greatest privilege of my privileged life. I had parachuted into the story that I had always wanted to write, crammed with exceptional characters and powerful colliding forces. Truth and mendacity, justice and expediency, fall and redemption, the power of the state and the force of morality: Ben's is a David and Goliath story that could only take place in a country that yearns for justice and continuously wrestles with its demons.

And the *heroes*—this story is crowded with heroes. The businessman who was rolled by a Times Square prostitute and went on to launch the modern innocence movement. The lawyers and investigators who worked for years, and for nothing more than the prospect of undoing a wrong. The convicted felon who risked his life by siding with Ben over his murderous friend, and the drug trafficker in federal prison who believed his central purpose in life was to exonerate Ben. The jury foreman who condemned Ben to life, and then thought again. The judge who found a Black man innocent of killing a white man in deep red Texas. The district attorney who risked his career to free Ben, and the prosecutor who patiently gathered shards of truth, like panning for gold in the swift current of deception and indolence.

At the center, of course, are Ben and Debra. We spent many hours together: at church and lunch with their friends every Sunday; dinners at their favorite restaurants and lunches on a park bench; formal interviews and simply hanging out. This sort of "immersive journalism" allowed me to catch glimpses of their bumpy passage and chronicle Ben's transition from Coffield prison to Debra's home in the suburbs of Dallas. Often, I felt ambivalent about my role. In my forty years of journalism, I had never spent so much time with, and felt such genuine affection for, the subjects I covered. These were not characters in a novel; their lives were not the narrative spine of a five-minute story on NPR. They were two people who had experienced decades of trauma and were finding their way forward.

In the ultimate example of the reverse-observer effect, Ben Spencer kept my mother alive. She was ninety-nine years old when I arrived at her Washington, DC, apartment on Monday, February 15, 2021. She was sitting in her favorite chair, wearing her quilted mint-green robe, a ribbon in her hair, a picture of elegance. For her entire life, until recently, Mom thought deeply and spoke eloquently about everything—politics, social mores, religion, her children's lives. She was also fiercely original in her opinions: In 2008, at the age of eighty-seven, the lifelong Republican fell in love with Barack Obama after listening to his speech on race and cast her first-ever vote for a Democrat. Her instinctual outrage at injustice— an innate and singular trait among her upper-middle-class friends—drew her to Ben's story, and for the better part of four years, I had been giving her regular updates.

Now, nearing one hundred, her hair was so wispy that I could see her scalp. She rarely talked. The words she had marshaled for a lifetime had abandoned her. But there was one topic that always engaged her, the only topic that she invariably remembered: the story of Ben Spencer. Her one wish, when she could still wish aloud, was that she might see him walk out of prison. Now her life had narrowed to a pinpoint, with a single piece of unfinished business: Ben's release.

"Mom, Ben sent you a letter," I said as I settled into a chair that frigid February evening. "This may be his last letter from prison. Shall I read it?"

She took my cold hand in her warm bony grasp and pulled it toward her in silent assent. Ben began his letter with a brief introduction of his case and a statement of his faith in God and in truth to prevail. "After being wrongfully convicted of this offense twice and being sentenced to life in prison, I really didn't think I could make it," he wrote. "All praise to God for He has surely proven me wrong, I'm still alive and there's hope for me."

I glanced at Mom. She was staring at me—cognizant, deep in his story. I had come to expect a level of lyricism in Ben's letters, but what surprised me about this one was his emotional intelligence—as if he could imagine my mother sitting mutely, her silent fears on the cusp of the unknown, her need for assurance and gratitude. I had told him she was following his story, that she believed in him, that she prayed for his release. And for three pages he recounted how much he appreciated Mom and her regard for his plight, her courage and faithfulness, her wisdom. "Thank you for the love and concern that you have shown, thanks for the love you have exhibited," he wrote. "Having your support has meant more to me than you can imagine. Thank you, Ms. Mary Ann Bradley."

I looked up. Mom's eyes were brimming, a rebellious tear breaking free and running down her cheek. As I dabbed her face with a tissue, I thought, Here is a man who has been incarcerated for nearly thirty-four years—where did he develop empathy? Not in the jungle of prison, or from the other inmates, or from the guards; it must be internal to him, a product of his wiring and his faith. He prays for her every day, he wrote. "I look forward to meeting you one day soon."

Mom closed her eyes and rested her head against the back of the chair. She sat quietly for a few moments, as if contemplating the letter, then opened her eyes and smiled.

Mom never met Ben in person, but she did see him on Zoom the day after he was released from prison. She was dressed in her favorite periwinkle sweater and a matching ribbon, but she seemed distant, half in this world and half in another. Ben understood. He, too, is living in two worlds, captivity and freedom, a dichotomy that few of us experience. But perhaps, thanks to Ben Spencer, we can appreciate the paradox, just a little.

## ACKNOWLEDGMENTS

On March 12, 2021, the day Benjamine Spencer walked out of the Dallas jail, I detected a soft sound, like a breath; upon reflection, I realized it was Jake Morrissey's sigh of relief traveling from New York City to Dallas. Jake had commissioned this book long before we knew the outcome; he had gambled that Ben would be freed and that the book's ending, if not the first three hundred pages, would be redemptive. I am grateful for that trust, and for so much more: Jake's keen questions helped direct my research; he cheered me on as I slogged through mountains of material; he had the patience of Job (except that time when he didn't) in pulling me over the finish line. British in style if not by birth, Jake is ever polite, witty, with the gifts of a writer, but not the ego. He edits kindly. He blew away the chaff and shaped this book to be both leaner and smarter.

I could hardly believe my good fortune when Raphael Sagalyn, agent to the intelligentsia, took me on as an untested author nearly twenty years ago. My fortune continued, as Rafe instantly understood the value of Ben Spencer's story. He walked me through every part of the process, by finding a home for the book, thinking through the organization, encouraging me to weave the larger story of injustice into Ben's narrative, arguing for more time, and suggesting titles. Rafe is as skilled as he is elegant, and has always looked out for my interests.

Had I known how much research this book would require, I might have cut and run. Instead, I turned to the National Registry of Exonerations. The Registry reminds me a little of the Phillips Collection in Washington, DC. Small, elegant, filled with unexpected treasures, you turn the corner and there's the exoneration equivalent of a Picasso or a Cezanne or a van Gogh. Each of the three-thousand-plus carefully researched stories tells of a tragedy born of serious flaws in the system. The depth of the Registry's research is matched only by the generosity of the experts there: Maurice Possley, Simon Cole, Rob Warden, and Samuel Gross, who answered every one of my questions quickly and in detail.

Stephen Bright, a legal pioneer who teaches at Yale Law School and defended death-row inmates as the director of the Southern Center for Human Rights, helped me navigate the judicial complexities. Richard Leo at the University of San Francisco generously offered his insights and research on the history of the innocence movement, of which he is an expert. I was also lucky to stumble on several young, brilliant researchers. Michelle Pitcher, a Pulitzer Prize winner, and Tana Geneva, a fine magazine writer, dug up historical facts, court precedents, and all manner of studies about the causes of wrongful convictions. Maggie Rossberg tracked down witnesses and financial information from the 1980s, before heading off to law school at the University of Virginia. Joanna (JoJo) Duchesne should be canonized for transcribing dozens of interviews, all the while working full-time on Capitol Hill.

Journalists rely on the kindness of strangers, and Celia and Jim Crank were among the most generous. They invited me to stay in their charming garage apartment in Dallas for three months, giving me the time and flexibility to immerse myself in my research and in the lives of Ben and Debra Spencer. Richard Shlackman, a retired general counsel at Ross Perot's EDS, emailed his colleagues repeatedly to learn whether Perot had given money to the state's star witness, Gladys Oliver. He never found a definitive answer, but I found a friend. Chase Baumgartner at the Innocence Project of Texas patiently explained the process of matching old DNA to the crime scene. Tasha Tsiaperas, the district attorney's media relations manager, far exceeded her job requirements. As a former reporter, she understood my needs and made my life easy, and we spent several evenings over drinks, swapping war stories. I consider her a friend.

In 1988, I was a twenty-nine-year-old reporter covering the Justice Department for *The Christian Science Monitor*, filing stories on Reagan-era scandals that were distant and bloodless. Then Errol Morris released *The Thin Blue Line*, an infuriating documentary about a wrongful conviction, the first film of its kind. Under Morris's deft questioning, the witnesses who put a man on death row bumbled and recanted on camera; the misconduct of Dallas County prosecutors was laid out like roadkill; and the young, shifty jailhouse informant all but confessed to the murder. As the credits rolled, I thought: You can do this? You can reinvestigate a conviction, and show the criminal justice system is flawed and indifferent to executing an innocent man? It opened my mind to the possibilities of journalism. Morris became my hero.

When I told Errol Morris in 2021 that *The Thin Blue Line* changed my life, he laughed. "Changed mine, too," he quipped. I talked with Morris twice, at length, about the corrupt justice system in 1980s Dallas. His reflections ended up on this book's cutting room floor, a phenomenon Morris knew well, but it saddened me. He generously agreed to help with a documentary on Ben's experience. That documentary is still a dream, but a viable one. Arielle Lever, a television agent at Creative Arts Agency, believed in this project from the get-go. Ethan Goldman, founder of Anchor Entertainment, has invested heavily in the project, as have director Alphonzo Wesson, producer Keayr Braxton, and Linzee Troubh, the development director at *The Atlantic*. My close friend Jody Hassett, an acclaimed filmmaker and former award-winning producer at ABC and CNN, flew to Dallas during the storm of the century to cover Ben's possible release from prison. Together we bought most of our meals from 7-Elevens, which have—who knew?—a decent wine selection.

I could not count all the friends who listened to my updates on the book ad infinitum, but two stand out: Wade Goodwyn, my dear friend at NPR, and Sharon Sandell Goodwyn, a pediatric critical care doctor. I spent many evenings in their home in Dallas, Wade sitting in his reclining chair, Sharon on the couch, me on the floor with their two dogs, Bella and Miles, talking through the holes in my research and how to fill them. Wade lost a long battle with cancer in 2023 at age sixty-four. I think of him and Sharon every day.

It's a big ask to get someone to read your manuscript. My friends did not flinch. What everyone knows of Mary Breed is her athletic prowess—she has won five national championships in cycling—but what I appreciate is her keen intellect. She served as a proxy for you, the reader. Steve Drummond—the best editor at NPR and an author in his own right—made my manuscript crisper and more lyrical. Steve Levin, a former federal prosecutor and now a defense attorney, saved me from mangling the law, and insisted that I maintain a driving narrative. Liaquat Ahamed, who authored the Pulitzer Prize–winning *Lords of Finance*, took the thirty-thousand-foot perspective and prompted me to restructure. Readers should be grateful I have such talented friends.

My family has been knee-deep in the Ben Spencer story from the beginning. Many days, I would meet my brother, David Bradley, at my mother's apartment and they would listen to me recount my investigation as it unfolded. He and his wife, Katherine, were so smitten with the story that they invested in the documentary project. Vivian Hagerty and Griffin Anderson, my stepdaughter and son-in-law, have spent many hours around the dinner table listening to details and suggesting ideas, but mainly they are the source of incalculable happiness. My world is bursting with color because of them. Patchett (dog, not author) stretched out by my side most mornings before dawn as I wrote, until it was time to play ball.

And Devin: You made this book possible. You believed in it, and in me, from the moment you heard of Ben's plight. You held down the fort when I traveled to Dallas. You befriended Ben and Debra, read my early drafts, told me not to worry about anything, just tell the story. *Bringing Ben Home* is your book as much as mine.

# NOTES

+———+

## PART 1: CONVICTION

### Chapter 1: A Murder in Dallas

1. All dates and times come from the police notes of Detective Jesus Briseno and his colleagues, as well as two sets of trial transcripts: *State of Texas v. Benjamin John Spencer*, 283rd Judicial Court of Dallas, Texas, Mar. 21, 1988, and *State of Texas v. Nathan Robert Mitchell*, 283rd Judicial Court of Dallas, Texas, Mar. 29, 1988.

   The state spelled Spencer's first name Benjamin, but when not quoting the official documents, we will use his preferred spelling: Benjamine.
2. This information comes from the testimony of the victim's widow, Jamee Young, in Benjamine Spencer's first trial. That trial transcript has been lost, but the information was recorded in notes taken by the prosecutors and by Ben Spencer during the trial.
3. *Texas v. Spencer* trial transcript, 1988, vol. 2, 55.
4. In a July 25, 2017 email, BMW Group confirmed that a person locked in the trunk could escape: "We have just looked at a comparable vehicle. It is technically possible to open the trunk from the inside. The latching can be actuated by a finger. However there is no mention of this function in the manual. Thus in our estimation it is not an 'official' function, but an 'inside trick.'" They added in a later email: "A trapped person who fumbles around could be able to find the latch with a little luck and skill."
5. *Texas v. Spencer* trial transcript, 1988, vol. 2, 175.
6. *Texas v. Mitchell* trial transcript, 1988, vol. 2, 18.
7. Dallas Police Department investigative notes in the death of Jeffrey Young, March 23, 1987.
8. For his part, Aaron Perkins was not available to testify. He had been terminated, and moved to Los Angeles. "We heard rumors he is in California singing," Hutchinson explained.
9. See testimony of Officer Jeffrey L. Hutchinson, *Texas v. Mitchell* trial transcript, 1988, vol. 2, beginning on page 395.

### Chapter 2: The Day After

1. Dallas Police Department investigative notes into homicide of Jeffrey Young, Mar. 24, 1987.
2. West Dallas boasted a storied history of crime. Bonnie and Clyde lived in West Dallas and launched their criminal careers there. The area, also known as the Devil's Back Porch, was a cauldron of criminal enterprise and provided an escape route for gangsters running from the law. When Dallas grew glamorous and rich with oil, West Dallas collapsed into itself, a lawless and murderous land.
3. Jeri Clausing, "Congressional Panel Opens Dallas Hearings," UPI, May 9, 1987.
4. See "Archive—the Dallas Drug War | Drug Wars | FRONTLINE | PBS," n.d., pbs.org/wgbh/pages/frontline /shows/drugs/archive/dallas.html.
5. "Archive—the Dallas Drug War." In 1986, a Dallas police officer shot and killed seventy-year-old Etta Collins after she called 911 to report a robbery in progress. The next year, police officers shot David Horton, an eighty-one-year-old crime-watch volunteer: Horton died by a dumpster near his apartment house. South and West Dallas became war zones in which both Black people and Dallas cops were killed—although not in equal numbers, and generally with impunity for the police.

6. Dallas Police investigative notes, Mar. 23, 1987, 19–20.
7. Dallas Police investigative notes, 20–21.

**Chapter 3: Defying Gravity**
1. Letter from Ben Spencer to Jerry and Jinna Lancourt, Sept. 5, 2016.
2. Letter from Ben Spencer to author, Aug. 27, 2017.
3. Letter from Ben Spencer to Debra Spencer, Sept. 29, 2005.
4. Letter from Ben Spencer to Debra Spencer, Dec. 20, 2004.
5. Letter from Ben Spencer to the author, July 30, 2017.
6. Letter from Ben Spencer to Debra Spencer, Jan. 4, 2005.

**Chapter 4: A Break in the Case**
1. Affidavit of Gladys Oliver, Mar. 25, 1987.
2. Dallas Police investigative notes, Mar. 23, 1987, 2–3.
3. Statements by Jimmie Cotton, Donald Merritt, and Charles Stewart come from their trial testimony in *Texas v. Spencer.*
4. Dallas Police investigative notes, Mar. 26, 1987, 29.
5. See Affidavit in Support of Spencer Arrest, Exhibit 53, *Ex Parte Benjamine John Spencer*, Application for Post Conviction Writ of Habeas Corpus, 293rd Judicial District, Dallas, Texas, CAUSE NO. F-87-96524-UT, 2004, 83–84.
6. *United States v. Wade*, 388 US 218 (1967), 228.
7. See Lindsay Knowles and Alison Spann, "Falsely Accused: Mistaken Eyewitness Accounts Make Up Majority of Wrongful Convictions," July 16, 2021, wlox.com/2021/07/16/falsely-accused-mistaken-eyewitness-accounts-make-up-majority-wrongful-convictions.

   PNAS has similar statistics: Thomas D. Albright, "Why Eyewitnesses Fail," *Proceedings of the National Academy of Sciences* 114, no. 30 (July 25, 2017): 7758–64, doi.org/10.1073/pnas.1706891114.
8. Keith A. Findley and Michael S. Scott, "The Multiple Dimensions of Tunnel Vision in Criminal Cases," *Wisconsin Law Review* 291 (2006): 348, media.law.wisc.edu/m/hyjb3/findley_scott_final.pdf.

   Studies show that on those rare occasions that defense attorneys petition to exclude an eyewitness' identification, the courts rarely comply—less than 6 percent of the time. See Stephen G. Valdes, "Frequency and Success: An Empirical Study of Criminal Law Defenses, Federal Constitutional Evidentiary Claims, and Plea Negotiations," University of Pennsylvania Law Review 153, no. 5: 1709, 1730–31 nn. 123, 124, and 125 (basing results on surveys of judges, prosecutors, and defense lawyers).
9. Hugo Münsterberg, *On the Witness Stand: Essays on Psychology and Crime* (New York: McClure, 1908).
10. James M. Doyle, *True Witness: Cops, Courts, Science, and the Battle against Misidentification* (New York: Palgrave Macmillan, 2005), 18.
11. Münsterberg, *On the Witness Stand*, 39.
12. Münsterberg, *On the Witness Stand*, 39–43. Münsterberg stated that the burglars had entered through a cellar window and taken little: "They had started in the wine cellar and had forgotten under its genial influence, on the whole, what they had come for" (41). They had visited several rooms at nighttime, a fact he surmised from the candle wax on the second floor. They intended to take, but abandoned, a large mantel clock, which they had packed in wrapping paper and left on the dining room table. They took very few clothes. A few days later, the police arrested the culprit, who revealed these facts: The single burglar had broken a lock and entered through the cellar door, not a window; had left wax in the attic, not the second floor; had wrapped the clock in a tablecloth, not paper; and had absconded with a closetful of suits, which Münsterburg had missed entirely.
13. See Münsterberg, *On the Witness Stand*, 49–51. Münsterberg gives few details about the experiment, but Franz von Liszt's famous experiment matches, which took place in 1902. See Siegfried L. Sporer, "Lessons from the Origins of Eyewitness Testimony Research in Europe," *Applied Cognitive Psychology* 22, no. 6 (September 2008):737–57, searchgate.net/publication/229547353_Lessons_from_the_origins_of_eyewitness_testimony_research_in_Europe.
14. Lest one discount the students' poor showing because of youth and inexperience, according to Hugo Münsterberg, a similar experiment was done on forty unsuspecting jurists, psychologists, and physicians at a scientific meeting in Göttingen "two years ago," which would have been in the first five years of the twentieth century. In the street outside, revelers were enjoying a carnival. In the middle of the meeting, "a clown in highly coloured costume rushes in in mad excitement, and a negro with a revolver in hand follows him." They shout "wild phrases," one jumps on the other, the gun fires, and they dash out of the room. "The whole affair took less than twenty seconds." When the witnesses wrote their accounts, they contained statements that were either wrong or completely invented; few of these "scientifically trained observers" accurately recalled what the two adversaries

were wearing or what they said, and some observers said the altercation lasted several minutes. In the end, the majority of the witnesses—all men—omitted or falsified about half the details of an event that unfolded directly in front of them. See Münsterberg, *On the Witness Stand*, 51–53.

15. Innocence Project, "The Psychological Phenomena That Can Lead to Wrongful Convictions," Nov. 18, 2018, innocenceproject.org/the-psychological-phenomena-that-can-lead-to-wrongful-convictions.

16. Dan Simon, *In Doubt: The Psychology of the Criminal Justice Process* (Cambridge, MA: Harvard University Press, 2012), 63.

17. There is an avalanche of studies on bad eyewitness testimony, but a good review of contaminated memories can be found in Mark Godsey, *Blind Injustice: A Former Prosecutor Exposes the Psychology and Politics of Wrongful Convictions* (Oakland: University of California Press, 2017), 125–28.

18. Simon, *In Doubt*, 62.

19. Simon, *In Doubt*, 54, citing Stephen E. Clark, Ryan T. Howell, and Sherrie L. Davey, "Regularities in Eyewitness Identification," *Law and Human Behavior* 32, no. 3 (2008), 198–218.

20. Thomas J. Nyman et al., "A Stab in the Dark: The Distance Threshold of Target Identification in Low Light," *Cogent Psychology* 6, no. 1 (2019).

21. K. Pezdek and S. Stolzenberg, "Are Individuals' Familiarity Judgments Diagnostic of Prior Contact?" *Psychology, Crime & Law* 20, no. 4 (2014): 302–14.

22. Simon, *In Doubt*, 62.

23. "If an eyewitness had a poor view of a perpetrator or paid little attention to the incident at the time, the witness likely had a poor memory of the perpetrator. But if the witness nonetheless were to attempt an identification by examining a clear picture of a suspect in a photo spread, or a good view of the suspect in a live lineup, the witness would likely replace the original, low-quality memory of the suspect with a clearer image from the identification procedure." Findley and Scott, "The Multiple Dimensions of Tunnel Vision in Criminal Cases," 318–19, citing Erin M. Harley, Keri A. Carlsen, and Geoffrey R. Loftus, "The 'Saw-It-All-Along' Effect: Demonstrations of Visual Hindsight Bias," *Journal of Experimental Psychology: Learning, Memory, and Cognition* 30, no. 5 (2004): 966–67.

## Chapter 5: No Excuse

1. Dallas Police investigative notes, Mar. 26, 1987, 28.

2. Dallas Police investigative notes, Mar. 26, 1987, 30.

3. Benjamin Spencer, Personal History, letter written to Centurion Ministries (1990), 8.

4. Brandon L. Garrett, *Convicting the Innocent: Where Criminal Prosecutions Go Wrong* (Cambridge, MA: Harvard University Press, 2011), 156.

5. Garrett cites the case of Brandon Moon, who was accused of rape in 1988: He claimed that he was on his college campus in El Paso, Texas, without a car; his girlfriend testified they met up fifteen minutes after the assault. "A guilty man knows what happened," his lawyer told the jury. "He can explain it away. An innocent man wasn't there. . . . He can't explain it away, because he has no earthly concept of what occurred." Moon was convicted and served seventeen years in prison before DNA evidence collected from the rape kit cleared him. Garrett, *Convicting the Innocent*, 156.

6. Garrett, *Convicting the Innocent*, 156.

7. Garrett, *Convicting the Innocent*, 164.

8. See Jim McCloskey and Philip Lerman, *When Truth Is All You Have: A Memoir of Faith, Justice, and Freedom for the Wrongly Convicted* (New York: Doubleday, 2020), 246–58.

9. A more famous example is Walter McMillian, who gained fame as the lead character in Bryan Stevenson's *Just Mercy: A Story of Justice and Redemption* (New York: One World, 2014). McMillian presented six alibi witnesses when he was tried for murder in Alabama in 1988. They all swore he was at a family fish fry on the day that a young woman was killed. He was convicted by a jury of eleven whites and one Black and sentenced to death, before being exonerated five years later.

10. Dan Simon, *In Doubt: The Psychology of the Criminal Justice Process* (Cambridge, MA: Harvard University Press, 2012), 165.

11. Juror Dallas Fry, quoted in "What Jennifer Saw," Frontline, PBS, Feb. 25, 1997.

12. For an excellent account, see Keith A. Findley and Michael S. Scott, "The Multiple Dimensions of Tunnel Vision in Criminal Cases," *Wisconsin Law Review* 291 (2006). Findley was Avery's post-conviction lawyer who enabled his release.

13. In those rare cases in which a suspect can corroborate his alibi with physical evidence, it remains a hard sell to juries. Even police records don't suffice. Seventeen-year-old Daniel Taylor was accused of shooting and killing two people in 1992, but Chicago jail records showed that he was in police custody when the crime occurred. Nonetheless, a Cook County jury convicted him and he served eighteen years before he was exonerated. See

"Daniel Taylor," National Registry of Exonerations, law.umich.edu/special/exoneration/Pages/casedetail.aspx?
caseid=4212.

Then there's Timothy Durham. When an eleven-year-old girl was raped at her home in Tulsa, Oklahoma, in
1991, local police zeroed in on Durham, who had a history of firearms and parole violations. But on the day of the
assault, Durham was in Dallas more than 200 miles away at the Pan American skeet shooting competition.
Eleven people swore to his whereabouts, and he produced credit card receipts for the gas, for dinner with his
parents, and for clothes he bought in Dallas. The prosecution claimed the witnesses were mistaken or colluding.
Durham was convicted and sentenced to 3,100 years in prison before DNA exonerated him and implicated another man. See Garrett, *Convicting the Innocent*, 157.

14. Letter from Benjamine Spencer to the author, July 30, 2017.

### Chapter 6: Entering the Tunnel

1. There are too many examples of tunnel vision to count, but the case of Marvin Anderson is typical. On July 17,
1982, a twenty-four-year-old white woman was brutally raped by a Black man in Hanover, Virginia. After approaching her on a bicycle, he dragged her off, threatened her with a gun, beat her, and raped her. She reported the
crime, adding that the assailant told her that he "had a white girl." That clue led the detective to eighteen-year-old
Marvin Anderson. According to an exhaustive review of the case by the Innocence Commission of Virginia,
Anderson was the only Black man the officer knew who lived with a white woman. Anderson had no prior record, and thus no mugshot, so police retrieved his photo from his employer. His complexion was darker than the
man the victim had described; he was taller, and he had no mustache or scratches on his face. Moreover, his photograph was the only one in color in the photo lineup. The victim selected his photo. Thirty minutes later, police
set up a live lineup that included Anderson, and told the victim to "go and look at the people in the lineup and to
see if she could pick out the suspect." He was the only person whose photo had also been included in the photo
array, and the victim identified him again. See Innocence Commission for Virginia, *A Vision for Justice: Report
and Recommendations Regarding Wrongful Convictions in the Commonwealth of Virginia* (2005), 77, available at
prisonlegalnews.org/media/publications/innocence%20commission%20of%20va,%20wrongful%20convic
tions%20report,%202005.pdf.

See also Keith A. Findley and Michael S. Scott, "The Multiple Dimensions of Tunnel Vision in Criminal
Cases," *Wisconsin Law Review* 291 (2006): 296–99, media.law.wisc.edu/m/hyjb3/findley_scott_final.pdf.

Her identification placed Anderson in a vise that no other evidence could break. And there was plenty of
conflicting, exonerating evidence. Aside from the physical differences between Anderson and the actual rapist,
Anderson's blood type did not match the type found in the semen. (This was before DNA testing.) Anderson
offered an alibi: Four witnesses—his girlfriend, his mother, and two neighbors—saw him washing his car at the
time of the rape. Worse, it seemed that everyone in the neighborhood knew, or suspected, who had actually assaulted the victim. John Otis Lincoln matched the physical description; he was seen riding a bicycle near where
the attack occurred; he had been convicted of one sexual assault and was awaiting trial for another. Yet the police
never considered him, and in 1982, an all-white jury convicted Marvin Anderson of rape. He was sentenced to
210 years in prison.

Six years later, John Otis Lincoln came forward and testified in court that he had been the rapist. The judge
dismissed his testimony. Only in 2002, when DNA excluded Anderson and identified Lincoln as the perpetrator,
was Anderson's name cleared. Peter Neufeld, codirector with Barry Scheck of the Innocence Project in New
York, said that Anderson's conviction was "the single worst case of police and prosecutorial tunnel vision in the
10 years we've been appealing these cases." See Francis X. Clines, "DNA Clears Virginia Man of 1982 Assault,"
*New York Times*, Dec. 10, 2001.

2. Mark Godsey, *Blind Injustice: A Former Prosecutor Exposes the Psychology and Politics of Wrongful Convictions*
(Oakland: University of California Press, 2017), 11.

3. Plea bargains are also confessions, and 97 percent of criminal cases are resolved by plea bargains. Only about 3
percent of suspects risk a trial. Someone accused of a crime in the United States makes a calculated decision—a
few years in prison with a plea, or a longer prison term, possibly life—after a jury trial. These negotiations take
place in private, and while the guilty plea is read in open court, we don't know the minute details of the negotia-
tion. We don't know if the suspect falsely confessed to avert a severe penalty. After that, in the vast majority of
cases, when a suspect pleads guilty, he forfeits his right to appeal later. We will never know—as we do with people
who risked a trial, were convicted, and were exonerated—how many people confessed to a lesser crime they never
committed as part of the plea.

4. For example, in one study, Appleby and Kassin, found that when potential jurors were told that a suspect falsely
confessed, but the DNA evidence excluded him, they voted to convict only 15 percent of the time. But when the
prosecutor offered an explanation for the exculpatory DNA evidence—for example, that the woman had had sex
with someone else but the suspect killed her—they voted to convict 45 percent of the time. See Sara C. Appleby

and Saul M. Kassin, "When Self-Report Trumps Science: Effects of Confessions, DNA, and Prosecutorial Theories on Perceptions of Guilt," *Psychology, Public Policy, and Law* 22, no. 2 (May 2016): 129.

"A confession is like no other evidence," Supreme Court Justice Byron White observed. "Indeed, the defendant's own confession is probably the most probative and damaging evidence that can be admitted against him." Confessions have profound impact on the jury, he wrote, "so much so that we may justifiably doubt its ability to put them out of mind even if told to do so." *Arizona v. Fulminante,* 499 US 279, 296 (1991) quoting *Bruton v. US,* 391 US 123, 139–40 (1968).

5. According to the National Registry of Exonerations, 22 percent of the innocent prisoners who were wrongly convicted of murder confessed to those murders. See False Confessions, Murder in the National Registry of Exonerations, law.umich.edu/special/exoneration/Pages/about.aspx.

The Innocence Project puts it higher: 29 percent of those exonerated by DNA falsely confessed. See Innocence Project: DNA Exonerations in the United States. Fast Facts, innocenceproject.org/dna-exonerations-in-the -united-states/#:~:text=29%25%20involved%20a%20misidentification%20through,misidentification%20by% 20a%20surviving%20victim.

6. According to Saul Kassin, young people are particularly susceptible to "internalized false confessions"—that is, confessions where police persuade the suspect that he had committed the crime, when he hadn't.

In the internalized confessions, police start with a vulnerable suspect, often someone who is young, traumatized, mentally fragile—someone like seventeen-year-old Marty Tankleff. On Sept. 7, 1988, his first day of his senior year of high school, Tankleff awakened to find all the lights on in his home. He and his family lived in an affluent neighborhood in Long Island, New York. The family was close, and the young man had no criminal record. He walked to his parents' bedroom and found blood everywhere. His mother had been bludgeoned to death. He found his father in his study, stabbed, unconscious, but still alive. He called 911.

The detectives drove Tankleff to headquarters and seated him in an interrogation room. About six hours into the interrogation, the detective began "a strategy of lies," says Kassin, who became involved in the case in the 1990s. The detectives told Tankleff that his mother had hair in her grasp. "We analyzed the hair. It's yours." That confused him; he hadn't touched his mother. The detectives tried to get him to admit he took a shower after he bludgeoned his parents, because the boy was clean as a whistle. "We just did a humidity test on the shower and it shows it was used this morning," the detectives stated. That also confused him because he didn't recall taking a shower.

Eventually, one detective left the room, staged a phone call, and returned. "Marty, I've got good news and bad news," he reported. "The good news is I spoke to the hospital. Your father has regained consciousness. The bad news is he said you did this." That was a lie. His father never regained consciousness. He died about a week later.

Kassin says that's when Marty Tankleff broke. "My father never lies," the boy told the investigators. "If he said I did it, I must have done it." He wondered aloud how he had brutally attacked his parents without remembering it. "Sometimes people wake up and sleepwalk and do things, go back to sleep, and they don't remember what they did," the detective suggested.

The detectives wrote up the confession, but as Tankleff was about to sign it, his uncle, a lawyer, burst into the room. He advised his nephew not to sign, and the young man took the advice. Still, based on that unsigned confession, Tankleff was convicted and sentenced to fifty years to life in 1990. Tankleff sought, and received, pro bono help from investigators, lawyers, and from Saul Kassin, who exchanged letters with him for years and offered testimony as an expert witness on false confessions. Tankleff's new legal team compiled evidence that his parents were killed by a business partner, who fled, changed his name, and faked his own death. In 2008, after eighteen years in prison, Marty Tankleff was exonerated and released.

7. "The fact that the police misrepresented the statements that [the state's witness] had made is, while relevant, insufficient, in our view, to make this otherwise voluntary confession inadmissible." *Frazier v. Cupp,* 394 US 731 (1969), at 739.

8. *Ashcraft v. Tennessee,* 322 US 143 (1944).

9. The silence begs the question: Were police in Detroit allowed to aggressively interrogate a learning-disabled fourteen-year-old named Davontae Sanford for the better part of two days and nights? Could they interview him without his parents present, until he finally confessed to a quadruple murder? Yes. It's legal for police to make implied threats: *Things will go badly for you if you don't confess.* They can make implicit promises: *I just want to get you home to your mom,* as they said to Sanford, when it's obvious to most people, if not a learning-disabled fourteen-year-old, that someone charged with a quadruple murder isn't going home after confessing. Sanford did not make it home for more than a decade. He was convicted of all four murders and sentenced to up to ninety years in jail. He served eleven years before being exonerated.

Megan Crane, an expert on interrogations who worked on Sanford's postconviction litigation as the codirector of Northwestern University Pritzker School of Law's Center on Wrongful Convictions of Youth, sees very little progress in recent years. Only two states have outlawed lying to minors during interrogations. Even though police can no longer physically abuse suspects to extract confessions, she believes they are "just getting smarter or savvier"—otherwise, why would more than a quarter of innocent people cleared by DNA have confessed to a crime they didn't commit? See Innocence Project, "DNA Exonerations in the United States (1989–2020)," innocenceproject.org/dna-exonerations-in-the-united-states.

"It's almost worse than the old days, when police could beat suspects into confessing, because it's so much harder to prove," she says. "You're not going to have photos that document the bruises and cuts that resulted from the physical beating, because it's become much more sophisticated."

10. "The Confessions," Frontline, PBS, Nov. 9, 2010.

### Chapter 7: Witnesses for Sale

1. For example, in 1979, the governor appointed Perot chairman of the Texans' War on Drugs task force. With characteristic verve, he plunged into the problem and landed squarely on the side of the police. Through the 1980s, Perot offered some eye-catching solutions. He proposed giving police helicopters infrared detectors to fly over minority neighborhoods and detect drugs. "Pick a night for covert action and cordon off a section of South Dallas," he suggested to a *Dallas Times Herald* columnist. "Send hundreds of police officers—however many it would take—into the area to 'vacuum it up.' Shake down everybody on the street. Search every house and apartment. Confiscate all drugs and weapons." See Laura Miller, "More Ideas from the Amazing Ross Perot," *Dallas Times Herald*, Mar. 13, 1988.

He caught flack and backed off these statements, briefly, but then revived his ideas. The constitutional issues could be settled later, he told NBC's *Today* show on Oct. 25, 1989. "You simply declare civil war, and the drug dealer is the enemy. There ain't no bail. You go to POW camp. You start dealing with the problem in straight military terms."

2. The number of misidentifications has grown significantly since this analysis by the National Registry of Exonerations was completed, but it is revealing. See Kaitlin Jackson and Samuel Gross, "Tainted Identifications," National Registry of Exoneration, Sept. 22, 2016, law.umich.edu/special/exoneration/Pages/taintedids.aspx.

3. Jackson and Gross, "Tainted Identifications."

4. See National Registry of Exonerations, "Robert Jones," law.umich.edu/special/exoneration/Pages/casedetail .aspx?caseid=5096.

5. Omar Saunders, eighteen, received life without parole, as did a fourteen-year-old friend, Calvin Ollins. Larry Ollins (Calvin's sixteen-year-old cousin) received life, and seventeen-year-old Marcellius Bradford was sentenced to twelve years. See National Registry of Exonerations, "Omar Small," law.umich.edu/special/exoneration /Pages/casedetail.aspx?caseid=3615.

6. For example, one girl accused a fifteen-year-old boy of fatally shooting the owner of a pet store in Wilmington, North Carolina, in 1988. Police paid her $850. He served twenty-seven years before being exonerated. See National Registry of Exonerations, "Johnny Small," law.umich.edu/special/exoneration/Pages/casedetail.aspx?ca seid=4983.

In Council Bluffs, Iowa, a teenager testified against his two friends, both Black, swearing that they shot a security guard in 1977. The reward: immunity from prosecution and five thousand dollars. The two young men served twenty-five years before they were exonerated. See National Registry of Exonerations, "Terry Harrington," law.umich.edu/special/exoneration/Pages/casedetail.aspx?caseid=3280.

When a cashier at a Chevron station in Louisville, Kentucky, was robbed and killed in 1993, police zeroed in on a twenty-one-year-old Black man. After he offered an alibi and several witnesses failed to pick him out of a lineup, police approached two other "witnesses"—both of them crack addicts—and offered them a thousand dollars each. The young man was convicted of capital murder and served fourteen years before he was exonerated. See National Registry of Exonerations, "Edwin Chandler," law.umich.edu/special/exoneration/Pages/casede tail.aspx?caseid=3098.

7. In the pantheon of jailhouse informants, Danny Edwards was a hack who generated dime-store mysteries with clichéd story lines and improbable plot twists. Yet, about the time that Edwards was narrating his indictment of Ben Spencer, a truly great informant was routinely bending his mind to create plausible stories—stories that would ensure a fellow inmate's conviction and secure his own freedom.

By his early thirties, Leslie Vernon White had managed to escape long sentences for his various crimes by trading information—concocted confessions from other inmates—for furloughs, cash payments, and freedom. He seduced juries with his sincerity, persuading them to convict the innocent as well as the guilty. His wiles proved that he, and the jailhouse informant system itself, were fixtures of the criminal justice system.

In the fall of 1988, White demonstrated for a Los Angeles Sheriff's deputy how easily he could gather information to fabricate a murder confession from another inmate. All he needed was a pay phone, which inmates had access to at all times. The deputy sheriff gave White the last name of a murder suspect, one he was certain White did not know, and White went to work. Posing as a bail bondsman, he called the inmate reception center at the

Los Angeles County jail and elicited the first name of the suspect, the booking number, the charge, the court, the bail, the date of arrest, and the name of the county jail where he was staying. Next, posing as "Deputy DA Michaels, from court upstairs," he called the district attorney's records office and learned the name of the prosecutor assigned to the case and when the crime occurred. Then, identifying himself as a sheriff's sergeant assigned to the jail, he called the sheriff's homicide squad and learned the name of the victim. After that, he called the deputy district attorney assigned to the case and, identifying himself as a police sergeant, told the prosecutor that some of his jail inmates were talking about the case and he needed to confirm their stories. The prosecutor supplied him with details about the murder, and within a few minutes, White had everything he needed to spin a convincing confession.

One detail remained: He needed to prove that he and the inmate had been in the same location so that he could have heard the confession. For this, he called a sheriff's deputy working as a bailiff in a suburban court and, identifying himself as a deputy district attorney, told him that he needed to interview two inmates: Leslie Vernon White and the murder suspect. The bailiff agreed to arrange transportation, placing the two men in the same holding cell, to await the fictitious prosecutor's arrival and interrogation. White was ready to testify in court. See Ted Rohrlich, "Review of Murder Cases Is Ordered: Jail-House Informant Casts Doubt on Convictions Based on Confessions," *Los Angeles Times*, Oct. 29, 1988.

White made a similar demonstration on camera to CBS News *60 Minutes* in 1989. He elicited details about the crime, and threw in a bonus for the viewing audience: a call to the coroner, who pulled photos of the body to show him, noting that the victim—a twenty-eight-year-old Black man—suffered three gunshot wounds, the fatal one to the femoral artery.

"It's a highly competitive business," White told correspondent Harry Reasoner. The inmates compete to offer confessions to the police and prosecutors, often colluding to corroborate each other so both can work off their time. "This is 'Let's Make a Deal.'" See "The Snitch," CBS News, *60 Minutes*, February 26, 1989.

Even after police and prosecutors learned how frequently White lied and put him on a list of undesirable informants, the Los Angeles Police Department used him "extensively," he told CBS. In 1986 alone, he testified in six murder trials. Asked if his testimony had put innocent men in prison, he told Reasoner, "Yes," adding: "Two of them for murder.

White's revelations sparked an uproar. A Los Angeles County grand jury investigated for a year, interviewing 120 people and combing through thousands of documents, and released an excoriating report that found that prosecutors and sheriffs "failed to fulfill the ethical responsibilities" in managing the informants and knowingly or unknowingly elicited false testimony. See Report of the 1989–90 Los Angeles Grand Jury, Investigation of the involvement of Jail House Informants in the Criminal Justice System in Los Angeles County, 6.

The district attorney reopened cases involving 140 defendants in which questionable snitch testimony was used, and defense lawyers compiled a list of 225 people convicted of murder based in part on informant testimony. The grand jury report called for the creation of a centralized database of informants that would list any benefits they received, the number of times they testified, and all favorable actions taken on their behalf. All these reforms were ignored. See Katie Zavadski and Moiz Syed, "30 Years of Jailhouse Snitch Scandals," ProPublica, December 04, 2019, projects.propublica.org/graphics/jailhouse-informants-timeline.

8. Alexandra Natapoff, *Snitching: Criminal Informants and the Erosion of American Justice* (New York: New York University Press, 2009).

9. *Illinois v. Perkins*, 496 US 292 (1990). The US Supreme Court held that the suspect, Perkins, had no right to be Mirandized, even though he was being interrogated by a state agent, because he didn't know he was speaking to an agent. This rule means that jailhouse informants can interrogate suspects on behalf of the government in ways that police are forbidden from doing without Miranda warnings.

10. *Massiah v. United States*, 377 US 201 (1964).

11. For a superb account of Willingham's case, see David Grann, "Trial By Fire," *The New Yorker*, August 31, 2009, newyorker.com/magazine/2009/09/07/trial-by-fire.

12. R. Scott Moxley, "Public Defender Scott Sanders Explains How He Solved OC's Snitch Scandal," *OC Weekly*, October 5, 2017, ocweekly.com/public-defender-scott-sanders-on-how-and-why-he-exposed-decades-long-cheating-by-ocda-and-ocsd-8475224.

13. The scandal prompted the US Justice Department to open an investigation into some one hundred cases in Orange County. The ACLU sued. A grand jury, which heard only the state's side of the story, concluded the snitch scandal was a "myth," but in an internal investigation, the Orange County district attorney's office found misconduct. The DA lost his reelection. The sheriff decided not to run again.

14. Perhaps most disturbingly, the biggest beneficiaries are notorious killers. For example, a convicted murderer named Ramon Alvarez was freed in 2022 after his lawyer discovered that a government-directed informant had lied at trial, and that the police detective handling him had paid the informant eleven thousand dollars on a check issued by the Santa Ana Police Department. The detective claimed (under oath) that the money was not for

the informant's testimony, but for future burial costs. The judge ordered a new trial, and the district attorney's office agreed to drop the case.

15. Letter from Ben Spencer to Lucille Spencer, October 29, 2013.

### Chapter 8: Alternatively

1. Prosecution report by Dallas Police Department Detective M. E. Jones, Apr. 9, 1987, Arrest # 87-23239/2, Service # 176249-U.
2. Except where otherwise indicated, these quotes come from my interviews with Kelvin Johnson and Ferrell Scott.
3. Affidavit of Kelvin R. Johnson, undated and unsigned, 1987.
4. The caller was likely Jeffrey Young's friend Troy Johnson, letting Jeff know he could access the computer.
5. Amina Memon, Aldert Vrij, and Ray Bull, *Psychology and Law: Truthfulness, Accuracy and Credibility*, 2nd ed. (Hoboken, NJ: Wiley, 2003), 63 n.4 (quoting I. K. McKenzie, "Regulating Custodial Interviews: A Comparative Study," *International Journal of the Sociology of Law* 22 (1994): 239, 249).
6. There is some confusion about when Ferrell Scott allegedly talked with the detectives. He believes it was in late summer or early fall of 1987, after he was bailed out for his drug arrest. But there is also a Crime Stoppers report that contains the same information Ferrell Scott relayed: The date on that is March 29, 1988—after Ben's second trial had begun.
7. Testimony of Ferrell Scott, in *Ex Parte Benjamine John Spencer*, in the 283rd District Court, beginning July 24, 2007 (henceforth called *Ex Parte Spencer* 2007 writ hearing), vol. 2, 168.
8. Affidavit of Jesus Briseno, Jan. 13, 2005.
9. Scott's attorney testified in a 2007 hearing that he did not recall driving with Ferrell Scott to police headquarters. In that hearing, Scott said they drove in the attorney's silver Cadillac Alante, a convertible with burgundy interior, which was accurate. Questioned twenty years later about a possible meeting, Ferrell's attorney testified he could not specifically recall a meeting. He did confirm Ferrell's description of his Cadillac: "Only got forty thousand miles on that one," he lamented. See *Ex Parte Spencer* 2007 writ hearing, vol. 3, 35.
10. Samuel Gross, Maurice Possley, Kaitlin Jackson Roll, and Klara Huber Stephens, "Government Misconduct and Convicting the Innocent: The Role of Prosecutors, Police and Other Law Enforcement," National Registry of Exonerations, Sept. 1, 2020, law.umich.edu/special/exoneration/Documents/Government_Misconduct_and _Convicting_the_Innocent.pdf, 18.
11. See National Registry of Exonerations for Yusef Salaam: law.umich.edu/special/exoneration/Pages/casedetail .aspx?caseid=3604; Korey Wise: law.umich.edu/special/exoneration/Pages/casedetail.aspx?caseid=3761; Raymond Santana: law.umich.edu/special/exoneration/Pages/casedetail.aspx?caseid=3610; Kevin Richardson: law .umich.edu/special/exoneration/Pages/casedetail.aspx?caseid=3578; Antron McCray: law.umich.edu/special /exoneration/Pages/casedetail.aspx?caseid=3423.

### Chapter 9: A Noble Cause

1. Letter from Ben Spencer to Debra Spencer, Feb. 24, 2007.
2. Letter from Ben Spencer to Debra Spencer, Apr. 25, 2005.
3. Dallas Police investigative notes, June 14, 1987, 52.
4. Dallas Police investigative notes, Mar. 27, 1987, call from David Lennox, 32.
5. Dallas Police investigative notes, Apr. 5, 1987, 47.
6. Dallas Police investigative notes, Apr. 16, 1987, 40.
7. Grand Jury testimony by prosecutor Jeffrey Hines, May 21, 1987, 3–4.
8. Correspondence between Harry and Maureen Young and District Attorney John Vance, July 29, 1987.
9. Correspondence between Harry and Maureen Young and District Attorney John Vance, July 29, 1987.
10. Letter from Ben Spencer to Jerry and Jinna Lancourt, Oct. 29, 2013.
11. Grand jury testimony by Jesus Briseno, Apr. 21, 1987.
12. Grand jury testimony by Jesus Briseno, Apr. 21, 1987.
13. See Charles Stewart testimony, *Texas v. Spencer* trial transcript, Mar. 21, 1988, vol. 2, 172–73.
14. Stuart Taylor Jr., "For the Record," *American Lawyer*, Oct. 1995, 71.
15. Stephen W. Gard, "Bearing False Witness: Perjured Affidavits and the Fourth Amendment," *Suffolk University Law Review* 41 (2008): 448.
16. See, for example, Joseph Goldstein, "'Testilying' by Police: A Stubborn Problem," *New York Times*, March 18, 2018.
17. Editorial Board, "Police Perjury: It's Called 'Testilying,'" *Chicago Tribune*, July 5, 2015.
18. Philip Bump, "How the First Statement from Minneapolis Police Made George Floyd's Murder Seem Like George Floyd's Fault," *Washington Post*, April 20, 2021, washingtonpost.com/politics/2021/04/20/how-first -statement-minneapolis-police-made-george-floyds-murder-seem-like-george-floyds-fault.

19. Email from Samuel Gross to author, July 13, 2022.

20. Email from Samuel Gross to author, July 13, 2022.

21. Samuel Gross, Maurice Possley, Kaitlin Jackson Roll, and Klara Huber Stephens, "Government Misconduct and Convicting the Innocent: The Role of Prosecutors, Police and Other Law Enforcement," National Registry of Exonerations, Sept. 1, 2020, law.umich.edu/special/exoneration/Documents/Government_Misconduct_and _Convicting_the_Innocent.pdf, 1.

22. Gross et al., "Government Misconduct and Convicting the Innocent," 12.

23. National Registry of Exonerations, "Juan Johnson," law.umich.edu/special/exoneration/Pages/casedetail.aspx ?caseid=3331.

24. National Registry of Exonerations, "Debra Brown," law.umich.edu/special/exoneration/Pages/casedetail.aspx ?caseid=4222.

25. National Registry of Exonerations, "Peter Rose," law.umich.edu/special/exoneration/Pages/casedetail.aspx?ca seid=3598.

26. Mark Godsey, *Blind Injustice: A Former Prosecutor Exposes the Psychology and Politics of Wrongful Convictions* (Oakland: University of California Press, 2017), 141, 145–47.

27. D. M. Loney and B. L. Cutler, "Coercive Interrogation of Eyewitnesses Can Produce False Accusations," *Journal of Police and Criminal Psychology* 31 (2016): 29–36.

28. Stéphanie B. Marion et al., "Lost Proof of Innocence: The Impact of Confessions on Alibi Witnesses," Law and Human Behavior (Aug 24, 2015).

29. Gross et al., "Government Misconduct and Convicting the Innocent," 82.

30. Gross et al., "Government Misconduct and Convicting the Innocent," 83. In May 1989, James Richardson Jr. rescued a three-year-old from a burning house next door to his own home in Cross Lanes, West Virginia. He called the police, who found the girl's mother bound, raped, and beaten to death in the house. They arrested Richardson for murder. Richardson was convicted based in part on testimony from Fred Zain, a state police forensic analyst who was eventually discredited. After Zain's fall from grace, the case was reopened and Richardson's attorney found that the police had concealed a blood-covered flashlight they found at the scene. DNA testing of the blood showed that it came from someone other than Richardson or the victim. Richardson was exonerated in 1999.

31. Gross et al., "Government Misconduct and Convicting the Innocent," 82. In June 1994, Eric Robinson was convicted of murder in a drive-by shooting in Los Angeles. His postconviction attorneys were able to obtain the complete police file for the case. The file showed that within days of his arrest the police had excluded him as a suspect. Months before his trial, police learned the identity of the real shooter. Finally, they threatened to arrest witnesses or beat them if they did not identify Robinson. All of this was hidden from the prosecution as well as the defense. He was exonerated in 2006.

32. Letter from Ben Spencer to Jerry and Jinna Lancourt, April 12, 2014.

### Chapter 10: In the Shadow of Henry Wade

1. Sarah Giddens, "Judging John Vance," *D Magazine*, March 1, 1990, dmagazine.com/publications/d-magazine /1990/march/judging-john-vance.

2. Eric Miller, "Who Will Follow Henry Wade?," *D Magazine*, May 1, 1986, dmagazine.com/publications/d -magazine/1986/may/who-will-follow-henry-wade.

3. The memo has surfaced in bits and pieces. The largest excerpt is in the death penalty case of Thomas Miller-El. In 2003, the US Supreme Court cited the memo as evidence that Miller-El's trial had been poisoned by racism during jury selection. See *Miller-El v. Cockrell*, 537 US 322 (2003).

4. See *Dallas Morning News*, March 9, 10, and 11, 1986, for the series and sidebars.

5. Steve McGonigle and Ed Timms, "Race Bias Pervades Jury Selection," *Dallas Morning News*, Mar, 9, 1986.

6. McGonigle and Timms, "Race Bias Pervades Jury Selection."

7. Speech by Henry Wade, Institute of Law Enforcement, Apr. 13, 1959. See Henry Wade Papers, Briscoe Center, University of Texas, digitalcollections.briscoecenter.org/collection/692.

8. *Harris v. Texas*, 467 US 1261 (1984), 1264.

9. *Batson v. Kentucky*, 476 US 79 (1986), 99.

10. *People v. Randall*, 283 Ill. App. 3d 1019, 1026 (Ill. App. Ct. 1996), 1025–1026.

11. Elisabeth Semel et al, "Whitewashing the Jury Box: How California Perpetuates the Discriminatory Exclusion of Black and Latinx Jurors," Berkeley Law Death Penalty Clinic, June 2020, law.berkeley.edu/wp-content/up loads/2020/06/Whitewashing-the-Jury-Box.pdf.

12. A 2020 study of nearly four hundred criminal trials in Louisiana and Mississippi found that Black potential jurors were more than three times as likely as white potential jurors to be excluded by prosecutors for cause. Louisiana prosecutors used 59 percent of their challenges to remove Black prospective jurors, even though only 33

percent of the potential jurors were Black. It was worse in Mississippi: Prosecutors used 80 percent of their challenges to remove Black prospective jurors, even though only 34 percent of prospective jurors were Black.

Thomas Ward Frampton, "For Cause: Rethinking Racial Exclusion and the American Jury," *Michigan Law Review*, 118, no. 5 (2020): 796–98, 796 n.44, michiganlawreview.org/wp-content/uploads/2020/04/118MichLRev785_Frampton.pdf.

Will Craft, "Mississippi D.A. Doug Evans Has Long History of Striking Black People from Juries," *APM Reports*, June 12, 2018, features.apmreports.org/in-the-dark/mississippi-da-doug-evans-striking-black-people-from-juries/#:~:text=Using%20information%20on%20more%20than,rate%20it%20struck%20white%20people.

13. Ronald F. Wright, Kim Chavis, and Gregory S. Parks, "The Jury Sunshine Project: Jury Selection Data as a Political Issue," *University of Illinois Law Review* (2018): 1407, 1426.

14. See Catherine M. Grosso and Barbara O'Brien, "A Stubborn Legacy: The Overwhelming Importance of Race in Jury Selection in 173 Post-Batson North Carolina Capital Trials," *Iowa Law Review* 97, no. 5 (2012).

15. *State v. Marcus Robinson*, Appendix to Petition for Writ of Certiorari, at 12a and 14a, No. 411A94-6 (N.C. Supreme Court).

16. Samuel R. Sommers, "On Diversity and Group Decision-Making: Identifying Multiple Effects of Racial Composition on Jury Deliberation," *Journal of Personality and Social Psychology* 90, no. 4 (2006).

17. Research conducted in Florida found that all-white juries convicted Black defendants in four out of five cases, whereas white juries convicted white defendants only two thirds of the time; in other words, white juries sent Black defendants to prison 25 percent more often. But when juries had at least one Black juror, the conviction rate was the same: 76 percent of the Black defendants and 77 percent of the white defendants were convicted. See Shamena Anwar, Patrick Bayer, and Randi Hjalmarsson, "The Impact of Jury Race in Criminal Trials," *The Quarterly Journal of Economics* 127, no. 2 (May 2012), 1017–55. See also Ashish S. Joshi and Christina T. Kline, "Lack of Jury Diversity: A National Problem with Individual Consequences," American Bar Association, Sept. 1, 2015, nacdl.org/Media/Unlocking-the-Jury-Box-(1).

18. Judge Timothy Walmsley faced the strictures of *Brady* in the 2021 trial of three white men in Georgia who chased down and shot a Black man named Ahmaud Arbery. Judge Walmsley noted that the attorney for the white defendants used their peremptory challenges to dismiss Blacks and try to seat, as the attorneys put it, more "Bubbas or Joe six-packs" on the jury. "There appears to be intentional discrimination in the panel," the judge said in a hearing. "Quite a few African American jurors were excused through preemptory strikes exercised by the defense, but that doesn't mean that the court has the authority to reseat." To do so, he would have to find that defense lawyers are "disingenuous . . . or otherwise are not being truthful with the court, when it comes to their reasons for striking these jurors." He could not make that finding. The jury included eleven whites and one Black.

19. No account of jury-rigging would be complete without the story of Curtis Flowers. On July 16, 1996, four people were shot at the Tardy Furniture store in Winona, Mississippi. The investigation quickly zeroed in on Flowers, a Black man who had recently worked at the store. The county was 45 percent Black. But the district attorney, Doug Evans, managed to seat an all-white jury, which convicted Flowers in 1997 and sentenced him to death. The Mississippi Supreme Court reversed the conviction based on prosecutorial misconduct. Evans retried Flowers in 1999 and won the death penalty from a jury with eleven whites and one Black. The high court reversed again. Evans tried a third time, in 2004, before another jury of eleven whites and one Black. This time, the Mississippi Supreme Court ruled that the prosecutor illegally rejected Black jurors based on race, and the conviction was reversed. Significantly, the next trial, in 2007, ended in a hung jury: The jury pool consisted of five Blacks and seven whites. Not to be deterred, Evans tried a fifth time in 2008, but the jury of three Blacks and nine whites also hung. In 2010, in the sixth trial, Evans got the jury and verdict he was looking for: The jury of eleven whites and one Black convicted Flowers and sentenced him to death, and the Mississippi Supreme Court upheld the decision. All this time, Flowers had been imprisoned on death row.

Enter journalist Madeleine Baran and *In the Dark*, an investigative podcast produced by American Public Media. The podcast revealed that District Attorney Evans used forty-one of his forty-five peremptory challenges to strike Blacks. The podcast looked at his entire career and found that, in the more than two hundred cases where they found information about jury selection, Evans used 71 percent of his strikes to dismiss Blacks, 29 percent to strike whites; put another way, half of all prospective jurors who were Black were dismissed versus only 11 percent of whites. To arrive at race-neutral reasons, Evans grilled the potential jurors who were Black: In the sixth trial, he asked twenty-nine questions to each struck Black prospective juror, but asked an average of one question to each white juror who was seated. See Madeleine Baran, *In the Dark*, podcast, season 2, beginning May 1, 2018, features.apmreports.org/in-the-dark.

Finally, the US Supreme Court stepped in. In 2019, in a seven-to-two decision, it reversed the sixth conviction. "We cannot ignore that history," Justice Brett Kavanaugh wrote for the majority. *Flowers v. Mississippi*, No. 17-9572, 588 US ___ 2019, Slip Opinion, 22. *Flowers v. Mississippi*, 21. "The state's relentless, determined effort to rid the jury of black individuals strongly suggests that the state wanted to try Flowers before a jury with as few black jurors as possible, and ideally before an all-white jury." Justice Clarence Thomas dissented: "If the Court's opinion today has a redeeming quality, it is this: The State is perfectly free to convict Curtis Flowers again." *Flowers v. Mississippi*, 42. It didn't. The state dismissed the charges and Curtis Flowers was freed, after twenty-three years, nearly half his life, on death row.

### Chapter 11: The Shell Game

1. I tracked down the court reporter who transcribed the court proceedings; she said she threw out the transcripts after fifteen years, as permitted by law.
2. Letter from Ben Spencer to Centurion Ministries, Apr. 13, 1990.
3. "The Cask of Amontillado," by Edgar Allan Poe, published in 1846, comes to mind. In Poe's story, the secretly vindictive narrator, Montresor, plots revenge against an unsuspecting friend, Fortunato, for an unnamed "insult." Enticing him with the promise of tasting amontillado, a special sherry wine, Montresor leads him through the catacombs to a fictional wine cellar. He thrusts Fortunato into a small alcove, chains the surprised comrade to the wall, and uncovers building stones and mortar hidden beneath the debris. He begins to wall up the entrance, stone by stone, tier by tier. Montresor continues to work, pausing briefly to attend to the screams from the terrified form chained to the wall, then picks up his trowel once again. At midnight, his task is nearly accomplished. "There remained but a single stone to be fitted and plastered in. I struggled with its weight; I placed it partially in its destined position."

   "For the love of God, Montresor!" shouts the victim.

   "'Yes,' I said," "'for the love of God!'"

   "I hastened to make an end of my labour," the narrator recalls. "I forced the last stone into its position; I plastered it up." *In pace requiescat*, he concludes. May he rest in peace.
4. District attorney's handwritten notes, 24.
5. District attorney's handwritten notes, 12.
6. One other witness sealed Ben Spencer's fate—erroneously. At the end of the trial, prosecutor Jeffrey Hines called on the personnel manager at Spencer's company, Mistletoe Express. The witness stated that Spencer did not work for the company after March 20, two days before Jeffrey Young's murder. She brought along the paperwork showing Spencer's name was not in their records. This, the state said, proved Spencer had a motive: Without a job, he needed money. "Here I was testifying that I was employed during the time that this offense was committed and that it was pointless for me to have been involved in such a crime," Spencer wrote later to an investigator. "The bottom seemingly fell out of my defense." After Ben was convicted, the personnel manager rechecked her files and found Spencer's name on the payroll. This mistake, along with perjury by Gladys Oliver, prompted the judge to declare a mistrial.
7. *Berger v. United States*, 295 US 78 (1935), at 88.
8. *Brady v. Maryland*, 373 US 83 (1963), at 87.
9. *Giglio v. United States*, 405 US 150 (1972).
10. Samuel Gross, Maurice Possley, Kaitlin Jackson Roll, and Klara Huber Stephens, "Government Misconduct and Convicting the Innocent: The Role of Prosecutors, Police and Other Law Enforcement," National Registry of Exonerations, Sept. 1, 2020, law.umich.edu/special/exoneration/Documents/Government_Misconduct_and _Convicting_the_Innocent.pdf, 32.
11. See National Registry of Exonerations, "Kristine Bunch," law.umich.edu/special/exoneration/Pages/casedetail .aspx?caseid=4085.
12. In 1987, Michael Morton received a life sentence for murdering his wife, Christine, in northwest Austin. In pretrial hearings, his defense lawyers suspected that Ken Anderson, the Williamson County district attorney, was withholding exculpatory evidence, in violation of *Brady v. Maryland*. The judge asked him directly if he had any such evidence. He replied that he did not. In 2011, DNA tests on a bloody bandanna found near the house excluded Morton and identified a convicted felon as the killer. Morton was exonerated in 2011 and freed after nearly twenty-five years.

    A court of inquiry convened to determine whether Anderson, by that time a judge, had failed to turn over the complete file. When the records were unsealed, the exculpatory evidence tumbled out. There was a police report from neighbors who said they saw a man park a green van in front of their house and walk into the woods behind the Mortons' house several times in the days before the murder. There was the report that someone attempted to use Christine Morton's credit card at a store in San Antonio, Texas, while Morton was in custody. Crucially, there was a transcript of a recorded phone conversation between the victim's mother and the lead detective, in which she stated that her three-year-old grandson said a "monster" killed his mother, accurately described the crime scene, and insisted the monster was not his father.

    One fact makes this case sui generis. Anderson was punished. He was disbarred and spent four days in jail for hiding evidence. I could find only one other case in which a prosecutor was criminally sanctioned for misconduct. In 2006, Mike Nifong, the Durham, NC, district attorney, falsely accused three members of Duke University's men's lacrosse team of rape. When his case began to fall apart, Nifong concealed DNA evidence that excluded the college students. He was disbarred and served one day in jail.

Notably, what these two cases share is the race of the victims. Michael Morton was a middle-class white man; the Duke students were white with wealthy parents. For a superb account of Michael Morton's case, see Pamela Coloff's two-part series in *Texas Monthly*: "The Innocent Man, Part 1," Nov. 2012, texasmonthly.com/true -crime/the-innocent-man-part-one and "The Innocent Man, Part 2," Dec. 2012, texasmonthly.com/true-crime /the-innocent-man-part-two.

13. But often, the Brady violations are so egregious that one strains to imagine that the misconduct was inadvertent. In 2000, Kenneth Kagonyera was convicted for shooting a man in his home near Asheville, North Carolina, during a break-in. The prosecutor concealed a confession by the true perpetrator and a DNA report that excluded Kagonyera; he also taped over and destroyed part of a surveillance video that could have cleared Kagonyera. His lawyers unearthed the exculpatory evidence eleven years later, and the prisoner was released. See National Registry of Exonerations, "Kenneth Kagonyera," law.umich.edu/special/exoneration/Pages/casedetail.aspx?caseid= 3817.

14. *United States v. Olsen*, 737 F.3d 625 (9th Cir. 2013), 631–32.

15. See National Registry of Exonerations, "John Thompson," law.umich.edu/special/exoneration/Pages/casedetail .aspx?caseid=3684.

16. *Connick v. Thompson*, 563 US 51 (2011).

17. A word about plea bargains. In Dallas in the 1980s, 90 percent of criminal cases ended in a plea. In the 2020s, plea bargains represent almost all the convictions in the United States: 97 percent of criminal cases are resolved this way. The state always has the advantage, because it doesn't have to show its evidence during plea negotiations. The suspect has no idea if the "eyewitnesses" lied for a reward or a jailhouse informant traded his false accusations for lenience. He can't tell if the police tampered with witnesses or the prosecutors hid evidence. He will not be told if DNA excludes him. The suspect—and the public—will never know: Any information that benefits the suspect or damns the state will almost never surface, because in the vast majority of cases, when the suspect pleads guilty, he forfeits his right to appeal later. Still, innocent people routinely plead to crimes they never committed. Of the 375 men and women exonerated by DNA analysis, for example, 12 percent had pleaded guilty. See Innocence Project, "DNA Exonerations in the United States (1989–2020)," innocenceproject.org/dna-exonerations -in-the-united-states. The National Registry of Exonerations has identified more than 800 exonerees who pleaded guilty—one out of every four.

18. See "The Trial Penalty: The Sixth Amendment Right to Trial on the Verge of Extinction and How to Save it," National Association of Criminal Defense Lawyers, 2018, nacdl.org/Document/TrialPenaltySixthAmendment RighttoTrialNearExtinct.

## Chapter 12: What the Jury Saw

1. Keith Findley and Michael S. Scott point out that empirical research reveals that prior to trial, mock jurors predict a 50 percent chance of voting to convict. If they had taken the presumption of innocence at face value, they would have predicted the chances of conviction closer to zero percent. See Keith A. Findley and Michael S. Scott, "The Multiple Dimensions of Tunnel Vision in Criminal Cases," *Wisconsin Law Review* 291 (2006): 348.

See also Michael J. Saks and D. Michael Risinger, "Baserates, the Presumption of Guilt, Admissibility Rulings, and Erroneous Convictions," *Michigan State Law Review* 1051 (2003) (citing T. M. Ostrom, C. Werner, and M. J. Saks, "An Integration Theory Analysis of Jurors' Presumptions of Guilt or Innocence," *Journal of Personality and Social Psychology* 36, no. 4 (1978), 436).

The late Daniel Givelber, a law professor at Northeastern University, posited that "jurors take the logical position that they are in equipoise concerning the defendant's guilt and will await the presentation of evidence before reaching a verdict." Daniel Givelber and Daniel James, "Meaningless Acquittals, Meaningful Convictions: Do We Reliably Acquit the Innocent?," *Rutgers Law Review* 49, no. 2 (1997), ssrn.com/abstract=10712.

2. A related psychological phenomenon is called "coherence," which Dan Simon defines as a "psychological process by which we process information and reach decisions in the face of complexity." Every person in every stage of a criminal trial—the victim's family, the police officers, the prosecutor, the defense attorney, the jury, the trial judge, and eventually, the appellate judge or judges—tries to assemble bits and pieces of the raw data they hear and create a coherent narrative. When the story they land on is correct, you get a fair verdict. But when all these people are persuaded to believe a *false* narrative, then coherence leads to "tunnel vision." People focus on one answer, blinded to all alternatives. Coherence has been called the unified theory of wrongful convictions, because it explains why innocent people can be suspected, prosecuted, and convicted; lose their appeals; and remain trapped in prison.

3. *Texas v. Spencer*, trial transcript, vol. 2, Mar. 21, 1988, 287–88. When quoting the transcripts, I have on occasion streamlined the sentences to make them comprehensible, but never altered the meaning or connotation.

4. *Texas v. Spencer*, trial transcript, vol. 3, Mar. 22, 1987, 308, 310–11.

5. Simon cites several studies showing that jurors give great weight to witnesses' confidence in their identifications. One study found that eyewitness confidence in their identifications was a stronger predictor of jurors' decisions than the actual accuracy of their identification. The study involved students who witnessed a staged theft and played the role of witnesses. They were examined and cross-examined by experienced prosecutors and defense attorneys. Other students played the role of jurors and found that the more *confident* witnesses were more persuasive than *accurate* witnesses.

   In another study, simulated jurors trusted the identification by confident witnesses twice as often as identifications by nonconfident witnesses (63 percent versus 32 percent). In another, witnesses who were perceived as "completely certain" were three times more likely to be judged as accurate as those who reported being "somewhat uncertain" (83 percent versus 28 percent).

   Witness confidence tipped jurors heavily toward convictions: Conviction rates were almost 50 percent higher when the prosecution eyewitness stated that he was "100 percent confident" than when he "could not say that he was 100 percent confident." Not surprisingly, conviction rates were higher (62 percent versus 38 percent) when the eyewitness stated that he was "absolutely certain" in his identification of a perpetrator than when he stated he was "not certain at all." See Dan Simon, *In Doubt: The Psychology of the Criminal Justice Process* (Cambridge, MA: Harvard University Press, 2012), 153.

6. *Texas v. Spencer* trial transcript, vol. 3, 316–17.

7. *Texas v. Spencer* trial transcript, vol. 3, 351.

8. *Texas v. Spencer* trial transcript, vol. 3, 351.

9. *Texas v. Spencer* trial transcript, vol. 3, 361.

### Chapter 13: The Defense Rests

1. *Texas v. Spencer* trial transcript, vol. 3, 422.

2. *Texas v. Spencer* trial transcript, vol. 3, 424.

3. As Dan Simon put it in his seminal article on juries: "Jurors' hearts and minds become the battlefield for a fierce barrage of heuristic persuasion, oftentimes packaged in compelling narratives and drenched in both genuine and contrived affect and emotion." See Dan Simon, "On Juror Decision Making: An Empathic Inquiry," *Annual Review of Law and Social Sciences* 15 (Oct. 2019): 415–35.

4. *Texas v. Spencer* trial transcript, vol. 3, 430.

5. *Texas v. Spencer* trial transcript, vol. 3, 432.

6. *Texas v. Spencer* trial transcript, vol. 3, 433.

7. *Texas v. Spencer* trial transcript, vol. 3, 567.

8. *Texas v. Spencer* trial transcript, vol. 3, 587.

9. *Texas v. Spencer* trial transcript, vol. 3, 565–66.

10. According to the National Registry of Exonerations, prosecutors lied, elicited perjury, or gave improper (i.e., inflammatory or false) closings in 14 percent of the convictions of innocent people—that is, more than 330 times.

    See Samuel Gross, Maurice Possley, Kaitlin Jackson Roll, and Klara Huber Stephens, "Government Misconduct and Convicting the Innocent: The Role of Prosecutors, Police and Other Law Enforcement," National Registry of Exonerations, Sept. 1, 2020, law.umich.edu/special/exoneration/Documents/Government_Misconduct_and_Convicting_the_Innocent.pdf, 33.

    Clarence Brandley's prosecutor offered up this insinuation in his final argument: He noted that Brandley had a second job at a funeral home and suggested that he was a necrophiliac who had raped the teenage victim after she was dead. The defense attorney objected, but the judge allowed it. On February 13, 1981, Brandley was convicted and sentenced to death. He was later found innocent. See National Registry of Exonerations, "Clarence Brandley," law.umich.edu/special/exoneration/Pages/casedetail.aspx?caseid=3044.

    Scaring jurors is also verboten, a fact that another district attorney in Texas forgot in the prosecution of Ronald Taylor for rape. "Do you want this defendant, the bottom line, to go home with you today and go down that elevator with you? Is that what you want? Because that is what a 'not guilty' verdict will do." The appeals court approved the statements as a "proper plea for law enforcement." The defense objected to this as inflammatory, but was overruled by the judge. Taylor was later exonerated. See Brandon L. Garrett, *Convicting the Innocent: Where Criminal Prosecutions Go Wrong* (Cambridge, MA: Harvard University Press, 2011), 171.

    I only found two cases in which an appellate court found the prosecutor had ventured too far during closing arguments. In each case, the defendant was in fact innocent. In the murder case against Curtis McCarty, the Oklahoma prosecutor allowed his imagination to roam free: "I wonder if [the defendant] was grinning and laughing that night when he murdered [the victim]. He killed that girl. He needs to pay for it." The appellate court in this case found misconduct. See Garrett, *Convicting the Innocent*, 171.

An appellate court in California found misconduct in a child sex-abuse case. In his closing arguments against Ricky Lynn Pitts, the prosecutor read at length from the Bible and said, in essence, that Christ took the side of children over adults. The appellate court reversed in part because the prosecutor had "turned Christ into an unsworn witness for the children's credibility." See Court of Appeal, Fifth District, California, *The People v. Ricky Lynn Pitts et al.*, No. F006225. Decided Sept. 5, 1990.

11. The Innocence Project looked at twenty-two cases in which the (exonerated) defendant had raised prosecutorial misconduct during closing arguments in challenging their convictions. Not one appellate court found in their favor. See Daniel S. Medwed, *Barred: Why the Innocent Can't Get Out of Prison* (New York: Basic Books, 2022), 91.

12. *Texas v. Spencer* trial transcript, vol. 3, 557.

13. *Texas v. Spencer* trial transcript, vol. 3, 561.

14. *Texas v. Spencer* trial transcript, vol. 3, 590.

15. *Texas v. Spencer* trial transcript, vol. 3, 594.

16. *State v. Mitchell* trial transcript, vol. 3, 289.

17. *State v. Mitchell* trial transcript, vol. 3, 302.

18. *State v. Mitchell* trial transcript, vol. 2, 611.

19. Specifically, the police did not take photos or draw a map of the BMW's position in the alley before towing it to the police lot. They never confirmed that Gladys Oliver could see it. There was testimony that a camper blocked her view, but the defense could not prove it without a map or photos. Also, the BMW was left in pouring rain all night before being dusted for fingerprints. And of course, West found the critical witness who saw the perpetrator running away and swore it was not Ben Spencer: Sandra Brackens.

20. Sometimes the pressure to convict among jurors lacks any subtlety. Consider the treatment of one juror in the rape trial of Arvin McGee in Oklahoma. For hours, they told her that the defendant had their names and might rape their family members. They took the "not guilty" jury forms away from her. She finally said, "Whatever you want to do, you go ahead and do it."

In the capital murder trial of Rolando Cruz, one juror said: "Half of the jurors had their minds made up before the trial even started." The jury foreman announced, because he was a defendant, he "must have done something," and that deliberations were "a mere formality, so we might as well get on with it." Both men were convicted. Both were later exonerated. See Garrett, *Convicting the Innocent*, 173.

21. According to a study of 222 cases in which jurors spoke to researchers after the trial, if the majority voted to convict on the first ballot, the jury convicted 94 percent of the time. Dan Simon, *In Doubt: The Psychology of the Criminal Justice Process* (Cambridge, MA: Harvard University Press, 2012), 197.

22. This study involved 225 criminal cases in Chicago and Brooklyn. Studies of other juries in Indiana and Kentucky found similar results. Simon, *In Doubt*, 197.

### Chapter 14: A Brief History of Innocence

1. *Texas v. Spencer* trial transcript, vol. 4, 6 (Debra) and 12 (Lucille).

2. *Texas v. Spencer* trial transcript, vol. 4, 14.

3. *Texas v. Spencer* trial transcript, vol. 4, 15.

4. *Texas v. Spencer* trial transcript, vol. 4, 19.

5. *Texas v. Spencer* trial transcript, vol. 4, 26–27.

6. Borchard concealed Katzman's identity in his book. As Marvin Zalman notes in his article about the origins of the book: "Astute readers could infer a veiled allusion to Frederick G. Katzmann, who prosecuted Sacco and Vanzetti, and see the book as an attack on both of their unfair trials. Yet, Borchard strategically decided to veil Katzmann's identity and avoid any reference to the trials. In a few letters, however, he wrote that his 'innocence project' was a reaction to the Sacco-Vanzetti case. After enactment of the federal compensation law, he wrote to George Soule, editor of *The New Republic*: 'The effort [to pass compensation legislation] received a new lease of life through the statement made by the District Attorney in the Sacco-Vanzetti case, who remarked that "Innocence Men [*sic*] are never convicted …" That dogmatic statement led me to undertake the research which resulted in the book "Convicting the Innocent." A very cursory examination of cases in our state and federal courts disclosed about 200 which seemed airtight. Of these I published some 65 from various jurisdictions presenting various types of cases so as to let the public judge of the accuracy of the statement of the District Attorney.'" Marvin Zalman, "Edwin Borchard's Innocence Project: The Origin and Legacy of His Wrongful Conviction Scholarship," *Wrongful Conviction Law Review* 1, no. 1 (2020): 142, wclawr.org/index.php/wclr/article/view/6.

7. Borchard was as precocious as he was energetic. Born in 1884, raised in New York City, the son of a prosperous Jewish immigrant from Prussia who imported coffees and teas, "Eddie" entered the College of the City of New

York at age fourteen; earned his law degree, cum laude, from New York Law School at twenty-one; then earned a second BA at Columbia, topping his academic career off with a Columbia PhD at age twenty-nine. In his spare time, he married, helped raise two children, avidly collected stamps, and played violin in the Philharmonic Society. He served as the law librarian for the Library of Congress before moving to Yale to teach law at the seasoned age of thirty-three.

Special thanks to Richard Leo at the University of San Francisco for his excellent work in his forthcoming book about the history of the innocence movement.

8. Edwin Montefiore Borchard, *Convicting the Innocent: Sixty-five Actual Errors of Criminal Justice* (New Haven: Yale University Press, 1932).

9. Borchard, *Convicting the Innocent*, 110–19. In "Dogskin Does Ten Years," Borchard tells the story of John A. "Dogskin" Johnson—a "barroom hanger on" who had done two stints in an "insane asylum." He was arrested in 1911 for abducting and killing seven-year-old Annie Martin of Madison, Wisconsin. He swore that he was home with his family that night. But a few days later, during the police interrogation in jail, Dogskin abruptly confessed, telling officers that a "devilish impulse" caused him to break the window next to Annie's cot, snatch her from her room, and throw her in the bay a few blocks away. He insisted on moving from the jail to the prison "today." As soon as he arrived in prison, he reasserted his innocence. It was later revealed that the police had played on his terror of being lynched, telling him that an angry crowd had assembled outside his jail window. He confessed "to save himself from death at the hands of the mob which, the officers said, was after him." A decade into his lifelong prison sentence, a former judge looked into the case and found no evidence against him. Rather, the girl's father had killed her while he was drunk. The governor pardoned the prisoner.

Borchard concludes, with some prescience, "A community does not like to be baffled, and when some plausible culprit is caught in the toils, especially if his record is unsavory, social pressure demands a conviction." He added that police "preyed on Johnson's weak mind until he finally caved in . . . he was psychologically 'beaten' into a confession."

10. In the 1980s, members of the McMartin family, who operated a preschool in Manhattan Beach, California, were falsely charged with hundreds of acts of sexual abuse of children in their care. The allegations were bizarre and some were physically impossible, but the Los Angeles police and district attorney investigated and arrested family members from 1984 to 1987. The trials ran from 1987 to 1990, and resulted in no convictions. All charges were dropped in 1990. The case was part of the day-care sex-abuse hysteria, a moral panic over alleged satanic ritual abuse in the 1980s and early 1990s that touched many people who took care of children for a living.

11. Borchard, *Convicting the Innocent*, 14–21. "A Corpse Answers an Advertisement" introduces the Boorn brothers, a famous case among innocence aficionados. They were convicted of murdering their brother-in-law, Russell Colvin, who had disappeared from Manchester, Vermont, in 1812. After seven years, Colvin was considered dead. What brought the Boorn brothers to the brink of extinction was a series of weird mistakes and intentional errors, involving a dream about Colvin's "ghost," a dog that dug up bones, a jailhouse informant who testified that one Boorn brother described the murder, and the inexplicable false confessions of both brothers. They were sentenced to hang on January 28, 1820. The matter would have ended there, had not the defense attorney placed an ad in the newspaper seeking the alleged victim's whereabouts. A reader in New York recognized the victim, who was now living in Dover, New Jersey. Colvin returned to Manchester, and seeing the fetters on his brothers-in-law, asked: "What is that for?" "Because," one of the condemned brothers said, "they say I murdered you."

12. According to the National Registry of Exonerations, by 2024, more than thirteen hundred people had been convicted and exonerated for a crime that never occurred. Most often, these cases involved child sex abuse, rape, and drug crimes.

13. Borchard, *Convicting the Innocent*, 1–6, "Seventeen Witnesses Identified Him."

14. The Innocence Project reports that of 69 percent of people later exonerated by DNA were convicted in part by mistaken eyewitness identification. See Innocence Project, "How Eyewitness Misidentification Can Send Innocent People to Prison," Apr. 15, 2020, innocenceproject.org/news/how-eyewitness-misidentification-can-send -innocent-people-to-prison/#:~:text=Eyewitness%20misidentification%20is%20a,cause%20of%20these %20wrongful%20convictions.

The National Registry of Exonerations found that mistaken witnesses contributed to three out of four wrongful convictions. See law.umich.edu/special/exoneration/Pages/taintedids.aspx.

15. Borchard, *Convicting the Innocent*, 367.

16. Borchard, *Convicting the Innocent*, 62–65, "Justice by Elimination."

17. This case also demonstrates the dicey nature of line-ups. The two witnesses were the Wolf sisters, who worked at the bank. The police placed Flood in a "show-up cage," where the sisters examined him under bright lights. The police told him to turn his coat collar up, "put on a cap not his own and pull it down over his eyes, stretch his hand forward and say, 'Stick 'em up.'" The sisters confirmed he was one of the bandits. The lineup performance proved "too persuasive [for the jury] to resist," Borchard noted.

Lineups have improved, thanks to science and the nearly six hundred innocent people who have been erroneously identified through that process and then convicted. But they still offer many opportunities for misidentification, with their toxic combination of unspoken pressure and people's limited ability to store accurate memories when facing danger.

18. Borchard, *Convicting the Innocent*, 28–31. On Washington's birthday, 1900, Borchard begins, the city recorder of Atlanta, Nash R. Broyles, "received a letter which he considered so obscene that he immediately turned it over to the Federal authorities." Mr. Broyles suspected one particular "negro," but the case against him collapsed when it was discovered the suspect was unable to write. "But the police were equal to the occasion," Borchard observes wryly, and they indicted his literate friend, William Broughton. Three "experts"—Broyles, a banker, and a traveling auditor—testified that Broughton's handwriting shared "incriminating and unmistakable similarities" with that of the obscene correspondent. If there were differences—and there were—it was due to the defendant being "a very sharp and intelligent negro" who was trying to disguise his handwriting. Eventually another man was confronted and confessed.

19. Borchard, *Convicting the Innocent*, 373.

20. Borchard, *Convicting the Innocent*, 369.

21. *United States v. Garsson*, 291 F. 646 (S.D.N.Y.1923), 649.

22. Erle Stanley Gardner, *The Court of Last Resort* (1952; repr. ed., New York: Open Road Integrated Media, 2017), 15.

23. Gardner, *The Court of Last Resort*, 15.

24. Gardner, *The Court of Last Resort*, 151.

25. The refrain:

> Here comes the story of the Hurricane
> The man the authorities came to blame
> For somethin' that he never done

26. National Registry of Exonerations, "Rubin Hurricane Carter," law.umich.edu/special/exoneration/Pages/casedetailpre1989.aspx?caseid=408.

27. For a detailed account of Lenell Geter's case, see chapter 10; see also "Lenell Geter's in Jail," CBS News, *60 Minutes*, Dec. 4, 1983, cbsnews.com/video/lenell-geters-in-jail.

28. Among others, *60 Minutes* chronicled several wrongful convictions in Texas, including the conviction of Clarence Brandley, a school custodian singled out for raping and killing a white teenager because he was Black; he was sentenced to death until the broadcast flushed out new, exonerating, witnesses. It also profiled the erroneous murder conviction of Joyce Ann Brown, who also was Black, and revealed the depth of ineptitude by Dallas investigators. Both were exonerated.

## PART 2: APPEAL

### Chapter 15: No Harm, No Foul

1. See Texas Department of Criminal Justice, Death Row Information, tdcj.texas.gov/death_row/dr_executed_offenders.html.

2. Witnesses described six-inch flames shooting from Jesse Joseph Tafero's head: "Florida Execution Becomes Gruesome Display," *Tampa Bay Times*, May 5, 1990, tampabay.com/archive/1990/05/05/florida-execution-becomes-gruesome-display. And foot-long flames consumed Pedro Medina's mask: Associated Press, "Condemned Man's Mask Bursts Into Flame During Execution," *New York Times*, March 26, 1997, nytimes.com/1997/03/26/us/condemned-man-s-mask-bursts-into-flame-during-execution.html. For a list of botched executions, see deathpenaltyinfo.org/executions/botched-executions.

3. *Benjamin John Spencer v. The State of Texas*, Court of Appeals, Fifth District of Texas at Dallas, NO. 05-88-00397-CR, May 3, 1989, 7–8.

4. Take, for example, the prosecutor's closing argument, in which he claimed that Ben cruelly prevented Jeffrey Young from being buried with his wedding ring on; this crossed the line, since it was a powerful, inflammatory allegation that had not been proven. However, the appellate court found it fair play, because the defense attorney did not pursue his objection.

Or, when the judge allowed the prosecutor to imply Ben had had threatened to burn Christie Williams's house down if she did not vouch for him—an unproven accusation that she had denied—that, too, passed muster: "A reasonable deduction could be drawn from the evidence that Christie was aware of the alleged threats made by Spencer and that her testimony was influenced by such threats." See *Spencer v. Texas*, 16.

5. William Blackstone, *Commentaries on the Laws of England* (Oxford: Clarendon Press, 1765), Book 4, Chapter 27, "Of Trial, and Conviction," lonang.com/library/reference/blackstone-commentaries-law-england/bla-427/#fn57u.

6. The statistics are from 2010, the most recent year available. See Nicole L. Waters, Anne Gallegos, James Green, and Martha Rozsi, "Criminal Appeals in State Courts," US Department of Justice, Office of Justice Programs, Bureau of Justice Statistics, Sept. 2015.

7. The authors note that the percentage of reversals has dropped significantly in recent decades, as courts have become more skeptical of defendants' arguments, and more bound by the restrictions imposed by the US Supreme Court. See Nancy J. King, Michael Heise, and Nicole A. Heise, "State Criminal Appeals Revealed," *Vanderbilt Law Review* 70 (2017): 1947.

8. Blackstone, *Commentaries*, 379.

9. *United States v. Barnard*, 490 F.2d 907 (9th Cir. 1974), 912.

10. M. B. Hoffman, "The Myth of Factual Innocence," *Chicago-Kent Law Review* 82 (2007): 663–90, at 664.

11. *Tanner v. United States*, 483 US 107 (1987), 115.

12. *Tanner v. United States*, 120.

13. *Tanner* presents an extreme example, but appellate courts typically defer to juries, even if their verdict defies reasoning. The case of Jeffrey Deskovic is one example. Sixteen-year-old Deskovic was accused of raping and killing a fifteen-year-old girl in Peekskill, New York. Detectives interviewed the teenager, who was a "loner" and psychologically troubled, for eight hours, with no lawyer or parent present. Eventually he confessed. When the session ended, the teenager lay under a desk in a fetal position, sobbing uncontrollably. Deskovic quickly recanted, and a few days after he was indicted, the FBI laboratory report found that DNA testing had excluded him as the source of the semen. Untroubled by this development, the state prosecuted him, telling the jury—without evidence— that the fifteen-year-old victim had consensual sex with a classmate before Deskovic killed her.

The jury convicted Deskovic and sentenced him to fifteen years to life in prison. In 1994, the New York appellate court unanimously affirmed the conviction. Despite the DNA evidence, the judges found "overwhelming evidence of the defendant's guilt." See *People v. Deskovic*, 201 A.D.2d 579 (N.Y. App. Div. 1994), 580.

In 2006, more sophisticated DNA testing identified the assailant, who—in yet another tragedy from wrongful liberty—strangled another woman to death while Deskovic languished in prison. Deskovic was exonerated and freed, after spending half his life incarcerated. The case illustrates the near blind deference that juries grant to prosecutors, including dismissing the most compelling forensic evidence—DNA—as disposable. It also shows the deference appellate judges give to jury decisions.

14. *Strickland v. Washington*, 466 US 668 (1984), 689.

15. Henry Weinstein, "A Sleeping Lawyer and a Ticket to Death Row," *Los Angeles Times*, July 15, 2000.

16. Weinstein, "A Sleeping Lawyer."

17. *Ex parte McFarland*, 163 S.W.3d 743 (Tex. Crim. App. 2005), 760.

18. Take the case of Harry Miller. In 2000, an elderly white woman said she was robbed of fifty dollars by a young Black man outside a Salt Lake City convenience store. Three years later, she identified forty-seven-year-old Harry Miller. Miller lived in Louisiana and happened to be visiting his brother when he was arrested. Two weeks before the robbery, Miller had suffered a stroke, leaving him incapacitated and requiring in-home care. Several people could testify that he was home in Louisiana, including a nurse who had visited him the day before the robbery. The prosecution argued that Miller jumped on a plane to Utah two weeks after his stroke, robbed the woman of fifty dollars, and flew home the same day. The defense neglected to call a single alibi witness. The jury convicted Miller and sentenced him to five years to life in prison.

On appeal, Miller claimed that his lawyer was ineffective. The judge dismissed his complaint. "Although the evidence makes it unlikely that Petitioner committed the crime, there was no reasonable probability of a different outcome at trial even if [the alibi witnesses] had testified." Prosecutors agreed to retry him, but a week before retrial, they dropped the charges, four years after Miller was imprisoned. See Daniel S. Medwed, *Barred: Why the Innocent Can't Get Out of Prison* (New York: Basic Books, 2022).

19. Mewed, *Barred*, 65, 279, footnote 10.

20. *Chapman v. California*, 386 US 18 (1967).

21. In 1982, Danny Brown was accused of raping his girlfriend and strangling her to death in Toledo, Ohio. The sole witness was the woman's six-year-old son, who identified "Danny" as one of the two men who were in the apartment that night. Based on that testimony—which the trial judge described as replete with "glaring inconsistencies"— Brown was convicted and sentenced to life.

On direct appeal, Brown raised fifteen claims of error. The Ohio Court of Appeals for the Sixth District affirmed the conviction. While the judges agreed there were three significant errors, "no trial is perfect," they opined. "These errors related largely to collateral matters, and we conclude that they are harmless beyond a reasonable doubt." See Medwed, *Barred*, 96.

In a scathing dissent, Judge Peter Handwork acknowledged that an accused person is not entitled to an error-free trial. "But he does enjoy the absolute right to be tried fairly—to a fair trial," the judge wrote. "An unfair trial is not made 'fair' because the jury found the defendant guilty and an appellate court, retrospectively, can rationalize it." See Medwed, *Barred*, 97.

Centurion Ministries, the first national organization to reinvestigate questionable convictions, accepted Danny Brown's case in 2001. DNA tests excluded him and identified another assailant, who killed another woman while Brown was serving time.

22. See Innocence Project, "New Report: Prosecutorial Misconduct and Wrongful Convictions," Aug. 25, 2010, innocenceproject.org/new-report-prosecutorial-misconduct-and-wrongful-convictions.

23. National Registry of Exonerations, "Shawn Henning," law.umich.edu/special/exoneration/Pages/casedetail .aspx?caseid=5768; National Registry of Exonerations, "Ralph Birch," law.umich.edu/special/exoneration /Pages/casedetail.aspx?caseid=5769.

24. Unpublished opinion, *Birch v. Warden*, No. TTDCV01817907S (Conn. Super. Ct. June 21, 2016).

25. *Henning v. Comm'r of Corr.*, 334 Conn. 1 (Conn. 2019), 32, casetext.com/case/henning-v-commr-of-corr?end Date=1577836799999&p=1&q=Shawn%20Henning%20v%20Commissioner%20of%20Correction&sort= relevance&startDate=1546300800000&type=case&ssr=false&scrollTo=true.

26. In 2023, a federal judge ruled that Dr. Lee was liable for fabricating evidence: See: Pat Eaton-Robb, "Judge Finds Henry Lee Liable for Fabricating Evidence in 1985 Murder Case," Associated Press, July 24, 2023, forensicmag .com/598677-Judge-Finds-Henry-Lee-Liable-for-Fabricating-Evidence-in-Murder-Case.

27. See National Registry of Exonerations, "Ronnie Long," law.umich.edu/special/exoneration/Pages/casedetail .aspx?caseid=5801.

### Chapter 16: The Priest of Justice

1. These quotes and descriptions come from interviews with the author, and from Jim McCloskey and Philip Lerman, *When Truth Is All You Have* (New York: Anchor, 2020).

2. McCloskey and Lerman, *When Truth Is All You Have*, 37.

3. Alfonso A. Narvaez, "New Evidence Ends Jersey Man's Life Term," *New York Times*, Nov. 6, 1986.

4. Benjamine Spencer letter to Centurion Ministries, autobiography, 1990, undated.

5. On August 23, 1980, a sixteen-year-old white girl named Cheryl Ferguson was found in the loft of the high school auditorium in Conroe, Texas. She had been raped and strangled to death. Two janitors, one Black and one white, found her. When a Conroe police officer arrived on the scene, he said: "One of you two is going to hang for this." Then, turning toward the Black janitor, a military veteran named Clarence Brandley, he said, "Since you're the nigger, you're elected."

The police called in the Texas Rangers, and a week later a Ranger met with the other (white and Hispanic) janitors. They came up with a simple story: The four janitors saw Brandley, the head janitor, follow the victim up the stairs. No physical evidence connected Brandley to the crime, since the state lab had destroyed the semen taken from the victim before it could be tested. In 1981, an all-white jury convicted Brandley and sentenced him to death.

Jim McCloskey arrived in Conroe three weeks before Brandley's execution date and quickly found exculpatory evidence. He found one janitor, wracked with guilt, who told McCloskey that the investigator had tampered with the witnesses, synthesizing their testimony. "He takes them on a walk-through at the high school and rehearses collectively with all of them together what their story is going to be," McCloskey says. "It was all rehearsed." That janitor told McCloskey that two other janitors followed the girl and heard her screaming for help. McCloskey found that prosecutors had hidden other exculpatory evidence. For example, the medical examiner had tied Brandley to the crime by testifying the victim had been strangled with a belt he owned; however, the Texas Rangers hid photographs showing that Brandley was *not* wearing the belt on the day of the murder.

A crew from *60 Minutes* happened to be following McCloskey for a profile and included in its story some interviews pointing to Brandley's innocence. As McCloskey would say about his clerical collar, the *60 Minutes* broadcast "didn't hurt." After the segment aired, more witnesses came forward. Six days before Brandley was to die by lethal injection, a divided Texas Court of Criminal Appeals vacated the conviction. The state eventually dismissed the charges, and Brandley was exonerated in 1990.

Because of state misconduct, both inadvertent and intentional, Clarence Brandley had lived under the shadow of execution for nine years.

6. By sheer, unlucky coincidence, the getaway car had been rented to a Joyce Ann Brown—of Denver, not Dallas. The state was untroubled by the geographical problem and, with the help of a jailhouse informant, convicted the Dallas Joyce Ann Brown of murder in 1980. When McCloskey met her in 1988, he abandoned the rigorous process and trusted his instincts. Before reading a single document, he took her case. "This is like a marriage, Joyce," he said. "You and Centurion Ministries are together until death do us part—or at least until we bring you home to your mama and daughter . . . I promise you. We will free you."

7. Everything pointed to the victim's jealous ex-lover: An eyewitness placed him at the scene, he was obsessed with the victim, and he was prone to violent outbursts. But a jury sentenced Cook to death in 1978. The prosecutor branded Cook a "little pervert," telling the jury: "I wouldn't be surprised if he didn't eat [the victim's] body parts." See Center for Wrongful Convictions, "Kerry Max Cook," law.northwestern.edu/legalclinic/wrongful convictions/exonerations/tx/kerry-max-cook.html.

Eleven days before he was to be executed, in 1988, the US Supreme Court stayed the execution on constitutional grounds. Enter Jim McCloskey, who dug up evidence that the forensic expert had lied, as had the jailhouse informant, and that a witness told police she saw someone fitting the description of the ex-boyfriend that night. Cook was tried again, and in 1994, a second jury convicted him and sentenced him to death. Two years later, this conviction, too, was overturned by the Texas Court of Criminal Appeals, which found that "the prosecutorial and police misconduct has tainted this entire matter from the outset." See *Cook v. State*, 940 S.W.2d 623 (1996), 627.

Prosecutors promised to try him a third time. Cook pleaded no contest to a lesser charge and was freed. Later, prosecutors revealed the results of a DNA test in the rape kit: They excluded Kerry Max Cook and implicated the victim's lover. See McCloskey and Lerman, *When Truth Is All You Have*, 230.
8. Letter from Ben Spencer to Jim McCloskey, April 9, 1990.
9. McCloskey and Lerman, *When Truth Is All You Have*, 7.

*Chapter 17: Double Helix*
1. James Strong, dir., "Cracking the Killer's Code," *Real Crime* (television series), July 29, 2002. The docudrama included appearances by Alec Jeffreys.
2. "The History of Genetic Fingerprinting," le.ac.uk/dna-fingerprinting/history.
3. Video interview with Sir Alec Jeffreys, University of Leicester, Sept. 9, 2014, youtube.com/watch?v= EGMg6i8nUxI.
4. Jane Gitschier, "The Eureka Moment: An Interview with Sir Alec Jeffreys," *PLOS Genetics* 5, no. 12 (2009): e1000765, journals.plos.org/plosgenetics/article?id=10.1371/journal.pgen.1000765.
5. Gitschier, "The Eureka Moment."
6. Video interview with Sir Alec Jeffreys, Sept. 9, 2014.
7. Ian Cobain, "Killer Breakthrough—the Day DNA Evidence First Nailed a Murderer," *Guardian*, June 7, 2016.
8. Cobain, "Killer Breakthrough."
9. Strong, "Cracking the Killer's Code."
10. For an excellent account, see Center on Wrongful Convictions, Rob Warden, "Gary Dotson: First DNA Exoneration," law.northwestern.edu/legalclinic/wrongfulconvictions/exonerations/il/gary-dotson.html.
11. Barry Scheck interview with Harry Chrysler (host), "Conversations with History: DNA and the Criminal Justice System," July 25, 2003, presented by the Institute of International Studies, University of California at Berkeley. youtube.com/watch?v=3Jp-mbGRxhM.
12. Richard A. Leo and Tom Wells, unpublished manuscript, 45.
13. Peter Neufeld interview with Harry Chrysler (host), "Conversations with History: A Passion for Justice," Apr. 27, 2001, presented by the Institute of International Studies, University of California at Berkeley, youtube.com /watch?v=1NRaNBjc0AI.
14. Neufeld interview with Chrysler.
15. Much of the background comes from the thorough work of Richard Leo, who generously provided his unpublished manuscript.
16. His freedom was short-lived. In 1997, Kotler was sentenced to twenty-one years in prison after being convicted of a different sexual assault in 1995. He was linked to that crime by DNA evidence.
17. Jonathan Rabinovitz, "Rape Conviction Overturned on DNA Tests," *New York Times*, Dec. 2, 1992.
18. As law schools were setting up their own innocence projects, Scheck and Neufeld schooled them in the nuts and bolts of wrongful convictions. Long before the internet, with streaming not even a fantasy, they sent out videotaped lectures given by the intellectual founding fathers of the innocence world. Scheck and Neufeld explained the use of DNA testing in forensic cases. Gary Wells, the premier scholar in the area of eyewitness identification, described the science of misidentification. Academics Richard Leo and Saul Kassin examined false confessions. Stephen Bright, who specialized in death penalty cases, covered bad lawyers. Forensic scientist Bill Thompson explained junk science. "And a little-known activist lawyer named Bryan Stevenson did race," Scheck said.
19. Transcript of Barry Scheck's closing argument in the O. J. Simpson trial, Sept. 29, 1995, simpson.walraven.org /sep28.html.
20. Leo and Wells, unpublished manuscript, 209.
21. David Margolick, "A Simpson Lawyer Makes New York Style Play in Judge Ito's Courtroom," *New York Times*, Apr. 17, 1995.
22. David Plotz, "Barry Scheck," *Slate*, Nov. 9, 1997.

### Chapter 18: A Punitive Turn

1. Peter Neufeld interview with Harry Chrysler (host), "Conversations with History: A Passion for Justice," Apr. 27, 2001, presented by the Institute of International Studies, University of California at Berkeley.

2. The 10 percent figure is thrown around often, but I have not found a study focused on this issue. Two sources that cite the figure are Thomas J. Gardner and Terry M. Anderson, *Criminal Evidence: Principles and Cases*, seventh ed. (Stansted, UK: Wordsworth Publishing, 2010), 271; and Daniel S. Medwed, *Barred: Why the Innocent Can't Get Out of Prison* (New York: Basic Books, 2022), 8, in which he writes that biological evidence is collected in 10 to 20 percent of cases, then often lost or destroyed. He cites "Death Penalty Overhaul," hearing before the Senate Committee on the Judiciary, 107th Congress, June 18, 2002 (statement of Barry Scheck).

3. For all the quotes in the Ada, Oklahoma, story, see the two-part series: Barbara Bradley, "Role of DNA Evidence Overturning Two Oklahoma Convictions," *All Things Considered*, NPR, Dec. 28, 2000, and Barbara Bradley, "Murder Convictions in Which There Was No DNA to Test," *All Things Considered*, NPR, Dec. 28, 2000. John Grisham later told the story of the four defendants in his nonfiction book *An Innocent Man* (New York: Doubleday, 2006).

4. The DNA of Glen Gore, who accused Williamson and Fritz and testified against them, matched that found on Debbie Carter. He was convicted in 2003.

5. The men were granted a new trial, but the prosecutor successfully explained away the discrepancies. For example, in explaining that she was shot and not strangled, as the defendant "confessed," the prosecutor told the jury that she was likely shot by a stray hunter's bullet after she was buried. The men were convicted again.

6. In 2018, some three hundred pages of documents were discovered in the Ada police evidence room. Under the *Brady* rule, they should have been turned over to the men's lawyers before trial, since the records showed that police had identified alternative suspects, including some who matched the sketches of the woman's abductors and had prior felony convictions. (Tommy Ward had a clean record.) The defense attorneys believed these represented a fraction of the evidence and interviews that were conducted. A state judge overturned Ward's conviction, ruling he did not get a fair trial. But in 2022, the Oklahoma Court of Criminal Appeals affirmed the conviction. See Clifton Adcock, "Attorneys in Ada 'Innocent Man' Murder Case 'Blown Away' by Content of Newly-Discovered Documents, Ask for Public's Help," *The Frontier*, May 16, 2019, readfrontier.org/stories/attorneys-in-ada-innocent-man-murder-case-say-they-were-blown-away-by-content-of-newly-discovered-documents-ask-for-publics-help.

   And Clifton Adcock, "Attorneys in 'Innocent Man' Case Eye Federal Court After Lower Court's Order Is Reversed," *The Frontier*, Aug. 31, 2022, readfrontier.org/stories/attorneys-innocent-man-case-eye-federal-court-after-lower-courts-order-is-reversed.

7. James Q. Wilson, *Thinking About Crime* (New York: Basic Books, 1975), 235.

8. *Herrera v. Collins*, 506 US 390 (1993), at 401.

9. *Herrera v. Collins*, 419.

10. *Herrera v. Collins*, 419.

11. Leonel Herrara was executed four months after the Supreme Court's decision. Just before the chemicals began entering his body, he said: "I am an innocent man and something very wrong is taking place tonight." Texas Department of Criminal Justice, Death Row Information, Leonel Torres Herrera, Last Statement, tdcj.texas.gov/death_row/dr_info/hererraleonellast.html.

12. David Garland, "The Limits of the Sovereign State: Strategies of Crime Control in Contemporary Society," *The British Journal of Criminology* 36, no. 4 (Autumn 1996): 445–71.

13. In 1981, Ricky Ray Rector shot and killed a man in a restaurant in Conwy, Arkansas, fled, and agreed to turn himself in. But when he met with the police officer, he shot the officer in the back and killed him, then shot himself in the head—the frontal lobe—effectively giving himself a lobotomy. He was tried and convicted of both murders.

14. Sheryl Gay Stolberg and Astead W. Herndon, "'Lock the S.O.B.s Up': Joe Biden and the Era of Mass Incarceration," *New York Times*, June 25, 2019.

15. James Boswell, *The Life of Samuel Johnson* (abridged) (London: Penguin Classics, August 30, 1979). Johnson made the remark in reference to an Anglican clergyman named William Dodd.

16. See National Registry of Exonerations, "Anthony Porter," law.umich.edu/special/exoneration/Pages/casedetail.aspx?caseid=3544.

17. "New DPIC podcast: Former Illinois Governor George Ryan on Commuting Death Row and His Journey from Death-Penalty Supporter to Abolitionist," Death Penalty Information Center, Oct. 15, 2020, deathpenaltyinfo.org/news/new-dpic-podcast-former-illinois-governor-george-ryan-on-commuting-death-row-and-his-journey-from-death-penalty-supporter-to-abolitionist.

18. Neufeld interview with Harry Kreisler, 2001.

19. "Governor Ryan Declares Moratorium on Executions, Will Appoint Commission to Review Capital Punishment System," Governor's office Press Release, Jan, 31, 2000. illinois.gov/news/press-release.359.html.

### Chapter 19: A Network of Innocents
1. Letter from Ben Spencer to Debra Spencer, Apr. 13, 2006.
2. *Strickland v. Washington*, 466 US 668 (1984).
3. "Bat Wielding Robbers," map of attacks, *Dallas Morning News*, Feb. 1, 1995.

### Chapter 20: Batman and Robbery
1. *State of Texas v. Michael Eugene Hubbard* trial transcript, Criminal District Court Number 3, June 24, 1996, vol. 2, 185.
2. *Texas v. Hubbard* trial transcript, vol. 2, 187.
3. *Texas v. Hubbard* trial transcript, vol. 2, 164.
4. *Texas v. Hubbard* trial transcript, vol. 2, 202.
5. *Texas v. Hubbard* trial transcript, vol. 2, 206.
6. *Texas v. Hubbard* trial transcript, vol. 2, 208.
7. The following accounts are detailed in court documents and trial testimony in *Texas v. Hubbard*.

Tuesday, Oct. 4, 1994, 5:00 a.m.: A businessman was knocked unconscious by a blunt instrument. He did not see his assailant, and awakened to find $450 taken from his wallet.

Monday, Oct. 31, 7:45 p.m.: The victim was walking from his office to his car when the attacker jumped from behind the car and hit the victim with a baseball bat, knocking him to the ground. He dragged him behind a dumpster, beating and kicking him, breaking the victim's jaw, lacerating his liver, and leaving bruises all over his body before running off with his wallet and watch.

Friday, Nov. 4, 6:00 p.m.: The assailant slammed an aluminum bat on the victim's head as he left his office. He beat him repeatedly as the man lay on the ground, leaving a three-inch laceration on the victim's face, then took car keys (but not the car) and the victim's eyeglasses.

Sunday, Nov. 13, 8:00 p.m.: The attacker jumped out from behind a wall as the victim walked to his car, hitting him again and again, shouting, "I'm going to kill you!" The victim suffered a broken left elbow, broken right wrist, a skull fracture, and a large abrasion on top of his head. The assailant netted a briefcase.

Sunday, Dec. 11, 9:00 p.m.: The victim was leaving the office when he was hit from behind with a baseball bat on his head and arm, leaving relatively mild injuries, including lacerations and swelling on his face and arm. The perpetrator took his wallet with ten dollars and a Timex wristwatch.

Monday, Jan. 2, 1995, 9:25 p.m.: Hidden underneath an external staircase, the attacker ran from behind the victim, who was leaving his office, and hit him on the left side of his head. As the victim lay on the pavement, the attacker leaned down and said, "Don't move, motherfucker, or I'll kill you. Where is your money?" When the victim didn't respond, he pulled him up by the hair. The victim pulled out a three-inch pocketknife and tried to slash his attacker, but it fell on the ground, provoking a frenzied beating before the assailant fled with nothing. The victim received twelve staples on the left side of the head.

Saturday, Jan. 14, midnight: As the victim was leaving the back door of his office, a man ran toward him and hit him on the head without saying a word, fracturing his skull, and kept beating him with a baseball bat. The victim later said the man was "vicious" and thought he was trying to kill him. The assailant took six hundred dollars from the victim's wallet and fled on foot. The victim did not know how he got home, but was found the next day by a neighbor, who took him to the hospital.

Saturday, Jan. 14, 4:00 a.m. Four hours later, an unknown man entered the back door of a bakery, where the baker confronted him. The intruder said, "Give me your money, motherfucker!" and hit the baker over the head with a club and—once the victim was on the ground—kicked him in the ribs and ran away. The victim suffered a laceration on his forehead, a bruise to his left cheek, and swelling in his right rib cage. The baker was the first victim to be able to identify his assailant.
8. Stan McNear interview with Jim McCloskey, Mar. 13, 2002, and McCloskey memorandum, Mar. 20, 2002.
9. The Batman's fifth victim suffered lifelong trauma and nearly met with Jeffrey Young's fate eight years earlier.

On November 24, 1994, Thanksgiving Day, Keith Sloan, a regional sales manager for Colonial Printing Ink, dropped by his office to finish some paperwork and grab his checkbook before the family gathered for the holiday meal. He called his wife to let her know he was leaving, locked up, and was walking toward his new Chevrolet Suburban when someone smashed a baseball bat into the top of his head. He collapsed and the attacker clubbed his head more than ten times before he fell unconscious. A few minutes later, Sloan awakened and managed to crawl to his car, drive to the road, and put the emergency lights on. A passerby found him soaked in blood and drove him to the hospital. Sloan did not enjoy the luck of the other men with fractured skulls. To control the life-threatening bleeding, the doctors removed a small part of his right frontal lobe. He had to learn to walk and talk again.

Nearly a decade later, Paul Henderson, a Pulitzer Prize–winning journalist who had brought his investigative skills to Centurion Ministries, tracked down Keith Sloan in Lee's Summit, Missouri. Sloan told him that the attack was "devastating" and changed his life forever. He lost his job. His wife filed for divorce. He was forced to move back to Missouri to be closer to his family "because I needed so much help." The former executive now bagged groceries, scrubbed out aquariums at a pet store, and worked as a janitor.

"Here I am mopping floors and cleaning mirrors," he told Henderson, "and nine years ago, I was sitting at a desk in charge of things. When I start dwelling on this, I try to put it out of my mind."

The investigator took photos. One of them shows Keith Sloan, with thick brown hair and a full beard peppered with gray, sitting on his bed in his Kansas City Chiefs T-shirt and white shorts. His bedroom looks like a hurricane passed through, every inch strewn with clothes, boxes, papers, and shoes. He looks at the camera, grinning, a man-child, unaware, it seems, of the chaos around him, but keenly aware of how small and solitary his life has become.

"Michael Hubbard damaged part of my brain," he told Henderson, "and when [my wife] left me, it ripped out my heart."

See Paul Henderson interview with Keith Sloan, March and May 2004 (submitted May 10, 2004), and Keith Sloan affidavit, May 24, 2004, in the files of Jim McCloskey.

10. *Texas v. Hubbard* trial transcript, vol. 4, 585.
11. *Texas v. Hubbard* trial transcript, vol. 4, 586.
12. *Texas v. Hubbard* trial transcript, vol. 3, 386.
13. The two investigations also share an uncanny number of details. Consider the ineptitude and indolence of the police. The fingerprint experts in Dallas could not seem to get a match to save their souls in 1987, and fared just as poorly in 1995. The detectives in each case—Jesus Briseno in 1987, Stan McNear in 1995—simply gave up when Michael Hubbard declined to provide a statement.

    Some parallels raise questions about Hubbard's guilt, just as they had undercut Spencer's conviction. In both cases, the police relied on eyewitnesses who identified the perpetrator under imperfect conditions. Ben Spencer's supporters insisted the eyewitness testimony is unreliable: Gladys Oliver was mistaken, they said, or more likely she made it up. Could the same be said about Ben Carriker? Could the dark night and the adrenaline have distorted his vision? In addition, Ben Carriker's description on the night of the attack was incorrect in a key respect: Hubbard's physique. Hubbard was six feet tall and 170 pounds. Karo Johnson seized on this point, noting in his closing: "He told those police officers that the person who . . . attacked him was about five foot eight, two hundred pounds and stocky. Do you see anybody in the courtroom that looked like that?" (*Texas v. Hubbard* trial transcript, vol. 4, 637).

    The DNA evidence on the bat also excluded Michael Hubbard. If DNA had been found in 1987 and excluded Spencer, his friends and family would be clamoring for his release. Spencer's supporters accused the police of succumbing to tunnel vision. Could the same be said in the Batman investigation?

14. All the letters quoted here are in excerpt; the correspondence between Harry Young and Ben Spencer runs to ninety pages.

### Chapter 21: Down to the Studs

1. I have on rare occasions edited the letters for brevity, but have not changed words and never changed the meaning.
2. Oliver was convicted of shoplifting in 1960. In 1975, she pleaded guilty to third-degree felony theft of $2,060; she had to make restitution to the victim and was given four years' probation. In 1985, she passed a bad check of $300, a misdemeanor, and was given six months' probation.
3. *Texas vs. Spencer* trial transcript, vol. 3, 590. This is Andy Beach's closing argument, where he touched on the integrity of the witnesses: "If there had been information [defense attorney Frank Jackson] has readily access to, that any of those individuals had ever become a convicted felon, they would have brought that to your attention. I'll guarantee you, if Charles Stewart or Jimmie Cotton or Donald Merritt or Gladys Oliver had ever been convicted of a crime, you would have found out about that. Those pathological liars, people that lived out there, the slime that Mr. Jackson called them, had ever been convicted, ever got up in front of somebody like this, like Benjamin Spencer did, 'I am guilty of a felony,' and go to the pen for six years, you would have heard about that."
4. Dr. Paul Michel, Report Re: *Texas v. Spencer*, 1988 Case # 87-96524-UT June 3, 2003, 5.
5. Michel, Report Re: *Texas v. Spencer*, 5.
6. Michel, Report Re: *Texas v. Spencer*, 5–6.
7. In Detective Briseno's notes, she had said between five feet eight inches and six feet tall.
8. Affidavit of Sandra Brackens, June 27, 2002.

9. Affidavit of Sandra Brackens, July 31, 2006.
10. *Ex Parte Benjamine John Spencer*, District Court 283rd Judicial District, Dallas County, Texas, Application for Post-Conviction Writ of Habeas Corpus, Cause no. F-87-96524-ut, 103–104.
11. Dec. 18, 2000, letter from Frank Jackson to Marcia Poole at Centurion Ministries.

### Chapter 22: A New Story

1. The investigators found them all. Jerry Fuller was "flat weeding" the gardens and fields in prison with Ben when he mentioned that everyone in West Dallas knew that Hubbard was the killer. Curtis Jones (aka C-Money) sat in the barber's chair while Ben gave him a trim, and told him that "Big Rob (Robert Mitchell) is in prison doing time for a crime that Michael Hubbard committed," unaware that Ben Spencer was serving life for the same crime. Artice Washington (aka Ice Tea), who had worked for the local drug dealer, used to see Hubbard as a regular customer. "Ben wasn't a hang-out kind of guy," Washington later told Henderson. "He always had a job. He was always a straight dude. I always knew he wasn't the killer."
2. The following account comes from a memo by Jim McCloskey about Michael Hubbard, Mar. 20, 2002, as well as interviews with the author.
3. Affidavit of Ferrell Damon Scott, July 20, 2004. He waited until he was out of prison before signing the document.
4. Ben Spencer letter to Debra Spencer, Aug. 16, 2005.
5. Ben Spencer letter to B.J. Spencer, Oct. 30, 2005.
6. Ben Spencer letter to Debra Spencer, May 21, 2006.
7. Dallas police routinely used polygraphs in their investigations—for example, to gauge whether would-be witnesses or suspects were lying. Dallas prosecutors relied on them when they negotiated deals with defendants, and judges often based the terms of probation on whether or not the polygrapher deemed the accused sincere in his promises. The polygrapher of choice was Rick Holden.
   On September 5, 2003, Holden traveled to Coffield Unit to polygraph Ben Spencer. Of the dozens of questions Holden asked, he dropped in five relevant questions, like a spy sussing out the territory behind enemy lines.
   *Were you inside Jeffrey Young's BMW at any time the night he was killed?*
   *Were you inside Jeffrey Young's BMW in that alley where it was abandoned on or about March 22, 1987?*
   *Did you take part in the assault on Jeffrey Young on or about March 22, 1987?*
   *Did you inflict any injuries on Jeffrey Young on or about March 22, 1987?*
   *Were you physically in the area of Jeffrey Young's office on March 22, 1987?*
   His analysis showed Spencer to be truthful in answering all the relevant questions: Holden told McCloskey that the score for Ben Spencer's truthfulness was "one of the highest I've ever seen."

### Chapter 23: Lost in Space

1. Affidavit of Jesus Briseno, Jan. 13, 2005.
2. Two critical sentences were identical in the affidavits of Gladys Oliver (Jan. 19, 2005) and Jimmie Cotton (June 29, 2005): "If I was asked to testify today about what I saw that night, my testimony would be the same as it was when I testified in Benjamin Spencer's trial. I testified truthfully regarding what I saw on the night of the offense."
3. Charles Stewart's account had been seriously compromised when he testified in Robert Mitchell's trial, but Centurion was never able to interview him to confirm that he never saw Spencer or Mitchell driving the BMW, or that he accused the two men at the behest of Gladys Oliver.
4. More promising still, the crime laboratory had clipped the victim's fingernails and preserved the clippings. If there was a struggle, the victim might have scratched the perpetrator and snagged his DNA under his fingernails. If so, the DNA, a hardy type of evidence that can last for centuries, might identify the assailant. This would emerge as a critical issue later.
5. For more on Bloodsworth's story, see chapter 18.
6. The Dixmoor Five were convicted even though DNA excluded them before the trial. They were eventually exonerated in 2011, after the DNA identified the real perpetrator, a serial rapist. Even so, Cook County State's Attorney Anita Alvarez insisted the actual rapist might have had sex with the victim's corpse after the young men had killed her. The real killer was convicted in 2016, after the young men had spent a collective eighty-five years in prison. See National Registry of Exonerations, "Jonathan Barr," law.umich.edu/special/exoneration/Pages /casedetail.aspx?caseid=3840; National Registry of Exonerations, "Robert Veal," law.umich.edu/special/exonera tion/Pages/casedetail.aspx?caseid=3827#:~:text=After%20serving%20a%20total%20of,source%20was %20identified%20as%20Willie.

7. Barry Laughman was fifteen years into his life sentence for murder and rape when his lawyer learned that the DNA sample had not been destroyed, but turned over to a Penn State professor who had moved to Germany. The samples cleared him. See National Registry of Exonerations, "Barry Laughman," law.umich.edu/special/exonera tion/Pages/casedetail.aspx?caseid=3373.

8. Reggie Cole was nineteen years old when he was convicted of shooting a man in Los Angeles in 1994. More than a decade later, his post-conviction lawyer tried to find the court records and the physical evidence (bullet casings), but was told they had been discarded. Eventually, the records were found in a janitor's closet at the Compton Courthouse. As to the shell casings, a *Los Angeles Times* reporter who had been following the police that night had pocketed them, unaware of their importance. The ballistic evidence linked the killing to another man. See National Registry of Exonerations, "Reggie Cole," law.umich.edu/special/exoneration/Pages/casedetail.aspx ?caseid=3113.

9. Johnny Briscoe was convicted of sexually assaulting a woman in St. Louis in 1983. Beginning in 1997, he petitioned the state to locate the evidence and test it, including three cigarette butts found at the scene. The prosecutor declined, advising Briscoe's attorneys, "We will neither conduct searches of our records nor turn over information unless. . . . ordered by a court to do so." Officials at the crime laboratory were more civil if not more helpful: In 2000 and 2001, they reported the evidence had been destroyed. And then the power grid intervened. In 2004, the St. Louis County Crime Lab experienced a power failure to its evidence storage freezer, which triggered an inventory of the items in the freezer at the time. The three cigarette butts from the Briscoe case were listed as items on the inventory sheet stored in the freezer. They were tested two years later and excluded Briscoe while matching to a convicted rapist already in prison. Briscoe was released after twenty-three years. See National Registry of Exonerations, "Johnny Briscoe," law.umich.edu/special/exoneration/Pages/casedetail.aspx?caseid= 3052.

10. Calvin Johnson Jr. had served sixteen years of a life sentence for rape in Georgia. He was exonerated after a summer intern at the district attorney's office retrieved an evidence box from the dumpster. See Jan Reiss, "A Matter of Conviction," *Harvard Public Health* (Winter 2016), hsph.harvard.edu/magazine/magazine_article/a-matter -of-conviction. See also Innocence Project, "DNA Exoneration Cases Where Evidence Was Believed Lost or Destroyed," Feb. 23, 2007, innocenceproject.org/news/dna-exoneration-cases-where-evidence-was-believed -lost-or-destroyed.

11. For a summary of Marvin Anderson's story, see footnote 1 in chapter 6.

12. By the end of 2013, ten other men—Julius Ruffin, Curtis Moore, Victor Burnette, Arthur Whitfield, Willie Davidson, Philip Thurman, Thomas Haynesworth, Calvin Wayne Cunningham, Bennett Barbour, and Garry Diamond—also had been exonerated as a result of the testing of evidence in Burton's files. In 2018, Roy Watford III became the twelfth person to be exonerated by DNA evidence in Burton's files. In 2019, Winston Scott became the thirteenth person exonerated by DNA evidence in Burton's files.

13. Oral arguments in *Arizona v. Youngblood*, 488 US 51 (1988), 44, supremecourt.gov/pdfs/transcripts/1988/86 -1904_10-11-1988.pdf.

14. *Arizona v. Youngblood*, 43.

15. *Arizona v. Youngblood*, 58.

16. Even when there is evidence of deliberate bad faith, an innocent prisoner can't get around *Youngblood*. Clarence Moses-El discovered this unhappy fact after he was convicted of raping a woman in Colorado in 1988. In prison, he raised a thousand dollars from other inmates to fund DNA testing. A judge ordered the biological evidence to be turned over to a lab for testing. The box containing the rape kit, bedsheets, and other physical evidence was labeled "DO NOT DESTROY." A few weeks later, someone at the Denver Police Department tossed the box into a dumpster, eliminating any possibility of Moses-El proving his innocence through DNA. Adhering to the Supreme Court's *Youngblood* reasoning, Colorado courts denied Moses-El's claim that discarding the evidence violated his constitutional rights. Eventually, he won a new trial, and acquittal, based on other grounds, but it would take twenty-eight years. See National Registry of Exonerations, "Clarence Moses-El," law.umich.edu/spe cial/exoneration/Pages/casedetail.aspx?caseid=5034.

17. Teresa N. Chen, "The *Youngblood* Success Stories: Overcoming the "Bad Faith" Destruction of Evidence Standard," *West Virginia Law Review* 109, no. 2 (2007), researchrepository.wvu.edu/cgi/viewcontent.cgi?article= 6199&context=wvlr.

18. Barbara Bradley, "DNA Exonerations Reduce Public Confidence in Other Evidence," *Morning Edition*, NPR, Aug. 29, 2000.

19. Daniel S. Medwed, *Barred: Why the Innocent Can't Get Out of Prison* (New York: Basic Books, 2022), 176.

20. Susan Greene, "Mothers of Victims Face Life Without Answers," *The Denver Post*, July 24, 2007.

21. Marc Bookman, "Does an Innocent Man Have the Right to Be Exonerated?," *Atlantic*, Dec. 6, 2014, theatlantic .com/national/archive/2014/12/does-an-innocent-man-have-the-right-to-be-exonerated/383343.

22. Medwed, *Barred*, 178.

### Chapter 24: A Second Bite at the Apple

1. Caveat: Some CIUs exist in name only. Indeed, as of 2022, of the nearly one hundred CIUs, more than half had never exonerated anyone. See National Registry of Exonerations, "Conviction Integrity Units," law.umich.edu /special/exoneration/Pages/Conviction-Integrity-Units.aspx. Still, in 2007, the promise was bright.
2. Ben Spencer letter to Debra Spencer, May 13, 2007.
3. *Ex Parte Benjamine John Spencer*, 283rd Judicial District of Dallas County, Texas, Cause No. W87-96524, July 24, 2007, vol. 2, 257–258.

   Here's the exact exchange:
   THE COURT: Is it conceivable that any of the three witnesses could have had better than standard vision?
   THE WITNESS: No.
   THE COURT: Is it conceivable they have had better than standard night vision?
   THE WITNESS: No.
4. *Ex Parte Benjamine John Spencer*, vol. 4, 152.
5. *Ex Parte Benjamine John Spencer*, vol 4, 77.
6. Edwards had signed an affidavit for Centurion Ministries stating that he lied at trial, but at the hearing, he reverted to his original testimony.
7. *Ex Parte Benjamine John Spencer*, vol. 3, 87.
8. *Ex Parte Benjamine John Spencer*, vol. 4, 182.

   The detective admitted he had concerns about Danny Edwards's credibility. Why, Judge Magnis seemed to wonder, did Briseno believe Edwards over Johnson?
   Here's the exchange:
   THE COURT: Edwards talks about there being a bag of gold coins.
   THE WITNESS: Yes.
   THE COURT: Johnson talked about there being a jam box, twenty-six dollars . . . Did you have any evidence that a bag of gold coins or gold chains were ever in Mr. Young's possession?
   THE WITNESS: No, not to my knowledge.
   THE COURT: But you did have evidence that should not have been leaked that there was some jam box and a small amount of cash?
   THE WITNESS: Yes . . .
   THE COURT: Johnson talks about the telephone ringing which you knew was true?
   THE WITNESS: Yes.
   THE COURT: Edwards doesn't say anything about that; is that correct?
   THE WITNESS: That's correct.
   THE COURT: Edwards also talks about somehow being a Mafia deal.
   THE WITNESS: Yes. He mentioned something to that effect.
   *The judge asked Briseno to consider Kelvin Johnson's account and Danny Edwards's account side by side.*
   THE COURT: What I am asking you is . . . which one seems more credible under those circumstances?
   THE WITNESS: Probably . . . Johnson's.

### Chapter 25: Judgment Day Redux

1. Willie Green had spent twenty-four years in prison for a murder he did not commit. law.umich.edu/special /exoneration/Pages/casedetail.aspx?caseid=3262.
2. *Ex Parte Benjamine John Spencer*, "Findings of Fact and Conclusions of Law," Mar. 28, 2008, 15.
3. *Ex Parte Benjamine John Spencer*, "Findings of Fact and Conclusions of Law," 5; *Ex Parte Benjamine John Spencer*, vol. 2, 168. Questioned twenty years later about a possible meeting, Ferrell's attorney testified he could not specifically recall a meeting. He did confirm Ferrell's description: a convertible silver Cadillac Allante with burgundy interior: "Only got 40,000 miles on that one," he lamented. *Ex Parte Benjamine John Spencer*, vol. 3, p. 35.
4. *Ex Parte Benjamine John Spencer*, "Findings of Fact and Conclusions of Law," 9.
5. *Ex Parte Benjamine John Spencer*, "Findings of Fact and Conclusions of Law," 36.
6. *Ex Parte Benjamine John Spencer*, "Findings of Fact and Conclusions of Law," 40.
7. *Ex Parte Benjamine John Spencer*, "Findings of Fact and Conclusions of Law," 42.
8. Ben Spencer letter to Debra Spencer, Mar. 31, 2008.
9. Ben Spencer to Debra Spencer, Apr. 6, 2008.
10. Ben Spencer to Debra Spencer. July 8, 2008.
11. Ben Spencer letter to Debra Spencer, Aug. 10, 2008.
12. Ben Spencer letter to Debra Spencer, Feb. 7, 2010.
13. Ben Spencer letter to Debra Spencer, July 11, 2010.

***Chapter 26: Ground Truth***

1. See National Registry of Exonerations, "Steven Chaney," law.umich.edu/special/exoneration/Pages/casedetail
.aspx?caseid=5489.

2. Brandon Garrett, *Autopsy of a Crime Lab: Exposing the Flaws in Forensics* (Oakland: University of California
Press, 2021), 42.

3. *People v. Jennings*, 252 Ill. 534 (1911).

4. Eventually, the US Supreme Court tightened the rules—theoretically, at least. They made judges the gatekeepers,
the ones to decide what is valid science and what is not. In theory, the science must be generally accepted and reliable, more than speculation or opinion, subject to peer review and having a known error rate that shows how
accurate, say, dentists are at matching teeth to bite marks. But in practice, judges generally have little scientific
training and aren't equipped to assess the "science." Faced with the question of whether microscopic hair evidence should be presented to the jury, judges stick to the familiar. "Judges are typically not going to consult the
scientific literature," Fabricant says. "What they're going to do is consult the law and the precedent. Once legal
precedent is established that this is good stuff, that this is valid and reliable, it comes in."

5. Brandon Garrett, *Autopsy of a Crime Lab: Exposing the Flaws in Forensics* (Oakland, CA: University of California Press, 2021, 52. See also Ryan Gabrielson, "The FBI Says Its Photo Analysis Is Scientific Evidence. Scientists
Disagree," *ProPublica*, Jan. 17, 2019. propublica.org/article/with-photo-analysis-fbi-lab-continues-shaky-foren
sic-science-practices.

6. For the account of Kevin Keith's conviction, see Barbara Bradley Hagerty, "Did James Parsons Kill His Wife?,"
*Atlantic*, June 2022, theatlantic.com/magazine/archive/2022/06/how-reliable-is-forensic-science/629632.

7. Citations to the trial transcript refer to the jury trial conducted in August 1993. A copy of the transcript was filed
with the clerk of courts in Sixth District Court of Appeals Case No. CA 930047 on Feb. 10, 1994. James Parsons
trial transcript, 1993, 1124.

8. Memo to Paul A. Ferrara, superintendent of the BCI, from Daniel L. Chilton, assistant superintendent, May 11,
1989.

9. Handwritten notes of investigation and meeting with Michele Yezzo, Aug. 9, 1993.

10. Parsons's daughters brought a civil suit against Michele Yezzo and the state of Ohio, alleging that they violated
Parsons's civil rights by failing to disclose exculpatory evidence and "maliciously" prosecuting him. In a deposition for that case, Yezzo was asked why she did not photograph the enhanced images, which were the only link,
forensic or otherwise, connecting Jim Parsons and his wife's murder.
  "This is one time that I didn't manage to get it soon enough, because I didn't anticipate having it well
enough," she responded, adding: "Operator error."
  See *Debra O'Donnell, et al., v. G. Michele Yezzo, et al.*, United States District Court for the Northern District of Ohio, Western Division, case no. 3:17-cv-2657, Judge Hames G. Carr, The videotaped deposition of G.
Michele Yezzo, 180, Monday, January 27, 2020.
  A federal judge dismissed the complaint against Yezzo; it's nearly impossible to sue a state employee for errors
performed in the course of his or her duties. But in January 2022, the Sixth Circuit Court of Appeals ruled that
she could be sued, noting that "a reasonable logical inference is that Yezzo fabricated the 'N' and 'S' results."

11. The chemist was Annie Dookhan, and this particular case involved Leonardo Johnson. See Shawn Musgrave,
"Judge Ordered Dookhan to Pay $2 Million to Wrongly Convicted Man," *Boston Globe*, June 21, 2017.

12. The supervisor was Fred Zain. The National Registry of Exonerations lists seven innocent people who were convicted by Zain's testimony: Gilbert Alejandro, Dewey Davis, Gerald Davis, Jimmy Gardner, William Harris,
James E. Richardson Jr., and Glen Woodall.

13. "Court Invalidates a Decade of Blood Test Results in Criminal Cases," *New York Times*, Nov. 12, 1993.

14. In re Renewed Investigation of the State Police Crime Laboratory, Serology Division, 219 W. Va. 408 (W. Va.
2006), 409.

15. Surely one of the most notorious "bad apples" was Michael West, a forensic odontologist who claimed he could
identify bite marks on a victim and then match those marks to a specific person. West's unique technique came to
light in a videotaped autopsy of a twenty-three-month-old girl, described in detail by Radley Balko and Tucker
Carrington in their superb book, *The Cadaver King and the Country Dentist*. The video shows West taking a
dental mold that he had made of the suspect's teeth and pressing it into the toddler's cheek, her elbow, her arm,
scraping it across her face and body at least fifty times. The defendant in that case was convicted and served fifteen years in prison before his appellate lawyers unearthed the evidence. West testified prolifically for prosecutors across the South; his testimony convicted at least nine innocent people who were later exonerated. But even
after he was disgraced and suspended by the American Board of Forensic Odontology, prosecutors continued to
call him as an expert witness and judges continued to allow his bite-mark testimony. See Radley Balko and
Tucker Carrington, *The Cadaver King and the Country Dentist: A True Story of Injustice in the American South*
(New York: Public Affairs, 2018), 174–75.

16. In 2004, a series of explosions blew up four trains in Madrid, killing nearly two hundred people. The Spanish national police recovered a partial, smudged fingerprint on a bag of detonators and asked the FBI to analyze it. The FBI assigned three top fingerprint examiners to the case. The fingerprint database offered up twenty possible matches. The first examiner found several minutiae in common with the fingerprints of Brandon Mayfield, a lawyer in Oregon who had converted to Islam. After reviewing the analyst's conclusions, two other examiners agreed. The FBI launched an investigation and soon arrested Mayfield.

    The Spanish police didn't see what the FBI saw, even after the FBI sent examiners to Madrid to argue that it was a "100 percent positive identification." Soon the Spanish police arrested an Algerian national. Two weeks after bringing Mayfield in, the FBI admitted its error and released him; the federal government later paid Mayfield two million dollars in a settlement. See Eric Lichtblau, "US Will Pay $2 Million to Lawyer Wrongly Jailed," *New York Times*, Nov. 30, 2006, nytimes.com/2006/11/30/us/30settle.html.

    A 2006 inspector general's report acknowledged that Mayfield's religious background likely contributed to the FBI's failure to reconsider its position after "legitimate questions" were raised. See Office of the Inspector General, "A Review of the FBI's Handling of the Brandon Mayfield Case (Unclassified and Redacted)," Mar. 2006, oig.justice.gov/sites/default/files/archive/special/s0601/PDF_list.htm.

    Mayfield was "incredibly fortunate," says Sandra Thompson, author of *Cops in Lab Coats*. If he had been tried in an American court, the jury would have heard that he converted to Islam and that three FBI examiners had found a perfect fingerprint match. "That would have been more than enough evidence to convict him of a crime beyond a reasonable doubt."

17. Itiel E. Dror, David Charlton, and Ailsa E. Péron, "Contextual Information Renders Experts Vulnerable to Making Erroneous Identifications," *Forensic Science International* 156, no. 1 (Jan. 2006): 74–78, pubmed.ncbi.nlm .nih.gov/16325362/.

18. Sherry Nakhaeizadeh, Itiel E. Dror, and Ruth M. Morgan, "Cognitive Bias in Forensic Anthropology: Visual Assessment of Skeletal Remains Is Susceptible to Confirmation Bias," *Science & Justice* 54, no. 3 (May 2014): 208–14.

19. Eitan Elaad, Avital Ginton, and Gershon Ben-Shakhar, "The Effect of Prior Expectations and Outcome Knowledge on Polygraph Examiners' Decisions," *Journal of Behavioral Decision Making* 7, no. 4 (1994): 279–92, researchgate.net/publication/227639045_The_effect_of_prior_expectations_and_outcome_knowledge_on _polygraph_examiners'_decisions.

20. Itiel E. Dror and Greg Hampikian, "Subjectivity and Bias in Forensic DNA Mixture Interpretation," *Science & Justice* 51, no. 4 (Dec. 2011): 204–08, pubmed.ncbi.nlm.nih.gov/22137054.

21. In 1989, nineteen-year-old Steven Barnes was convicted of murder and rape in Utica, New York, based largely on junk science. The analyst testified that she conducted a "photographic overlay" from the fabric on the victim's blue jeans and found a similar pattern on his muddy truck. She compared soil samples from his truck and compared them with soil samples from the crime scene a year later, and determined they had "similar characteristics." And two hairs collected from Barnes's truck were microscopically similar to those of the victim. See National Registry of Exonerations, "Steven Barnes," law.umich.edu/special/exoneration/Pages/casedetail.aspx?caseid=3013.

22. Ray Girdler was convicted in 1982 of burning down his trailer home in Yavapai County, Arizona, a fire that killed his wife and two-year-old daughter. Experts said the that heat-warped metal, burn patterns on the trailer floor in the shape of pools of liquid, and multiple locations where the fire appeared to start were indications that the fire was the result of arson. He was convicted and given two life sentences before experts admitted ten years later that the science was bogus. Arson cases—which gained some notoriety with the execution of Cameron Todd Willingham in Texas—put dozens of people behind bars. See National Registry of Exonerations, "Ray Girdler," law.umich.edu/special/exoneration/Pages/casedetail.aspx?caseid=3796.

23. Timothy Bridges was convicted of raping the elderly woman in Charlotte, North Carolina, in 1991. The state ignored a bloody palm print found in the home, which matched neither the victim nor Bridges. Instead, they relied on an FBI-trained analyst who testified that two hairs found at the scene came from Bridges. The expert said he could make a "strong identification" that the hair at the scene was Bridges's hair and that there was only a one-in-a-thousand chance that another person could have left those hairs. Bridges, then twenty-three years old, was sentenced to life in prison. See National Registry of Exonerations, "Timothy Bridges," law.umich.edu/special /exoneration/Pages/casedetail.aspx?caseid=4845.

24. The report has been described as a bombshell, but it went largely unnoticed. The Obama administration ignored most of the recommendations, such as removing crime laboratories from state and local law enforcement agencies and making them independent. When the President's Council of Advisors on Science and Technology (PCAST) reported in 2016 that many areas of forensic disciplines have "scant scientific underpinnings," the Justice Department essentially rejected the report. And what befell the National Commission on Forensic Science, which was created in 2013 to raise the standards of science used in courts? The Trump administration shut it down in its first three months.

25. Garrett, *Autopsy of a Crime Lab*, 15.

26. For the 15–16 percent study, see Garrett, *Autopsy of a Crime Lab*, 63. For the 63 percent error rate study, see Chris Fabricant, *Junk Science and the American Criminal Justice System* (Brooklyn, NY: Akashic Books, 2022), 105; and C. Michael Bowers, "Problem-Based Analysis of Bite Mark Misidentifications: The Role of DNA," *Forensic Science International* 159, supplement 1 (2006): s104–s109.

27. R. Austin Hicklin et al., "Accuracy and Reproducibility of Conclusions by Forensic Bloodstain Pattern Analysts," *Forensic Science International* 325, article 110856 (Aug. 2021). sciencedirect.com/science/article/pii /S0379073821001766#.

28. Press Release, "FBI Testimony on Microscopic Hair Analysis Contained Errors in at Least 90 Percent of Cases in Ongoing Review," Apr. 20, 2015, fbi.gov/news/press-releases/fbi-testimony-on-microscopic-hair-analysis -contained-errors-in-at-least-90-percent-of-cases-in-ongoing-review.

29. The lab in Washington, DC was shuttered in 2021 and reopened in December 2023.

   If asked why labs fail, critics finger two culprits among many. First, the overwhelming majority of crime labs suffer from the poverty born of being a stepchild to law enforcement. They're tucked into the police department or state law enforcement and depend on them for funding, never mind the psychological pressure analysts feel to help their colleagues catch and prosecute the bad guys. Second, no one from the outside is rigorously checking their work. Most laboratories have received certification by an oversight organization. But many critics, such as Garrett, consider accreditation a seal of approval that is bought for a fee. The audits are scheduled in advance, the tests are easy, and the focus is on having the right procedures on paper, not arriving at the right answer.

30. The headline has since been changed. Adam Liptak, "Houston DNA Review Clears Convicted Rapist, and Ripples in Texas Could Be Vast," *New York Times*, March 11, 2003, nytimes.com/2003/03/11/us/houston-dna -review-clears-convicted-rapist-and-ripples-in-texas-could-be-vast.html?searchResultPosition=1.

31. See Death Penalty Information Center, "Executions by County," deathpenaltyinfo.org/executions/executions -overview/executions-by-county.

32. Rodriguez was convicted in 1987 of raping a fourteen-year-old girl and sentenced to sixty years in prison. The experts at the Houston Police Department Crime Lab testified the blood typing of the swabs taken from the victim showed that Rodriguez committed the crime, and that the hair found in the rape kit was "microscopically similar" to Rodriguez's. In 2004, seventeen years later, DNA testing proved the scientists were dead wrong—he was *not* a contributor—and that they erroneously excluded the real perpetrator. See National Registry of Exonerations, "George Rodriguez," law.umich.edu/special/exoneration/Pages/casedetail.aspx?caseid=3591.

33. See National Registry of Exonerations, "Josiah Sutton," law.umich.edu/special/exoneration/Pages/casedetail .aspx?caseid=3672.

34. Michael Bromwich, "Crime Lab Proposal Is a Major Step Toward Independence," *Houston Chronicle*, Mar. 23, 2012.

35. As of 2022, seven states have enacted laws to clarify that wrongfully convicted people can get back into court based on discredited forensic evidence. These include California, Connecticut, Michigan, Nevada, Texas, West Virginia, Wyoming.

   California: In 2014, California enacted a law that allows convicted people to seek relief based on flawed forensic evidence used in their convictions.

   Connecticut: In 2018, Connecticut enacted a law removing the three-year time limit in the motions for new trial law to permit the introduction of new, non-DNA evidence after conviction. The new law includes a provision to clarify that new evidence may include new scientific research, guidelines, or expert recantation.

   Michigan: In 2018, Michigan amended its court rule that dictates post-appeal relief. The changes now allow a person to file a post-conviction motion for relief based on new scientific evidence, including but not limited to shifts in a field of scientific knowledge, changes in expert knowledge or opinion, and shifts in a scientific field used in a conviction.

   Nevada: In 2019, Nevada passed a law creating an avenue for people to present new, non-DNA evidence of factual innocence beyond two years after a conviction. The law clarifies that new evidence may include relevant forensic evidence that was not available at trial or that materially undermines forensic evidence presented at trial.

   Texas: In 2013, Texas passed the first law in the nation allowing people to challenge their convictions based on new scientific evidence or old scientific evidence that has since been discredited.

   West Virginia: In 2021, West Virginia passed a law creating an avenue for people to present new forensic or scientific evidence that provides a reasonable probability of a different result at trial. The law clarifies that this new evidence can include evidence that was not available at the time of trial or that undermines forensic evidence relied upon by the state at trial.

   Wyoming: In 2018, Wyoming enacted a "factual innocence" law to remove the state's two-year time limit for introducing new, non-DNA evidence. The law includes a provision that new evidence may include new scientific research, guidelines, or expert recantations that undermine forensic evidence used for convictions.

36. The Texas Forensic Sciences Commission now accredits laboratories, audits their performance, and licenses the analysts. It works with prosecutors, lab technicians, scientists, legislators, judges, and defense attorneys to try to carve out solutions for thorny problems, both in the law and the science. And it holds forensic science roundtables, touching on subjects like bite marks or hair evidence, as well as larger ethical issues.

37. See Texas Forensic Science Commission, "Forensic Bitemark Comparison Complaint Filed by National Innocence Project on Behalf of Steven Mark Chaney—Final Report," Apr. 12, 2016, txcourts.gov/media/1454500/finalbitemarkreport.pdf.

### Chapter 27: No Way Out

1. See discussion of *Herrera v. Collins* in chapter 18, "A Punitive Turn."

2. *Ex Parte Spencer*, 337 S.W.3d 869 (Tex. Crim. App. 2011), concurring opinion by J. Price, 881.

3. *Ex Parte Spencer*, 881.

4. The ninth judge, Charles Holcomb, had stepped down to run for US senator, leaving the court one vote short.

5. *Ex Parte Spencer*, 876.

6. *Ex Parte Spencer*, 879.

7. Steve McGonigle and Jennifer Emily, "Texas Criminal Appeals Court Says Man Thought Innocent by Lower Judge Should Remain Behind Bars," *The Dallas Morning News*, Apr. 20, 2011.

8. See discussion of the Supreme Court's interpretation of the Anti-Terrorism and Effective Death Penalty Act (AEDPA) in chapter 18, "A Punitive Turn."

9. Letter from Rick Magnis to Parole Board, Oct. 24, 2014.

10. Letter from Alan Ledbetter to Parole Board, Oct. 23, 2014.

11. Letter from Bruce Anton to Parole Board, Nov. 24, 2014.

12. Letter from Rafael Anchia to Parole Board, Oct. 28, 2014.

13. Letter from Andy Beach to Parole Board, Oct. 3, 1989.

14. Letter from Andy Beach to Parole Board, Nov. 1, 2006.

15. Letter from Andy Beach to Parole Board, Apr. 18, 2013.

16. Letter from Karen Wise to Parole Board, Apr. 18, 2013.

17. Ben Spencer to Debra Spencer, April 17, 2011.

18. Ben Spencer to Debra Spencer, Feb. 1, 2011.

19. Ben Spencer to Debra Spencer, May 2, 2014.

20. Ben Spencer to Debra Spencer, June 11, 2016.

21. Ben Spencer to Ann Hallstrom, June 25, 2016.

22. Ben Spencer to Jinna and Jerry Lancourt, Nov. 24, 2012.

23. Ben Spencer to Jinna and Jerry Lancourt, Dec. 3, 2014.

24. Ben Spencer to Ann Hallstrom, June 25, 2016.

25. Ben Spencer to Jinna and Jerry Lancourt, June 23, 2015.

26. Ben Spencer to Jerry Lancourt, Sept. 5, 2016.

27. He is referring to *McQuiggin v. Perkins*, 569 US 383 (2013), which the Supreme Court handed down on May 28, 2013. The court ruled that the Antiterrorism and Effective Death Penalty Act (AEDPA), which restricts prisoners' habeas corpus rights, contains an "actual innocence" exception. Under AEDPA, a prisoner must file a habeas petition within one year of the loss of a direct appeal or within one year of discovering new evidence through the exercise of due diligence. In a 5-4 decision written by Justice Ginsburg, the court held that "actual innocence, if proved, serves as a gateway through which a petitioner may pass," meaning that a prisoner who can show proof of innocence may file a petition outside of the statute of limitations and a court may consider the merits of the claims.

28. In *Finley v. Johnson*, 243 F.3d 215, 218 (5th Cir. 2001), the US Court of Appeals (Fifth Circuit) held that if a prisoner can show that he is actually innocent of the charges against him, the prisoner can appeal to the federal court, and procedural bars do not apply to his case.

29. Susan Hawk, a Republican, resigned on September 6, 2016, after suffering a mental breakdown.

## PART 3: DARKNESS AND LIGHT

### Chapter 28: The Surge

1. Sandra Brackens also recalled that she saw Robert Mitchell driving his car—alone, without Spencer—and park it across the street, where he lived with his family. A few minutes later, she noticed the BMW in the alley, and she walked with Robert Mitchell and two other people to inspect the car—an account, if correct, that conflicts with the narrative that Spencer and Mitchell drove the BMW to the alley and ran away.

2. Jennifer Thompson and Ronald Cotton (with Erin Torneo), *Picking Cotton* (New York: St. Martin's Press, 2009), 15.

### Chapter 29: Innocence Deniers

1. Danny Edwards met Spencer on March 27, 1987. According to the jail records, on March 30, the informant talked with Detective Briseno and told him that Spencer had confessed to the killing. Only *later that day* was Edwards appointed a lawyer, and nearly two weeks later, Edwards agreed to his plea deal: His charges were reduced from aggravated to non-aggravated robbery, and instead of spending up to twenty-five years in prison, he faced a maximum of ten years.

2. Even if Beach did not know that the logs undermined Edwards's story, he still violated the law, according to Gary Udashen. *Brady* applies whether there was bad faith or not. In other words, if Beach believed that Edwards had his deal before he met Spencer, but it turns out he was wrong, he still committed a *Brady* violation by not determining the truth of when Edwards got his deal and revealing that to the defense.

3. Andy Beach email to author, Aug. 16, 2017. Beach was troubled for another reason. He thought the entire deal was suspicious. No one in the DA's office should have made a deal at all. He explained that prosecutors never gave informants a deal before the trial; otherwise, the state would lose all leverage over the wily informants. By withholding the deal, the prosecutor could claim—as Beach did in this case—that the informant was not receiving a benefit for his testimony.

4. See Lara Bazelon, "The Innocence Deniers," *Slate*, Jan. 10, 2018, slate.com/news-and-politics/2018/01/inno cence-deniers-prosecutors-who-have-refused-to-admit-wrongful-convictions.html; and Lara Bazelon, "17 Cases of Denied Innocence," *Slate*, Jan. 10, 2018, slate.com/news-and-politics/2018/01/innocence-deniers-seventeen -cases-of-prosecutors-fighting-exoneration.html.

5. *Berger v. United States*, 295 US (1935), 88.

6. Leon Festinger discussed this phenomenon in his groundbreaking books *When Prophecy Fails: A Social and Psychological Study of a Modern Group That Predicted the Destruction of the World* (1956) and *A Theory of Cognitive Dissonance* (1957). He identified the phenomenon in the Great Disappointment, when a lay Baptist preacher named William Miller convened a large group of people in Exeter, New Hampshire, to welcome the return of Jesus on October 22, 1844, only to find the Lord stood them up. They adjusted their beliefs, created a new church, and decided that the date marked the beginning of Jesus' final work of atonement leading to the Second Coming. The new church is called the Seventh-Day Adventist Church.

7. See National Registry of Exonerations, "Juan Rivera," law.umich.edu/special/exoneration/Pages/casedetail .aspx?caseid=3850.

8. See National Registry of Exonerations, "Rolando Cruz," law.umich.edu/special/exoneration/Pages/casedetail .aspx?caseid=3140, and National Registry of Exonerations, "Alejandro Hernandez," law.umich.edu/special/ex oneration/Pages/casedetail.aspx?caseid=3292.

9. Jerome Morgan, then seventeen, was at a sweet-sixteen party in a hotel ballroom in 1993 when a gunman shot another teenager and fled the room. Morgan was convicted based on the testimony of two teenagers. Nineteen years later, the two eyewitnesses had recanted, saying they had been pressured by police to identify Morgan. (Morgan's attorneys found other exculpatory evidence that had not been turned over to the defense.) When a new trial was granted, and Morgan was released on bail in 2014, District Attorney Cannizzaro said he would try Morgan again. He threatened to prosecute the two witnesses for perjury. According to Lara Bazelon, his assistant district attorney stated: "They either put an innocent man in jail for twenty years or they lied to get him out." The threat had the intended effect: The witnesses, afraid of going to prison for perjury, refused to testify at the retrial. The DA then accused Morgan's attorneys of coercing false recantations and asked that they be removed as Morgan's counsel. The judge rebuffed the request as "outrageous." In May 2016, two weeks before Morgan's retrial, Cannizzaro's office dismissed the charges against him, saying the high court's ruling had tied his hands. He prosecuted the witnesses for perjury, and they were acquitted.

### Chapter 30: No Justice for Some

1. Since 2017, the pain has abated considerably, but it was ever-present when I was meeting Ben Spencer for the first time in 2017.

2. The two people were Sandra Brackens, who told us that Charles Stewart admitted he lied for the reward money, and Daryl Tennison, a neighbor and friend of Charles Stewart, who testified at Robert Mitchell's trial that Stewart admitted he knew nothing about the crime and only signed the papers because "Gladys told me to." See *State of Texas v. Nathan Robert Mitchell*, 283rd Judicial Court of Dallas, Texas, Mar. 30, 1988, vol. 2, 611.

3. Barbara Bradley Hagerty, "Can You Prove Your Innocence Without DNA?" *Atlantic*, Jan.–Feb. 2018, theatlan tic.com/magazine/archive/2018/01/no-way-out/546575.

### Chapter 31: Fresh Eyes

1. David Harris was convicted of killing Mark Mays in Beaumont, Texas, in 1985, while Randall Dale Adams was in prison. Harris was executed in 2004.

2. For years, no one really noticed how powerful elected district attorneys were. They try 95 percent of criminal cases, and their decisions about whom and what to charge can change the local justice system in a heartbeat. Larry Krasner, a longtime defense attorney in Philadelphia, upended the system when he was elected in 2018. He and other "progressive prosecutors" had long been troubled by the disparate treatment of people of color in policing and sentencing (particularly involving drug crimes), and beginning in 2016, voters started to elect more liberal DAs.

Twin factors—the candidacy of Donald Trump and the number of Blacks killed by police—threw the movement into overdrive. On the campaign trail, Trump told police officers, "Please don't be too nice" to a suspect by shielding his head when guiding him into the back seat of a police car; rough him up a bit. At the same time, the number of Blacks killed by police—often captured on video—astonished and outraged the public.

3. Memo from Gary Udashen to Cheryl Wattley and Jim McCloskey, May 30, 2020.

4. See *Ex Parte Benjamine John Spencer* in the 283rd District Court of Dallas County, State's Amended Response to Application for Writ of Habeas Corpus, Jan. 21, 2021.

State's Exhibit 19: Affidavit of Assistant District Attorney Karen Wise, Dec. 20, 2020: ". . . Mr. Stewart's grandmother's house had a long driveway that was closest to the alley where Mr. Spencer was seen getting out of the victim's car; the house was on the far side of the driveway, further away from the alley. . . . We agreed that, because Papa Lee's house blocked the view, we could not see far enough into the alley where the victim's car was apparently parked when Mr. Spencer got out of the car. Our crime scene visit was never mentioned during the writ hearing that started the next day and, thus, nothing about our crime scene visit was in the record of the writ hearing. Consequently, I did not discuss the crime scene visit in my response to the writ filed by Mr. Spencer because I was bound by the facts in the record."

State's Exhibit 23: Affidavit of Assistant District Attorney Kevin Brooks, Jan. 14, 2021: "Prior to the writ hearing, I went out to the crime scene with others from my office. I recall standing at various points in his grandmother's driveway where Charles Stewart could have possibly stood (based on his trial testimony), and I developed the opinion that Charles Stewart did not have a line of sight to the victim's BMW that had been parked in the alley. Even though the scene had changed through the years, the house that would have obstructed his view in 1987 was still there when we visited the scene in 2007. Others who were present also came to the same conclusion. Consequently, I did not believe that Stewart could have seen what he said he saw, and subsequently testified to. I believe I expressed my opinion to Spencer's attorney at that time."

5. See *Ex Parte Spencer*, State's Amended Response. Exhibit 14: Affidavit of Seancory Patton, Jan. 14, 2021.

After Oliver snubbed the district attorney, Daryl Parker and I visited Oliver's last known address in Forney in November and December of 2020. The first time, her granddaughter said she lived in the same apartment she had for years. We checked; not so. Three weeks later, the same granddaughter said she lived with another relative, but would not say whom. I returned alone a third time with cookies, a strategy I call my "cookie offensive." She accepted the cookies and asked me to leave.

6. See *Ex Parte Spencer*, Memorandum in Support of Application for a Writ of Habeas Corpus Seeking Relief from Final Felony Conviction under Code of Criminal Procedure, Article 11.07, Sept. 1, 2020.

Ground 1: That Gladys Oliver testified falsely at trial, saying she only received $580 in reward money when she actually received $5,000 to $10,000.

Ground 2: That Jimmie Cotton now admits he lied at trial when he identified Ben Spencer.

Ground 3: That Danny Edwards now admits he lied at trial when he said that Ben Spencer confessed to the assault.

Ground 4: That advances in visual science since the evidentiary hearing in 2007 prove that none of the three neighbors could have identified a face in poor lighting. The chances of correct identification at nighttime drops to zero at 65 feet, and all three witnesses were much farther away. District Attorney Creuzot considered that ground, and talked with the scientist, Geoffrey Loftus, for more than two hours; but in the end, he felt it was too close to an innocence claim, the science was not well enough established, and he did not want to muddy the waters.

## Chapter 32: And Then There Were None

1. Debra Spencer to Ben Spencer, Oct. 4, 2020.

2. Gary Udashen memo to Cynthia Garza, Nov. 12, 2020. He also noted that usually Danny Edwards lied when it served his interest, but "it was clear that Barb Hagerty was just a reporter who could do nothing for him. So he had no reason to lie to her the way he lies to DAs, police officers, judges, and lawyers."

3. See *Ex Parte Benjamine John Spencer* in the 283rd District Court of Dallas County, State's Amended Response. State's Exhibit 37: Written statement of Shona Grigsby (aka Leilani Edwards), Dec. 4, 2020.

4. In my interview with Leroy Perry, he told me he had spent hours trying to figure out what happened to Jeffrey Young that night. He recalled loading up his wife and daughter in the car and driving through West Dallas, just

looking for . . . what? Clues? Peace? Proper homage to a colleague? He was to testify in Robert Mitchell's trial in March 1988, and out of curiosity, he attended Spencer's second trial the week before. That's when he met Harry Young.

"We were sitting out in the hallway during one of the breaks, kind of seeing what each other thought would happen," he recalled. "And then he told me that they've got the right people because his company put up the money for any information that would lead to the arrest and conviction of whoever did the crime. And that they gave it to the lady who actually lived on the street that Jeff was found. Ten thousand dollars, that's the number I was told.

"I go, 'You know, she could be lying. I mean, if her incentive is just to get the money. If these two guys lived behind her, why would they drive the car over to their neighborhood and drop the car off? That made no sense to me at all. I would go as far away from there as possible."

"What did Jeff's dad say to you when you said she could be lying?" I asked.

"I don't remember that part. He was very emotional."

5. This was how John Williams, who composed the soundtrack for the movie *Jaws,* described the soundtrack: "the tuba grinding away at you, just as a shark would do, instinctual, relentless, unstoppable." See Lester D. Friedman, *Citizen Spielberg* (Chicago and Urbana: University of Illinois Press, 2006), 174.

6. Woe to Assistant District Attorney Karen Wise. Recall that Wise wrote four letters to the parole board opposing Spencer's release. She served as second chair during Spencer's 2007 evidentiary hearing. In Wise's files, Garza found a sheet of personal note paper with a handwritten question: *Was Gladys Oliver paid by EDS and Crime Stoppers? EDS—yes, Crime Stoppers—?* Garza interviewed Wise, who agreed it was her handwriting, but she did not recall when she wrote it. She said she received the information from a prosecutor who interviewed Gladys Oliver and believed Oliver had received the entire twenty-five thousand dollars.

Garza learned that another prosecutor, Christina O'Neal, interviewed Gladys Oliver sometime between 2004 and 2007, and relayed the information to Karen Wise. When Garza asked to speak with O'Neal, she demurred, saying she was too busy and wanted written questions in advance. She asked if she would be a witness in a hearing. Garza opted not to pursue this further.

Not only was this the *third* confirmation that Oliver had received reward money, but it also appeared that prosecutors knew for years and had sat on the information.

7. It doesn't matter if Beach knew or not, according to Gary Udashen. "There is no bad-faith requirement in order to establish a Brady violation." A prosecutor can be acting in good faith and doing everything he can to comply with *Brady,* but if he fails to reveal something that should have been revealed, it is still a *Brady* violation."

8. Gary Udashen argued this point in a memo to DA Creuzot and Cynthia Garza on Nov. 12, 2020. First, *Ex Parte Chabot,* 300 S.W.3d 768 (Tex. Crim. App. 2009), changed the law concerning the presentation of false testimony by the state.

Prior to 2009, in order to receive writ relief based on the presentation of false testimony by the state, the applicant was required to prove that the state knew the testimony was false. In *Chabot,* the Court of Criminal Appeals changed that ruling to recognize that the *unknowing* presentation of false testimony by the state is also a due process violation. Therefore, as of 2009, if the state presented false testimony but did not know it was false, that is nonetheless a ground for writ relief.

9. The deadline for claiming it had officially passed, and Beach went to bat for her.

### Chapter 33: Reprieve

1. Barbara Bradley Hagerty, "'An Awful Mistake' Might Soon Be Fixed—Finally," *Atlantic,* Jan. 28, 2021.
2. Debra Spencer to Ben Spencer, Feb. 2, 2021.
3. Jody Hassett, a former ABC News producer and an award-winning documentary filmmaker, was also there. A close friend and fellow journalist, she was helping gather video for a potential documentary film.

### Chapter 35: State of Play

1. See TX Crim Proc Art. 39.14, juvenilelaw.org/wp-content/uploads/2017/06/Michael-Morton-Act.pdf, and deathpenaltyinfo.org/news/texas-enacts-michael-morton-act-intended-to-reduce-wrongful-convictions.
2. "Tracking Use of Certain Testimony," TX Crim Proc. Art. 2.024, effective Sept. 1, 2017.
3. "Corroboration of Certain Testimony Required," TX Crim Proc. Art. 38.075, effective Sept. 1, 2009: A defendant cannot be convicted on informant testimony "unless the testimony is corroborated by other evidence tending to connect the defendant with the offense committed. . . ." In addition, the state must tell the defense about evidence of a crime that the informant may have committed, and that evidence can be used to impeach or undercut the informant at trial.
4. "Electronic Recording of Custodial Interrogations," TX Crim Proc. Art. 2.32, effective Sept. 1, 2017.

5. See National Registry of Exonerations, "Conviction Integrity Units," law.umich.edu/special/exoneration /Pages/Conviction-Integrity-Units.aspx. The figure includes 147 people who were exonerated in Houston for drug possession. Prosecutors secured plea bargains from suspects before the results of their drug tests were complete, and in these cases, the drug tests were negative. Houston alerted all the prisoners and exonerated them. Excluding them, Texas has exonerated 64 people for violent crimes. New York wins the prize for most erroneous convictions, mainly murders, with 75 exonerations—almost half from Brooklyn's Conviction Integrity Unit.

6. "Procedure Related to Certain Scientific Evidence," TX Crim Proc. Art. 11.073, effective Sept. 1, 2013. The law allows a prisoner to challenge his conviction based on "relevant scientific evidence [that] is currently available and was not available at the time of the convicted person's trial because the evidence was not ascertainable through the exercise of reasonable diligence by the convicted person before the date of or during the convicted person's trial. . . . Had the scientific evidence been presented at trial, on the preponderance of the evidence the person would not have been convicted."

7. Timothy Cole Act, 2009, Tex. Civ. Prac. & Rem. Code, §103.001 to 103.154.

8. Although these individuals were innocent of these crimes, approximately 25 percent had falsely confessed and 11 percent had pleaded guilty. These exonerees spent an average of fourteen years in prison—10 percent of them spent twenty-five years or more in prison—for crimes they didn't commit. See innocenceproject.org/research -resources/#:~:text=Although%20these%20individuals%20were%20innocent,crimes%20they%20didn't% 20commit.

   The National Registry of Exonerations found that more than 20 percent of the people convicted of murder and later exonerated had falsely confessed. See innocenceproject.org/research-resources/#:~:text=Although% 20these%20individuals%20were%20innocent,crimes%20they%20didn't%20commit.

9. See Innocence Project, innocenceproject.org/search/eyewitness+identification+reform+25+states.

10. For an up-to-date list of the reforms on jailhouse informants, see Natapoff's website, snitching.org/legislation.

11. According to Rebecca Brown at the Innocence Project, those states are Texas, California, Connecticut, Nevada, West Virginia, Wyoming, and Michigan.

12. *Arizona v. Youngblood*, 488 US 51 (1988).

13. See: Connick v. Thompson, 563 US 51 (2011).

14. *McCleskey v. Kemp*, 481 US 279 (1987).

   In *McCleskey*, the prisoner, Warren McCleskey, received the death penalty for killing a white police officer. He presented a groundbreaking empirical study by University of Iowa law professor David Baldus. The study of twenty-five hundred murder cases in Georgia showed that people accused of killing a white person were 4.3 times more likely to be sentenced to death than someone convicted of killing a Black person. Justice William Brennan cited the unadjusted data in his dissent, which showed that Blacks convicted of killing whites were sentenced to death at nearly twenty-two times the rate of Blacks who killed other Blacks. Baldus also showed that prosecutors sought the death penalty for 70 percent of Black defendants with white victims, but for only 15 percent of Black defendants with Black victims, and only 19 percent of white defendants with Black victims.

   The majority ruled that statistics were immaterial: A defendant must point to evidence of specific discrimination to get relief in his case. "What the court says essentially," Vincent Southerland says, "is that because you can't say there were some racists out there who said 'We want to convict all the Black people,' the court was essentially powerless to act."

   This leaves the courts helpless to address discrimination that is obvious to the most casual observer. "Despite seeing our prisons and jails filled with a disproportionate number of Black and brown people compared to their percentage of the population, despite what we know about the ways in which the criminal system operates, the way in which police are deployed to particular neighborhoods because of the racial dynamics of those neighborhoods, we can't do anything about that in the law, because we can't point to some bad actor who says, I'm going to arrest all the Black people or charge all the Black people with much more severe crimes."

15. Four years after the first DNA exoneration, the Court ruled that evidence of innocence, without a constitutional violation, was insufficient to get one's case before a federal judge. See *Herrera v. Collins*, 506 US 390 (1993). Recall that the US Supreme Court ruled six to three that a claim of actual innocence does not entitle a petitioner to federal habeas corpus relief by way of the Eighth Amendment's ban on cruel and unusual punishment.

   Congress tightened the hatches when it passed the Antiterrorism and Effective Death Penalty Act (AEDPA). It required federal courts to largely defer to the rulings of state courts and set up a maze of procedures and time limits to thwart prisoners from bringing their cases before a federal judge. Over the years, the US Supreme Court has interpreted the law to block one exit after another, trapping innocent prisoners as well as guilty ones.

16. In *Shinn v. Ramirez*, the court combined two cases involving death row inmates. One involved Barry Jones, who was tried for sexually assaulting and killing the four-year-old daughter of his girlfriend. His court-appointed attorney barely investigated on his client's behalf, and after Jones was convicted and sentenced to death, his

appellate attorney provided an equally limp defense. Years later, a federal judge held an evidentiary hearing and determined that the girl's injuries were inflicted on a different day than the prosecution had claimed, at a time in which Jones could not have inflicted them, and that other forensic evidence presented by the prosecution was false. The federal judge found that both Jones's trial counsel and his state post-conviction counsel had provided ineffective assistance for failing to investigate and present this evidence earlier in the case. As a result, the court granted Jones federal habeas relief. A three-judge panel of the US Court of Appeals for the Ninth Circuit unanimously affirmed that ruling.

In 2022, the US Supreme Court reversed, saying that the federal hearing never should have occurred. It ruled that because Jones did not raise the issue of ineffective assistance of counsel in state court, he was barred from federal court. See: In Shinn v. Ramirez, 596 US ___ (2022), supremecourt.gov/opinions/21pdf/20-1009 _19m2.pdf.

17. *Shinn v. Ramirez*, 22 of majority opinion.
18. *Shinn v. Ramirez*, 19, Dissent. Sotomayor was joined by Justices Stephen Breyer and Elena Kagan. She described the decision as "perverse" and "illogical," writing that it "eviscerates" controlling case precedent and "mischaracterizes" other decisions of the court (page 14 of dissent).

"The court's decision will leave many people who were convicted in violation of the Sixth Amendment to face incarceration or even execution without any meaningful chance to vindicate their right to counsel," Sotomayor warned, also noting that the ruling "all but overrules two recent precedents," *Martinez v. Ryan* and *Trevino v. Thaler* (page 1 of dissent).
19. On June 15, 2023, Jones was freed after serving twenty-nine years for a crime that the Arizona attorney general agreed he did not commit. The US Supreme Court's decision did not prohibit the AG's office from independently reviewing the case. The office reached a settlement agreement in which Jones pleaded guilty to second-degree murder for failing to take the young girl to a hospital while she was in his care, after which she died from her fatal internal injury. In exchange, he was released from prison for time served.

See "Barry Jones Freed from Arizona's Death Row after 29 Years," Death Penalty Information Center, June 16, 2023, deathpenaltyinfo.org/news/barry-jones-freed-from-arizonas-death-row-after-29-years.

The next year, the Supreme Court doubled down in *Jones v. Hendrix*. It ruled that a prisoner who is completely innocent of a crime may not appeal his conviction if he has used up his appeals, relegating him to serve out his sentence. Once again, Justice Thomas wrote for the majority, placing the onus on the legislature: "Congress has chosen finality over error correction." *Jones v. Hendrix*, 599 US ___ 2023, Slip Opinion, 12, supremecourt .gov/opinions/22pdf/21-857_4357.pdf.

Writing for the three dissenters, Justice Ketanji Brown Jackson charged that the ruling is "stunning in a country where liberty is a constitutional guarantee and the courts are supposed to be dispensing justice" (page 67 of dissent).
20. Those six are Chicago, Houston, Brooklyn, Detroit, Dallas, and Philadelphia. The CIUs in Texas account for 30 percent of the national total.

### Chapter 36: A Partial Justice

1. The laboratory compared the DNA from Jeffrey Young's fingernails with another sample from Young. The second sample produced results at only three of the twenty-three tested locations, resulting in a total of four alleles. The four alleles are consistent between both of Young's samples, which is why the test suggests the DNA under Young's fingernails is his own. The chances of the four alleles from the second sample coming from someone else are low: between one out of 206 people and one out of 21,020 people are expected to have those same four alleles.

The state is not allowed to run the DNA from underneath Young's fingernails through its database, because it is not allowed to upload profiles that may belong to a victim. The state could compare Michael Hubbard's DNA with the DNA from the crime directly. However, the prosecutor would have to show probable cause for the "search" to obtain a warrant for Hubbard's DNA sample. In the end, the DNA did not contradict Ben Spencer's assertion of innocence but did not solve the crime either.

# INDEX

+———+